The Maestro Myth

Great Conductors in Pursuit of Power

NORMAN LEBRECHT

A BIRCH LANE PRESS BOOK
Published by Carol Publishing Group

A Birch Lane Press Book
Published by Carol Publishing Group
Birch Lane Press is a registered trademark of Carol Communications, Inc.
Editorial Offices: 600 Madison Avenue, New York, N.Y. 10022
Sales & Distribution Offices: 120 Enterprise Avenue, Secaucus, N.J. 07094
In Canada: Canadian Manda Group, P.O. Box 920, Station U, Toronto, Ontario M8Z 5P9

Queries regarding rights and permissions should be addressed to Carol Publishing Group, 600 Madison Avenue, New York, N.Y. 10022

First published in Great Britain by Simon & Schuster Ltd in 1991

Carol Publishing Group books are available at special discounts for bulk purchases, for sales promotions, fund raising, or educational purposes. Special editions can be created to specifications. For details contact: Special Sales Department, Carol Publishing Group, 120 Enterprise Avenue, Secaucus, N.J. 07094

Manufactured in the United states of America
10   9   8   7   6   5   4   3   2

Library of Congress Cataloging-in-Publication Data

Lebrecht, Norman, 1948-
      The maestro myth : great conductors in pursuit of power / Norman
   Lebrecht.
            p.   cm.
      "A Birch Lane Press book."
      Includes bibliographical references (p.   ) and index.
        ISBN 1-55972-108-1
        1. Conductors (Music) 2. Conducting. I. Title
   ML402.L4   1992
   784.2'145—dc20   91-43651
                                                              CIP
                                                              MN

Contents

The Making of a Myth

EVERY AGE INVENTS heroes. The warrior, the lover and the saintly martyr captivated medieval minds. Romantics worshipped the poet and explorer; industrial and political upheavals set the scientist and social reformer on a pedestal. The advent of mass media enabled idols to be custom-made for separate consumer groups: pop stars for adolescents, screen goddesses for the lovelorn, cardboard soap-opera characters for couch potatoes, sports champions for the more energetic, terrorist hijackers for the world's oppressed, pop-philosophers for the chattering classes.

Heroes act as a safety valve in the social pressure-cooker. They allow small men in spectacles to identify harmlessly with Sylvester Stallone instead of throwing a punch at the boss, and shy girls to fantasize away their chastity in the flaunted sexuality of Marilyn Monroe and Madonna. Such dreams are unrelated to any concrete reality. The once-ubiquitous bedroom-wall portraits of the South American guerrilla leader, Che Guevara, did not signify incipient juvenile revolution in suburbia. Guevara as a political force was a minor irritant to remote regimes. As an icon, however, he vented the frustrations and yearnings of affluent youngsters in the decadent West.

Such popular heroes are literally mythical, in the sense that they are either insubstantial or wholly fictitious. Cultural gods are no different. Andy Warhol and Jeff Koons have demonstrated that an artist need not be distinctively original in order to be celebrated; the name of Karlheinz Stockhausen is known to music-lovers who have never heard a note he composed. Their fame lies less in anything they invent, than in the myth they represent.

The 'great conductor' is a mythical hero of this kind, artificially created for a non-musical purpose and sustained by commercial necessity. 'Orchestral conducting as a full-time occupation is an invention – a sociological not an artistic one – of the 20th century,' acknowledged Daniel Barenboim, an eminent practitioner. 'There is no profession which an impostor could enter more easily,' wrote the astute and long-suffering violinist, Carl Flesch. The conductor exists because mankind demands a visible leader or, at the very least, an identifiable figurehead. His musical *raison d'être* is altogether secondary to that function.

He plays no instrument, produces no noise, yet conveys an image of music-making that is credible enough to let him take the rewards of applause away from those who actually created the sound. In musical terms, argued the polemicist Hans Keller, 'the conductor's existence is, essentially, superfluous, and you have to attain a high degree of musical stupidity in order to find watching the beat, or the conductor's inane face for that matter, easier for the purpose of knowing when and how to play than simply listening to the music'. That heresy, phrased less politely, can be heard wherever orchestral players gather to drown their multitude of sorrows. 'Too many of these guys are masters of the brilliant wave,' grumbled the former Berlin Philharmonic flautist, James Galway. A bad conductor is the bane of a musician's daily life; and a good one is not much better. He gives orders that are redundant and offensive, demands a level of obedience unknown outside the army and can earn at a concert as much as his entire orchestra is paid.

Yet, when work has to be provided and a season organized, it is the players themselves who elect conductors and invent them. The myth begins with their mute submission. Orchestral musicians are a hardened lot who melt at the wave of a wizard's wand. They would say that Arthur Nikisch had merely to enter the room for an orchestra to sound better. Musicians talked of 'this magic thing' that set Arturo Toscanini and Wilhelm Furtwängler apart from other mortals. Leonard Bernstein, one conceded, 'makes me remember why I wanted to become a musician'. By some wordless impulse, an exceptional conductor could change the human chemistry in his orchestra and audience. The anti-authoritarian philosopher Elias Canetti viewed it as a manifestation of almost godlike authority:

> His eyes hold the whole orchestra. Every player feels that the conductor sees him personally and, still more, hears him . . . He is inside the mind of every player. He knows not only what each *should* be doing but what he *is* doing. He is the living embodiment of law, both positive and negative. His hands decree and prohibit. . . . And since, during the performance, nothing is supposed to exist except this work, for so long is the conductor ruler of the world.

To the listener in the stalls, the conductor represents a dual form of escapism: the longing to lose oneself in music combined with an urge to sublimate in the actions of that all-powerful figure on the podium. The conductor is an obvious hero whose gestures are unconsciously imitated with a finger on the arm of the concert-hall seat or, back home, waving one's arms before the bathroom mirror to the accompaniment of recorded sound. Replicated on disc and video, the maestro myth evolved into a money-spinning worldwide cult.

It is a highly refined form of worship. The conductor has never been a mass-hero, but the idol of an élite. To the average fan on the football terraces and the single parent subsisting on state support, he signifies, if anything, an unattainable aura of privilege and fastidiousness. Only Toscanini and Bernstein were as famous as rock stars, and for reasons that had nothing to do with their craft. The conductor is not a popular hero but a hero's hero: the incarnation of power in the eyes of the all-powerful. 'There is no more obvious expression of power than the performance of a conductor,' noted Canetti. 'Every detail of his public behaviour throws light on the nature of power. Someone who knew nothing about power could discover all its attributes, one after another, by careful observation of a conductor.'

Powerful figures became devoted fans. Margaret Thatcher, the British prime minister, openly envied the absolutism of Herbert von Karajan. Richard Nixon, in the toils of Watergate, took time out to send a get-well card to Leopold Stokowski and bask in the sound of the Philadelphia Orchestra that he founded. Every notable maestro who set foot in western Germany while Helmut Schmidt was in power was summoned to dinner at the Chancellery. Even France, described by its minister of culture as an unmusical nation, found the attention of its presidents occupied by the repatriation of Pierre Boulez and the installation of Daniel Barenboim at the Bastille. Karajan's festivals at Salzburg were a shrine for heads of heavy German industry. A Japanese electronics magnate became his acolyte. One of Britain's top defence manufacturers would be flown by company jet to wherever Riccardo Muti was conducting.

Maestros were showered with baubles and titles. 'People have the desire to give him gifts,' reported a Bernstein associate. The British establishment, while neglecting composers, bestowed knighthoods on countless conductors and made Karajan a Doctor at Oxford for no discernible contribution to scholarship. Bernstein, who did precious little for France, was awarded the coveted Légion d'Honneur. Lorin Maazel, one of the least diplomatic of musicians, was made Ambassador of Good Will by the United Nations secretary-general; Riccardo Muti became ambassador-at-large for the High Commissioner for Refugees, never having seen the perimeter fence of a refugee camp in his busy life.

These honours may be meaningless, but they are listed religiously in the conductors' press releases and serve to reinforce their myth. They signalled a sharing of power and status with the mightiest persons on earth. In exchange, potentates and presidents hoped to share some of the maestro's indefinable magic, the legendary aspects of his myth. In addition to sagacity and an inexplicable skill, conductors were alleged to possess the key to eternal life and vigour. Pierre Monteux, at eighty, sought a 25-year contract from the London Symphony Orchestra, renewable by mutual consent. Stokowski, at 91, signed a ten-year exclusive recording deal with RCA. Toscanini and Otto Klemperer kept on into their mid-eighties. The fact that many others died in early middle age – Gustav Mahler at fifty, the Hungarians Istvan Kertesz and Ferenc Fricsay at 43 and 48, and the founding fathers Bülow and Nikisch in their sixties – did not disturb the myth, nor did the sight of old Karl Böhm catnapping in his podium while the orchestra played on regardless. Senior maestros shared with politicians a noted reluctance to make way for younger men.

Their mystique was further enhanced by rumours of sexual rapacity. Klemperer was attacked in his podium by a jealous husband and Malcolm Sargent was forever fondling the wives of colleagues. Nikisch had a permanent twinkle in his mesmeric eye and Furtwängler was said to take a different woman to his room before every concert. At the same time, their communion with the spirit of dead composers endowed maestros with a priestly aura and their concerts with the solemnity of a convocation. Mixed together, this cocktail of spiritual power and physical prowess produced a hero whom music-makers and listeners alike could envy and secretly emulate. The conductor, a golem created for a specific purpose, responded readily to their changing tastes. He might seem to live upon Olympus, but was ever-sensitive to the popular whim and adapted in order to survive. Each important conductor was identifiably a child of his own time, conditioned by its social climate and personifying its prevalent ethos.

In a time of territorial expansion, Hans von Bülow was the bluff imperialist, Nikisch and Richter the colonial administrators. Immovable generals – Stokowski, Koussevitsky – captured the podium during the First World War. They were followed in the age of dictators by a tyrant, Toscanini, and a woolly appeaser, Wilhelm Furtwängler. George Szell and Fritz Reiner were cold warriors for an age of austerity. Herbert von Karajan, moulded by the Nazis, turned defeat into a personal economic miracle. The libertarian sixties produced the Bernstein heyday, love and peace and flower-shirts at rehearsal. The materialist fixations of the next decades yielded offshore conductors who behaved like takeover merchants and lived like Donald Trump. 'Those aren't artists,' said an outsider, overhearing the author's conversation about conductors with a senior Berlin player, 'they're businessmen.'

The triumph of capitalism has brought conducting to its lowest ebb. A bare handful of prospects under the age of forty have come forward to take the helm in the next century, as the profession fails to replenish itself. 'Where have all the conductors gone?' demand banner headlines over despondent articles.

Richard Strauss: the musician as hero

The crisis in conducting is twofold. There is a dearth of fresh talent, and an alarming superficiality in the state of symphonic interpretation. Brahms, Bruckner and Mahler are performed more than ever before, with far less penetration. The crisis does not exist in isolation but originates in the societies that bred the maestro and his myth. The conductor is no more than a magnifying mirror of the world in which he lives, *homo sapiens* writ large. As such, his development reveals more about the nature of twentieth-century society and morality than it does about twentieth-century music.

The history of the conducting profession is inseparable from that of the institutions it directed. Great conductors create great orchestras; feeble appointments send them into speedy decline. The litmus test of any maestro's ability is his impact on an established company. A 25-year-old novice called Simon Rattle transformed a cantankerous and demoralized ensemble in Birmingham into a standard bearer for the city. Leonard Slatkin performed a similar feat in St Louis, Missouri, as did Mariss Janssons in Oslo.

Berlin enjoys precedence among orchestras thanks to its extraordinary succession of Bülow, Nikisch, Furtwängler and Karajan. It shares the summit with the Vienna Philharmonic, the Concertgebouw of Amsterdam, one at any given time of London's four orchestras, and America's Big Five: Boston, Chicago, Philadelphia, Cleveland and the New York Philharmonic.

La Scala held sway consistently in Italian opera under Toscanini, De Sabata, Serafin and Abbado; Vienna led the way in international opera from Mahler's directorate through Strauss and Bruno Walter, to Karajan, Maazel and Abbado. Covent Garden and the Metropolitan Opera in New York make up the four pillars of the grand operatic establishment.

Other contenders rose and fell with the calibre of their conductor. The Czech Philharmonic was outstanding under Talich and Kubelik, the BBC Symphony under Boult and Boulez, Dresden Opera in the era of Fritz Busch and Minneapolis when Dmitri Mitropoulos was in charge. None held on to their eminence after the music director's departure. 'There are no bad orchestras,' said Mahler contentiously, 'only bad conductors.'

The profession was formed in the middle of the last century when composers abdicated responsibility for directing their scores, which grew too unwieldy for orchestras to play unguided. Breaking free of the composer's psychological grip, the emergent conductor made his role first as a municipal figurehead, then as a national one, and ultimately as a multinational enterprise in tune with the spirit of the modern age. His ideals modulated over the course of a dozen decades, from achieving the fleeting illusion of a perfect performance, to engraving on indelible surfaces a 'definitive' concept for all eternity of how music should be played.

Records and films won the conductor worldwide celebrity, along with the accolade of greatness. The concept of The Great Conductor is a fiction perpetrated for the preservation of musical activity in an era of multiple leisure pursuits. Over the past half century, the number of professional orchestras around the world has doubled to around five hundred; and the number of capable conductors has diminished inexorably. Every orchestra has to sell upwards of thirty thousand seats a season and each needs star conductors to haul concertgoers away from their hi-fis and television sets ('Stars is a stupid word,' says Georg Solti. 'Stars are just stars because they are travelling too much'). In the absence of real talent, orchestras fall back on the hype of competing record companies, each of whom pretends for commercial reasons to have ten or more conductors of world class.

The players become parties to this deception, much to their individual chagrin. Their professionalism has risen in inverse proportion to the quality of conductors they face. Musicians in major orchestras recognize six maestros at most as being fit to lead them; with the rest, they grit their teeth and stare fixedly at the score. 'It's very difficult for an orchestral musician after thirty years of having worked with the greatest to have someone new come along and do a Brahms symphony,' explained an eminent concertmaster. 'Working with a mediocre conductor, I go in thinking: we're faced with two days of this, and I have to create a nice feeling for the orchestra . . .' Knowing that livelihoods depend on selling tickets, no player is rash enough to risk a hundred jobs by denigrating conductors.

Orchestras and record labels are only partly to blame for promulgating the Great Conductor myth. For all the attention they attract, classical record companies are relatively small and idealistic concerns with a couple of hundred staff and a turnover in the low millions. Although most are owned by multinationals, the place of DG or Decca within the mighty Philips parent, which employs thirty million people around the world, is prestigious but minuscule. Anxious to find conductors, record executives fall prey to be manipulated by artists' agents who push forward something that looks like a maestro in which they have a substantial financial interest of ten to twenty per cent.

The rise of the all-powerful agent is one of the most worrying aspects of the conducting crisis, and arguably its major cause. In the past twenty years, as the quantity and quality of top conductors has declined, maestros have become infinitely richer and their personal managers much more powerful.* If an agent controls enough conductors, he can dictate terms to promoters and record producers, and foist counterfeits on an innocent public. Fake maestros have begun to abound in the podium, earning their greatest fame and fortune in Japan where musical discrimination is least refined among the concertgoing public. Recent developments have proved Abraham Lincoln wrong: in conducting these days, apparently you *can* fool all of the people all of the time.

How, then, does one distinguish genuine talent from a flashy impostor? Given the nebulous and indeterminate nature of conducting, the art of a good conductor is impossible to define. Rattle, for example, cannot explain much of what he does. 'There are some things that one has to glory in their tenuousness, and music is one of those. If you try to pin it to the wall, you've had it,' he says. 'It's a strange feeling, everyone should experience it,' said Riccardo Muti. 'You give a gesture in the air – and the sound comes out . . .'

No-one has ever explained how one man with a physical flourish can elicit an exhilarating response from an orchestra while another, with precisely the same motions and timing, produces a dull, unexceptional sound. It is not enough to be a musical genius. Composers from

*See Chapter 16.

Beethoven onwards have been humiliated in the podium, and brilliant soloists have slunk back shamefaced to their instrument. 'What I have above all conductors,' announced James Galway, embarking hope-filled on a podium career, 'is that I have played in the best orchestra in the world, the Berlin Phil, under some of the greatest artists of the century. And I know there are some things I can do better.' He was proved wrong, and so were many other fine players who tried in vain to make the transition. The physical act of conducting can be easily learned; the intangible, spiritual side has to come from somewhere within. An imposing personality is not enough to impress an orchestra. Experienced players say they can tell in ten minutes if a newcomer has 'got it' or not. 'When a new man faces the orchestra, we know whether he is the master or we, from the way he walks up the steps to the podium and opens the score – before he even picks up his baton,' wrote the father of Richard Strauss, a Munich horn player and conductor-baiter.

Historically, what outstanding conductors have had in common is an acute ear, the charisma to inspire musicians on first acquaintance, the will to get their own way, high organizational ability, physical and mental fitness, relentless ambition, a powerful intelligence and a natural sense of order which enables them to cut through thousands of scattered notes to the artistic core. This ability to obtain an overview of the score and convey it to others is the essence of interpretation. Since order is, in Alexander Pope's phrase, 'heaven's first law', its imposition is perceived as a quasi-divine act that bestows on the conductor an ethereal glow in the minds of his players.

Not every important conductor possessed all the requisite traits. Many, past and present, have been poorly read and averagely intelligent – Hans Richter and Serge Koussevitsky, for example. Some were hopelessly disorganized, physically weak and lacking all ambition but sufficiently over-endowed in other characteristics to succeed. The prerequisites of the profession have changed surprisingly little in a century and a half.

Players knew the moment they put bow to strings when they were joined by an exceptional communicator. Members of a chamber orchestra which worked with humdrum directors found themselves playing Mozart for two weeks in Switzerland with Georg Solti. Not only did their timbre alter instantly, but players said they retained the Solti sound in their playing for two months afterwards. Some believe they can still hear Klemperer in the playing of the Philharmonia, almost twenty years after his death. A visitor rehearsing *Tristan* at La Scala asked Victor De Sabata to take the baton while he tested the sound from the centre of the auditorium. Needless to say, the sound he heard was totally different from the one he had produced. De Sabata, without uttering a word, asserted his dominance of the orchestra just by standing there. That is one mark of a major figure.

Another is his ability to give life to new art. On 19 November 1923, to mark the jubilee of Buda's union with Pest, the Hungarian composer-conductor Ernst von Dohnányi gave three important premières: his own Festival Overture, Zoltan Kodály's exciting *Psalmus Hungaricus* and, in between, Bartók's Dance Suite, which suffered 'a shocking failure'. Dohnányi 'could not find his way in this music, and so of course the players could not find theirs either,' wrote the celesta player. Bartók, on hearing the chaos, said: 'Well, it seems I cannot orchestrate.'

Soon afterwards, the Czech Philharmonic came to Budapest. In the interests of neighbourly relations, a recent Hungarian score, Bartók's Dance Suite, was programmed by Václav Talich. The audience, initially apprehensive, went wild after his performance and forced Talich to repeat the Suite from start to finish. Bartók said: 'Well, it might seem that I *can* orchestrate.' Talich had played the same score as Dohnányi, but was clearly a superior conductor, applying a heightened sensibility to difficult rhythms. He was trusted blindly by Leos Janáček to improve his scores, and re-instrumented most of the love tragedy *Katya Kabanova*. One measure by which a great conductor can be assessed is in the new music that he brought into being.*

Some maestros communicated with their eyes, others with their whole body; some would speak and shout, others said little or nothing. Of Richter it was held that he had no secret: 'simply, he knew his job, he was a great economizer of time, and he was a stern disciplinarian'. Musicians in other orchestras could not understand how Berlin Philharmonic players were able to decipher Furtwängler's wavery arm motions that gave no literal indication of the number of beats in a bar. Toscanini, his antipode, had a beat like a metronome. Both were outstanding conductors, and neither can be explained in scientific terms. They shared an inexplicable mystique that reinforced a collective myth.

The sustenance of a myth requires the connivance of compliant writers. Music critics have contributed significantly, if unwittingly, to the cult of the Great Conductor, not only by adopting the term as a cliché but by tailoring their collective attitude and even their vocabulary to strengthen the mythology. Every critic has his favourite performer, who, likely as not, is the next-door critic's *bête noire*. Such partisanship is the spice of musical literature and the controversy helps hone the critical faculties on both sides.

Towards conductors, however, there is a predisposed sympathy. Tenors

*Major premières are listed in the biographical entries in the Appendix, p. 329.

may be safely ridiculed and the pomposity of pianists pricked with a satirical pin, but maestros as a breed are sacrosanct, their virtues inflated, their sins concealed. Some writers are evidently overwhelmed by charisma, others by wealth and power. Toscanini was thirty years dead before anyone wrote a serious criticism of his conducting. Furtwängler is still revered as a demi-god. Critics tolerated, even adulated, the bestial behaviour of Koussevitsky and Szell; they lauded the 'spiritual' qualities of men whose fiscal and social dealings verged on the criminal; they protected the inept and praised the barely competent.

They may decry a particularly lame specimen from time to time, but towards the profession as a whole they extend a reverence shown to no other group. Interviews for record magazines are conducted in a manner that is both obsequiously ingratiating and self-abasing. The magazines themselves are dependent on record company advertising and frequently degenerate into a travesty of trade journalism, reporting nothing except what advertisers want the readers to know.

Writers on music have actually altered their language when it comes to reporting the activities of maestros. A conductor never goes job hunting; he *accepts an invitation* to become music director. He does not break contracts that fail to pay enough but is said to have 'relinquished his post for private and domestic reasons'. He never bullies record executives into reissuing his old discs but 'gives permission for a special edition to be released'. If he feels jaded, he will not take a night off but declares himself *indisposed*, delaying the announcement and allowing his name to be advertised, knowing that people are paying at the box-office to hear a poor substitute.

This is by no means the worst deception committed by modern conductors and concealed by journalists. The word 'commitment' itself is fraught with ambiguity. Music directors proclaim themselves 'totally committed' to the orchestra under their command at that moment, conveniently ignoring their polygamous attachment to an opera house in another country. A music director may not see his orchestra for nine months on end, or know the names of half his staff, while drawing two salaries worth half a million dollars each and wearing his life away in jet-lag. 'Why does this happen to conductors?' demanded the editor of an independent journal. 'Is it personal greed, or the greed of agents and record companies which drives them to distraction, if not destruction?'

The fault lies equally with those who fail in their duty to scrutinize and criticize. There is a conspiracy of silence surrounding conductors, a conspiracy based on self-interest and unstated fear. The case of Charles O'Connell has not been entirely forgotten. O'Connell, a respected record producer, dared to discuss the vanities of conductors in a memoir published in 1947. He admitted shortly afterwards: 'I think I have written myself out of the music business' – as indeed he had, never working again. The only other memoir of comparable revelation, by the British producer John Culshaw, appeared after its author's death. Conductors wield real power, and would-be iconoclasts are easily scared off by libel suits and threats to their livelihood.

The purpose of this book is to examine the origins and nature of the conductors' power, and its influence on the present decline of their profession. Over the past ten years, I have discussed the subject with musicians, record producers, agents, orchestral managers and the leading maestros themselves in an occasionally naïve attempt to understand the relation between the exercise of power and musical performance.

This is not an anti-conductor treatise; far from it. Nor is it an art-critical history of the occupation, subjecting its successive luminaries to technical and interpretative scrutiny. Indeed, several familiar names are virtually absent from these pages, having made but a marginal contribution to the evolution of power politics in the global podium. Among the more notable omissions are the Swiss Stravinskian Ernest Ansermet and his compatriot Charles Dutoit, the Hungarians Antal Dorati and Istvan Kertesz, and any number of capable Germans from Karl Muck and Fritz Busch to Rudolf Kempe, Eugen Jochum, Erich Leinsdorf and Wolfgang Sawallisch. These, together with other eminent conductors, are widely renowned and recorded, but have done little to mould the character of their profession.

Rather than assembling yet another catalogue of conducting 'greats', my aim here has been to delve beneath the mechanics of conducting into the social, psychological, political and economic dynamics of an infinitely fascinating *métier* – to analyse it in plain language without euphemisms, technical flummery and honorifics. Taken from start to finish, the story of conducting is a chronicle of individual endeavour and ambition, modulated by violent circumstances in the surrounding society. Conducting, like most forms of heroism, rests on the use and abuse of power for personal benefit. Whether such heroism is desirable in music, or a necessary evil, remains open to debate. Its future is now, in any event, immediately in doubt. 'Unhappy is the land that has no heroes,' sighed Andrea in Bertolt Brecht's *Life of Galileo*. 'No,' contradicted the astronomer, 'unhappy is the land that *needs* heroes.'

CHAPTER 1

The Tears of a Clown

THE ROT, REMARKED a recent composer, started with Beethoven. Deaf, disorganized and half-demented with the anguish of ostracism, the ailing composer ventured beyond the capabilities of existing orchestras. His symphonies required ever-larger ensembles, but their intricacy demanded a coherence that could only be supplied from without. It was no longer enough for the players to follow their own seated leader when he remembered to look up from whatever part he was playing. They needed an objective non-player to create order amid mounting chaos. As Beethoven's attempts to conduct his music collapsed in tear-streaked farce, the composer ceased to be regarded as the natural leader of musicians and a new profession was born.

Ever since men first made music together,* one of their number was designated to give a lead to stop them falling out of time and tune. The Psalms of King David are punctuated by the cry of 'Selah', uttered by the chorus leader to call for a change of pace, mood or instrumentation. The ancient Greeks, when making music, watched the snap of the senior player's fingers or the rhythm of a dancer's steps. Pictures exist of pre-Christian Sumerian musicians taking an explicit cue from a *primus inter pares*, a colleague who is clearly directing them.

In medieval Europe, choirmasters began physically beating out time with a roll of paper or a short stick. Instrumental Baroque bands would follow their first fiddler. The post of *maestro di capella* (master of the chapel) was created in Venice for Claudio Monteverdi, father of modern opera and much else, to define his responsibilities for hiring the best musicians and making sure they played together. His title was translated into German as *Kapellmeister*, a term that would endure to designate the functions of the first generation of real conductors.

The composer was expected to participate in and direct his own music. Wider executive powers were conferred at the court of the Sun King on

---

*The suppression of female talent is considered in Chapter 13.

the frivolous Florentine, Jean-Baptiste Lully, who held a lifetime mon-opoly over opera productions in Paris and absolute mastery over the royal chapelle. A fine violinist and fabulous dancer, he disdained waving a bow or tapping a foot to beat time, but stood in front of the band and banged heavily on the floor with a wooden staff, a practice that would be observed in France for the next century. For Lully, however, it proved fatal. Bashing his foot during a Te Deum composed for Louis XIV's recovery from illness, he contracted gangrene, suffered several ampu-tations and died in protracted agony.

Other leaders devised an airy downward gesture to denote an accented beat and an upward motion for an unemphasized note. The paper scroll was adopted as a directional wand but proved ineffectual in obtaining precise entries. Vivaldi, Bach and Handel performed their works from a sedentary position of near-parity with the players, leading concertos from the violin or keyboard. Given the manageable size of their orchestras, rarely exceeding thirty musicians, and the music's straightforward linearity, the composer's dual responsibilities as player and director were not unduly taxing.

Handel was fiercely attached to his leadership role and once sword-fought a friend who denied him the prerogative. Haydn plainly enjoyed the authority and led concerts from the keyboard, even though his first violinist in London, Johann Peter Salomon, was a competent leader and technically his employer, having financed the entire concert series. Mozart was so fond of improvisation that his leadership required an extra effort of concentration from the other players. With Beethoven, the composer's *jus primae noctis* over his own music came to an end. Once a brilliant pianist, his hearing had so deteriorated by his mid-thirties that he could no longer distinguish wrong notes from right.

He suffered also from a weak memory, and was wretchedly clumsy. A rival composer, Ludwig Spohr, heard him perform a new piano concerto:

> At the first sforzando he threw out his arms so wide asunder that he knocked both lights off the piano upon the ground. The audience laughed, and Beethoven was so incensed at this disturbance that he made the orchestra cease playing and begin anew. [The composer, Ignaz] Seyfried, fearing that a repetition of the accident would occur at the same passage, bade two boys of the chorus place themselves on either side of Beethoven and hold the lights in their hands. One of the boys innocently approached nearer, and was reading also in the notes of the piano-part. When therefore the fatal *sforzando* came, he received from Beethoven's out-thrown right hand so smart a blow on the mouth that the poor boy let fall the light from terror. The other boy, more cautious, had followed with anxious eyes every motion of Beethoven and, by stooping suddenly at the eventful moment, he avoided the slap on the mouth.

The audience roared with laughter. Beethoven crashed his forearms on to the fortepiano, snapped its strings and aborted the rest of the concert. In the fifth and sixth symphonies he faced near-rebellion from the orchestra; in the seventh he resorted to histrionics, crouching to the ground to show that he wanted a passage played quietly and leaping into the air for a forte. When no sound came through, he looked around bewildered and realized he had lost his place in the score.

By the ninth he was so handicapped that his presence was merely symbolic. The massed musicians and chorus took their lead either from the keyboard player or first violinist. One of the soloists grasped Beethoven by the arm at the end to show him the audience wildly applauding. He had not heard a sound. Neither the orchestra of the ninth symphony nor its message of human brotherhood were conductable from the perspective of a single instrument. Such magniloquence demanded preparation, interpretation and application, professional skills that increasingly eluded those who wrote the music.

Although composers predominated in the podium for much of the nineteenth century, many were fallible when it came to conducting. Schumann was a disaster as music director in Düsseldorf, his perilous mental state undermining an already limited performing talent. Mendelssohn, much-admired conductor of the Leipzig Gewandhaus and London's Philharmonic Society, was criticized by colleagues for the uniform speeds of his performances. Tchaikovsky was an unreliable interpreter of his own late symphonies, and had to be rescued by professionals.

The early stars of the small stick were lesser composers like Spohr – once ranked with Beethoven but soon relegated to a much lower division – who pioneered the modern baton after despairing of the paper scroll and the violinist's bow. Otto Nicolai, composer of a Shakespearian comic opera, *The Merry Wives of Windsor*, formed the Vienna Philharmonic Orchestra in 1842; he abolished the concertmaster's irritating habit of stamping on the floor and gave the city its first account of Beethoven's Ninth for twenty years.

Still louder noises came from Gaspare Spontini, an opera composer whose *ffff*s were the wonder of Berlin, and the French lunatic Louis Jullien, who invented the promenade concert in London, joined the Barnum circus in America and pretended that the trees on his estate played Beethoven's *Eroica* when the wind was in the right direction. Each exerted a formative influence on the last two composers to define the art of conducting. Hector Berlioz was introduced to England by Jullien and remembered him fondly despite some unpaid fees. Berlioz hated earning a living as a critic. Conducting gave him opportunities to travel abroad and occasionally perform his own music, which at home was either ignored or mutilated. In Paris, he related, he had to leap on to the platform to rescue his Requiem when the conductor, François Antoine Habeneck, paused at a critical moment to take a pinch of snuff. Since Habeneck was an excellent musician who had built up one of Europe's best orchestras, Berlioz concluded that his compatriots were out to sabotage his music.

His conducting was fired by an enthusiasm that infected the weariest of players and was applauded from London to St Petersburg. Although the archetype of a Romantic personality, he demonstrated a classicist's attention to detail and devotion to accuracy, weeding out corrupt practices and misreadings. He lacked any aptitude for playing an instrument and was the first to regard conducting as a skill in its own right, as difficult to perfect as playing the violin. In an essential treatise on the art, he likened the conductor to the captain of a ship.

Richard Wagner was initially full of admiration for Berlioz, with whom he shared a wary camaraderie while down and out in Paris and London. His views on conducting had been moulded by childhood encounters with Carl Maria von Weber, the undervalued architect of modern orchestral seating who died in London with tubercules the size of breakfast eggs in his lungs. The effects wrought by Weber's contemporary, Spontini, made an indelible impression. As soon as he had an opera house to call his own, Wagner brought the ageing Italian to Dresden to conduct his opera *La Vestale* so that he could study his technique. The so-called 'Napoleon of the orchestra' told him to fix the front-desk players firmly with his eye and never wear glasses no matter how short-sighted he became. While in Dresden, Wagner also repatriated Weber's bones for something resembling a state funeral.

His experience and philosophy of conducting stemmed from six years in the Saxon capital, where he developed a violent antipathy to the dominant musician at nearby Leipzig, the epicentre of music since Bach's time. Wagner abhorred Felix Mendelssohn on racial, personal, local and musical grounds. His manifesto 'On Conducting', written quarter of a century later, amounts to little more than a sustained attack on a long-dead enemy and his 'elegance' as a conductor. Wagner's approach to directing an orchestra, by contrast, was hyper-Romantic. He advocated the explicit extrapolation of ideas inherent in great music for the edification of a mass audience. If Beethoven intended the *Eroica* symphony to be heroic, then let the public at large experience sensations of heroism by means of subtly manipulating the musical texture. He would never 'glide through the score' like Mendelssohn, but performed it with grit and fire (he laughingly ascribed the conflagration at his opera house during the 1848 revolution to the burning passion of the previous night's Beethoven Ninth). He came to dismiss Berlioz as dull and others as 'kapellmeisters'. Only Liszt, who premièred *Lohengrin* at Weimar while

Caricature of Wagner by W. Bithorn

its composer was on the run, was exempted from his strictures. He spouted theories about energy and intelligence in conductors, the essential relation of tempo to *melos* (song) and the inability of Jews to appreciate either.

Wagner was widely regarded as the supreme conductor of his time and a paramount influence on conducting style. Yet when he finally received the call from King Ludwig of Bavaria to come to Munich and achieve the *Gesamtkunstwerk* he had preached – the mystical union of all the arts – he laid down the baton and left the execution of *Tristan* and the *Ring* to subsidiary conductors. Even Wagner seemed to have accepted that conducting was a specialist occupation, separate from the act of creation.

The first professional conductor was a born loser. Blessed with a tiny gift for invention and the wit to perceive its limitations, he insinuated himself into the widening communication gap between composer and orchestra. Aware that he could not create deathless works, and unwilling merely to re-create, he applied himself to the service of greater men, who exploited and humiliated him.

Hans Guido Freiherr von Bülow, scion of an ancient line, was an anti-hero in a romantic era. He was not a conqueror of hearts but a rape victim, not a potentate but a pathetic figure mocked across dinner-tables. 'The best abused musician of our day,' wrote a eulogist, 'he has been more misunderstood, more laughed at, and even sneered at, than any other.'

The archetype conductor evolved as much out of personal crisis as musical necessity. From the wreckage of a marriage paraded across the front pages and an emotional state that trembled perpetually on the brink of collapse, he formed two world-class orchestras, premièred two Wagner operas and a Brahms symphony, rescued the toughest piano concerto from the waste-bin, nurtured the juvenile Richard Strauss and inspired Gustav Mahler's Resurrection Symphony. On any reasonable reckoning, these are enormous achievements, perhaps immortal ones. In his own eyes and the judgement of history, Bülow was a failure, a man who introduced himself as *nur der Taktstock Wagners* – 'only Wagner's baton'. Alternately servile and domineering, humble and haughty, sentimental and sadistic, he personifies the dilemmas and dichotomies of future conductors. Their collective insecurity and much of their mystique are rooted in Bülow's contradictory, cantankerous character, bred in the human soil that gave rise to Hitlerism.

He grew up like the 'dreamy, delicate child, frightened of everything and troubled frequently by earache' of Heinrich Mann's *Man of Straw*, a fictional case-study of the perfect Imperial German. He was 'poor Hans', the sickly son of a squabbling Dresden couple, and suffered childhood attacks of 'brain fever' at the onset of domestic strife. All his life, he was physically prostrated at the hint of any emotional crisis. Grandfather Bülow was a wounded war hero. His son Eduard turned into a literary liberal whose humanitarianism was spiked by a hasty temper. Bülow's mother, Franziska, by quirk of marital misery, became a church-going reactionary. She brooked no dissension, showed no compassion. Buffeted between them, Hans learned to bow before the mighty and accept their will, asserting himself only over social inferiors.

> The workmen used to laugh when he passed the workshops after having been punished, crying loudly, his face swollen with tears. . . .
> He would say to himself: 'I have got a beating but from my papa. You would be glad to be beaten by him, but you are not good enough for that.'

Bülow's brutal upbringing, amounting to actual child abuse, was typical of child-rearing methods that are today acknowledged as having been a nursery for Nazism. German parents were encouraged to exercise total control over their children, who learned unthinkingly to obey and, when their turn came, coldly to command. Adolf Hitler was a product of this system, wielding unfettered power by day yet shrieking in his sleep at nightmare memories of childhood.

Young Hans took refuge in music, reading piano scores in bed instead of fairy tales. Mesmerized by Liszt's visits to his home, he took piano lessons from Clara Schumann's father and sent his juvenile compositions to the court conductor, Richard Wagner, who responded encouragingly. His parents tolerated his musical interests as a social grace that might assist his future career. One of the few things they shared was a determination that Hans should study law, with a view to obtaining a secure position in government service.

The revolutions of 1848–9 finally tore the Bülow ménage apart as Eduard and Franziska confronted one another across the political ramparts. Although 19 when they divorced, Hans remained subject to their will. Eduard remarried a field-marshal's daughter and went to live in a Swiss castle, while Franziska moved in with her son in Berlin, where he was resentfully studying law and surreptitiously writing songs, playing the piano and submitting concert reviews to a leftish newspaper. Wagner had joined the revolution and escaped into exile.

On a visit to his father's Schloss, Hans suddenly disappeared. 'He is gone to Wagner in Zurich,' guessed Eduard, and set out in hot pursuit. He burst into Wagner's studio, where Hans fell 'at his father's feet and implored him to let him become a musician'. Apoplectic Eduard was won over by Wagner, who also petitioned the indomitable Franziska to leave Hans to study with him for six months 'in a special and sacred cause'. Liszt sent a persuasive letter the following week. Hans begged her 'not to follow your antipathies . . . make me some concessions, I pray', and Franziska, for once in her life, yielded.

Hans now submitted to an extra master. 'The greatest artist who has appeared in our age,' he told his sister, 'has awaked in me ambition, self-confidence and the spring of life. It became clear to me that I was able to *share the spirit* of this man, that I was able to become his pupil, his apostle; and with such an aim as this before me, life appeared to me worthy of living.' The moment his half-year elapsed, Eduard cut off his allowance and told him he could starve. Franziska returned his letters unopened. Their resistance melted only when he began to gain acclaim as a concert pianist. He was reconciled with his mother, but Eduard died before they were reunited, leaving Hans inconsolable at the loss of his 'truest, best and dearest friend' and desperately seeking a father-surrogate.

Richard Wagner embodied the fearful severity that the 23-year-old self-styled 'orphan' expected from a parent. He had worshipped Wagner ever since seeing *Rienzi* when he was 12 years old. To children growing up in the stuffy little Kingdom of Saxony, the republican music director was a symbol of rebellion, and his operas of forbidden love seemed unimaginably wicked. Bülow's English-born schoolfriend, Jessie Taylor, developed a teenage crush on Wagner that flared briefly into a love affair. She would later help Hans rebuild his life from the ashes of his tragic adoration.

While staying with Wagner in Zurich, Bülow had acquired the rudiments of conducting along with the ideal of service to a superior being. On his return to Berlin, he moved back in with his mother, taught piano at the Stern Conservatory and promoted the dangerous new music of his mentor. He opened his first orchestral concert with the *Tannhäuser* overture and, when the audience murmured, fainted dead away on the stage.

Franziska took in lodgers and was delighted when Liszt sent her his two teenaged daughters, Blandine and Cosima. The girls and their brother Daniel, fruits of his stormy liaison with the Countess Marie d'Agoult, had been turned over to him when French law rejected their mother's natural rights over her illegitimate children. As soon as he had won the case, Liszt left the children for seven years with his elderly mother and a succession of governesses and swung off on a continental tour. He finally settled in Weimar with Princess Carolyne von Sayn-Wittgenstein, who had no interest in his children but was jealous of her predecessor. When Marie approached her children, who lived near her home on the Champs Elysées, Liszt's mistress took fright and ordered him to remove them from Paris to a place of moral safety.

Nothing, it seemed, could be more secure than the Berlin apartment of the devout Frau von Bülow, where their education would be rounded off with piano lessons from her harmless son, Hans. He was 25 when Cosima arrived and she was 17. They were drawn to one another instinctively as victims of impossible parents. Within weeks Hans asked Liszt for permission to court his daughter. This was no love story, however. Love hardly crossed the threshold. 'For me,' Hans told her father, 'Cosima Liszt transcends all other women not only because she bears your name but also because she so resembles you, because she is in so many ways the exact mirror of your personality.' He added: 'I swear to you that, however much I feel bound to her by my love, I should never hesitate to sacrifice myself to her happiness and release her were she to realize that she had made a mistake in regard to me.' He would be called to honour this pledge in circumstances more agonizing than anyone could envisage.

Liszt, mildly alarmed, postponed the wedding for a year. He had no right to play the protective father, but was sensitive enough to feel uneasy and indicated to Frau von Bülow that Hans might make himself a better match elsewhere. Neither, however, cared enough to forbid the marriage, which took place in Berlin on 18 August 1857. From the Catholic church, the young couple went straight to the railway station to catch a train for Zurich and seek the blessing of Richard Wagner.

Cosima knew Wagner as her father's best friend and resented his hold over her frail bridegroom. Wagner was emotionally preoccupied with Mathilde Wesendonck, wife of his Swiss patron and inspiration of *Tristan und Isolde*. He asked Hans to prepare a piano score of the opera and let him conduct the unfinished prelude with a makeshift ending of his own at a national convention of composers in Leipzig. Wagner moved to Paris to supervise a disastrous *Tannhäuser* production, hauling Bülow back and forth from Berlin to prepare his parts and play Sancho Panza in high society to his own Quixote. 'Poor Bülow,' muttered Berlioz, 'Wagner bitterly hates everyone who has humiliated him by rendering him a service.'

Cosima in Berlin nursed her dying brother and named her first child Daniella Senta, after Liszt's son and Wagner's *Flying Dutchman* heroine. 'It would be my own and my wife's greatest happiness to dedicate her one day to your service,' Bülow told Wagner. Cosima's next confinement was nightmarish, following the death in childbirth of her only sister. 'I hardly dared tell Hans that I was pregnant, so unfriendly was his reaction, as if his comfort were being disturbed,' she wrote years later in her diary, adding: 'only Richard, far away, was concerned about me, and I did not know it.' By now Wagner was sleeping with a Viennese actress, Friederike Meyer, while wooing a wealthy lawyer's daughter, Mathilde Maier. He did not spare much thought for Cosima.

On his next visit to Berlin, in November 1863, he was thrown against Cosima while riding in a bumpy carriage to Bülow's concert. They fell into each other's arms and 'with tears and sobs sealed our vow to live for each other alone' – or so he dictated to her when she took down his memoirs.

Months later, Cosima was all but forgotten when the 18-year-old King Ludwig II of Bavaria summoned Wagner to Munich and gave him a house, a salary and the chance to stage his unseen operas. Wagner told the Bülows he was too busy to see them that year and continued flirting with Mathilde Maier. When she resisted, he invited the Bülows to his summer villa beside Lake Starnberg. Cosima turned up with her two small daughters and they became lovers before Bülow joined them a fortnight later. He was evidently apprised of the relationship. 'I wanted to try combining my former existence with my new life,' explained Cosima, and Wagner got the King to employ Bülow as his court pianist. Within three weeks of this social experiment, Bülow was seized by total paralysis.

He was put to bed in a hotel while Cosima went to Karlsruhe to consult her father, an international authority on extra-marital complications. The unshockable Liszt brought her back to Munich, where he met Wagner after a long estrangement. He ordered a temporary suspension of the *ménage à trois*, but Bülow was soon needed back in Munich for the Tristan première and Cosima was pregnant again. She gave birth to Isolde on 10 April while her husband conducted the first full rehearsal of *Tristan*. The baby was registered as Bülow's child with Wagner as godfather, each believing himself to be the father. Fifty years later Isolde sued Cosima to determine her paternity and stake a claim in Bayreuth; in 1945, her Swiss son was asked by the Allies to help cleanse the shrine of Hitlerism.

Although Cosima had slept with both men throughout the summer, Bülow wanted their marriage to continue. Cosima, however, could not make up her mind, and Wagner wanted the best of both worlds: Cosima in his bed, Hans in his pit. On 10 June 1865, Bülow conducted the first performance of *Tristan und Isolde*. Wagner, the master-conductor, had forsaken the podium to superintend the 'complete work of art' and Bülow conducted the four-hour score entirely from memory. He had, said Wagner, 'absorbed every last nuance of my intentions'. The profession of conducting was born that night.

Wagner's triumph was shortlived as foes at court drove him out of Bavaria. He moved to a Swiss lakeside house at Tribschen, near Lucerne, where Cosima in February 1867 gave birth to his daughter Eva, named after the heroine of *Die Meistersinger von Nürenberg* which he had just finished. 'I forgive you,' said Bülow, hastening to her bedside. 'What is needed is not forgiveness but understanding,' snapped his wife.

The conductor has received scant sympathy from historians. That he was a born victim is self-evident; that he was made to connive for five long years in his own victimization makes his position doubly poignant. The lies Cosima told to deceive the King were publicly endorsed by her cuckolded husband; when a newspaper dropped hints of adultery, Bülow challenged its editor to a duel. He fell in with the deception because he dared not confront the lovers. Having adopted Wagner as a surrogate for his domineering father and Cosima as his refuge from an icy mother, he was emotionally imprisoned by their inevitable relationship.

On 21 June 1868 he premièred *Die Meistersinger*. 'Bülow uses his whole body to indicate the nuances he wants and puts such ferocious energy into each gesture that one begins to tremble for the violinists and the lamps within his reach,' noted a journalist. Wagner berated him loudly during rehearsals and Bülow in turn flayed the orchestra with his acidulous tongue. When Franz Strauss, Munich's horn-player and father of a future composer, declared 'I can't go on', Bülow snarled woundingly, 'then why don't you retire?' At a recalcitrant singer, he spat out his most memorable aphorism: 'A tenor is not a man but a disease.'

Months later, Cosima took matters in hand and moved in with Wagner. Bülow wrote to her: 'You have preferred to devote your life and the treasures of your mind and affection to one who is my superior and, far from blaming you, I *approve* your action.' The time had come to redeem his betrothal pledge to Liszt. He told the piano-maker Carl Bechstein: 'I have been unavoidably forced by certain quite recent events to take a step which I would have made any humanly possible sacrifice to avoid on my Master and father-in-law's F. L.'s account. Before leaving Germany I *must* try to obtain a *dissolution of my marriage.* . . . Oh my dear Bechstein – everything within me is crashing! And it had to be!'

In a state of near-collapse, he was saved by his former classmate Jessie, cohabiting in Florence with an eminent German historian, Karl Hillebrand, yet still nursing her romantic Wagner grievance. Bülow, at her home, regained his bearings. 'I am somewhat crazy, am I not?' he inquired, quoting one of Jessie's English poets. 'But I got tipsy from the sun overhead, and the stars inside.'

His body would betray him repeatedly for the rest of his career as a conductor, but his mind held firm until the moment almost 15 years later when he was forced to accept the finality of his orphanhood. Barred from the Bayreuth *Ring*, he donated forty thousand marks from a concert tour in the hope of an invitation to *Parsifal*. Wagner, incensed, threw the money into a trust for Bülow's two daughters and applied to adopt them as his own. Instead of spending the summer of 1882 watching *Parsifal*, Bülow quietly remarried. His bride was Marie Schanzer, a young actress born in the year he had wedded Cosima. On their Danish honeymoon at Klampenborg, where he used to spend holidays with his first wife, Bülow fell apart and was committed to a mental asylum.

Cosima was consumed by guilt. 'I flee to my room and see Hans before me in that institution, and I feel like screaming, screaming to some God to help me! . . . I do not believe that I shall ever have, or deserve to have, another happy moment.' Wagner awoke that night shouting, 'I hate all pianists – they are my Antichrist!'

Against expectations, Bülow emerged from hospital in a matter of weeks, partially recovered. It was Wagner who died that winter. Cosima tried to starve herself to death in a paroxysm of grief, deterred only by Bülow's cable – '*Soeur, il faut vivre!*' ('Sister, you must live on!') – he advised in the French tongue they had always shared and that Wagner loathed. As heir to Bayreuth, she thought repeatedly of inviting her first husband, the supreme Wagner conductor, to conduct an opera – but never found the courage to ask him.

* * *

None of this would be worth relating here were it not germane to the emergence of a conducting prototype. Tortured by tyrannical parents and a callous composer, Bülow passed on the savage treatment he had received to his players, in the name of a superior authority. Subsequent conductors took their cue from him. Koussevitsky, at his most brutal, addressed his players as 'my children'. A terror to his musicians, Toscanini abased himself before great composers.

Bülow's independent career as a conductor was overshadowed by his divorce from Wagner. He burst into tears when a childhood friend berated him for somehow betraying 'an ideal to which *I* have remained faithful' and when a London hostess asked if he knew Wagner, he rasped: 'Ah, he married my widow.'

In Russia he met Tchaikovsky and persuaded him to retrieve the B flat minor piano concerto that he had thrown away when the Rubinstein brothers pronounced it unplayable. Bülow performed the concerto in Boston, bellowing instructions at his orchestra and audience until, gratified by the reception, he pounded out the entire finale a second time. Back in St Petersburg he gave Tchaikovsky the triumph of his life by conducting the Third Suite. 'Never had any of his works been received with such unanimous enthusiasm,' wrote the composer's brother.

Smetana, Dvořák and Stanford were among the symphonists he espoused. His ear was acute and his verdict irrevocable. When an English composer played him something commonplace, Bülow rushed outside and vomited on the pavement. He praised the conducting of the young Gustav Muhler when their paths crossed in Hamburg but found his compositions insupportable. He was not entirely deaf to modernism and crowned young Strauss Richard the Third. Wagner, of course, was the first Richard and after him there could be no second.

The nearest Bülow ever came to filling the Wagner void was in a flirtation with his detested antipode, Johannes Brahms. To Wagnerians, Brahms was an antichrist invented by the Viennese critic, Eduard Hanslick. Wagner represented the fusion of all arts in opera, whereas Brahms persisted with the symphonic form that Wagner pronounced bankrupt.

Bülow had known Brahms since the 1860s and did not think much of his chamber music. He revised his opinion when Brahms' long-awaited first symphony was performed at Karlsruhe in November 1876, months after the inaugural *Ring*. The two men met in Baden the following year and Bülow offered to conduct the symphony in Glasgow. In a letter to Jessie he acclaimed it as 'the Tenth Symphony' – the continuation of Beethoven – and talked of the 'three Bs' – Bach, Beethoven and Brahms – as the pillars of his musical faith. Brahms was 'jarred and outraged' on hearing of these flights of hyperbole.

In 1881, Bülow repaired their friendship with a priceless gift: free use of his new orchestra at Meiningen whenever Brahms wanted to try out

a new composition in private. He had been hired by the Grand Duke of
Saxe-Meiningen to turn his court band into something special. With
limitless rehearsal and fine players like the clarinettist Richard Mühlfeld,
for whom Brahms wrote his quintet and late sonatas, Bülow pursued an
ideal of perfection. He trained the four dozen men to play standing
upright and, like himself, entirely from memory. No sheet of paper was
seen on his stage. 'You should have the score in your head, not your
head in the score,' he told Strauss, 'even if you have composed the thing
yourself.' The orchestra was the first to undertake continental tours and
was universally applauded. Liszt, in a famous article, called the Meiningen Hofkapelle a 'miracle'.

In 1884 Brahms accepted an invitation to the Duke's summer residence
in Italy, where he started work on his fourth symphony. He conducted
it privately at Meiningen, before turning over the symphony to Bülow
for a German tour. As they came to Frankfurt, Brahms said that Clara
Schumann had specially asked if he could conduct the symphony in her
town. Bülow said he had never been so insulted in his life and raced out
into the night, refusing to sleep under the same roof as Brahms. The
next day he cabled the Duke: 'Since I cannot carry on grinding this
Brahms barrel-organ, I respectfully beg your Highness to accept my
resignation.'

On an imaginary matter of honour, he had tossed away a valued
friendship, a secure job and a fingerhold on posterity. The cause might
seem insignificant but he had plainly resolved never again to yield primacy
to a composer.

As the number of conductors increased, Bülow's excesses were decried
by would-be successors. Leading the charge was Felix von Weingartner,
a minor aristocrat who aimed to cleanse scores of the fanciful interpretations with which Bülow (and, by implication, Wagner) had decorated
them. Irascible, litigious, licentious and five times married, he was forever
involved in some form of intellectual, romantic or judicial disputation.
Pamphlets poured forth from his frenetic pen. So did compositions; he
judged fellow-conductors by their willingness to perform his music.
(Bülow charitably performed a string serenade.)

On seeing Bülow's 1887 Hamburg performance of *Carmen*, Weingartner suffered 'a feeling of acute discomfort, almost of horror' at the
conductor's podium antics. 'My aim in conducting has been and is to
reproduce the work soulfully and with the greatest simplicity and fidelity,
while making my own gestures so inconspicuous that the attention of the
audience is not drawn to me and away from the music,' he stated prig-
gishly. A pale, lanky figure, Weingartner would shut his eyes before a
symphony, the better to commune with its spirit. His interpretations

tended to be weighty and impersonal. Excess movement, he said, disturbed the audience and confused the players. 'Sensation-mongering in music began with Bülow,' he proclaimed sensationally, in an 1895 polemic that took its title, 'On Conducting', from Wagner's famous treatise. Most of it was an outright attack on Bülow, whom he blamed for

> the detestable illusion of the value of the personality which induces every little Nobody to claim special rights for himself so long as his behaviour is sufficiently unorthodox, and dazzles the talented weakling into committing absurdities.

He complained that people talked of 'Bülow's *Carmen*', rather than Bizet's. Bülow had given rise to a cult of conducting personality; Weingartner campaigned for precedence to be restored to composers. Their dispute rages on, in different guises, to the present day.

Weingartner's cause would deserve greater consideration had he practised what he preached. A man of impermeable vanity, he sliced huge chunks out of Wagner operas he conducted and wrote two books on Beethoven that are riddled with alterations to the composer's scoring, dynamics and tempi. In the symphonies, he inserted instruments unknown in Beethoven's day and emphases that were totally out of character. If anything, his approach was less pure than Bülow's, who told pupils: 'Learn to read the score of a Beethoven symphony *accurately* first, and you will have found its interpretation.'

Many of Bülow's annotations were based on original analyses made by Wagner. Liszt rejected criticism of Bülow's performances as 'devoid of foundation' and Strauss said,

> the exactitude of his phrasing, his intellectual penetration of the score . . . above all his psychological understanding of Beethoven symphonies and of Wagner's preludes in particular have been a shining example to me.

Mahler admired his conducting, while Bruno Walter – who stood in relation to Mahler as Bülow had to Liszt – was enthralled by his performance. 'I saw in Bülow's face,' wrote Walter,

> the glow of inspiration and the concentration of energy. I felt the compelling force of his gestures, noticed the attention and devotion of the players, and was conscious of the expressiveness and precision of their playing. It became at once clear to me that it was that one man who was producing the music, that he had transformed those hundred performers into his instrument and that he was playing it as a pianist played the piano. That evening decided my future . . . I had decided to become a conductor.

Just as his life seemed most meaningless, his Munich and Meiningen achievements all but forgotten, Berlin suddenly offered Bülow a passport to posterity. At the age of 57, he was on the brink of another breakdown, racked by headaches, insomnia and arm pains. 'He kept repeating that life was over for him, that he wanted to die, and it was only by continually telling him how much we all adored him . . . that I was able gradually to quiet him and put him to bed, where I sat holding his hands until early morning when he finally went to sleep,' recalled his American pupil Walter Damrosch.

To his daughter, Bülow half-joked of enduring 'a particularly painful chronic exhaustion and acute hypochondria', but violent swings of mood and outbursts of intense self-loathing threatened to put him beyond his second wife's devoted care and permanently into an asylum. Berlin may well have saved his life. Its Philharmonic Orchestra had lost all its instruments and scores in 1886 when fire swept through the Scheveningen casino, where it was entertaining tourists. All that survived, mocking the musicians' misery, was a singed sheet of a Johann Strauss waltz, *Freut euch des Lebens* ('Let life be joyful'). The great violinist Joseph Joachim headed a rescue operation with fund-raising recitals. The Mendelssohn banking family injected cash and the city's leading concert agent, Hermann Wolff, undertook to manage the entire season at his own risk if he was allowed to pick as principal conductor – Hans von Bülow.

Berlin had never enjoyed much in the way of musical merit; long gone were the days when Goethe pumped his friend Zelter for news of the latest premières and Carl Maria von Weber found his most receptive audience. Under the Iron Chancellery of Bismarck, the citadel of Berlin was dedicated to progress of a fiercer kind. It nurtured a vigorous scientific culture, with the phenomenal Hermann von Helmholtz in the university's chair of physics, but little in the way of artistic adornment other than Joachim's presence at the academy of music and the recitals of his world-famous quartet. Compared to London, Berlin was 'a dismal, ill-lit and second-rate city, with one good thoroughfare (Unter den Linden) flanked by palaces and public buildings of striking architectural aspiration but of cold and even repellent effect . . . The opera was poor [and] there were no first-rate concerts.'

Bülow's visits in the early 1880s with his Meiningen masterplayers had alerted the Reich's capital to what it was missing. Seated around tables laden with beer and sausages, Berliners greeted his concerts with 'tumultuous enthusiasm . . . applauded wildly, and shouted themselves hoarse'. Berlin gained its own Philharmonic when fifty of the 74 players in Benjamin Bilse's court-sponsored orchestra walked out in protest at being given fourth-class tickets for their rail journey to Warsaw. With Joachim's support, they drew up a charter of independence, appointed a compliant conductor, Ludwig von Brenner, and made their debut in October 1882. Beer and food were still served, though only in the intervals.

The string section shone under Carl Halir, a superb soloist who later premièred the final version of the Sibelius concerto, but the brass and woodwind were 'wretched', according to Richard Strauss. Joachim's concerts lent occasional lustre and Brahms appeared in January 1884. Six weeks later Bülow made a guest appearance at a Hermann Wolff subscription concert, though three more years would pass before he was offered the conductorship. Wolff had been involved with the orchestra since its formation, offering financial guarantees to the rebel bands and persuading two business friends to purchase a former skating rink and convert it into Philharmonic Hall. A multilingual former music critic, Wolff handled his clients like Dresden china, making them camomile tea at moments of stress and tucking them into bed to ensure a safe night's sleep.

Bülow was his most difficult artist, a challenge to anyone's ingenuity. 'It takes patience, self-control, intuition and pity to remain on his side,' Wolff confided to his wife. Putting him in a position of authority in Berlin would be commercially hazardous. The volatile, unstable Bülow, 'quick to love and quick to hate', could easily destroy the orchestra, chase away its supporters, outrage the imperial government.

'I can only justify my existence here by introducing reforms,' Bülow replied. He would expect the orchestra to be note-perfect at his first rehearsal so that he could 'get right to work on the music itself'. Concerts were to be shorter than customary, without fripperies and sweetmeats, only music that he, Hans Guido Freiherr von Bülow, considered essential. His opening concert consisted of three classical symphonies – Mozart's *Jupiter*, Haydn's *Clock* and Beethoven's *Eroica*. Bülow, with nothing to lose, had no reason to compromise.

He performed Beethoven's ninth symphony twice in the same concert to convince Berlin of its importance. Musicians were appalled, but the callow young Kaiser was intrigued (in Hamburg, Bülow had the doors locked to stop the public escaping after the first performance). Openly contemptuous of Berlin, he reserved special venom for the Royal Opera, calling it 'Hülsen's circus' and apologizing to the owner of Germany's largest circus for any unintended offence. Next time he went to the opera, Baron von Hülsen had him bodily ejected.

When the opera house set up rival 'Symphony Evenings of the Royal Orchestra', its resident conductor, Felix von Weingartner, discovered that 'Bülow had drawn to himself in the Philharmonic the whole of Berlin's musical public'. Unable to outplay Bülow, the operatic aristocrats and their friends at court stripped him of the honorary title of Court Pianist. He duly advertised his next recital as '*Volkspianist* Hans von Bülow'.

The People's Pianist began making impromptu speeches to his concert audiences. In the middle of his second season he confessed that, as court conductor in Munich and Meiningen, he had counted himself a failure. Berlin now enabled this child of 1848 to attain his ambition of becoming the People's Conductor. These were dangerously democratic sentiments in a society that did not recognize freedom of speech. Younger fans egged him on to ever-greater excesses.

At the close of his fiftieth concert on 28 March 1892, he favoured them with a lengthy address on the state of humanity, 'a dream that has borne enough bad fruit'. Of the *Eroica* that he had just conducted, he reminded them that Beethoven had originally dedicated the symphony to Napoleon but scratched out his name when the hero turned tyrant. We musicians, said Bülow, must now rededicate this work – 'to the greatest spiritual hero to arise since Beethoven himself, to Beethoven's brother, the Beethoven of German politics. We dedicate it to Prince Bismarck. *Heil!*'

Bismarck had been sacked two years earlier by the abrasive young Kaiser and was attempting a comeback, rousing the masses on whistle-stop nationwide tours that threatened to undermine the government. Berlin was split between his followers and die-hard royalists. There had been violent protests in the streets and the Emperor had defiantly ridden his horse through the demonstrators' ranks. Grumblers, declared William II, could kindly pack their bags and 'shake the dust of Germany from the soles of their feet'. His challenge became a slogan of the bold assertiveness of Imperial Germany. Watching the furore his remarks had provoked, Bülow whipped out a white handkerchief, flicked the dust off his shoes and left Berlin the next morning. 'Did my duty,' he cabled his wife. He repeated the concert and speech in Hamburg where, to his disgust, the mercantile class paid no attention.

After a year's absence, he returned to Berlin to conduct the *Eroica* for the benefit of his players' pension fund. At his final concert on 10 April 1893, he conducted the last three Beethoven symphonies, ending the ninth on its adagio without the uplift of choral liberation. He foresaw no happy ending for Germany, its music or himself. Frail and fractious, he returned to Hamburg where his health gave way. Sent to Cairo for convalescence, he died days after arrival, on 12 February 1894, of what turned out to be an undiagnosed brain tumour.

After a life of unstable relationships, he had founded in his final years a durable institution. 'My orchestra par excellence,' he called the Berlin Philharmonic. It was his supreme epitaph. Although others had helped in its formation, Bülow's intervention was decisive in creating a collective ethos and self-regard that prevail to the present day. Berlin became known culturally for the glory of its orchestra. The Philharmonic became the city's calling-card and trade representative, a propaganda tool during two World Wars and one Cold, the symbol of its society and an example to all cities that wanted to advance in the world's estimation. Bülow, whose only aspiration was musical excellence, did not live to see his ideal exploited. Like the rest of the world, Berlin had used his talents and shoved him aside. To further its pragmatic aims, it now required a different kind of conducting figurehead.

Original programme from the former ice-rink that became the Berlin Philharmonic

CHAPTER 2

Honest Hans and the Magician

ORCHESTRAL PLAYERS CALLED him the Magician and sat transfixed by his wand. Audiences watched him in wonderment, women's eyes following the proud sweep of his elongated baton. 'Now don't forget to tell me, Olga,' he overheard a Berliner whispering in the front row, 'the moment he begins to *fascinate*.'

To many in his own time and beyond Arthur Nikisch was the archetypal conductor, a tiny man with a huge crown of hair who conquered great orchestras with the flick of a wrist and strode the world stage with regal aplomb. Watching him, concertgoers became aware for the first time that the conductor's personality, an entirely subjective set of likes and dislikes, was actively shaping the sound of the music they heard. He loved telling how Brahms, at one of his Leipzig rehearsals, wandered about the empty Gewandhaus grumbling: 'Is it possible? Did I really write that?' But when the orchestra began to disperse, the symphonist advanced upon Nikisch beaming with pleasure and exclaiming, 'You have changed everything. But you are right. It *must* be like that.'

In a Nikisch performance, interpretation ceased to be a faithful elucidation of the composer's notes. It became a creative act in its own right, extrapolating the original idea and extending it in unsuspected, at times unpalatable, directions. Although his approach was often 'wrong and contrary to the intentions of the composer, Nikisch made [the music] convincing for the moment', wrote an American colleague. The modern conductor must create anew, said Nikisch in his eulogy for Bülow: 'that is why his individuality plays so significant a role'.

Purist reservations were swept aside by the sheer excitement he generated. Tchaikovsky's fourth symphony under his direction had a London audience jumping on to the Queen's Hall seats, 'stamping and shouting themselves hoarse; many chairs were broken'. After a twelve-hour working day, the London Symphony Orchestra found themselves playing Tchaikovsky's Fifth 'like fiends: when we reached the end of the first movements, we all did rise from our seats and actually shouted'.

Nikisch had rescued the Fifth from the waste-basket, after the composer botched its première in November 1888 and wrote the symphony off as a failure. Visiting St Petersburg soon afterwards, Nikisch beamed gently as the players protested long and loud at the work's inadequacy. They were still murmuring in the woodwinds when he raised the baton. With deep satisfaction and no little glee (he retold the story regularly), he observed a tide of interest rise slowly through the strings and into the winds and brass until the entire orchestra was taken by storm and gripped with unbroken concentration for a full hour. 'He does not seem to conduct,' said the composer, 'rather to exercise a mysterious spell.'

At his opening concert with the Berlin Philharmonic, Nikisch founded Tchaikovsky's popularity in Germany with a national première of the selfsame Fifth. Steering perilously close to *kitsch*, he achieved an orchestral tone that sent Russian critics reeling for one of Pushkin's highest accolades. They called it *nega* – 'bliss'. 'I can only conduct if I feel the music in my heart,' said Nikisch.

This intense relationship with a composer and a work lay at the heart of his magic. Like a lover in the throes of passion, he contrived to make his loved one bloom as never before. 'Make all your performances a grand improvisation!' he exhorted Henry Wood, sometimes called 'the English Nikisch'. 'If the critics don't like it, they can get a metronome to conduct.' Like lovemaking, Nikisch held that conducting required spontaneity, boldness, imagination and a profound feeling for the work in hand. Routine was abhorrent to him.

'My interpretation changes almost with every performance according to the powers of feeling aroused within me,' he said. 'Of course, it is only details that are altered. To experience a Beethoven symphony one way today and entirely differently tomorrow would be as laughable as it is illogical. The kind of trick a travelling jester would play.' 'This is wonderful but it isn't Beethoven,' was the reaction of a young English musician raised on drier performances. On hearing Nikisch conduct *Tristan*, the ultimate music of infatuation, Adrian Boult 'nearly went mad each night'.

Wherever he appeared, Nikisch was recognized by his flaming coiffure and the flash-white shirts with outsized cuffs that half-concealed his small, pale hands. He dressed elaborately, friends said, not to show off but because he was an aristocrat in all things. At the close of a concert, he did not rush for a drink in the artists' room but stood serenely on stage, alternately bowing and chatting to his front-desk players until the applause diminished to a level that he deemed appropriate for a measured departure.

Nikisch was not naturally good-looking. His supreme asset was a deep-set pair of dark eyes that drew men and women to him like a silken web: soft, brooding, somewhat sombre, unfailingly hypnotic. There was nothing demagogic in his look, just a seductive hint of infinite consolation, like a siren's distant song. The top of his baton became an extension of those remarkable eyes, hypnotizing the players with its slightest tremor as he stood almost motionless on the rostrum. After a searing Brahms symphony that Adrian Boult found 'rather too exciting', the aspiring conductor realized that Nikisch's hand had never once risen above face level throughout the explosive experience. 'It was all in the point of his stick,' said Boult. 'I remember people saying at the time that if you put Nikisch in a glass case and asked him to conduct an imaginary orchestra you could at once, in a few bars, tell what he was conducting.'

New players unfamiliar with his discreet stick feared they might miss the moment of attack, only to be drawn in unobtrusively by the little finger of his left hand, its diamond ring glittering. At the instant of climax, a half-clenched fist proved explosive. 'His right hand beats time,' wrote a Hamburg critic, 'the left makes the music.' He developed a new wrist and finger technique of conducting, and was the first to beat just ahead of the note, adding forward propulsion to the music. 'If one of my colleagues were to ask me after a concert how I produced this or that particular effect, I would be unable to answer,' he once said. 'When I conduct a work, it is the thrilling power of the music that sweeps me on. I follow no hard and fast rules of interpretation, nor do I sit down and work it all out in advance.'

High-minded musicians thought him stupid. 'In intellectual respects one would say he was somewhat primitive. He read little or nothing, was fond of cards, women and company . . . his ambitions were chiefly musical and social,' sniffed the violinist Carl Flesch. He may have lacked the curiosity of a Wagner or a Mahler, but Nikisch was no fool. His friends included the intellectual Pevsners of Leipzig – he gave a barmitzvah gift to the future chronicler of British buildings – and he encouraged his sons to study at university. The elder, Arthur, became a distinguished lawyer and a member of Thomas Mann's circle.

In common with many maestri, he stood little taller than a midget. 'His spiritual powers raised him above himself,' noted a Leipziger, 'when he stood on the podium he would grow before our eyes into an enormous, titanic figure.' He exhibited none of the compensatory aggression associated with diminutive men and, in contrast to the tinpot tyrants astride the podium, was unfailingly gentle with his players, never raising his voice, rarely uttering a stronger word of reproval than, 'Excuse me, gentlemen.' Musicians melted before him. The London Symphony Orchestra, a workers' co-operative formed in 1904 by a tough, underpaid gang of Queen's Hall rebels, 'gloried in playing for him'. His introductory session with the Boston Symphony Orchestra ended with the players exultant. 'We have heard today words that we did not hear in five years,' they informed a member of the board. 'What words?' she demanded. *'Sehr gut, meine Herren!'* ('Well done, gentlemen!')

'When he merely stood on the rostrum, the orchestra already sounded better than with other conductors,' reported Fritz Busch, who played under Nikisch at Cologne. Unlike a colleague who addressed his men by number – '32 in the woodwind, you cracked at fig. 17' – Nikisch would memorize the names and quirks of individuals in every orchestra he conducted. At Cologne, slowly peeling off his kid gloves, he announced that it was his life's dream to conduct 'this famous orchestra'.

> He suddenly interrupted himself, stretched his hand out towards an old viola player and cried out, 'Schulze, what are *you* doing here? I had no idea that you had landed in this beautiful town. Do you remember how we played the *Bergsymphonie* under Liszt at Magdeburg? Schulze did remember it and immediately resolved that with this conductor he would use the whole length of his bow, instead of playing with only half.

If ever he was late to rehearsal at Leipzig, he would fish into his pocket for a few gold coins and present them as an act of contrition to the musicians' pension fund. Players regarded Nikisch as one of their own and welcomed him to their backstage poker games.

His family life revolved around music. He married a mediocre Belgian soprano, Amélie Heusner, and accompanied her recitals to the disgust of his admirers. 'Apart from her voice, Mrs Nikisch was a charming and intelligent woman,' bitched a Boston friend. Amélie retired to compose operettas, which Nikisch loyally scored for her, having abandoned his own early compositions. Their second son, Mitya, was a gifted, short-lived pianist; the elder, Arthur, wed a singer; a daughter, Kaethe, married the Leipzig concertmaster.

But the eyes that entranced the world's orchestras roved wickedly when away from the podium. 'He was adored by the ladies of Paris,' reported his French follower, Pierre Monteux, 'and his conquests of the feminine heart both in Europe and America are well known.' Women found his air of 'melancholy sensibility' utterly irresistible and flocked to the shop of his Leipzig baton-maker to acquire sticks that had been wielded by *Der Magier* – 'this one for the *Pathétique*, that for the *Pastoral*'. Elena Gerhardt, whom he accompanied on far-flung recital tours, was among his paramours. 'Nikisch always used to say one cannot have too much of a good thing,' she wrote suggestively. There was little resentment of his successes, whether artistic or amorous, even among jealous rivals. Nikisch was recognized as possessing supernatural qualities.

He came from a family of Hungarian peasants, born in the village of Lébényi Szent Miklós in 1855 and sent as an eleven-year-old violin student to the Conservatory in Vienna. In May 1872, as he neared graduation, an outcast called Richard Wagner came to town. Nikisch and the more daring of his classmates had secretly studied *Tristan* and infiltrated themselves into the orchestra that Wagner conducted in Beethoven's *Eroica*. Ten days later, on Wagner's 59th birthday, Nikisch played in a Beethoven Ninth at Bayreuth to celebrate the laying of the Festival's foundation stone. Concertmasters of ten orchestras sat around him in the strings and the aspiring conductor Hans Richter blew second trumpet and beat the kettledrums because, said Wagner, 'no professional timpanist has yet understood the part'. Those two Beethoven concerts determined Nikisch's future. He would become a conductor and emulate the *Meister*. He left Bayreuth inspired, yet uncorrupted. Abnormally alert to potentially servile youth – Bülow was the tragic prototype, Richter his successor – Wagner failed to notice Nikisch. Somehow, the greatest *Tristan* conductor of his time would never raise a baton at Bayreuth.

For four years he fiddled for a living in the Vienna opera orchestra, his existence enlivened by Verdi's visit to conduct his Requiem and by occasional Philharmonic concerts under Brahms, Liszt and Bruckner. Otherwise, he found orchestral life humdrum and gave most of his wages to a deputy to relieve him of the tedium. His saviour was a Jewish ex-tenor, Angelo Neumann, who had taken over as manager of the Leipzig Opera and was looking for a chorus director. Nikisch, now 23, leaped at the opportunity and made himself so useful in Leipzig that Neumann went off on his summer holiday leaving him in charge of *Tannhäuser*. No sooner had he reached Salzburg than a telegram arrived: 'Orchestra refuses to play under Nikisch. Too young.' Neumann replied: 'Rehearse the overture with him, then resign if you like.' A few seconds with Nikisch was enough to convince. His success, wrote Neumann, 'was so unqualified that the musicians themselves begged him with a storm of cheers and congratulations to continue the rehearsal at once; and with this performance of *Tannhäuser*, Arthur Nikisch entered the ranks of the foremost conductors in Germany'.

For the rest of his life he dominated music in Leipzig, Wagner's birthplace and Bach's shrine. Rising out of the opera pit, he restored the Gewandhaus concerts that had faded since Mendelssohn's death and became the city's most popular personality. Hearing that he had been felled by a heart attack, the local electricity workers union called off a strike in order to sustain his life-support equipment. In Berlin, which Bülow meant to bequeath to Richard Strauss, he displaced the young composer from the Philharmonic and soon gave a performance of his *Also Sprach Zarathustra* that totally eclipsed its première under the baton of its creator. Strauss hailed him as 'the magnificent Nikisch'.

He inherited Bülow's other orchestra in Hamburg, was an annual fixture in the London season and travelled more widely than any previous conductor, touring both North and South America. This gave rise to suggestions that he was a brilliant improviser who lacked the patience to settle with an orchestra and train it to a consistently high standard. The charge is unfounded. Under his directorship, Germany's three top orchestras attained peak performance and the LSO found its feet. The only blot in his copybook was a four-year stint in Boston, where in 1889 he succeeded a rigid disciplinarian, Wilhelm Gericke, and was attacked on the one hand for encouraging slackness in the players and on the other for the 'almost constant overstress' of his Mozart and Haydn interpretations. Retrospectively, the Nikisch years were the brightest in the Boston Symphony's first quarter-century.

Splitting himself between several cities, Nikisch set a pattern that would be carried to outrageous lengths by jet-set successors. He also learned to watch his back for subversion in his absence. Early in 1887, while away sick, his Leipzig deputy stepped in with a breathtaking *Fidelio* and a *Siegfried* that earned twelve curtain calls. 'I am now on equal footing with Nikisch,' crowed the aspirant, 'and need have no qualms about fighting him for the upper hand, which I am certain to gain if only on grounds of physical superiority; I don't think Nikisch can stand the pace – sooner or later he will take himself off.'

Gustav Mahler was wrong on both counts. Nikisch returned to oust his deputy, who had terrified staid Leipzigers with his zealotry. He bore no grudge, however, and performed various of Mahler's compositions – thanklessly enough. 'Perhaps you can still retrieve these works from the grave where Nikisch hurled them,' Mahler begged another conductor.

Nikisch dealt with competitors by pandering to their ulterior ambitions, to the extent that he happily performed the derivative compositions of Felix Weingartner, conductor of Berlin's other orchestra. Weingartner succumbed to the Nikisch charm and would appear hand-in-hand with him to take bows. One rival, though, was unassailable. Hans Richter, Wagner's wand for the inaugural *Ring*, wore an unimpeachable authority. He knew Nikisch from Vienna and steered well clear of him.

Superficially, the two men seemed quite similar. Richter was born in Hungary, son of the Kapellmeister at Györ, and trained at the Vienna Conservatory. He, too, stood immobile on the rostrum and could conduct with his eyes alone. Both excelled in the same kind of music, while representing diametrically opposing styles of performance. 'Richter is German-Hungarian,' Nikisch would say, 'I am Hungarian-Hungarian.' Unable to dislodge one another, they carved up the continent of Europe like medieval barons and carefully avoided trespassing. Nikisch controlled northern Germany and Russia, made forays into France and Italy and visited the Americas. Richter reigned at Bayreuth and Vienna, and was welcomed in Budapest, Munich and Brussels. He crossed neither the

Atlantic nor the Urals and never left the European mainland, except to work England. London was the only place where the paths of these formative champions converged. The clash was brief but instructive and in the 1890s it turned the capital of 'the Land without music' into a focal point of the musical world.

The Bayreuth Ring of 1876 had left Wagner facing ruin. To raise cash, he arranged a series of eight concerts at London's new 10,000-seat Royal Albert Hall and Hans Richter went along to share the conducting. Socially, the venture was a tremendous success and Queen Victoria summoned the Wagners to Windsor. Monetarily, Wagner messed up his sums and emerged with just £700, one-tenth of the amount he needed.

Nor did he excel with the baton. With 169 players, many brought over from Germany by the concertmaster August Wilhelmj, rehearsals were chaotic. Deichmann, leader of the second violins, tapped angrily on a stand to call his English players to order, only for the ivory tip of his bow to fly off and hit Wilhelmj in the face, to the delight of the local contingent.

> Herr Wagner is by this time in a frenzy of passion. But this is the opportunity for that perfect tactician, Herr Richter, who, taking the great composer by the arm, leads him away, speaking in a soothing, conciliatory tone. . . . In a few moments the conductor returns without Herr Wagner and, with the baton in his hand, says only two words, 'Now, boys!'
>
> Every man in that orchestra looks back to the eye which seems to read into their very souls as, electrified by the wonderful personality of the great conductor, each one pushes his chair nearer to the music-stand and a volume of sound, as if from one instrument, conveys to the ear the glorious effects in that wonderful conception of one of the greatest musical and dramatic geniuses of the century. Now we know we are playing *Das Rheingold*, for we feel it illuminated by the soul of Richard Wagner.

The relief felt in the orchestra when Richter replaced Wagner was reported by a twenty-year-old music critic, George Bernard Shaw. His conducting was 'a revelation', wrote one player and London showered him with return invitations. No conductor could get so much out of British musicians, wrote a trumpeter:

> His beat is unmistakable; but his power is not there – it is in his eye and in his left hand. What a wonderfully expressive left hand it is! And he seems to have every individual member of the band in his eye; he misses nothing, and we do not seem able to escape from the influence of that eye for a single moment.

For Richter, England offered refuge from a more baleful influence. For a dozen years, ever since he was 23, he had been at the beck and call of Richard Wagner; London gave him the chance to become his own man. He had been a horn-player at the opera in Vienna when Wagner came looking for a menial who could copy out his scores. Richter moved to Triebschen, where Wagner was living in sin with Cosima and finishing *Meistersinger*. For the next three months he lived and ate alone, refused admission to the family table. All morning Wagner would compose, bringing sheet after wet sheet of his opera to the adjoining room for Richter to replicate. 'I never once heard the piano in his room,' he recalled, 'which proves that in composing or sketching his ideas he never made use of it.' He used Richter, however, to play the comically quick horn passage at the end of the second act and was overjoyed to hear that it worked.

Richter's relation to the Wagners remained one of worshipful servility. He was a witness at their wedding and played the Siegfried Idyll beneath Cosima's window on the morning of her next birthday but never earned her confidence. In January 1875, she jotted in her diary that Richter's fiancée 'is of Jewish origin'. Wagner praised the 'treue Hans' disingenuously to his face, while privately complaining that 'he is incapable of understanding *why* it should be thus and not otherwise', implying that Richter lacked the intelligence to interpret music.

As first conductor successively at Budapest Opera and the Vienna Court Opera he remained tied to Bayreuth. The man who freed him was a Joachim pupil, Herman Franke, who had played as Wilhelmj's deputy and was determined to bring Richter back to London. Franke sold his Guarnerius to raise the money, but was poorly rewarded and died not long after in a German lunatic asylum.

Richter's impact on London was instantaneous. He conducted Beethoven symphonies 'without a book' and, when a horn-player complained that his part was unplayable, grabbed his instrument and blew it perfectly. There is no better way to earn respect from an orchestra. 'Thick-set and broad-shouldered, slightly below medium height, his beard square-cut and of golden-brown tinge,' he became a national institution, portrayed on cigarette cards. His concert success led to Covent Garden, where he led *Tristan, Meistersinger* and *Ring* cycles, and in 1885 to the directorship of the Birmingham Festival – 'an affront to all of us English', complained Arthur Sullivan.

His presence proved decisive for British music. He premièred works by local composers – Stanford's *Irish* Symphony, Parry's Fourth – encouraging a stir of creativity and letting it be known that he was 'only too pleased to promote the work of an English artiste'. On 19 June 1899 he changed the course of music history in the United Kingdom. Richter's performance of Edward Elgar's *Enigma Variations* at St James's Hall

inaugurated a renaissance of English music that restored its credit in
Europe after a lapse of two centuries. Elgar's music was taken up by the
leading conductors, Nikisch, Fritz Steinbach and Richard Strauss; the
composer dedicated his first symphony

To Hans Richter, Mus. Doc.
True Artist & true friend

and portrayed him affectionately in a lumbering theme of the second as
'Hans himself'. He even managed to forgive Richter the calamitous
première of *The Dream of Gerontius*, of which he gave the most 'perfunctory rendering of a new work' ever heard by the doyen of critics, Hermann
Klein of the *Sunday Times*. Richter, it seems, had been unable to grasp
the structure of the oratorio.

To Richter, Elgar's First was 'the greatest symphony of modern times,
written by the greatest modern composer – and not only in this country'.
Nikisch called it 'a masterpiece of the first order', remarking that just as
Brahms first symphony had been dubbed 'Beethoven's Tenth' so could
Elgar's be considered Brahms' Fifth. But while Richter saw Elgar as the
great hope for the future, Nikisch perceived from the outset that he was
essentially a conservative, looking backwards at Brahms rather than in
any progressive direction.

Richter was popular with his players and would readily humour them,
warning the cellos not to play 'like married men' in *Tristan*. Conducting
the Tchaikovsky first piano concerto in Leeds, he swept his baton down
before the soloist had finished, pulling some musicians involuntarily into
a premature *tutti*. He immediately halted the performance, turned to the
audience and said: 'Ladies and gentlemen, do not blame the orchestra
for that mistake. It was my mistake and only mine.' The entire hall stood
up and cheered: they had never heard a conductor admit fallibility.

'If Richter looks like a prophet,' wrote Claude Debussy of his London
Ring in April 1903, 'when he conducts the orchestra he is Almighty God:
and you may be certain that God Himself would have asked Richter for
some hints before embarking on such an adventure.' He was not above
a little showmanship. In the tricky 5–4 beat of the second movement of
Tchaikovsky's *Pathétique* he once laid down the baton, dropped his arms
to his side and sustained the rhythm with his eyebrows.

This, then, was the Richter of legend: the man who premièred Wagner's *Ring*, two symphonies by Brahms, two by Bruckner and one by
Dvořák and Elgar, the conductor who enjoyed the confidence of great
composers. The reality was less glowing. For the last quarter of the
nineteenth century Richter was chief conductor in Vienna and became
imbued with its easy-going ways. By the time Mahler took over the Opera
in 1897, he was refusing to rehearse beyond midday so as not to miss the

first round of beers in the bar where his cronies gathered. Mahler removed him unceremoniously from the *Ring* and soon after from the opera house after seeing a *Meistersinger* in which Richter 'conducted the first act, where I enjoyed him enormously, like a master, the second like a schoolmaster, and the third like a master cobbler'. Grumbling to anyone whose ear he caught, Richter returned to England and read a headline that shouted, 'Arthur Nikisch Conquers Apathetic London'.

In his late fifties and unfit for a fight, he retreated to the north-west where a colony of German immigrants wanted him to conduct the Hallé concerts in Manchester. 'We preferred in those days to keep our heroes at a distance; consequently they grew in stature and dignity,' wrote a young concertgoer. He became a titanic cosmopolitan figure in an industrial backwater and Mancunians were encouraged to believe that they had the greatest orchestra and conductor in the world.

Nevertheless, the quality of his performances outside the mainstream of Wagner and Beethoven was erratic. 'A few things he interpreted admirably, a great many more indifferently and the rest worse than any conductor of eminence I have ever known,' recalled Thomas Beecham. Urged to perform French music, Richter insisted, 'there *is* no French music'. When he attempted Berlioz, the critic Ernest Newman reported that 'it was fairly obvious last night that Dr Richter was not thoroughly acquainted with the score'. Young musicians sent him their compositions 'but the parcels would come back weeks later unread and unopened; his mind never inquired; his intellect lay indolent'.

Despite the prudence of his programmes, eight of his twelve Manchester seasons yielded deficits. In 1908 he introduced Cosima Wagner's latest son-in-law as his deputy, to general derision, and four years later laid down his baton for the last time and retired to Bayreuth. At the outbreak of war, 'he threw in the face of England the honours our country had bestowed upon him'.

Richter was, in truth, never much of a crusader for new music, even with those composers on whom his reputation rested. Bruckner complained bitterly that he bent the knee to the powerful critic Hanslick – 'I told Herr Richter that if he wants to perform one of my symphonies, he can take one of those Hanslick has already ruined and he can do no more harm to.' It was Nikisch who gave Bruckner his first taste of success with the seventh symphony in Leipzig and Nikisch who conducted the first cycle of his symphonies in 1920. Nikisch introduced Debussy to hostile Germans, and when they whistled, bowed as deeply as if they had applauded. Although out of tune with modernism, he risked Schoenberg's chamber symphony in ultra-cautious Leipzig. 'I was particularly delighted,' said the composer, not renowned for his gratitude, 'when at the final rehearsal I realized you had applied yourself to my music with great devotion and warm interest . . . taking the trouble to get to know this score.'

'It was noticed that he never took scores home,' said his pupil, Adrian Boult; but friends travelling with him on holiday saw him poring through a pile of new music on the train. At his 25th anniversary concert in Berlin, after repeating his opening programme, he asked the cheering audience if they wanted him to continue as chief conductor. Populist that he was, he knew there could be only one answer: Nikisch was conductor for life in Berlin and Leipzig.

Where Richter left no musical progeny, Nikisch was the model for youngsters wherever he went. In Russia, he fired the imagination of Serge Koussevitsky, in France of Pierre Monteux, in Switzerland of Ernest Ansermet, in Germany of Wilhelm Furtwängler, in Hungary of Fritz Reiner. The mighty succession of Hungarian maestros – Reiner, Georg Szell, Eugene Ormandy, Ferenc Fricsay, Antal Dorati, Istvan Kertesz and Georg Solti – traced its origin to Nikisch. Both Karajan and Bernstein dropped his name as a token of their legitimacy.

His influence, however, was most pronounced on two pupils, whose low-key approach was formative in the advance of music in Europe. Václav Talich went from studying with Nikisch in Leipzig to play viola in the Bohemian String Quartet while serving a conducting apprenticeship in Laibach (Ljubljana). In the year Czechoslovakia achieved independence, he was named chief conductor of the reconstituted Czech Philharmonic and turned it into an outstanding ensemble. He later became music director at the National Theatre, where he championed the operas of Leos Janáček, who spent one of the happiest nights of his provincial life sharing the presidential box at a Talich concert with the venerable Tomas Masaryk.

Talich sought no celebrity beyond his native land. He spent a season with the Scottish orchestra and had a part-time attachment to the Stockholm Philharmonic, but he was wedded with unshakable fidelity to his orchestra and his country and stayed put through the six awful years of Nazi occupation. Banished by the Communists to Bratislava, he founded the Slovak Philharmonic. His reputation fell prey to the whim of party ideologists and for years on end his name was suppressed and recordings withheld in the land he loved. 'Believe me,' he told a friend in wartime, 'in all my artistic life I strove only after one thing: to serve, to serve. If bitter tongues endowed me with the nickname of virtuoso, they let themselves be misled by the apparent ease [of my work] without realizing that it is redeemed by an unusual industriousness, exhaustive attention to every detail of the picture and by a rigid refusal to yield in enforcing the eternal truth.'

Talich had the nonchalance and natural gifts of a Nikisch. 'He was a very powerful man,' said Herbert von Karajan. 'He had what seemed to me a great genius for drawing the orchestra together and controlling it as a single expressive instrument. I was fascinated to watch this . . . I tried to imitate it but I couldn't do it.' What Talich did, he did instinctively and unlearned, but the ethos he personified was that of Nikisch.

The more phlegmatic Adrian Boult applied his principles of player psychology. At rehearsal, he recalled Nikisch,

> would hardly ever strain to get the utmost out of his orchestra; it was all easy-going and placid. He very often adopted a rather slow tempo and the whole rehearsal seemed quite leisurely; and although the players were doing hard work, they hardly felt that they were. They were made to feel that it was very easy to work with Nikisch.

Some musicians felt the same about Boult, though they looked upon him as a 'dull fish' who lacked Beecham's wit and Malcolm Sargent's flair. He would share their table at the BBC staff canteen and grouse with them about the food. 'You can have meals with [players] and you can enjoy association with them at other times and still be their master at a performance,' he maintained. 'In fact, master isn't the word. I always feel the conductor is akin to the chairman of a committee.' Boult was primarily that: an efficient administrator who assembled the first radio orchestra of world repute and laid ground rules for the regular broadcasting of music.

Yet he was also a conductor of deceptive depth. None of his compatriots could perform the second and third Brahms symphonies with such profundity, or modern music with such sympathy. He might look a bit like the long stick he wielded, but Boult was a musician of exceptional sensitivity and intelligence, qualities that he hid behind the stiff British bristle that decorated his upper lip. Like Talich, he had little inclination to leave his own country and make a name for himself abroad.

In concert he stood stock still, letting the tip of the stick do the work, the last disciple to persist with immobility. Furtwängler, an incurable fidget, embodied his conviction that every performance must be 'a grand improvisation'. This ideal contradicted the standards of consistency required by the record industry for which, paradoxically, Nikisch was the first to conduct a complete symphony – his 1913 set of Beethoven's Fifth is a relic of an age when music was made to resonate in the memory, not be stored in the living-room cabinet.

The stature of Nikisch cannot be assessed in vinyl – nor should it, for recording was the least of his legacies. With Magyar wit and charm, Nikisch lifted the conductor out of the podium and set him on a pedestal in the centre of society. He liberated the music director from local servitude, gaining global fame and a comfortable fortune. The fee he demanded in 1912 for conducting an English opera – £150 – was more than a top conductor would command at Covent Garden forty years later. In order to retain his services, the London Symphony Orchestra had to guarantee Nikisch one hundred guineas per concert, the equivalent of $450, or more than half as much again as Gustav Mahler was getting in New York from the richest concert organization in the world. Nikisch was not necessarily greedy, but he knew his worth and never undersold himself. He represented a city, a society and a way of life – and they were expected to sustain his appearance of prosperity. With Nikisch, real money entered the maestro mystique.

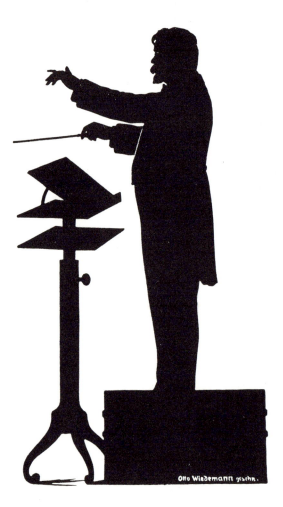

Nikisch motionless

CHAPTER 3

Masters of the House

THE MAP OF Europe has changed surprisingly little over the past five
centuries. Take out modern communications and conurbations, eliminate
political boundaries, and the centres of population and culture are much
the same as they were when Columbus departed to find a new world.
Mighty rivers and mountain ranges still determine in an era of high
technology where most people make their homes, away from dangerous
slopes and forests and close to a source of fresh water. All the great
capitals have retained their centrality, perched upon major waterways
and connected to their hinterland by multi-lane motorways built upon
the winding routes of medieval footpaths and horse tracks.

Beside these eternal roads, small towns sprang up to feed off passing
trade, providing nourishment for travellers, rural merchandise for salesmen and intimate services for the army garrison that protected the stra-
tegic artery. Towns like Iglau abound in every European land. Nothing
ever happens in them, and any native with a spark of talent or ambition
escapes as quickly as possible to the metropolis.

Iglau sits upon the main highway from Prague to Vienna. It has a
Gothic church dating from 1257 and a Renaissance town square in which
time stands breathlessly still. When Czechoslovakia became independent
in 1918, Iglau became Jihlava, reverting to the name it was first given by
Good King Wenceslas. Under German occupation, its synagogue was
promptly burned down on the orders of Gauleiter Seyss-Inquart (later
tyrant of Holland) and its Jews deported to their deaths. After the War,
Jihlava settled back into its historic torpor, oblivious to 'progressive'
slogans emblazoned on every public building by the Communist regime.
Gustav Mahler would find its present-day inertia unbearably familiar.

Mahler had more pressing reasons than most to leave the tight little
town. His home in Iglau was a living hell where his pious mother endured
crippling headaches and conjugal misery, his brothers and sisters were
carted off in coffins, while his father presided over drunken revelries in
the tavern he owned downstairs. Mahler's earliest composition, aged six,

was a merry polka – preceded by a funeral march. He sought solace in the surrounding woods and meadows and passed his boyhood in perpetual daydreams. 'What the flowers in the field tell me' became the title of a movement in his third symphony and his *Kindertotenlieder* expressed fury at adult apathy towards infant mortality.

He made his public debut in a piano recital at the age of ten in October 1870 and was sent away to Prague to improve his mediocre schoolwork, living with the Grünfeld family and its two budding virtuosos, Heinrich and Alfred. After six months he was brought home half-starved and terribly shaken, having disturbed the 19-year-old Alfred Grünfeld in *flagrante delicto* with a housemaid. Thinking the girl was being violently assaulted, he burst in to save her – only to be abused by both consenting partners. The episode taught him to be wary of sexual passions.

Prague was never to be more than a stepping stone on his path to posterity. His ambition ran beyond regional capitals and the limits of his own art. Asked as a child what he wanted to become, he replied: 'A martyr.' A messianic urgency became apparent in his teenage years. He picked up a stray idea from Schopenhauer and preached that unremitting service to art and ceaseless quest for the divine could bring about the redemption of mankind. He was, obsessively, a God-seeker. Had he not been a musician, friends believed, he might have become a great writer, statesman or saviour. When Arnold Schoenberg eulogized him as 'a saint', he meant it literally, in the sacred sense.

Like every youngster in a subdued, distant province he dreamed of glory in the gold-paved imperial capital. Like every musician, he looked to Vienna as the summit of his calling. Haydn, Mozart, Beethoven and Schubert had made Vienna pre-eminent and Brahms was now its presiding genius. Vienna, to Mahler, was the earthly Jerusalem, a vision never wholly dispelled by bitter experience. Admitted to its Conservatoire at 15, he thanked the man who introduced him for 'opening the gates of the muses' temple, bidding me enter and leading me into the Promised Land'.

He soon discovered that the land would not yield its fruits readily. Although he excelled at his studies and won prizes for composition, those who bucked the rigid structural and harmonic rules of Brahms' new symphonies had difficulty in starting their careers; a gifted classmate, Hans Rott, went mad of frustration and died at 26. Their gentle mentor Anton Bruckner, Brahms' detested antipode, hardly dared to have his expansive symphonies performed in Vienna for fear of its carnivorous chief critic, Eduard Hanslick. Wagner, whom the students adulated, was outlawed by respectable society and became an underground cult, his prohibited stew of theatrical, social and racial ideas bubbling furtively in many an unlikely corner. Mahler, under his spell, became vegetarian and wore woollen underwear, for a while.

He found further disillusionment in the prevailing standards of operatic performance and the stultifying effects of the Viennese character. The Austro-Hungarian capital could call upon the finest performers in Europe yet, with an indigenous blend of complacency and conservatism, provided seasons of mortifying dullness. The Court Opera, pride of the newly built Ringstrasse, presented its brilliant ensemble in static productions on antiquated sets. The conductor would sit at the very foot of the stage, his back to the superb orchestra, coaxing some semblance of cohesion from half-rehearsed singers. Unless Hans Richter directed, musical quality was variable. The lion of musical Vienna was Johann Strauss, and his waltzes required little finesse to make them whirl.

Mahler realized that, in order to succeed at the hub of Europe's largest empire, a young man needed more than genius. He needed power. Absolute control of the means of operatic production was essential if he was ever to achieve in Vienna the perfection that Wagner had envisaged, an alliance of all the arts in the *Gesamtkunstwerk*. Mahler's lust for power was limited to that specific purpose; perhaps, like Marx, he believed the power structure would wither away once its goal had been attained. Even at the height of his supremacy he showed no expansionist desire to rule anything beyond the Vienna Opera. His aims were idealistic and localized, confined essentially to the juvenile fantasy of every small-town aspirant, from Dick Whittington to Richard Nixon, to dominate the capital of his nation.

No conductor had ever sought the prerogative of executive power. At the great opera houses, the conductor was a salaried employee at the beck and call of aristocratic administrators who told him what to perform, when and with whom. His name did not even appear on the programmes. The idea that a conductor should be put in charge of a central imperial institution did not cross anyone's mind until Mahler came along with his impossible demands and preposterous ambition.

He took up the baton at the Conservatoire, abandoning the piano once 'he had become accustomed to mastering the orchestra in exactly the same way'. Unemployed and short of money, he refused to conduct at the Iglau theatre and was saved from penury by a fortuitous mid-season engagement at Olmütz (Olomouc), where the conductor had been sacked for an unmentionable offence. At this garrison town near the German border, he was talent-spotted by foreign visitors and hired as director of chorus at Kassel, where most operas were covered by his senior colleague and he was left with burlesque, vaudeville and ballet performances. When the shrewd ex-tenor Angelo Neumann became manager of the German theatre in Prague, one of his first inquiries came from Kassel's disconsolate chorus master. On the strength of a brief interview, Neumann named Mahler third conductor in Prague and started his meteoric ascent. Within a year he was taken on as Arthur Nikisch's deputy at the Leipzig Opera and presumptuously attempted an in-house putsch. At just 28 years old, he landed the Royal Hungarian Opera with a huge salary and untrammelled authority.

'The position offered me here is surprisingly good,' he informed his parents in Iglau. 'All-powerful master of an institution as large as the Vienna Opera – and, at the same time, first conductor. I shall be responsible only to the minister . . . [and] have at my disposition, with a single stroke of the pen, a treasury of one million florins.'

The Royal Hungarian Opera was, at the time, 'a completely discredited company' that nationalists wanted raised to equal status with Vienna as an indigenous, though internationally recognized, institution. The candidate least likely to achieve this was a callow Czech Jew who spoke no word of the Magyar tongue and openly endorsed Wagner's cult of Teutonic supremacism. In his opening address, Mahler promised to make the opera 'the focal point of Hungary's artistic endeavours and pride of the nation'. He gathered new casts to sing mostly in Hungarian, retrained the orchestra, revitalized stage production and conducted most performances himself. On the night of Hungary's first *Rheingold*, he carried on conducting regardless while half the stage went up in flames and the front rows fled. During his *Don Giovanni*, the great symphonist Brahms, notorious for his ostentatious snoring at the opera, snapped bolt upright on his couch in a private box and cried out 'admirable! splendid fellow!'.

Mahler actually turned in a profit by the end of his second season, as Viennese cognoscenti began sailing down the Danube to watch opera in the empire's second capital. In the streets of Budapest, people gawked as he walked by. 'Am I a wild animal, then, that everyone can stop and stare at me as in a menagerie?' he shouted at them. Suffering neither fools nor sluggards, he made as many enemies as admirers and had to refuse duelling challenges from musicians he had affronted. 'The orchestral players feared him because in artistic matters he made no concessions whatever and, in his unwearying diligence at rehearsal, was as reckless with his musicians as he was with himself,' reported a fellow-conductor. He slashed frenziedly with the baton, driving himself to the point of exhaustion, as if every note depended on his personal intervention. Newspaper caricatures began appearing of Mahler, the man with many arms. He was impetuous, inconsistent, incandescent: an astonishing conductor.

'Discipline, work; work, discipline,' were his watchwords. When his beloved mother died, he refused to take time off to attend her deathbed or funeral, but arranged for his younger siblings to be boarded out and funnelled his filial grief into the *Todtenfeier* opening movement of his second symphony, the *Resurrection*. His first symphony, premiered in Budapest the following month, was hooted down as 'an enormous aberration on the part of a mind of genius'.

It was inevitable that his honeymoon with the Hungarians would be short-lived. The appointment as artistic director of a one-armed nationalist pianist, Count Géza Zichy, ended Mahler's reign after three years. Zichy was so keen to be shot of him that he volunteered to pay his severance compensation out of his own pocket. Mahler, worn out by Hungarian wrangling, went to conduct at the municipal theatre in Hamburg where he took orders from an unscrupulous impresario but improved the company's standards and brought its *Ring* production to London in 1892. His counterpart at Hamburg's Philharmonic concerts was none other than Hans von Bülow, who eccentrically showed his appreciation of Mahler's efforts by sending a laurel wreath to 'the Pygmalion of the Hamburg Opera'. Frustration at the worthless operas he was forced to present was rinsed off in the 'Castilian spring' of his symphonies. 'God! I could endure everything if only the future of my works seemed assured,' he exclaimed while paying the Berlin Philharmonic to perform his second symphony. 'I am now 35 years old (unmarried, in case you're interested),' he wrote to a female fan, 'very uncelebrated and very *unperformed*. But I keep busy and don't let it get me down. I have patience; and I wait.'

At every unexpected ring on the doorbell, he would jump up crying, 'here comes the summons to the god of the southern zones', longing for the call that would restore him to Vienna. Brahms was dying and others were intriguing on his behalf around the café tables where Austria makes its vital decisions. In the meantime, he cultivated two teenaged protégés: a Berlin boy called B. W. Schlesinger, whom he taught to conduct and renamed Bruno Walter, and a breathtaking soprano, Anna von Mildenburg, with whom he fell in love.

Towards the end of 1896 conditions at the Vienna Court Opera turned from bad to critical. The veteran director, Wilhelm Jahn, was an elderly man of sedentary habits of whom it was rumoured that he once shortened an opera in order to finish a card game. The star singers were well past their best, but no-one dared retire them, and the lesser roles were lamentably sung. Years had elapsed since the last première of any significance. The Court Opera was losing money and earning no prestige. Negligence and neglect were evident everywhere in the magnificent edifice, a prime symbol of the Habsburg monarchy, and its decay was readily perceived as a metaphor of the crumbling state. For this reason, if no other, the opera had to be urgently reinvigorated.

As soon as Mahler learned of looming upheavals, he contacted every conceivable acquaintance and friend of friends who might possibly promote his candidacy. The former singing teacher of his girl-friend, Anna, became a key negotiator. Hungarian barons mobilized on his behalf, society hostesses sweet-talked royal princes, journalists spread beneficial gossip. Mahler posed before ministers as a pliable puppet and pretended to be Richter's greatest fan. In months of long-distance manoeuvring he displayed brilliant political skills. When success finally seemed certain, he quietly discarded his ancestral faith and converted to Roman Catholicism – a prerequisite for holding high office at the Habsburg Court. 'Mahler would have given anything to get to Vienna,' noted a confidante.

News of his appointment, in the spring of 1897, took Vienna by storm. The newcomer had never conducted in the capital, was nothing but a civic *Kapellmeister* in northern Germany, a Jew by birth, and at 36 was absurdly young for a position of such importance. Racialist newspapers militated against him, Cosima Wagner railed in vain at his installation and conservative musicians wrote off his compositions with disdain. Wilhelm Jahn was led to believe that the young fellow would serve as his assistant; within six months he had been pensioned off and Mahler was in sole charge of the Court Opera, answerable only to a handful of high-ranking courtiers and ultimately to the Emperor Franz-Joseph himself.

Mahler's era in Vienna set the standard by which all operatic regimes are judged. He introduced *esprit de corps*, animated stage direction, imaginative scenery and a nightly norm of performance that was never allowed to fall below his personal specifications, no matter who was holding the baton. 'Ensure [that] each performance is better than the last,' he exhorted the company. Every night had to be a gala.

Until he could appoint reliable assistants – notably Franz Schalk and Bruno Walter – Mahler did most of the work himself, conducting a hundred times in each of his first three seasons. He stamped his personality vigorously on the house, which trembled in anticipation whenever the lights dimmed and the tiny, intense figure of the Director was seen rushing into the pit. In a decade, he gave no fewer than 648 performances. By modern comparison, in his six seasons as head of the Vienna Opera, Herbert von Karajan conducted 168 times – less than half of Mahler's workload. It was a dangerously heavy burden that, towards the end of his third year in office, precipitated a near-fatal haemorrhage.

He had sought unlimited power and wielded it omnipotently. As well as ruling over orchestra, chorus, singers and repertoire, he extended his writ to every corner of the opera house, taking charge of production and stage design, costume departments, public facilities – even audience behaviour. His first edict abolished the claques of paid supporters with which star singers packed parts of the house. Next, he withdrew press tickets, making critics pay for their own seats and attracting gratuitous editorial hostility. Finally, from his inaugural *Rheingold* onwards, he closed the auditorium to late-comers, requiring them to wait in an isolated side-box – rather like a schoolmaster's sin-bin – until an appropriate break in the proceedings.

These punitive severities bemused the benign old emperor, who protested that 'after all, the theatre is meant to be a pleasure'. But the benefits of Mahler's revolution were obvious and Franz Joseph praised him for having imposed himself as 'master of the opera house, in no time at all'. Mahler could hardly believe his own achievement. 'It's like a dream to think that I really rule there as Lord and Master,' marvelled the young Director as he walked one day past his opera house.

His autocracy was absolute. When courtly superiors tried to secure roles for a well-connected soprano or make him perform an opera written by a distinguished public figure, Mahler said he accepted orders only from the emperor and would prominently advertise any acts of favouritism as being presented 'By Command of the All-Highest'. A specific request by Franz-Joseph for an opera by Count Zichy, his Budapest adversary, was bluntly turned down on grounds of musical competence. 'A chestnut tree,' said Mahler pithily, 'cannot be expected to produce oranges.'

He bypassed an entrenched hierarchy of artistic directors and flagrantly encroached on areas far beyond his contractual remit. In an aggressive memorandum to the chief comptroller of Court theatres, he argued that there could be no 'officially defined limits' to his power in any part of the opera house, since he bore responsibility for its achievements and failures. 'If the Director is given overall authority, he must be free to make his own decisions on matters of detail,' he concluded, and boldly ordered new costumes for *Der Freischütz* without going through the proper channels. In the early years, none dared resist him. 'Mahler burst over the Vienna Opera like an elemental catastrophe,' wrote one of its orchestral cellists, the composer Franz Schmidt. 'An earthquake of unprecedented intensity and duration shook the entire building from the foundation pillars to the gables. Anything that was not very strong had to give way and perish.'

Faltering singers and conductors, Richter included, were unsentimentally removed. Two-thirds of the orchestra were replaced within months by younger players. He nurtured a new constellation of stars: the fabulous coloratura Selma Kurz, the light soprano Marie Gutheil-Schoder, famous for her *Carmen*, and the Wagnerian tragedienne Anna von Mildenburg, with whom he severed intimate relations to avoid scandal. 'He was a martyr to the consuming flames of work,' grumbled the easy-going tenor, Leo Slezak, 'and he expected us to be the same.' He made the singers

Caricature of Mahler

act out their roles, refusing to tolerate immobile arias, and in rehearsal would leap back and forth between pit and stage to try out dramatic ideas. Before Mahler, the only directions written into the singers' scores in Vienna were: enter and exit.

Restraining his dictatorial tendencies, he sought a partnership with fellow-artists, the more intelligent of whom warmed to his challenge. 'He did not impose a domineering conception on either the work or the artists,' confirmed Marie Gutheil-Schoder, 'he left options open for individuals to develop without prejudice.' Each rehearsal and performance was unpredictably exciting and freshly conceived.

> Nothing irritated him more than someone objecting: 'Herr Direktor, yesterday you wanted it like this, and today you want it done differently.' To which he would say: 'I convinced myself yesterday that it could not possibly be done like that; you must go along with me.'

In every performance, he decreed, 'the work must be born again'. He ruthlessly eliminated vocal embellishments by vain singers and lovingly restored every cut made by his predecessors in Mozart and Wagner.

Mahler's *Götterdämmerung* lasted an hour longer than anyone else's but seemed to pass more swiftly. Stretches of dialogue were reinstated in *The Magic Flute* and *Carmen*. His *Fidelio* inserted the problematic *Leonore* overture ahead of the finale at the point of maximum dramatic impact. Any practice held sacrosanct as a long-standing tradition was rigorously re-examined and generally dismissed as corrupt. Tradition, he proclaimed, is usually an excuse for *Schlamperei* – a Viennese condition combining slackness, sloth, sloppiness and make-do. His contempt for the familiar provoked unease among middle-brow music-lovers who feared that their hallowed heritage was under threat.

Gradually, he began refreshing a stale repertoire with the latest operas by Puccini, Pfitzner and the controversial Richard Strauss, whom he championed to the point of threatening resignation over *Salome*, which Catholic censorship barred from Vienna as sacrilegious. Major works by Smetana and Tchaikovsky achieved their first popularity with German-speaking audiences. He conducted altogether 63 different operas, and *Figaro* more than any other.

When Richter's departure for England left a vacancy at the Vienna Philharmonic, Mahler lost no time in adding the symphonic season to his operatic duties. At his opening concert, he outlawed once and for all, with a wave of his hand, the custom of applauding between movements. He shocked listeners by orchestrating a Beethoven quartet and outraged musicians by adding extra wind instruments to the untouchable Ninth. Although fanatical in his devotion to textual precision, Mahler did not hesitate to amend a score to suit changing circumstances and technologies.

Performances of his own music drew crowds of curious youngsters and puzzled grimaces from the old guard. Crusty Eduard Hanslick began his review of the *Resurrection* with the verdict: 'One of us must be mad – and it is not me!' The orchestra found his symphonies impenetrable and his revisions unacceptable.

The Philharmonic were an autonomous band of men who democratically determined the concerts they played. In the opera pit, the same musicians were Mahler's employees, subject to his every tyranny. Grudges carried over from the opera house, a tide of negative reviews and a financially disastrous trip to Paris ended his tenure ignominiously. In April 1901, while he underwent emergency triple surgery for internal bleeding, the Philharmonic received rave notices under the ballet conductor, Joseph 'Pepi' Hellmesberger. Mahler refused to return unless he received a unanimous vote of confidence; the orchestra opted for Hellmesberger instead.

His workaholic schedule had left Mahler no time for social life. He remained an outsider in Vienna, dining alone after the opera at the Café Imperial, or walking home to eat supper with his sister, Justine. After his brush with death and Bruno Walter's arrival as second conductor, he began to ease up and show his face more often in society. At a dinner party given for him in November that year by Berta Zuckerkandl, daughter of a newspaper magnate and wife of a top anatomist, he met a girl of 21, barely half his age, who swiftly seduced him (capturing his virginity, she claimed) and fell pregnant.

Mahler's wedding to the flirtatious, fickle Alma transformed his life both privately and professionally. He gained the warmth of a family life but was left vulnerable to emotions he had long quashed. Pomp and pride crept into his middle symphonies, amid intimations of impending disaster.

Alma, daughter and stepdaughter of fashionable painters, mingled with artists who had declared war on the over-decorated Biedermeier style of the bourgeoisie. She introduced Mahler to Alfred Roller, whom he commissioned to design a new *Tristan und Isolde*, and with his spare and simple scenery invoked the second phase of his operatic revolution. Stripped of its clutter of props, Wagner's opera was revealed in naked muscularity. Kaleidoscopic colours and lighting brought out the intrinsic moods: reds for the love potion, blues for the palace and shades of grey for the death of love.

Alma awoke her husband to many of the creative sparks of her own generation, rebels like Arnold Schoenberg, Peter Altenberg and Max Reinhardt. To innovators in fin-de-siècle Vienna, Mahler became a patron and guiding light, the man who made change possible. Young composers elected him their president, writers dreamed of him at night. 'I have never sensed so deeply the heroic in a man,' remembered Stefan Zweig. A vagrant named Adolf Hitler was transfixed by his conducting.

Abroad, Mahler gripped the imagination of progressive Europeans. A clique of French politicians became his followers and their leader, General Georges Picquart, swore like a trooper when he was hauled out of watching *Tristan* and summoned to the Elysée to be appointed minister of defence. Dutch musicians led by Willem Mengelberg formed a fan club; a Mahler cult was started in England by the conductor Henry Wood and in Italy by the composer Alfredo Casella; his picture was published on postcards in Spain; he received ovations in St Petersburg; Thomas Mann considered him the first great man he had ever met.

The more his fame spread, the more isolated he became in Vienna, harried by reactionaries and resentful nobodies. Any pleasure at his achievements was outweighed by inevitable lapses and incessant intrigues. Where in Hamburg he had complained of 'the gross misery of [serving in] famous temples of art', he now concluded that 'a permanent opera company directly contradicts the principles of modern art'.

He longed 'to live only for my compositions', and conducted them all over Europe. 'A musical score is a book with seven seals,' he said.

JUBILEJNÍ VÝSTAVA V PRAZE R. 1908.
KONCERTNÍ SÍŇ

V sobotu dne 19. září o 7. hod. večer.

X. (POSLEDNÍ)
FILHARMONICKÝ KONCERT

GUSTAV MAHLER:
Symfonie č. 7. (E-moll.)

Prvnl provedení vůbec.

Řídi skladatel.

L. Úvod a prvnl věta.

II. Hudba nocl. (Andante sempre sostenuto.)

III. Scherzo.

IV. Hudba nocl. (Andante amoroso).

V. Rondo — Finale.

Programme for the world première of Mahler's 7th Symphony in Prague

'Conductors who can decipher it present it to the public soaked in their own interpretations. For that reason there must be a tradition, and no-one can create it but I.' But his presence on the podium conveyed entirely unwanted messages. 'Though I wished very much to admire the work of a composer whom I held in such esteem,' wrote the French philosopher Romain Rolland on hearing him conduct the fifth symphony at Strasbourg, 'I fear Mahler has been sadly hypnotized by *ideas about power* – ideas that are going to the head of all German artists these days.'

The aura of power had become inseparable from Mahler. 'His personality stood between his works and the public,' noted Hermann Bahr, husband of the jilted Mildenburg. 'His personal impact was so strong that most people could not reach over it to his work, some because of their admiration and love for him, others because of envy, fury and hatred. He had first to die for his work to become free.'

His conducting absences and an unexpected budgetary deficit gave his enemies the necessary ammunition. Early in 1907 Mahler, the small-town outsider, was forced out by city schemers and vested interests. 'What I leave behind is not what I dreamt,' he told his opera staff, 'something whole, something complete in itself, but fragments, unfinished things – as is man's fate.' Just before his final production, Gluck's *Iphigénie en Aulide*, a friend saw him gazing in childish delight at a street billboard, still unable to believe the good fortune that had brought him to the summit of Vienna's mighty Opera and the fulfilment of his childhood dreams. There was something holy that night about Mahler, said his companion.

* * *

Mahler's assumption of power made little immediate impact on conductors at other opera houses, ruled either by a royal chamberlain or a grasping businessman. Nor did his successors capitalize on the prerogatives he had seized.

The conductors shortlisted for his job were: Schuch of Dresden, Nikisch of Leipzig, Mottl of Munich and the wandering Weingartner, all Austro-Hungarians by birth. Ernst von Schuch was midwife to most of Strauss's operas and had moulded his orchestra to manage their ornate sonorities. Moderate by nature, he rarely let rip with a triple-forte and abridged most of his scores, habits that endeared him to divas rather than to composers. It was said of Schuch that 'he breathed with the singers' and reined in the orchestra to play in their shadow. Strauss, who was in his debt, called him 'a greatly talented conductor but a modest subaltern of a Kapellmeister'. Schuch was aware of his own limitations and resisted Vienna's offers, as did Nikisch, who was better off elsewhere.

Felix Mottl, the youngest assistant in Wagner's *Ring* of 1876, had built up an excellent ensemble in Munich. Many considered him the equal of Nikisch who, on hearing their praise, said: 'his technique is immense but here' – pointing to his breast – 'nothing'. Mottl disproved this slur by falling victim to romantic indulgence. Prone to powerful females, he met his nemesis in 1911 in the stately shape of Zdenka Fassbender, whose Isolde was so formidable that when she sang out 'Death-doomed head, death-doomed heart', her loving conductor suffered a heart attack and lived just long enough to marry her on his deathbed. Mottl had previously declined to succeed Mahler in Vienna. This left Felix von Weingartner, the cantankerous Liszt pupil who fancied himself as a composer of genius and imagined the world was conspiring to suppress his music.

Even the headstrong Weingartner refused Mahler's crown at first, before memories of his own boyhood ambitions in the little Dalmatian town of Zara made the prospect of ruling Vienna irresistible. He started out by tearing down the relics of Mahler's triumphs, starting with the epoch-making *Fidelio*. 'To my horror,' he explained, 'I learnt that Vienna had adopted the ludicrous practice of setting the great *Leonore* overture in the midst of the action. . . .' He pulled the overture from its perfect slot and ousted Alfred Roller, who went to Dresden to draw the definitive *Rosenkavalier* for Strauss and Schuch.

He performed Wagner and Mozart with gaping cuts that provoked hissing from the top galleries. The principal singers fled as soon as their contracts elapsed and the replacements that Weingartner hired were palpably inadequate. After three wretched seasons he was sacked, accused of unduly favouring a soprano, Lucille Marcel, who later became his third wife. He left in a huff, blaming his setbacks on Mahler's Jewish supporters and scattering libel writs left and right.

Weingartner had so undermined Mahler's musical reforms that few voices were raised in 1911 when the Court turned the clock back and installed as Director a theatrical administrator, Hans Gregor, who restored the *status quo ante* and reduced his musicians to minions. As the Habsburg Empire sank slowly into the mire of history, a stagnant Court Opera sang its swansong.

Mahler's disciples, meanwhile, spread their wings and carried his gospel across the continent. In Amsterdam, where the fount of music had virtually run dry since the Middle Ages, Willem Mengelberg applied Mahlerian management principles to turn his Concertgebouw orchestra into a world-leader. Red-haired and hot-tempered, he flung himself ferociously into every rehearsal and refused to compromise on technical perfection. He brooked no dissension from any quarter and sabotaged civic attempts to found an opera house opposite the Concertgebouw. 'Mengelberg was the king,' recalls Bernard Haitink, who grew up in an opera-free city. 'And he said: "No, the opera house will hurt *my* music-making with the orchestra and take *my* audience away from the concert hall." As a result, there is no opera tradition in Amsterdam.' Mengelberg ranked Beethoven and Mahler as the supreme composers and, when the good people of Amsterdam wanted to reward his first 25 years of service, he refused to accept anything for himself but demanded funds for his orchestra to perform the world's first cycle of Mahler symphonies, a milestone in the annals of concert music.

In return for putting up with his despotism, Holland found its way back onto the musical map and the orchestra claimed the unwavering commitment of an outstanding conductor for just under half a century – until his apparent endorsement of the Nazi occupation cast him into national disgrace. Of Rhenish ancestry and Teutonic sympathies,

Mengelberg raised his arm in the Hitler salute and condoned the deportation of 16 Jewish players, although their physical survival in the death
camps has been ascribed to his discreet influence. His muddled political
opinions did not cloud his musical ideals and, while rehearsing the Vienna
Philharmonic during the war, he loudly berated them for not playing 'the
most beautiful music that there is – Mahler's'.

Another of Mahler's apostles, Alexander Zemlinsky, joined the Court
Opera in 1907 just in time to see his hero disappear. 'He revered Mahler
like a god,' wrote Alma, who was his lover before she married. Zemlinsky
made a piano reduction of Mahler's sixth symphony and ultimately modelled his own *Lyric Symphony* on *Das Lied von der Erde*. He stayed on
in Vienna until the last hope of Mahler's return was extinguished, then
moved to Prague to succeed Angelo Neumann at the German Theatre. Over the
next sixteen years, he converted Prague into a hive of operatic modernism
where Schoenberg, Berg, Hindemith and Kurt Weill were performed alongside
Mozart, Wagner and Strauss. Established operas drew fresh breath from the
bustling winds of change. Igor Stravinsky 'was never inspired by a Mozart
performance until...I heard Alexander Zemlinsky conduct *Figaro* in Prague'.
His company stood above the swirling tides of nationalism and, when
Czechoslovakia threw off the Austro-German yoke in 1918, its founder-
president, Tomas Masaryk, personally provided state subsidies for the con-
tinuance of the German-speaking theatre.

Zemlinsky shared Mahler's affinity for Czech composers, taking Janáček's stark operas from the National Theatre and having them produced
in German. He regularly conducted the Czech Philharmonic, giving no
fewer than 35 concerts of Mahler symphonies but not daring to perform
his own. 'Zemlinsky can wait,' shrugged his brother-in-law Arnold
Schoenberg. Alma Mahler wrote him off as a weakling. 'I lack what it
takes to get to the very top,' he told her sadly. 'In this throng, it is not
enough to have elbows – you need to know how to use them.'

In his mid-fifties he was hauled into the limelight of Europe's liveliest
arts scene by Otto Klemperer, Mahler's youngest protégé, who planned
to harness his experience and conducting skill to a revolution he was fomenting
in Berlin. Klemperer, who had premiered one of Zemlinsky's operas at
Cologne, nominated the senior conductor to serve as 'musical conscience' at the
reopened Kroll Opera while he enacted there his own version of Mahler's
interrupted mission. The Kroll was Berlin's third opera theatre – the other two
were conducted by Erich Kleiber and Bruno Walter – and its purpose was to
reach a broad public with accessible works at affordable prices. It staged up to
ten productions a year and sold the bulk of its tickets far in advance to music
societies and workers' clubs. Klemperer had heard Mahler despair that no opera
house could be run at a high standard when a different work had to be staged

every night. At the Kroll, he was liberated from this obligation and the guaranteed subscription allowed him to innovate without fear of box-office collapse.

In the space of four seasons Klemperer turned the Kroll into the world's foremost experimental company, performing classics in controversially modern settings, staging a Schoenberg double-bill and Stravinsky triple-bill, and giving important national premières of *Oedipus Rex* and Janá-ček's *From the House of the Dead*. In the turmoil of social and national ideologies that swirled around Berlin, any new music was bound to strike someone as Bolshevist, and an accusation of tampering with Germany's cultural heritage invariably created uproar.

Klemperer's production of *The Flying Dutchman* in modern dress, with Senta wearing a simple skirt and sweater, provoked furious protests from the 'Wagner League of German Women', who failed to notice that he had restored Wagner's original score. His gaunt account of Beethoven's liberation opera was loudly derided as '*Fidelio* on ice'. Both productions blazed a trail for the styles of half a century hence. 'I didn't want an avant-garde opera,' said Klemperer retrospectively, 'I wanted to make good theatre – just that and nothing else.'

Nazis attacked the Kroll for peddling proletarian and Jewish perversions; Communists deplored abstract scenery that contradicted their emergent doctrine of realism. Between operas, Klemperer began giving all-Bach concerts, another dangerous novelty, or mixing Bach with new works by Hindemith and Weill. He conducted majestic Mahler performances, faced adversity on all sides and looked back on the Kroll as artistically the most important period in his life.

Klemperer remained in Berlin until a month after Hitler came to power. When the Gestapo began night raids on eminent opponents he escaped to Switzerland but, finding few openings in a Europe glutted with musical refugees, moved to America where he struggled with depressive illness and brutally recalcitrant orchestras. He joined the community of intellectual émigrés on the West Coast and directed the infant Los Angeles Philharmonic, cutting little ice in a company town whose prime concern was movies. His dedication to living music raged unabated and he favoured his adversary and neighbour Arnold Schoenberg with premières of his less taxing works – a suite for strings and his orchestration of Brahms' G minor piano quartet that Klemperer designated Brahms' fifth symphony. 'You know I have no cause to show you greater respect than you show me,' grumbled the surly composer.

Conducting Mahler's *Resurrection* Symphony in New York, Klemperer incurred a deficit heavy enough to damage his box-office potential on a national scale. One miserable Carnegie Hall night, recovering from brain surgery and dogged by malicious rumours of insanity, he paid to stage his own concert. Precious little other work came his way during the War. He did not make a single record in 15 years in America. 'My recollection is that he would arrive regularly at mealtimes,' noted the son of a fellow-conductor who was in similar straits.

Klemperer returned to Europe, conducting opera in Budapest and East Berlin until Communist interference forced him back to the United States, where his passport was confiscated while his Eastern bloc links were investigated by the FBI. Just then, a British record executive called Walter Legge threw him a lifeline. Legge needed conductors for his orchestra, the Philharmonia, which was making a name for itself in the concert hall as much as on the turntable. Failing to release Jascha Horenstein from a small record company, he turned to Klemperer who, in London theatres packed with former German refugees, and on internationally acclaimed recordings, belatedly found fame and professional satisfaction.

His acid wit and tough discipline earned him a wary affection among London musicians who recount numerous anecdotes of his eccentricities, some of them doubtless true. When a trumpeter was delayed in heavy traffic, he refused to rehearse until the wretched man breathlessly burst in, whereupon he turned to the strings alone and growled, 'now we can start – if you please, *Eine Kleine Nachtmusik*!' A player who kept looking at his watch on a sunny Saturday afternoon was asked, 'Is it going?' He was mortified to discover that recordings could be pieced together with takes from different performances. '*Lotte, ein Schwindel*!' he groaned to his daughter on watching the repair of a cracked horn note in one of his Mozart symphonies, and refused to condone the fraud.

The catalogue of his calamities continued. Forced to conduct sitting down, he was put out of action again by a geriatric appendectomy. While smoking in bed, he set fire to his room; then, trying to extinguish the flames, he sustained severe burns when he mistook a bottle of spirits for a water flask. A long sequence of skin grafts put paid to a *Tristan* he was planning with Wieland Wagner, who felt he came closer than anyone to the composer's concept. After every reversal, he somehow limped back.

His solidarity saved the Philharmonia from disbandment and he conducted it until his 87th year, engraving his image indelibly on twentieth-century music-making in monumental interpretations of great works – Beethoven symphonies whose architecture was magnificently revealed, Brahms and Bruckner and, above all, Mahler – performed unapologetically as a composer of the first rank.

A loner to the last, he cracked bitter witticisms at the expense of his colleagues. In 1954, after the deaths of Furtwängler and Kleiber, he sniped: 'It has been a good year for conductors.' Asked about his own place in musical history he growled – with po-faced irony and a German accent thick as leberwurst: 'I am the last of the classical school. When Bruno Walter died, I put my fees up.'

It was in 1920s Berlin that Klemperer came into conflict with Mahler's natural successor. Bruno Walter's long and close association with Mahler had lent his symphonic interpretations an unassailable hallmark of authenticity. He directed Mahler's music with supple flexibility, an easy-going lilt and a glow of nostalgia that grew warmer and more leisurely with the passage of time. He avoided some of the most unsettling works, like the third, sixth and seventh symphonies and the tortured fragments of the tenth. In Walter's performances, particularly the ones by which he is remembered on record, perilous precipices were made safe, ironies were muted and the anger toned down into mere grandeur. He lacked Mahler's febrile fanaticism and restless quest.

These limitations were scarcely mentioned during Walter's long lifetime, when his status as Mahler's mouthpiece was inviolate. Among the first to demur was Klemperer, who heard him give the première of *Das Lied von der Erde*. Dismayed at not having grasped the piece immediately, he decided that the conductor had come between him and the music. 'If only we could have heard the work once under Mahler,' he moaned to Alma.

When Klemperer took charge at the Kroll, Walter was conducting across Berlin at the Charlottenburg Opera and had an annual concert series with the Philharmonic. He was respected, popular and influential. Klemperer loathed him, though he took care to curb his waspish tongue. Side by side, each represented diametrically opposing aspects of their contradictory mentor, personally as much as musically. Walter was gentle, serene and unfailingly polite. Klemperer was acerbic, dogmatic, uncompromising, indomitable. He was ganglingly tall, thin and dishevelled, Walter was short, cuddlesome and perfectly groomed. Walter had friends in high places and neighbourly relations across the garden fence with Thomas Mann, Germany's Nobel prizewinner for Literature. Klemperer was an obstreperous iconoclast who repelled celebrities. He was pathologically manic-depressive, while Walter exuded an almost abnormal calm. Walter leaned politically to the right, Klemperer to the left. Klemperer keenly followed modern art and supported new talent, Walter stuck to what he knew.

Both were Jews who had adopted Christianity, but whereas Klemperer reverted to Judaism after the Holocaust and recoiled from ex-Nazis, Walter made great play of showing 'Christian forgiveness' towards musical collaborators. Unlike Mahler, both were womanizers, although

Klemperer chased skirts only when in a manic phase of his illness while
Walter kept a mistress. Klemperer played out his passions in full public
gaze and was once horsewhipped in the Hamburg Opera by Elisabeth
Schumann's jealous husband during *Lohengrin*; Walter posed as a doting
husband and father and took his pleasures furtively with the soprano
Delia Reinhardt and others. In a penetrating television interview, Klemperer was asked to distinguish between Walter and himself, 'Dr Walter is
a very great conductor,' he rasped wickedly. 'But he is a great moralist.
I am an immoralist. Absolutely!'

As musical personalities, they were polar opposites. Where Klemperer
conveyed an immutable logic in all he performed, Walter softened the
edges of the tonal argument to convey his conception of the work. Just
after the First War, a young composer, Berthold Goldschmidt, watched
both men perform Pfitzner's recent opera *Palestrina*:

> Walter conducted beautifully, very lyrical and silky, stressing all the
> melodious elements and establishing the medieval atmosphere in the
> prelude. Four weeks later I heard Klemperer perform it in Cologne.
> The first eight bars of the prelude were completely different. Klem-
> perer conducted sternly, sternly, and without any personal inflection,
> as if the passage had been composed by Josquin des Près, with
> none of the lyrical expressiveness that Walter had instilled. Both
> performances were marvellous. It was the first time that I realized
> the enormous difference a conductor can make to the sound and style
> of a music.

Walter's relations with Mahler were not as amicable as he liked to pretend. As a junior assistant in Hamburg he had been captivated by Mahler's 'irresistible power' and 'felt as if a higher realm had been opened
to me'. But he lived in terror of the man's unpredictable demon and
suffered under his autocratic will. He would accompany Mahler on long
country rambles, ate at his table, joined him on summer holidays and,
according to family tradition, fell in love with his youngest sister, Emma.
When Mahler discovered the romance, he married Emma off hastily and
unhappily to an orchestral cellist, Eduard Rosé. Aware of Walter's talent,
he did not want a potential competitor as brother-in-law. Nothing of this
connection is mentioned in Walter's memoirs. In the summer of 1896 he
lived with Mahler as he finished the Third Symphony in which Mahler
felt 'my savage and brutal nature reveals itself most starkly'. Walter
hardly ever performed it.

At the end of a two-year apprenticeship, Mahler sent him to make his
way in the world at Breslau, Pressburg and Riga, but when he summoned
him to join the revolution in Vienna, Walter unexpectedly refused. 'I felt
that it was necessary to become firmly rooted within myself before exposing myself again to the powerful influence of Mahler,' he wrote. This

was not entirely true. He had presumptuously demanded that Mahler announce him in Vienna as successor to the venerated Hans Richter – a move that would have been tantamount to Mahler posting his own obituary in the shop-windows of the Kärntnerstrasse. Mahler was appalled at his gall:

> What concern of yours is it whose *successor* you are, and for that matter what concern is it of the public? Apart from anything, you will not be a 'finished' conductor for another two or even ten years . . . It would be very important to me to have you before 1900 because I shall be dead by then [of exhaustion] if things go on the way they are now. So let me hear from you – *by return* and no excuses!

Walter did not relent until Mahler fulfilled his prediction and almost died of overwork. His arrival in Vienna ended 'the first and only discord in our relations' but his feelings remained ambiguous and he threatened on several occasions to leave, complaining that the critics were attacking him as a substitute for Mahler.

He was the only member of Mahler's pre-marital circle to survive the advent of Alma, whom he befriended in conscious self-interest, and she repaid in kind. He raised a young family of his own but found that domestic bliss mysteriously brought on an attack of near-paralysis in his conducting arm. Walter thought he was suppressing the 'Faustian' tendency in himself and went to see Sigmund Freud, who recommended a long holiday.

On Mahler's departure, he stayed on under Weingartner but quit when Vienna passed him over a second time for the top job. He replaced Mottl as head of the Court Opera in Munich and remained there for eleven years until driven out by mounting anti-semitism, a phenomenon he refused to recognize. He took up the baton in his home town, Berlin, replaced Wilhelm Furtwängler in Leipzig, led the German opera seasons at Covent Garden, visited America and brought back Shostakovich's first symphony from the Soviet Union. He was, of all conductors, 'first in the command over the affections of a large public in most parts of the world' and the music he made was characterized as 'noble and compassionate'. When the Nazis threw Walter out of Germany and Austria, free nations vied to grant him citizenship and employment. He spent the rest of his days opulently in the United States, returning occasionally to overwhelming ovations in post-War Europe, universally beloved, 'the conductor of humanity'.

Those who knew Walter at close quarters saw a different man. 'Walter was mean, nasty, a pig,' was how Anna Mahler remembered him and sculpted him in stone. Mahler's daughter abhorred his refusal to assist refugees less fortunate than himself and was outraged at his reluctance

to help old Arnold Rosé, veteran concertmaster of the Vienna Philharmonic who was left destitute in London after the *Anschluss*. When Alma
begged him to contribute to a subsistence fund for her former brother-
in-law and his own chamber music partner, Walter pleaded poverty and
eked out a few hundred dollars. The following year, basking in the
Californian sunshine, he demanded the return of his 'loan'.

An orphaned violinist in the Rosé clan was denied access to his Munich
rehearsals despite appeals on her behalf from Mahler's friends. Walter
exploited his position to grant privileges to the famous and was too
haughty to concern himself with the needs of young musicians and struggling composers. Mahler, by contrast, loved the company of bright youngsters and discreetly dug into his own pocket to feed Arnold Schoenberg's
hungry family. 'Walter is a great conductor,' admitted Schoenberg. '*In
private, however*,' he added, in a long-suppressed letter, '*he always was
a repulsive pig and I get nauseated just thinking about him*.' This porcine
metaphor found its way into a number of caricatures. Colleagues who
admired his art were contemptuous of his personality. Even Toscanini,
whose friendship he claimed, called him 'a sentimental fool'.

His outward respectability mirrored that of Thomas Mann, who closeted his homosexuality behind a brood of six children. Walter's daughters
paid the ultimate price for his paternal shortcomings. His younger girl
committed suicide after a disastrous marriage; the elder collapsed when
he announced, directly after her mother's death, 'well, now I can marry
Delia'. Seeing his child slumped prone on the floor, he sighed with relief
and murmured: 'Well, then, perhaps I won't have to.'

Walter was a hypocrite, the antithesis of Mahlerian morality masquerading as its mortal manifestation. The godly values and 'humility before
the work' expressed in his performances were mocked by standards of
personal conduct that, while unremarkable in a car-dealer, conflicted with
his aspirations to administer a sacrament. The Church, he wrote,

> knows why it calls upon the power of music at its most solemn
> functions. Music's wordless gospel proclaims in a universal language
> what the thirsting soul of man is seeking beyond this life. I have been
> vouchsafed the grace to be a servant of music.

These words, intended as his epitaph, have never been questioned and
the innocuous image that Walter made for himself survives largely intact.
Bruno Walter is proof positive that a great conductor does not need to
be a good man. His contribution to the art of conducting was to invent
an aura of spotless serenity. Maestro-makers took their cue from Walter,
whose very name was counterfeit, when constructing fake personae for
Herbert von Karajan and Leonard Bernstein. The euphemisms and
flummery that conceal the machinations of musical life from its consumers

are derived from Walter's veneer of benign geniality. This artificial *Gemütlichkeit* constitutes his principal legacy and underpins his enduring popularity in duplicitous Vienna and in an entertainment industry that thrives on his deceptions.

Mahler did not live to see his faith in Walter shattered, but saw the one contemporary he most respected forsake idealism for materialism. Richard Strauss and I, he used to say, 'are like two miners who dig a shaft from opposite sides [of a mountain] and finally meet underground'. Ever since their mid-twenties they had kept in touch and conducted each other's music. Strauss jocularly styled himself 'the first Mahlerian' and Mahler believed that Strauss was leading the way into a new operatic era.

As conductors, they were antipodes. While Mahler put every last ounce of energy into each rehearsal, Strauss steadily restricted his activity in the podium until he stood there immobile, giving the faintest of flicks with his baton. 'I perspire only in [Beethoven's] C minor symphony, the Ninth and the Eroica – and of course in *Tristan* and Act 1 of *Walküre*,' he confided in 1908. 'In everything else I don't lose my self-command and don't give out too much of myself.' He had the disconcerting habit of entering a green room in the interval, thrusting his hand under the conductor's armpit, and calling out 'amateur!' if it felt damp.

After the First War, Strauss was honoured to be named Director of the Vienna State Opera and referred to himself happily as Mahler's successor. Faced by an all-out strike, he reassured the Viennese that he would not be another Mahler: he had no wish to dominate, and left the daily management to his co-director, Franz Schalk. He was attacked for the size of his salary and the suggestion that his operas might be given undue prominence and gave up after five years, not without tears, having built himself a splendid palace in the centre of the city.

What had driven him apart from Mahler was, in addition to a memorable clash of wives, his delight in earthly possessions – the cheerful boast that his Garmisch home was paid for by Salome's striptease Dance of the Seven Veils, his readiness to compromise with any textual cuts and political demands that would allow his music to be performed and his family to live in comfort. Strauss had no desire to change the world. All he wanted to do was write music, make money, play cards and exercise his conducting arm for his own sweet pleasure.

His split with Mahler signified an irreconcilable division in their profession, the spiritual sundered from the material. Mahler believed in art for its own sake. Strauss, the son of an orchestral musician, expected to be paid for every note he played. Mahler, he told Otto Klemperer, was always seeking redemption. 'I don't know what I am supposed to be redeemed from,' said Strauss. 'When I sit down at my desk in the morning and an idea comes into my head, I surely don't need redemption. What did Mahler mean?'

*   *   *

The fate that befell Gustav Mahler in the first half of 1907 was an epic tragedy reminiscent of the biblical tale of Job. At the acme of his power and confidence and happiness, the summit of his Iglau dreams, Mahler was struck down by three swift blows that robbed him of everything he held dearest in life. Vienna, which dazzled the musical world under his directorship, turned upon him with pent-up racial venom and forced his resignation, returning him to a nomadic existence. His four-year-old daughter, Maria, caught diphtheria and died in agony. Alma collapsed; when a doctor came to examine her, he cast a diagnostic eye over Mahler and discovered an incurable heart condition that could prove fatal at any moment. He was ordered to give up all forms of violent exercise which, for a man who loved nothing more than swimming two miles across a lake after a long mountain hike, amounted to a second sentence of death.

He fled to Toblach in the high Dolomite mountains, leaving Alma to bury the child and sell the house while he searched for mental equilibrium in a book of Chinese poems that supplied the texts for *Das Lied von der Erde*. 'Is it bearable?' he asked, showing Bruno Walter the score. 'Will people not want to do away with themselves on hearing it?'

The child's death and his own fragility fractured the marriage. Alma, her fidelity weakened and fearing lonely widowhood, started consorting with younger men. Mahler consulted Freud, who told him he had a mother complex fixated on his wife. Alma was flattered, but continued seeing her lover, possibly with Mahler's connivance. Whatever resistance he could summon was channelled into two final symphonies of mortal struggle with the Creator who had so unjustly afflicted him.

When he left for America, a conclave of Vienna's progressive spirits gathered to wave him goodbye. '*Vorbei!*' muttered Gustav Klimt as his train pulled out, 'it's over!'

In New York, Mahler conducted initially at the Metropolitan Opera and subsequently at Carnegie Hall with skill and imagination but little of the fire that he had radiated in Vienna. Husbanding his resources, he survived three seasons without cancelling a performance. He produced a *Tristan* that entered operatic legend and his *Bartered Bride* was the first Czech opera in the New World, but he made cuts in most operas and accepted inferior orchestral playing. 'Where music is, the demon must be,' he exhorted the musicians but his baton arm dropped lower and lower and he needed milk and bananas to get him through a rehearsal.

He was hustled out of the Met by an Italian coup after declining to take on the executive responsibilities of its ailing German manager, Heinrich

Conried. Alarmed at the glitter of Oscar Hammerstein's Manhattan Opera Company, the Met directors signed up both the administrator and chief conductor of La Scala. Arturo Toscanini had engineered the metamorphosis of Milan with uncut productions, immaculate ensemble and defiant dedication. His assurances that he held Mahler 'in great esteem and would infinitely prefer such a colleague to any mediocrity' masked a constitutional inability to tolerate a rival.

He demanded to conduct *Tristan*. Mahler protested that he had 'lavished a great deal of effort on *Tristan* last season and may reasonably assert that the form in which the work now appears is my intellectual property'. He won the argument – and lost the war. While Mahler conducted the next run of *Tristan*, Toscanini made sure it was his last and, with the rich and rowdy support of New York's Little Italy, drove him out of the opera house.

In the urban jungle of the American miracle, where the fittest survived in splendour and the weak perished unheard, Toscanini presented himself as the bold new force of musical destiny, sweeping all before him. He was forty years old, handsome and fiercely determined. He would not be content merely to command an opera company in a capital city.

CHAPTER 4

Facing The Dictators

TOSCANINI WAS AN unloved child who demanded to be obeyed. When his wishes were thwarted, he threw infantile tantrums and sharp objects. Anything less than instant gratification and total acquiescence – whether by a paternalistic government or childlike musicians – provoked a violent response. He was brutal to orchestras and created a cult of brutality that other conductors copied as a token of their authority in an authoritarian era. He was a bully; but no coward. Exposed to hired thugs and the notionally superior might of the modern state, he kept his head stubbornly high above the parapet of history.

Many consider him the greatest conductor that ever lived. 'Music never sounded before . . . as it did when Arturo Toscanini conducted it,' asserts the daughter of one of his singers, 'and there are legions of us today who are witness that it has never sounded the same since.' More than forty years after his death he remains the only maestro of whom many people have heard, and his portrait still graces the postage stamps of the United States. Ignace Jan Paderewski, famed pianist and Polish prime minister, wrote: 'There is nobody to be compared with Toscanini for he is a transcendent genius – a genius of the first order. One cannot speak in any ordinary terms of Toscanini.' Conductors accepted that he was in a class of his own, uniquely combining the professionalism of Richter with the magic of Nikisch. 'He is supreme!' exclaimed a sceptical London orchestral player.

He was known simply as 'Maestro' – no definite object required, for he was the definitive object: the only conductor in the world. A New York record producer summoning a cab to 'Mr Toscanini's house' was severely reprimanded. 'MAESTRO, not Mister,' said Maestro. Power was his objective, though, not mere glory. He was at heart a humble man who said: 'I am no genius. I have created nothing. I play the music of other men. I am just a musician.' The deification of Toscanini was an American invention – made for a nation with global aspirations, mono-lithic media that thrived on simple-minded certainties, and a monotheistic faith in single idols – one Sinatra, one Garbo, one poet, one painter, one president at a time.

High in the broadcasting towers of the Avenue of the Americas where Toscanini's image was moulded, music was deemed to need a god-like intermediary if it was to reach a mass market. This totem had to be something more than a frock-coated musician. Ideally, he would be both a player on the stage of momentous world events – an ideological icon, the defender of democracy – and, at the same time, a man with whom Middle America could identify, the home-loving slippered patriarch who watched boxing on the television and played hide-and-seek in the garden with his grandchildren. Toscanini played along with both parts of this myth, and ultimately came to believe in it.

His omnipotence was founded on a public perception of his role, rather than on outright control of institutions. He preferred illusions of power to the mundane reality, shunning the practicalities of management and delegating the implementation of his wishes to a clique of terrorized lackeys. He was frustrated and bored when running an opera house or orchestra and resigned his positions all too readily. Not for him Mahler's ambition to achieve fleeting perfection in an imperial theatre that would serve an example to others. Toscanini, aided by sophisticated advertising techniques, projected *himself* as the personification of perfection, the sole arbiter of musical taste and rectitude. He alone could interpret the notes correctly and he alone would determine what counted as great music for public consumption. No-one dared suggest that the notes he played were often wrong, or that his musical menu was so unbalanced that it would provoke prolonged and possibly fatal arteriosclerosis in the American concert hall.

He ruled unchallenged and unrestrained, 'forgiven conduct that would have been tolerated in no other artist' and exerting a stranglehold on musical appreciation across the civilized world. Artistically and intellectually, he remains a massive paradox. He was the Great Dictator in an art and a society that shed blood, sweat and tears in its mortal effort to rid the world of great dictators.

Toscanini was the eldest child and only son of an impecunious couple in Parma, a town of 45,000 known for its cheese and ham rather than anything spiritual. The family belonged to the working-class Oltratorrente, the other side of the stream, the wrong side of the tracks. His father, Claudio, returned from Garibaldi's wars of liberation drunk on glory and dissatisfied with tailoring. He relied on his new wife, Paolina, to raise the family and look after the shop while he spouted political fantasies in sunlit squares. She had neither the time nor inclination to bestow much affection on her brood. Arturo, a sickly mite, was in any case not expected to survive. When a second baby was due and his parents went to try their luck briefly in Genoa, he was left behind in the care of grandparents. His mother, he confessed, 'never loved me. And I never loved her.' At the age of nine he won a scholarship to the Parma Conservatorio and moved into its dormitory behind the walls of a former Carmelite convent. Paolina never once crossed the river to visit him.

The frigidity of his upbringing, so unusual among Italians, stunted his emotional development. Although he grew up to be irresistible to women and availed himself prolifically of their charms, his sexual liaisons were (with one exception) swift and superficial. When he married, it was a calculated alliance that seemed to preclude passionate romance.

> He once told me [wrote a confidante] that he had waited until the age of thirty to marry because a man was not serious before then; and that he had chosen a woman ten years younger than himself 'so that my life would not be disrupted when I was old. I would certainly die before she did.'

His own longevity thwarted this design. He was devastated to find himself a widower at 84 and mourned his Carla in months of self-imposed isolation. Comtemptuous of the Church as a rule, he took a distinctly Catholic attitude to marriage, abominated divorce and abruptly terminated long friendships with the Austrian writer Stefan Zweig, who forsook his family to marry a secretary, and the German conductor Fritz Busch, who took a second spouse long after the demise of his first. 'A man can take a mistress but he must have only one wife all his life,' he adamantly proclaimed. On learning that his elder daughter was seeing a married man he battered her and boycotted her wedding, while continuing to indulge his own adulterous fancies.

He was a stern and unyielding father who blighted the lives of several descendants. The favourite granddaughter, with whom he frolicked for photographers, ended up taking an overdose in a hotel room (Sonia Horowitz was the only child of Toscanini's daughter, Wanda, and the pianist, Vladimir Horowitz). 'Toscanini loves no-one,' concluded a disgruntled collaborator. 'On his sleeve he wears not his heart but his spleen . . . he is not capable of love.'

The love he could not give his own parents or receive from them shifted vicariously and with unnatural intensity to the art that accepted him without question. At the Conservatorio, he endured draconian discipline and prison-like conditions, with rotting fish for supper and straw pallets to sleep on. In a vendetta against one of the masters, Toscanini and his classmates killed, cooked and ate his wife's cat. He learned at school that bestial savagery and dedication to music were inseparable. At 18 he graduated with high honours in cello-playing and composition and sailed to Brazil as principal cellist and assistant chorus master with a touring opera company. On reaching Rio, the singers went on strike against an inept local conductor and refused to perform. The audience received their protest as a national slur and chased off an Italian understudy. Riots seemed certain when the deputy chorus master, hauled from private pursuits in his *pensione* bedroom with a girl from the chorus, walked into the pit at 9.15 p.m. on 30 June 1886, seized the baton, sat down, waved away the score and struck up the overture to *Aida* to begin a sensational debut that echoed around the musical world.

He conducted for the rest of the tour but did not 'seriously think of myself as a conductor' and, on returning home, looked for work as a cellist. Even after giving Catalani's new opera *Edmea* in Turin, he slipped back into the La Scala orchestra to play cello in *Otello*, Giuseppe Verdi's return to opera after a sixteen-year silence. At the end of a first act rehearsal Toscanini, nudged by his neighbour, saw everyone standing up and found the great composer approaching him to criticize his playing in the concluding love duet. Play louder, said Verdi. Toscanini bit back a retort that the passage was marked *piano* in the score.

The long-awaited *Otello* was greeted by an explosion of patriotic fervour. Crowds carried its composer home on their shoulders and cheered the night away beneath his balcony. Toscanini packed his instrument, raced home, pulled Paolina from her bed and shouted, '*Otello* is a masterpiece! Get down on your knees, Mamma, and say *Viva Verdi!*' He had found himself a devotion more potent than mother-love.

Italian opera, at the peak of its fertility, was being sabotaged at home by indigenous lassitude. Finer performances could be seen in Paris or St Petersburg than in Rome and Milan, where slapdash playing, vain divas and personal rivalries conspired to wreck the productions. Every small Italian town had its own opera house – Turin at the time had a dozen – but the orchestras were made up of casual labour with casual attitudes and even La Scala had no permanent ensemble. Operagoing was a social habit devoid of musical meaning. The singers were all that counted and they were allowed to flaunt and distort at will. Verdi had endured a lifetime of such abuses. His librettist and fellow-composer, Arrigo Boïto, prayed aloud for a native conductor who would cleanse an art that had been 'befouled like the walls of a brothel'. An influential figure in Milan, Boïto pinned his hopes first on the shortlived and easy-going Franco Faccio, then on the 31-year-old Toscanini whom he named chief conductor at La Scala after a decade of peripatetic experience.

Alongside an administrator of his own age, Giulio Gatti-Casazza, Toscanini took over the house at the lowest ebb in its history, after a 16-month closure enforced by drastic cuts in its municipal subsidy. He opened with *Die Meistersinger*, performed uncut for the first time in Italy, and followed up with a *Norma* that he cancelled expensively after the dress rehearsal because the singing was unsatisfactory. A new rigour had imposed itself upon La Scala. In a couple of seasons it was numbered among the world's three or four outstanding companies, a position it has never since relinquished. Over the next half-century and more, it was dominated by the diminutive figure of Toscanini, whether or not he was connected with its season.

His triumph was augmented by the good fortune of finding the finest living tenor and bass-baritone, Enrico Caruso and Feodor Chaliapin, and the skill to apply their talent to apposite roles. Caruso made his impact in Donizetti's delightful though long-undusted comedy *L'elisir d'amore* while the huge Russian was an ominous Mefistofele in Boïto's opera of that name. Other stars were the baritone Antonio Scotti and the lyric soprano Rosina Storchio, who became Toscanini's tragic lover. With Verdi's death at the dawn of the century, Toscanini became the public face of Italian music – he, rather than Puccini and the verismists whose operas, though sensationally popular, were unexalted. In Toscanini, the conductor replaced the composer as the figurehead of music. Opposition rallied against his policies and his presumption. Local composers and their powerful publisher, Ricordi, campaigned xenophobically against his love for foreign operas, while operagoers resented his restraint on the repetition of popular arias. At the closing performance of the 1902 season, they insisted on a *bis* midway through the first act of *Un ballo in maschera*. Toscanini beat on regardless through mounting uproar and left the house at the interval. He arrived home, hours early and bleeding, having punched his fist through a window. 'What's wrong? Is it finished already?' asked his wife Carla. 'For me, it's finished,' said the conductor, and booked his passage to Buenos Aires, where he conducted the next four seasons.

He was not forgotten at La Scala. During the rowdy première of *Madam Butterfly* in February 1904, wags latched on to Rosina Storchio's obvious discomfort and, when the front of her kimono billowed out in the breeze, shouted: 'She's pregnant! with Toscanini's baby!' In fact, she had given birth to his child months earlier, a defective waif who died at 16 and hastened her premature decline. She sang *Butterfly* heart-rendingly in Buenos Aires and their love affair continued on both continents while Toscanini raised a family of his own. The sudden death in Argentina of his four-year-old son, Giorgio, provoked a crisis of guilt and priorities. He came out and conducted the next night as if nothing had occurred, but resolved to return to his duties at La Scala – on his own terms: no repeats, no applause, and the construction of a proper orchestral pit. Notices went up around the house that 'for reasons of order and artistic continuity' the management had decided 'to instruct the conductor not to grant any encores'. Just how readily he now received 'instructions' was shown at the end of his second season when he refused an order to perform two pieces by a lamented Milanese music professor at a memorial concert. Not only did he boycott the event but he sued the Scala directors for trespassing on his artistic domain.

The invitation to transfer his partnership with the pliant Gatti to the Met was both irresistible and face-saving, although the *New York Times* misnamed him as 'the most renowned of all Italian conductors, Mr TOS-CANELLI'. He inherited Mahler's marvellous cast and added few notable singers of his own.

His golden era at the Met glittered less as a result of his conducting, remarkable though it was, than for its unrivalled feast of great singing. Gatti's opening schedule for November 1908 read like this:

Sat 14	*Aida*	Farrar, Caruso	cond. Spetrino
Mon 16	*Aida*	Destinn, Louise Homer, Caruso, Scotti	c. Toscanini
Tue 17	*Bohème*	Marcella Sembrich, Caruso, Scotti	c. Spetrino
Wed 18	*Walküre*	Fremstad, Schmedes, Gadski	c. Hertz
Thur 19	*Butterfly*	Farrar, Caruso, Scotti	c. Toscanini
Fri 20	*Traviata*	Sembrich, Caruso, Pasquale Amato	c. Spetrino
Sat 21	*Tosca*	Emma Eames, Caruso, Scotti	c. Toscanini

Apart from Caruso's superhuman feat of singing six times and five roles in a week, the outstanding feature of this programme is the qualitative disparity between singers and conductors. Once he was rid of Mahler, Toscanini made sure that no conductor of substance would enter the Met (or La Scala*, for that matter). Francesco Spetrino was a hack hired from the Warsaw Opera, while Alfred Hertz's Germanic stolidity was a perpetual target for Toscaninian scorn. Pathologically jealous, he encouraged the press – with the aid of the Met's unscrupulous publicist, William Guard – to regard him as supreme, 'the commander-in-chief', earning 'almost twice the salary of the President of the United States'.

He broke with Gatti in 1915 over the manager's decision to remain in America and sailed home to apply himself selflessly to the war effort, leading military bands under fire and staging benefit galas for the casualties. The frustrated patriotism of his feckless father had finally found room for expression. He nevertheless persisted in playing Wagner and boycotted the city of Rome when it banned German music.

He took advantage of post-War confusion and inflation to evict the entrenched box-holders at La Scala and reconstitute the opera house as

---

*Vittorio Gui was the only noteworthy conductor to work with him at La Scala. Tullio Serafin served for half a season as junior repetiteur; Victor de Sabata did not appear in Milan until Toscanini had left.

an autonomous entity. His third period at La Scala lasted throughout the 1920s and earned the company and its conductor unstinted European laurels. Their 1929 visit to Berlin and Vienna with casts featuring Mariano Stabile, Toti dal Monte and Giacomo Lauri-Volpi was among the operatic high points of a vibrant decade in both countries. Otto Klemperer called it 'unforgettable' and for the astonished young Herbert von Karajan 'it was a revelation'. At Bayreuth and Salzburg, his Wagner was praised for its clarity and southern lyricism.

Wherever he appeared, Toscanini now outshone all of his singers. He was heralded as the greatest of conductors and the true fount of music, to the chagrin of colleagues like Wilhelm Furtwängler, who enumerated his faults and his fakery:

> In contrast to, say, Nikisch, he has no innate manual talent, and what he does have has been fought for and worked upon. But certain striking shortcomings have remained: above all the enormous waste of space in the *forte*. The size of his beat in the *f* is such that it makes any differentiation impossible. As a result, these *tuttis* are all the same . . . I do not hold with taking the conductor all too seriously as a person. It is of no consequence whether or not he is disciplined, whether or not he looks good . . .

This partisan and unpublished opinion was a lone voice of dissent in a wilderness of uncritical adulation that steadily swept the musical hemisphere. Any reservations were confined to a tiny fringe of individualists and avant-gardists, whose existence Toscanini generally ignored.

His receptivity to new music hardened with advancing age and weakened eyesight and he gave few further premières, with the notable and momentous exceptions of the posthumous *Turandot* and *Nerone* which established Toscanini as the living voice of the late Puccini and Boïto.

All the while, he kept his links across the Atlantic. When his position in Italy became unsettled, a US media giant headhunted the seventy-year-old Toscanini as a status symbol sitting atop its round-the-clock cocktail of news, soap opera and zappy tunes. The National Broadcasting Company (NBC) offered to create for him a 92-man virtuoso orchestra with which he would give ten live concerts from its studios. It cost NBC $50,000 a year in conductor fees and six times as much in musicians' salaries but it was money well spent in gaining kudos and heading off a Congresional inquiry into broadcasting standards. NBC also won exclusive rights to issue Toscanini's records on the label of its parent company, the Radio Corporation of America (RCA).

Initially suspicious of recording, Toscanini came to regard it as a means of affirming his superiority by achieving clearer sound and bigger sales than other conductors. Although he could not outsell Leopold Stokowski and the Philadelphia Orchestra in classical pops such as *The Blue Danube* and the *Nutcracker Suite*, in more serious repertoire, Toscanini's name on the sleeve exerted an altogether different tug at the consumer's purse-strings. Music performed by Toscanini carried a certificate of worthiness: it was guaranteed by all recognized authorities to be great music, perfectly played. The records could be bought with absolute assurance and displayed with total confidence on the living-room shelves as a sign of the householder's cultural values. They served in other words, as *kitsch*, – an art-substitute once defined (by Wilhelm Furtwängler) as 'the intellectual half-man's fear of . . . being duped'.

Phoney stories were fed to the press – 'World's Largest Drum Rushed to New York for Toscanini Concert' – even as his political stance in Europe made real news. He hit the cover of *Life* and *Time* and every magazine that counted. And, while he managed barely one-sixth of Bob Hope's radio audience, he polled twice the ratings of any broadcast concert series. Toscanini had become the first conductor for a mass audience and, for most people, the only one they could name. Fame, in media parlance, at least, was an acceptable surrogate for love.

Mass appeal did not affect Toscanini's musical authority, which was by now too huge to be enlarged by universal fame, or dented by demotic acclaim. He ruled music by a symbiosis of divine right and brute force. Acting in the name of the creator, he persecuted all who strayed from the one truth path – or what he, with superior wisdom, beheld as the one true path. He permitted no deviation from holy writ, no experimentation or textual criticism. He was a fundamentalist preacher of a faith of his own invention. Ever since he set out to rescue Verdi from his ravagers, Toscanini had propounded a doctrine of literalism that promised a precise account of what the composer had written. Whether the composer was Verdi or Beethoven, Puccini or a neophyte American called Samuel Barber, no mortal executant had the right to alter a crotchet of their inspiration, let alone colour a performance with individual mannerisms and mood. The conductor was a cipher, the servant of the written notes.

That, at any rate, was the theology. In practice, Toscanini – amid loud protestations of humility – developed a cult of his own personality as the living embodiment of musical deity*. 'They say that my character is like Verdi's,' he liked to brag, and an RCA sleeve-note headed 'Verdi and Toscanini' moved him to tears with its fawning account of their 'remarkable similarity of origin, intellect, temperament and character'.

There was no hypocrisy in this perception. He was genuinely devoted

---

*The cult is thoroughly examined in Joseph Horowitz's *Understanding Toscanini: or how he became an American culture-god* . . . (See Bibliography, p. 365).

to genius and conscious of his duties as its self-anointed deputy, delving continually for enlightenment into long-familiar scores. Once, failing to turn up at a post-concert reception in London, he was found sprawled on his hotel bed squinting at the notes of Beethoven's *Pastoral Symphony* that he had just magnificently performed. The compulsion of a Toscanini performance was rooted in a dynamism bred of absolute dedication and self-certainty. It was set in stone like the Ten Commandments, yet swept all before it like a Crusade. It constituted a hypnotic dichotomy of stasis and fluidity, eternal law in continuous evolutionary motion.

In the eyes of his audience he was more than just the composer's envoy. By conducting from memory, a practice forced on him by feeble eyesight, he gave the impression of having conjured the music from the recesses of his own imagination, as a retroactive participant in the act of creation. For want of a composer, he *was* the composer. Interpretative notions that enabled music to be played in subjective, variable manner, fired by the conductor's spontaneous inspiration, were anathema to him. 'Blessed are those works that don't need interpreters,' he scrawled in a child's autograph album. 'They cannot be vitriolized by histrionic mountebanks as happens very often to the divine art of music.'

His own performances, though, were notably individual. The music he made was vivid and explicit, unfailingly fresh – *'newly created for us'*, in the telling words of a Vienna Philharmonic player. The secret ingredient of this 'Toscanini sound' was kept in the family for thirty years after his death, when the New York Public Library acquired his scores at a knockdown price and researchers were finally able to examine them. Just how far he had departed from scripture was instantly visible. Many of his working scores are littered with red pencillings that subvert the texture of the music and alter its essential colouring. In Debussy's *La Mer*, he actually rewrote two whole pages of full score in green ink and pasted them into his copy in place of the authentic text. *La Mer* was a Toscanini trade-mark, a work he conducted in America more than any other except Wagner's *Meistersinger* overture. Yet what he conducted was not wholly Debussy. A first-edition copy of *Iberia* that the French composer had affectionately inscribed to him is extensively altered. Toscanini did not, as he pretended, faithfully recreate what the composer had written. Where he did not like what he read in the score, he rewrote it.

His account of the *Enigma Variations* provoked wonderment among English listeners – and no wonder, for his copy of Elgar's score is speckled with alterations. Even Beethoven was subjected to his ministrations; the timpani and brass parts were expanded in the vivacious opening movement of the Eighth symphony and, perversely, reduced in the finale of the Ninth. He habitually introduced extra instruments in climactic passages to enhance the impact of his orchestra and electrify the excitement of a Toscanini concert. Beethoven was deaf, he said, and could not know how his music should sound. Clearly, a schizoid duality was operating in Toscanini's brain. While upholding the inviolable sanctity of the text, he assumed – as high priest and creator's proxy – the absolute right to edit. 'His dedication to the composer transcended the score,' argues Massimo Freccia, one of his musical assistants. 'He felt he was serving the composer best by perfecting it.'

Composers protested at this presumption. Verdi himself muttered angrily about 'the tyranny of conductors' after reading his publisher's report of Toscanini's *Falstaff*. When Maurice Ravel rebuked him after the Paris première of *Bolero* for playing the orgasmic rhythms twice as fast as indicated, Toscanini retorted, 'it's the only way to save the work'. Dmitri Shostakovich, outraged by his wartime recording of the *Leningrad Symphony*, said: 'Hearing it made me very angry. Everything is wrong. The spirit and the character and the tempi. It's a sloppy hack job.' Mere composers, though, were powerless beside the might of Toscanini and most were wretchedly grateful for the favour of his attention. Ravel begged him to perform his next concerto; he received no reply.

Orchestral musicians and staff were aware of the contradiction between Toscanini's famous doctrine and his everyday practice. He told Freccia, 'change what you want, but don't tell anybody' and every string player could tell when someone had been tampering with his parts. Toscanini, noted the respectful BBC violist Bernard Shore, 'is not a purist in the rigid sense' and genuine purists were appalled at his interference with classical masterpieces. His recordings of Mozart symphonies were described by their studio producer, the man responsible for getting the notes right, as 'granitic, driven, steel-skeletoned, merciless and cold' – utterly alien to the composer's spirit.

Yet the public were assured by an entirely docile press and music profession that whatever Toscanini performed was uniquely and indisputably authentic. 'He strove earnestly to realize as exactly as possible the composer's intention as printed in the musical score,' wrote the *New York Times* in its obituary. To reconcile what they heard with the myth they sustained, music critics were obliged to perform stunning feats of mental acrobatics. 'Signor Toscanini's standard of complete faithfulness,' wrote *The Times* of his 1935 *Enigma*, 'sometimes resulted in too literal a reading of [Elgar's] markings.' Since Toscanini was the conductor, the performance had to be accurate; if the music sounded different, then the composer must have got it wrong. . . .

The only American to dissent from the critical tide of adulation was forced to write his notices in cipher. 'By praising him discreetly, indicate his shortcomings,' was the editorial warning given to Virgil Thomson of the *Herald Tribune*. Thomson, a competent composer, disliked the 'wow-technique' of the Toscanini sound, despised his attitude to modernism and detected technical faults in his conducting. In his view, Fritz Reiner of Pittsburgh was 'a sounder musician than Toscanini' – an opinion 'shared by many other musicians'. Not a murmur of such demurrals was printable at the time, when Toscanini exerted tougher thought-control in American media than Stalin wielded at *Izvestia*. He was the primary arbiter of fine music for the common man at a time of its proliferation on radio and record. Apologists deemed his dictatorship essential for the survival of music in America, and none who valued their musical jobs dared question its legitimacy.

Given that journalists are competitive, cynical and resistant to self-censorship, their wholesale complicity in manufacturing and maintaining the Toscanini mythology without so much as an arched eyebrow is puzzling in the extreme. Music critics were undoubtedly overwhelmed by the power of his performances, and their editors and proprietors understandably approved of his uncompromising posture on matters of principle. But the editorials supported him even when he was wrong and critics churned out the same glowing encomia long after the musicianship had lost its sheen and become erratic, as it did in the final years. He was depicted as a historic personality, comparable in music only to Beethoven himself: 'he was bigness and nobility, honesty and courage, sincerity and depth; and these human qualities are expressed in his art'. He was 'one of those splendid anomalies whereby nature, from time to time, deigns to rehabilitate the human race'. His 'heroism' was daily manifest in a relentless struggle for 'ever-new forms of perfection'. He was not just a great musician but, in the golden words of his concert announcer beamed to every American home, 'the greatest musical interpreter of our time – perhaps of all time'.

The hyperbolic unanimity of these hallelujahs would seem to indicate some sinister external manipulation, whether by New Yorks' Italian lobby or by commercial interests allied to NBC. But no evidence of large-scale orchestration has come to light, no threats uttered or bodies discovered, no writers sacked or advertising withdrawn. His stranglehold on press coverage was achieved not by overt pressure but by subliminal terror. The aura of fear he cast around his podium was so awesome as to subdue the rest of society into mesmerized submission. Toscanini's rehearsal rages were integral to his legend. Screaming like 'stuck bulls in a Chicago slaughterhouse', his fists and spittle flying in all directions, he would kick the rehearsal piano until aides feared that his legs, not its, would snap. No object was safe from his temper and no witness emerged unscathed.

Even today, listening to tapes of his tantrums leaves one feeling

physically sick, transfixed by a shrieking stream of foul invective punctuated by the smashing and ripping of musical paraphernalia. He was
sufficiently self-conscious to ban outsiders, especially women, from
rehearsals; the few friends who gained admittance were duly 'terrified'
and served to communicate his terror still further. He generally avoided
causing bodily harm, though once, while adjudicating a dispute between
NBC players, the septuagenarian conductor suddenly turned on one of
the men and began to pummel him. The musician 'stood dazed and
rooted to the spot, suffering the blows to rain upon his head', paralysed
by the ferocity of the attack. In Turin, he snapped a violinist's bow,
causing him facial injury and narrowly missing an eye. Signora Carla
rushed in with generous compensation and Toscanini apologized, but the
player sued him anyway for damages–and lost. Under some laughable Roman
law, the conductor was deemed to have acted as an 'artist prey to the
tyranny of the tragic (not individual) will' and was therefore not accountable.

In Toscanini's case, this verdict was doubly absurd for he never yielded
entirely to rage. A corner of his mind was always icy cool, attuned to
the possible consequences. Once, while rehearsing a Respighi rarity in
wartime,

> he picked up the score and was about to hurl it to the floor, but he
> stopped with it in mid-air, his hands uplifted. You could almost follow
> his thinking. 'I dare not destroy it. It's the only score in America.'
> He put it back on the stand with considerable care and then continued
> his tantrum.

Unable to break his baton in half, he would rip a pocket handkerchief
and, if it proved resistant, tear the coat off his back. Hearing it split
satisfyingly down the middle, 'he felt relieved and quietly asked the men
to begin the phrase all over again'. The cry of *basta!* from his long-
suffering wife rendered him instantly placid.

Many a sneak photographer suffered from his fear of flashbulbs. He
would 'knock the camera out of his hands, stamp on it, breaking it into
smithereens, let out a roar, then turn back with an angelic smile' to
resume his shipdeck conversation with a colleague's small child 'at the
very syllable he had interrupted it'. This mixture of searing rage and
sudden serenity, added to the hint of calculation behind his explosion,
only enhanced the terror of his tempers. There was never much warning
before an outburst and his musicians lived in a state of trembling anxiety
that cannot have improved their playing.

Some managed to convince themselves that the tyranny served a musical purpose. Others, deep down, 'admired his capacity to be so moved
and aroused by his feeling for his work'. The passions he vented on them
counted, in his mind and theirs, as a token of paternal affection. After

one tempest, provoked by a fractionally delayed brass entry at the close
of an otherwise magnificent *Bohème*, he summoned the players to his
dressing room and declared:

> I hide my head in shame, After what happen-ed tonight my life is
> finish-ed. For me it is impossible to look in the face of any*bawdy*.
> But *you* [and he pointed straight at the man at head of the dejected
> line] you will sleep with your wife tonight as if *nothing* happen-ed.

He once excused himself to a soloist by recalling the torments of his own
musical apprenticeship – 'oh, what I suffered, I suffered!' – and the
loveless childhood became a frequent refrain of his old age.

The kind of fear that makes grown men shiver in their seats and wet
their pants is confined to murderous despots, and the conduct of Toscanini
bears an uncomfortable resemblance to the horrifying rages by which
Adolf Hitler exercised his power. Hitler never chewed carpets when
thwarted in his desires; that was a figment of Allied propaganda. His
outbursts were in fact more ominous, less ridiculous. They were coldly
planned to arouse crowds to a frenzy of hate-filled hysteria, or to paralyse
potential adversaries, actually inflicting a heart attack on frail President
Hacha of Czechoslovakia. In serious setbacks, such as the Normandy
invasion, Hitler was unfailingly calm. His tantrums were, like Toscanini's,
triggered by tiny incidents or faults and designed to secure instant obedience from those around him. He would appear 'to lose all control of
himself' but was aware of the effect he was having and 'as suddenly as
he had begun he would stop, smooth down his hair, straighten his collar
and resume a more normal voice'.

Hitler's tantrums have been interpreted by psychoanalysts as 'the
weapons of a child', aimed at frightening his mother into compliance. He
shared with Toscanini the inability to have an emotional relationship with
any individual, only with a faceless mass. While it would be unjust to
pursue the comparison any further, a number of additional traits, such
as the humourless inflexibility that both men exhibited from an early age,
may have a common personality origin.

Toscanini craved power but was not a psychopath and never killed
anyone. He became Hitler's foremost cultural opponent and a living
symbol of the essential alliance between art and liberty. He was a world
hero, and rightly so. While standing up to the dictators, however, he
shamelessly copied their methods.

From the moment Benito Mussolini marched on Rome to the day his
body was strung up in the Piazzale Loreto in Milan, Toscanini was his
mortal enemy. 'If I were capable of killing a man, I would kill Mussolini,'
he said on the eve of the march. 'I wish-ed only to put my hands on his

neck and choke him,' he recounted of their last meeting. His detestation of Fascism was instinctive, implacable and initially isolated. The overwhelming majority of Italian musicians, great and small, accepted the régime so long as it left them alone; an invidious few, who included the clapped-out composer Pietro Mascagni and the great tenor Beniamino Gigli, were active supporters. Puccini proclaimed himself a Fascist but died before it meant much.

Paderewski saw Mussolini as Poland's last hope; the anti-Soviet Igor Stravinsky expressed sympathies with Fascism and, in 1935, 'joyfully' conducted its rabble-rousing hymn. Fritz Kreisler spent pleasant evenings playing for the Duce, who personally turned his pages. Unlike Hitler, Mussolini seemed less of an ogre than a jovial rogue who, with a flexing of muscles and a faint hint of regret, provided the discipline that made Italy's trains run on time.

Toscanini was taken in at first sight by the thrust of his oratory and his grandiose dreams. In 1919 he stood for parliament as a candidate of the embryonic *Fascio di Combattimento*, whose manifesto was modelled on Lenin's. This localized movement did not win a single seat and socialists jubilantly carried Mussolini's coffin through Milan in an election night mock-funeral. Months later, his black-shirted supporters swarmed on to the streets, creating the climate of disorder that led to their ultimate seizure of power. Toscanini broke with them well ahead of the 1922 coup, disillusioned by the violence and particularly by Mussolini's abandonment of anti-monarchism. His political beliefs amounted to the same Garibaldian simplicities his father had fought for: a united Italy, governed as a democratic republic.

With the New Italy he hit trouble within days of its inception. As he entered the pit on 2 December 1922 for the final act of *Falstaff*, a section of the Scala audience called for the Fascist anthem of national rejuvenation to be played. He ignored the disruption and prepared to resume the opera. When the noise persisted, he smashed his baton and stomped out. Order was restored by a managerial promise that the 'Giovinezza' would be played after the final curtain. Toscanini returned but would not conduct the hymn or allow his cast to join in the singing. Scala artists, he said, 'are not vaudeville singers' and the tune had to be tinkled out on the pit piano. A decree was issued from Rome that portraits of Mussolini and the King were to hang prominently in every theatre. In the premier opera house, the music director refused.

Mussolini, still insecure in his power, swallowed these snubs. He announced his intention in 1924 to attend the opening of *Turandot* and stipulated that the Giovinezza must be sounded on his arrival. Toscanini refused. Since the withdrawal of Italy's *gran maestro* from the swansong of its last famous composer would have occasioned international comment, the Duce once again backed down. On his next visit to La Scala, he treated Toscanini to a private harangue behind closed doors. The conductor prudently controlled his temper and said nothing. He knew that the cost of dissent was steadily rising.

Anti-Fascists were being roughed up and sometimes killed. One of his oldest allies, Giuseppe Gallignani, threw himself out of a window after being sacked from the Milan Conservatory by order of some witless functionary at the Ministry of Public Instruction in Rome. Toscanini turned Gallignani's funeral into a political demonstration, kicking the minister's wreath into the mud and refusing to allow an official eulogy. He shut La Scala for a night rather than play the odious anthem on a national anniversary and berated the Irish soprano Margaret Sheridan for having praised Italy in a Fascist daily. 'If you spouted less in political papers, you would be a better singer,' he told her. 'Maestro,' she replied boldly, 'may I also suggest that if you dabbled less in politics you would be an even greater conductor.'

His departure from La Scala to conduct the New York Philharmonic in 1930 ended an untenably tense co-existence. Mussolini was relieved to see him go, but party firebrands were burning to make Toscanini pay for his insolence. Their chance came in May 1931 when he went to Bologna to conduct two concerts without fee in memory of his friend, the composer Giuseppe Martucci. After the final rehearsal, he was told that, because a Fascist convention was being held nearby, various ministers were coming to the concert and he would have to perform the anthem. He balked, and a compromise was arranged that a local band would greet the dignitaries in the lobby.

As Toscanini drew up at the artists' entrance before the concert, he was accosted by Fascist youths who demanded to know whether he was going to play their tune. On hearing him utter 'No!' a journalist called Leo Longanesi bashed the old man in the face and neck. He was bundled into the car by his wife and driver and rushed to the hotel, where his wounds were bound. Uproar from the concert hall quickly spread into the streets and hundreds of black-shirts clamoured menacingly beneath his window. The composer Ottorino Respighi, sent out to mediate, brought back an ultimatum that Toscanini had to leave before dawn. On reaching home, he sent a cable of protest to Mussolini, whose reaction was to confiscate his passport and place him under effective house arrest.

This indignity, added to the previous night's injuries, aroused outrage in Italy and around the world. Koussevitsky cancelled his forthcoming concerts at La Scala and Fritz Reiner walked out of a Milan rehearsal to visit the prisoner. Dozens of Italian musicians defied the secret police and came knocking at his door. Around 15,000 messages of support were delivered by the postman, according to police records. The restrictions were soon lifted, but Toscanini did not perform again in his country as long as Mussolini was alive. 'I would rather die than conduct again in Italy,' he declared.

He extended this boycott to Germany in 1933 when Hitler began purging Jews from public life, switching his summer activities from Wagner's Bayreuth to Mozart's Salzburg – 'the deepest sorrow of my life'. When Austria joined the Reich, he withdrew to the Lucerne Festival in neutral Switzerland, blasting his Wagner concerts by radio into the subjugated neighbouring territories. While other artists hedged their bets in the early years of Nazism, Toscanini was unremitting in his opposition. He signed petitions and manifestos, raised money for refugees and in 1937 conducted the inaugural concerts of the Palestine Symphony Orchestra, comprised mainly of displaced European musicians. To their astonishment, he praised their playing warmly in the first two rehearsals. In the third, he hit the roof. The players were overjoyed: at last Toscanini was treating them like a real orchestra. As he refused payment, they showered him with a lifetime's supply of Jaffa oranges.

He insisted on returning the following year despite being warned off by the Zionist leader Chaim Weizmann, who feared for his safety during the Arab uprising. His courage and endurance were as indomitable as his convictions. He took his NBC orchestra on a gruelling South American tour, before the US entered the War, to counter Axis cultural propaganda. He made a rousing contribution to the war effort with a rumbustious new orchestration of the Star-Spangled Banner, the score of which he auctioned off for a million dollars in warbonds. When Mussolini was overthrown in 1943, he composed a painstaking message in English, 'To the People of America':

> I am an old artist who had been among the first to denounce Fascism to the world. I feel and believe that I can act as an interpreter of the soul of the Italian people – these people whose voice has been choked for twenty years. . . .

In Milan, his name was plastered across the façade of La Scala until Germany reinstated the Duce and the graffitists were tracked down and tortured. When American forces captured the city, they found slogans proclaiming 'Vogliamo Toscanini! – We want Toscanini!' His return to La Scala in 1946, having donated a million lire to help repair the house, was an occasion of national awakening. He was no longer just a conductor, nor even the 'greatest conductor in the world', but, in the assessment of his most objective biographer, a living symbol of that 'healthiness, severity and humanity which had given their country a Dante, a Michelangelo, a Verdi'.

In the course of his campaign, his motives and beliefs were never closely examined, and triumphant victory gave him a certain immunity to objective study As a diehard nationalist, he had shared Mussolini's ambition to extend Italy's borders and believed in the supremacy of the Italian race, to the detriment of others. 'All Slavs are primitives,' he repeated to a friend who was fighting for Czech freedom. Nor did he take kindly to his daughter Wanda marrying a Jew, snarling a xenophobic aphorism from his distant youth – 'wife and cattle from your own village'. His was the Alf Garnett/Archie Bunker type of gut-racism that needs only a spark of opportunity to ignite into oppression.

If his antipathy to Fascism was neither ideological, pacific nor entirely humanitarian, it can only have been provoked by personal factors. What aroused him against Mussolini was not bloodshed nor demagogic posturing but the state challenge to his own authority within a domain where he had made it absolute. He refused to play the Giovinezza because the demand to perform it encroached on his own prerogative. His opposition to the Nazis was rooted in their attempt to dictate which musicians were racially fit to perform in his productions. Hitler's concession that he could keep Jewish players at Bayreuth was counter-productive, since it only confirmed his fear that the government had seized the function of deciding who might or might not make music. His resignation note to Winifred Wagner spoke of 'painful events *which have wounded my feelings* as a man and as an artist'. There was never any reference to principles, ethics and human rights. His attitude was, in the view of an Italian sympathizer, 'a personal, human reaction which became political' – a defensive response to an external, quasi-parental authority.

His courage caught the imagination of half the world and harnessed the power of music to the fight for freedom. All it lacked was moral conviction, an underlying sense of purpose that might have sustained the cause of justice among musicians after the immediate struggle was won. Toscanini had no such aims. His only post-War political intervention, a brief and futile protest, was to cancel concerts in Paris and London to convey his unhappiness at Italy's new borders. The fate of his country's musical institutions, shackled to democratic parties more firmly than they had ever been to the Fascists, was of no concern to him. His struggle had been personal, its spiritual aspects invented and embellished by his many mythologists. He was not a moral figurehead like Pau Casals or Albert Schweizer but the musical equivalent of a warlord pursuing the narrow objective of military victory. In his regained Italian homeland, he enjoyed its fruits for a few last years, remaining to the end 'as simple, as selfish, and as savage as a child'.

*   *   *

If Nature meant to invent an antidote to Toscanini, it could not have produced a more extreme contrast than Gustav Heinrich Ernst Martin Wilhelm Furtwängler. His names alone signify a cultured, comfortable background, worlds apart from the hovels in which Toscanini was raised. The Furtwänglers were well-established members of the German intellectual middle classes. His grandfather had published a book on 'The Idea of Death in Myths and Artistic Monuments'. His father, Adolf Furtwängler, was a distinguished archaeologist who had dug at Olympia and would die there of dysentery; his mother, daughter of a friend of Brahms, was a gifted painter. Every stage of Willy's infant progress was lovingly recorded in her diary. At six weeks old, she noted, he laughed out loud – a reflex rarely repeated in his photographs. His was a studious childhood and a contemplative life. Had his musical gifts been less convincing, he might have found a niche as a philosopher or theologian.

He was, in every physical and psychological respect, the negative of Toscanini. Tall, gangling and fair where the Italian was compact and swarthy, his movements were ungainly and vague, Toscanini's sleek and tigerish. He went jogging, skiing and kept to a demi-vegetarian diet; Toscanini was a sedentary carnivore. One was dreamily ruminative, the other remorselessly determined; one theorized, the other strategized.

Furtwängler's ambition was to be a composer. Conducting caught his imagination only because it achieved a comparable creative purpose. A symphony could not exist on paper, he said: 'the meaning of music still lies in its playing'. His role as interpreter amounted to something like Wagner's task in musically piecing together Siegfried's sword. 'The work can only be reconstituted,' explained Furtwängler, *'by forming it entirely anew.'* He saw himself as a partner in the act of creation. Each time he conducted, a work of art was born. Toscanini's avowal that the conductor was a humble servant of the work was 'nonsense' – he was its master. Conversely, where Toscanini teemed with masculine aggression, Furtwängler saw his function as 'more female'. He spoke of 'the passive act of immersing oneself in a work . . . from which rebirth follows of its own accord'. He was, in this sense, a receptacle for the composer's spirit.

Toscanini's fundamentalist loyalties offended Furtwängler's faith in a living, fertile art. 'A formula for the correct rendering of everything, which can become a universal law, applicable to every case – no, there is not such a thing, though many people assume there is,' he expostulated in a BBC interview, passion tripping up his scripted English. In the fateful opening of Beethoven's ninth symphony, depicting 'chaos: the primeval beginning of time, out of which everything evolved', Toscanini might devote ten whole minutes of rehearsal to getting his strings to play in perfect unison. The result, said Furtwängler, was that 'one heard this passage exactly as it stands in the score, with merciless clarity: but

Beethoven's idea just vanished'. His own rendition was opaque, tremulous, pregnant with manifold possibilities.

'A curious mixture of artistic instinct and intuition, and deliberating intellect' went into his approach. Where a composer started with a universal idea and worked his way down to details, the conductor had to fight through the tiny notes to begin 'his real work – the weaving of all the particulars into an organic whole'. He memorized his concert scores and directed them with eyes closed, as if at prayer. 'When Furtwängler appeared on the rostrum, tall and haggard, dressed in a long cassock-like *Gehrock*, a friend sitting next to me exclaimed, "But that is a priest, not a conductor!" ' recalls a Berlin composer. In the opera pit, on the other hand, unseen by the audience, his eyes remained glued to the score. He was not unconscious of his effect on the watching public.

From his Munich concert debut as a twenty-year-old with Bruckner's still-unfamiliar ninth symphony and his own Adagio for large orchestra, it was obvious that Furtwängler differed markedly from any known species of conductor. He weaved all over the box, dancing, sometimes singing, and making circular motions with his arms that could not remotely be construed as a firm beat. His own composition was an instant failure but the Bruckner interpretation left an indelible impression. He caught the ear of the composer Hans Pfitzner and became his assistant conductor at German-ruled Strasbourg, where his 'deep, genuine musicality' was spotted by Bruno Walter and commended for higher office. In the northern port of Lübeck he performed his first concerto with the clear-sighted violinist Carl Flesch, who was entranced by his 'sublimated sensuousness' and found him 'nearest to my heart of all conductors . . . honest through and through'.

He was not yet thirty when he succeeded Artur Bodzansky (who was leaving for the Met in New York) as music director at Mannheim. He soon took over Willem Mengelberg's concert season in Frankfurt and Richard Strauss's role as concerts director with the Berlin opera orchestra. The *Gesellschaft der Musikfreunde* that controls concert activity in Vienna installed him as its director. In 1922 when Arthur Nikisch died, the fast-rising Furtwängler was unhesitatingly chosen by both his orchestras, in Leipzig and Berlin, to the dismay of the better-qualified Bruno Walter and his agent, the widow Louise Wolff, who retained her long-deceased husband's grip over the Berlin Philharmonic. Mounting its podium, the new chief conductor would invariably bow, half-ironically, towards Queen Louise's permanent box.

'Furtwängler moved Heaven, Hell and sundry other spheres to get the jobs,' grumbled Walter. 'I was awkward and shy,' reflected the victor. 'My colleagues did not consider me dangerous. When they finally realized that I was indeed a danger to them, it was far too late.' Furtwängler headed Leipzig's concerts for six years and Berlin's for the rest of his life, achieving a level of communication with the players that transcended mutual comprehension and approached a mystical symbiosis. They never fully understood the wavering, wandering motions of his spider-like arm but somehow sensed when to put bow to strings. How do you know when to begin? demanded fellow-musicians. 'We get used to it,' they shrugged. Various clues were offered to newcomers: start when the stick reaches the third button in his waistcoat – count 17 from the moment he raises his arm – wait until you can absolutely wait no longer.

On occasion players would request him for a precise beat in a tricky passage. 'How did you like that?' they asked proudly after a crisp entry. 'Not in the slightest,' he muttered. 'It sounded so dreadfully direct.' He would go white with anger when the music failed to sound right and actually spat at the orchestra in impotent rage; the front desk talked of equipping themselves with 'Furtwängler umbrellas'. Much of his rehearsal time was devoted to getting transitional passages working smoothly so that he could enter a concert without worrying about technical problems and concentrate purely on structural and spiritual dimensions.

He spoke very little at rehearsal and what he said was often as vague as his beat. London Philharmonic players who worked with him in 1938 complained of his 'reluctance to go to the root of the problem, to trace the primary cause to its source . . .

> If a passage fails to give him satisfaction he will break off with a characteristic fluttering wave of his left hand, saying impatiently, 'Noch 'nmal, noch 'nmal' and will repeat the offending bars. If this time also it fails to reach the desired standard, he will go over it again . . . eventually he will shake his head in a despairing way and continue the rehearsal without having analysed the weakness.

Precision playing was of no value to a man who sought a glow of shared commitment. He was, said an arch-enemy, 'the first conductor who divided the responsibility for interpretation between himself and the orchestra'. He told singers: 'You are waiting for me to give cues. I am not giving cues. You are to come in, and I come with you. I want you to take over!' Chronic vacillation undermined the practical and moral quality of his leadership. Confronted with urgent demands he would mumble 'J' . . . ein,' a shifty amalgam of Ja and Nein. When tested by forces of evil, his response proved almost fatally indecisive.

While too remote a figure for musicians to love as they had once loved Nikisch, he nonetheless inspired undying loyalty. The cellist Gregor Piatigorsky never forgot how, at his Berlin audition, 'Furtwängler put his arms around me, and as we walked off the stage together, asked me to become the first cellist of the Philharmonic.' A rear-desk violinist, Fritz

Peppermüller, volunteered to become his unpaid factotum, running all manner of delicate and discreet errands for the helplessly unworldly music director. Furtwängler would board a tram and, finding his pockets empty, borrow the fare from the conductor. Taxi drivers treated him like a lost child. He finally learned to drive and bought himself a Daimler-Benz that he propelled at high speed without ever being quite sure which pedal was the accelerator and which the brake. Beaming with pride, he drove Richard Strauss to lunch down Unter den Linden, only to smash straight into the brand-new parked car of an apoplectic Prussian prince.

He shared with Toscanini an appetite for sexual adventure, but was too hesitant to proposition a girl directly and would send the faithful Peppermüller to solicit her to join him for 'a long chat'. A conductor, he felt, 'should be aware of his attraction' to the opposite sex; he had five children out of wedlock, all of whom he honourably acknowledged. His marriage to a vacuous Danish divorcee, Zitla Lund, broke up childless after eight years; his second wife, Elisabeth Ackermann, was a war widow with four children who happily bore him a fifth.

It was on honeymoon, in Milan in 1923, that he made the acquaintance of his antipode. Both men expressed sentiments of mutual esteem and established cordial relations that lasted, superficially at least, for a dozen years, except when they trespassed on one another's territory.

In January 1925 Furtwängler made his US debut in a Brahms first symphony that 'swept everything before it by reason of its vitality, the irresistible and unbroken current of its rhythms, and the spirit of greatness and heroism that informed every measure'. He was re-engaged by the New York Philharmonic for two further seasons and believed he had acquired a secure dollar-base to protect him from a resurgence of Weimar stagflation. Toscanini, meanwhile, unaccustomed to reading *New York Times* encomia for any conductor but himself, rapidly arranged to return to New York after a decade's absence. The Philharmonic and press cooled perceptibly towards Furtwängler. A Beethoven Ninth that he was meant to conduct was taken over by Toscanini, newly appointed chief conductor of the combined Philharmonic and Symphony orchestras. Furtwängler left the United States on 7 April 1927, never to return. Questioned in Germany about the quality of American orchestras, he replied, '*unangenehm virtuös*' – 'uncomfortably brilliant'.

He blamed the Maestro for his displacement and was overheard 'flaying Toscanini alive, blood dripping from very word'. When German critics fell prostrate before the Italian, he sat down and wrote a scathing analysis of Toscanini's concerts and personality, evidently intending it for publication:

> His greatness lies in his character. This helps him in the eyes of the world, but it does not, unfortunately, help art. One can say with certainty that if he were a greater artist, if he had deeper insights, a

livelier imagination, greater warmth and devotion to the work, he would not have become so disciplined. And this is why his success is disastrous.

Working side by side at Bayreuth, Toscanini was full of praise for Furtwängler's Wagner performances which, though very different from his own, he held to be equally valid. Their relations became tenuous only upon Hitler's accession to power. In the third month of the Reich, Toscanini protested over the plight of Jewish musicians and was blacklisted by the Nazis. Furtwängler took the opposite course of conciliation. Days after the Toscanini ban he wrote to Josef Goebbels: 'If the fight against Jewry is directed chiefly against those artists who are themselves rootless and destructive, who seek to impress through trash and sterile virtuosity, this is only correct . . . But when this attack is directed against real artists as well, it is not in the best interest of our cultural life.' No country could afford to dispense with Walter, Klemperer and Max Reinhardt: such men 'must be enabled to have their say in Germany in the future'. His letter was published by the Minister for Propaganda and Enlightenment alongside his own disingenuous reply, promising 'warmest support' for 'real artists'.

Taking Goebbels at his word, Furtwängler invited foreign Jewish soloists to play in his next season – and was uniformly rebuffed. His old friend, the violinist Bronislaw Hubermann, issued Furtwängler's letter and his own stinging response to the British press. Furtwängler, undeterred, went to Vienna to confront Hubermann and the pianist Artur Schnabel at a public reception. To his loudly reiterated invitation, Schnabel replied that if all musicians who had been sacked on political or racial grounds were restored to their positions in Germany, he would happily return. 'To my great amazement,' he recalled, 'Furtwängler replied – and this was obviously not prepared – that I was mixing art and politics.'

By now, Furtwängler had conducted a celebratory *Meistersinger* for the inauguration of the Third Reich ('lackey!' groaned the exiled Thomas Mann in his diary). He would soon perform on film in front of the blood-red swastika flag, raise his arm in a halfway Hitler salute, accept titles from the regime and confer privately with the Führer, whose favourite conductor he was. He could hardly pretend to be keeping politics out of art. Abhorrent though he found Nazi rowdiness and street thuggery, he viewed the government as a German administration dedicated to upholding German values. Its Chancellor shared the same German forename as his own revered father and was more devoted to Wagner than any leader since Ludwig of Bavaria. He was also beguiled by Goebbels, 'this small, morose little man whom he thought rather charming'.

For almost two years, Furtwängler co-existed peaceably with the Nazis, doing his quiet best to help disenfranchised musicians and retaining by special privilege some Jews in his orchestra. He conducted 'decadent music' with impunity and advised Erich Kleiber to transfer the première of Alban Berg's *Lulu* Suite from the opera house on Unter den Linden to the Philharmonic, which could cope more capably with officialdom. In a parallel sidestep, he performed a symphonic suite based on Paul Hindemith's opera *Mathis der Maler*, which had been banned for a variety of reasons that included its modernist score, a subversive libretto dealing with the artist's role in a repressive society, Goebbels' personal dislike for the composer, and the racial origins of his wife.

Encouraged by the suite's 'wildly enthusiastic' reception and angered by renewed Nazi criticism, Furtwängler wrote another of his open letters to Goebbels calling for a review of 'The Hindemith Case.' His appeal, couched again in Nazi phraseology – 'one must consider him a "German composer" and he is, in fact, in bloodline terms, purely Germanic' – appeared on the front page of the *Deutsche Allgemeine Zeitung*, on a November Sunday in 1934 when Furtwängler was due to conduct *Tristan* at the Berlin State Opera in the presence of both Goebbels and Hermann Goering. As he entered the pit that afternoon, he was greeted by a twenty-minute ovation, the significance of which was not lost on the Nazi chieftains.

Adept in the arts of mental torture, they devised a cruel and unnatural punishment that Furtwängler would suffer until his death, exactly 20 years later. For ten days, he was left awaiting a response. Then, summoned to Goering's office, he was harangued and physically threatened by the Prussian overlord. Goebbels, in a mass rally at the Sportspalast, violently castigated his interference in matters of national policy. Furtwängler was forced to resign from the State Opera, but ordered to remain at the Philharmonic. Chastised with one hand, he was cherished with the other. A senior government official called at his home to convey the Führer's personal request that he postpone a planned holiday in Egypt with English friends. The curb was softened by its flattering acknowledgement of his personal importance to the head of state. He was not a prisoner but the victim of sophisticated psychological attrition.

The final blow was delivered somewhat more crudely. Two Nazis knocked on the door of Dr Berta Geissmar, his indispensable secretary, and ordered her out of Berlin by nightfall. Days later, the Gestapo confiscated her passport. A capable, ugly woman of Jewish extraction, Geissmar had been Furtwängler's closest associate since he befriended her as a schoolgirl in Mannheim. She bought the ring for his wedding, trailed along on the honeymoon, took the decisions that he shirked. She once slapped down his hand as he was about to shake on a deal with the Vienna Philharmonic. Goering said: 'If Furtwängler were to be deprived of his Geissmar, his whole musical personality would collapse like a house of cards.'

Her fate, perhaps her life, hung on his good conduct. In March 1935, Furtwängler went to see Goebbels and put his name to a public apology for the Hindemith Affair. At the end of the year Dr Geissmar was given a passport and left for London, where she became secretary to Sir Thomas Beecham. Furtwängler, meanwhile, encountered by a leading soprano in a train compartment, begged her tearfully for help with unanswered correspondence.

The ploy had worked: he was a ship adrift. For the remainder of their Reich, the Nazis were able to do with him virtually as they pleased. He was the last internationally recognized conductor in Germany – Erich Kleiber had quit over the Hindemith case – and they used him blatantly for propaganda purposes. He conducted at party functions and, in two occupied countries, was driven to his concerts in an SS motorcade. 'He has done us great service abroad,' noted a satisfied Goebbels. Months into the War he added: 'Furtwängler reports on his trips to Switzerland and Hungary. He met with triumphal success everywhere. We can put him to good use, and at the moment he is very willing. He intends now to keep an eye on the music world in Vienna. And to go to Prague to raise our musical prestige.' Berlin, the Reich capital, gloried in his music.

Goebbels grumbled about his intercessions on behalf of Nazi victims but was always able to bring him back into line by playing on his pathological insecurity and bottomless jealousy of any rival, notably the rising Herbert von Karajan. A Nazi scribe, Walter Abendroth, was chosen to elicit his views on music, for a book the conductor endorsed as his personal credo.

Furtwängler's resistance was inconsequential and uncoordinated. He refused the gift of a house from Hitler and several cars from Goering, retired from conducting for some months to compose a symphony and held on to a handful of Jewish players in Berlin until the writing on street walls convinced them to emigrate; in Vienna he was unable to save Jewish members of the Philharmonic from the gas chambers.

Why didn't he leave Germany? He had, after all, plenty of opportunities to defect while working and holidaying abroad. He was famed throughout the musical world, had a house in St Moritz and friends in free countries; unlike other émigrés, he would have faced a secure future. In 1936 he was thrown a lifeline when Toscanini nominated him as his successor at the New York Philharmonic, apparently in the hope of detaching him from the Nazi domains and saving his mortal soul.

Furtwängler first consulted Goebbels, then accepted the offer – on condition that he could continue conducting in Germany. His appointment on these terms provoked protests from New York's large Jewish population and, a week later, he cabled his withdrawal:

> Political controversy disagreeable to me. Am not politician but exponent of German music which belongs to all humanity regardless of politics. I propose to postpone my season in the interest of the Philharmonic Society until the time public realizes that politics and music are apart.

Toscanini remonstrated with him to change his mind but Furtwängler was adamant. Making music in Germany was his paramount concern and he dared not jeopardize it., Goebbels had reportedly told him: 'You are welcome to leave, but so long as we are here – and we have founded a Thousand-Year Reich – you will never be allowed back on German soil.' Toscanini, at least, was still allowed back each summer to his Italian villa.

Toscanini sought unsuccessfully to exclude him from the 1937 Salzburg Festival. 'Everyone who conducts in the Third Reich is a Nazi!' he snarled at him, ignoring the inconvenient fact that several of his own Salzburg singers came from German companies. After the War, he led a campaign to block Furtwängler from conducting at the Chicago Symphony and Metropolitan Opera.

In a rambling defence prepared for his denazification tribunal, Furtwängler contended that Arnold Schoenberg and Max Reinhardt had both urged him to stay behind to protect their common heritage. Reinhardt's agent gave evidence on his behalf. Schoenberg said: 'I am sure he was never a Nazi. He was one of those old-fashioned *Deutschnationale*...Also, I am sure he was no anti-Semite – or at least not more so than every non-Jew. And he is certainly a better musician than all the Toscaninis, Ormandys, Kussevitskis and the whole rest. And he is a real talent, And he *loves* music.'

In his naïve and muddled mind, Furtwängler had sought to defend 'the superior intellectual life of Germany' from Nazi domination. 'Those who became emigrants or demanded that one should emigrate believed . . . that one had to leave a Nazi Germany. But this is precisely what is incorrect. Germany was never a Nazi Germany but a Germany ruled by Nazis.'He seemed unable to grasp that no-one had left their homeland willingly.

Elisabeth Furtwängler maintained that he risked his life in Berlin under Allied bombing to give concerts that were rallying points for members of the anti-Hitler Resistance. 'His public was never a Nazi public,' she asserted. 'A Furtwängler concert every week or two was a reason for staying alive,' said devotees. His final programme in the old Philharmonie before it was flattened contained a premonitory performance of

Beethoven's violin concerto by his concertmaster Erich Röhn in which a thunderous, Götterdämmerung-like tremor in the finale portended certain destruction (unknown to the authorities, the cadenzas played were by the Jewish violinst Joachim; the only available alternatives were by the equally tainted Kreisler). In the last winter of the Reich, he took a hint from the Armaments Minister Albert Speer and fled to Switzerland to avoid possible retribution by Nazi diehards. He was, by his own admission, no hero.

Did Furtwängler make a pact with Hitler? demanded Berlin's newspapers after the War. He firmly denied it:

> I knew that Germany was in a terrible crisis; I felt responsible for German music, and it was my task to help it survive this crisis . . . Does Thomas Mann really believe that in 'the Germany of Himmler' one should not be permitted to play Beethoven? Could he not realize that people never needed more, never yearned more, to hear Beethoven and his message of freedom and human love . . . ?

The exiled composer Hanns Eisler accused him of using his art and abusing the great works of German's classic composers to prettify Hitler's bloodstained hangmen regime. In Eisler's view he was an accomplice in 'murder, arson, robbery, theft, fraud, torture of the defenceless and, above all, silencing the truth'.

Although vindicated by Allied courts – the Soviets were notably keen to entice him to their sector of Berlin – Furtwängler could not escape insistent charges of collaboration that embittered and probably shortened his life. From his Swiss base, he resumed pre-eminence in Berlin and Salzburg and conducted regularly in London, pursued by a stain that refused to fade. He told a British journalist:

> A single performance of a great German masterpiece was a stronger and more vital negation of the spirit of Buchenwald or Auschwitz than word. Please understand me correctly: an artist cannot be entirely unpolitical. He must have some political convictions, because, after all, he, too, is a human being. As a citizen it is an artist's duty to express these convictions. But as a musician I am more than a citizen. I am a German in that eternal sense to which the genius of great music testifies.

In his German loyalty and his constitutional indecisiveness, Furtwängler had helped Hitler masquerade as the legitimate custodian of Germany's musical heritage. Music was a key element in forging the *Volksgemeindschaft*, the people's community that would bind pagan, Aryan society in an indivisible unity of leader-worship.

Whether in a racially pure Bavarian village or in a Polish concentration camp, music was performed to express Germany's spiritual supremacy and to instil disciplined obedience in its subjects and slaves. The official abhorrence of jazz stemmed as much from its improvisatory freedoms as from its negroid origin. 'Germany is the most music-loving and creative land on earth,' wrote Wehrmacht Major-General Paul Winter in mid-War, 'and the German soldier knows that he is risking his life not only for the safety of his fatherland *but also for the survival of German music.*'

In Furtwängler the Nazis retained an interpreter who performed German music with undiminished conviction while genocide was committed in its name. By opting to remain, he endowed the Nazis with cultural respectability at a crucial moment in their ascent, and in wartime gave moral sustenance to their cause. In his confrontations with tyranny, Furtwängler proved a feeble adversary who was all too easily manoeuvred into outright collusion. The humanity he expressed in music was traduced and travestied by his paymasters. His legacy as a performer may well be among the most significant in the annals of conducting, but his conduct under political pressure compromised the very profession on which he wielded so formative an influence.

*   *   *

The role of the conductor was never at issue in the Soviet bloc: Marxism could not contemplate a power base on the podium and reduced the music director to a cipher, or a stooge. Unlike his fellow-tyrant Hitler, whose system was run on a grid of Gauleiters under a hierarchical 'leadership principle', the Great Leader and Teacher crushed any alternative symbol of authority. Conductors became faceless technicians. If Stalin decided one day that the finale of Beethoven's Ninth was 'the right music for the masses', then it would be performed, shorn of its preceding movements, endlessly across the Union The conductor was employed to beat time; his personality was immaterial. The only musicians allowed to acquire a distinctive identity were composers, who paid for it heavily in the Zhdanov purges, and a handful of vocalists and instrumentalists who were sent abroad to earn hard currency.

Soviet conducting has never recovered from Stalinist paranoia. In the 1980s it was official policy to downgrade conductors against other export-quality musicians. At the time of Leonid Brezhnev's death, only four conductors were allowed to pursue international careers; one' was a chronic alcoholic who had to be propped up on the podium, and another was the son-in-law of a Politburo member.

Yevgeny Mravinsky, the most accomplished of Russian conductors, was rarely let out of the country. On just five western excursions in half a century with the Leningrad Philharmonic, he was able to demonstrate that a singular style was somehow being kept alive in Russia. His Tchaikovsky recordings of 1956 are landmarks in a line of authenticity that harks back to Nikisch's St Petersburg revelations. Mravinsky survived by keeping a tight lid on his feelings, musically as much as personally. 'He has a heart but it doesn't show,' said Kurt Sanderling, his deputy for twenty years. At rehearsals he was icily remote, conveying his wishes by sheer force of personality. 'You could see the chandeliers vibrating,' players said, when Mravinsky wordlessly hinted at intense emotion. Little is known of his private life or political opinions. Even with Dmitri Shostakovich, for whom he premièred five symphonies, Mravinsky discussed only 'the finest points of orchestration, interpretation, symphonic structure'.

He would spend months on end in the countryside staring at the flat landscape, listening to the birds. He apparently avoided joining the Party and would boycott its festive October Revolution concerts – according to Mariss Jansons, son of another of his deputies and his hand-picked heir. 'He never made compromises,' says Jansons. 'For some people it would have been dangerous to refuse [such concerts]. But he knew there wouldn't be the right artistic conditions.' When his string section emigrated en masse in the 1970s, he doggedly repaired the ensemble and sustained its standards.

Jansons was favoured by the players as his successor, but the Party in 1988 imposed Yuri Temirkanov, who had never worked with the orchestra and tended to dismiss Mravinsky. 'I don't think many people realize that the Philharmonic has been virtually leaderless for the last ten or 15 years,' he declared. Temirkanov's appointment – though he told western journalists he was no Party member – showed that little had changed in the state of Soviet music under Mikhail Gorbachev's perestroika.

Most of the finest conductors had fled the country, led by key members of Shostakovich's inner circle. The composer's son, Maxim, settled in New Orleans; his closest musical friend, Mstislav Rostropovich, was embraced by the National Symphony Orchestra in Washington; Kirill Kondrashin, who premièred the Babi Yar symphony, found a niche at the Concertgebouw, where he soon died of a post-concert heart attack. The only conductor of genuine charisma left in the USSR, Gennady Rozhdestvensky, toyed for years with the idea of defection but always pulled back from the brink.

In younger socialist states, Stalinist controls were less stringently applied to the podium and talented conductors continued to flow from Poland, Hungary and Czechoslovakia. During the continental collapse of Communism in 1989, it was a conductor who delivered the *coup de grâce* to the hard-line German Democratic Republic. Despite a credit-starved economy, the regime sustained three dozen opera houses and 88 orchestras ostensibly for a population of just 16 million, though more pertinently for external prestige. The GDR portrayed itself as cradle of musical civilization and guardian of the Bach, Handel, Wagner and Schumann birthplaces. Its Brechtian theatres exported 'revolutionary' operatic directors who came to dominate western stagecraft. Artistic endeavour conferred a kind of national legitimacy to an insecure state.

When the regime built a wall across Berlin to stop its citizens escaping and protect them from material desires, it recalled Kurt Sanderling from Leningrad to turn the unknown Berlin Symphony Orchestra into the equal of the opposite side's Philharmonic. Eminent musicians in the GDR were obliged to join the Party and participate in the lie of two Germanies – one shiningly perfect and redeemed, the other rooted in the despicable Nazi past. They played along with the system and took their place among its élite. The Leipzig music director Kurt Masur was a favourite of Party strongman Erich Honecker, who built him a brand new concert hall.

The collusion between musicians and megalomanes cracked open when the reformist Gorbachev visited Berlin for the GDR's fortieth anniversary on 7 October 1989, encouraging a wave of public dissent. That night, protests were brutally dispersed in several cities. A quarter of a million people poured the following day on to the Leipzig streets. Honecker warned his people on television to 'remember what happened in China' earlier that year, when troops massacred students in Tienanmen Square. He put the armed forces on alert and ordered them to open fire if marchers massed again in Leipzig's Karl Marx Square, between the state opera house and his new Gewandhaus hall.

The next afternoon, 9 October, Kurt Masur convened three party bosses, a priest and a cabaret artist in his apartment to discuss how violence might be averted. As the evening column of protestors converged on the square, Masur took the decision to throw open his concert hall and invited the demonstrators inside to air their grievances in the first open forum for four decades. The silence of repression had been broken. Honecker was toppled, the Berlin Wall breached, and Masur became a national hero and, briefly, a presidential candidate. 'Am I so bad a conductor that I have to become a politician?' he quipped.

Contrary to his fears, heroism positively enhanced his artistic allure. Masur had been widely known as a highly capable performer of romantic repertoire, though lacking the gloss of flair and flexibility that amounted to star potential. Now, overnight, he became a contender for major positions and took over the New York Philharmonic for a king's ransom of more than seven hundred thousand dollars, wealth undreamed of in the shattered eden of human equality.

The significance of his courage, however, was not confined to the career of a single conductor. In defying the tanks, Masur began to reclaim the forsaken moral rectitude of his profession. After generations of music directors who caved in to political pressure, one man stood up and behaved as á leader should. Kurt Masur may never go down in history as a towering figure but he will be remembered as the music director who called a halt to compromise and collaboration when many of his colleagues hid their heads behind a score. 'In a way,' he reflected mildly, 'I was only carrying on those principles that I try to uphold when I conduct Beethoven's hope in the Choral Symphony.'

* * *

Towards the end of 1989, as the geographical wounds of two world wars began to heal on the face of Europe, a senior record industry figure was heard bemoaning the dearth of good conductors. 'Among the four million who went up in smoke at Auschwitz,' he mused over a light salmon lunch and fine Chablis, 'there must have been half a dozen potentially great conductors, and many others who could capably run the lesser orchestras. A few more froze to death in the Gulags. That's why we have so few around today.'

Between them, Hitler and Stalin had destroyed the breeding grounds, traditions and aspirations that nourished the art of conducting. There may be other reasons for the lack of conductors but there is no denying that the seemingly endless flow of talent somehow ran dry in the decades after 1945. And for want of innate resources, aspirants began to mimic the mannerisms of the last monoliths, Toscanini and Furtwängler, in the hope that something would rub off on to their music. Toscanini-clones and Furtwängler-copies briefly abounded until the next wave merged their opposing traits into a hybrid 'Tosc-wängler' style.

Herbert von Karajan was probably the parent of this ugly mongrel. Supremely opportunistic, he admired Furtwängler's seamless flexibility and fervent spirituality but 'attempted to superimpose' Toscanini's rigorous perfectionism on the Berlin Philharmonic in order to obliterate his predecessor from musical memory. For two decades after his death, Furtwängler existed as a fad for esoteric collectors who swapped pirate tapes of his performances. His recordings fell into such commercial disrepute that an English entrepreneur was able to launch his own label with discs unwanted by the major companies.

The pendulum of posterity started to swing back when conductors who heard Furtwängler in their impressionable student days surged up the career ladder late in Karajan's life. Furtwängler-worship became an article of faith for a clique of non-Karajanites led by Daniel Barenboim, Zubin Mehta and Vladimir Ashkenazy. 'It's not a cult,' explained Mehta defensively. 'It's a clan. There's nothing unhealthy about it.' As Furtwängler's stock revived, even would-be Toscaninis like the Neapolitan Riccardo Muti began to pay homage to the German's mastery. The wheel came full circle when, on compact disc, the latest gadget from the industry he had created, Toscanini was hugely outsold by an antagonist who had disdained records as a manifestation of earthly materialism.

Toscanini's end came in the most pathetic manner when the infallible memory failed during a live broadcast, choked off by a transient ischemic attack (TIA), a neurological condition then unknown to medical science. As he floundered in mid-Wagner, and America listened aghast, NBC technicians mercifully substituted a Brahms record. His NBC resignation was followed with indecent haste by the disbandment of his orchestra and the total removal of classical music from American mass media. The audience he had hoped to build switched passively to game shows and soap-operas. Never again would serious music be proselytized (or prostituted) as an ersatz religion that competed on equal terms and ratings with the tambourines and ticker-tape of the televangelists.

'I think that Mr Toscanini has had a baneful effect on musical beliefs and standards in America,' wrote a disillusioned record producer in 1947. He had narrowed the repertoire to a single gauge, where it remained stuck. The star system he espoused as a means of glamorizing music steadily cannibalized the music itself – until people paid to hear Pavarotti not Verdi, Perlman not Prokofiev. On his own records, Toscanini's name was blazoned much larger than the composer's, all pretence to humility long abandoned.

By a contrary quirk, the fundamentalism he preached was taken up by the very musicians he least appreciated – academic performers of medieval, baroque and early classical music. Let us play, said these scholarly souls, exactly what the composer wrote: on the instruments he had in mind and in the original pitch and style. Their Early Music Revolution, launched on a self-righteous tide of literal interpretation, valued authenticity above beauty and spiritual depth. When Roger Norrington recorded the Beethoven symphonies on original instruments, he was likened by an American critic to Toscanini for his 'inspired literalism' and considered preferable to Furtwängler's imprecise 'variability'.

For some years after Toscanini's death, conductors continued terrorizing American orchestras, believing that this was how a great conductor had to act. Georg Szell, known as 'the chemist among conductors' for his analytical ear, was an awesome taskmaster who could hear whether instruments were tuned at 420 or 424 vibrations per second. 'What we feared most was his beastly competence,' says one assistant. He made his Clevelanders wear three-piece suits at all times while on tour.

Arthur Rodzinski introduced himself to the New York Philharmonic by sacking 14 players and spent his only season in Chicago in a state of permanent warfare. Fritz Reiner was hated by the Chicago players for nine long years. Georg Solti, himself a Toscanini acolyte, heaved a sigh of relief when the musicians 'lost that kind of Reiner fear that the music director is a natural enemy'. The fact that these tyrants were themselves refugees from political violence gave their brutality a faint edge of madness.

More than three decades after his death Toscanini is still the one conductor whose name everyone knows. For Toscanini, glory was the route to power, and power was the means by which he brutally extracted the sound he wanted and brought music into contention as a commercial and political force. He taught conductors that their influence need not be confined to the podium. Personally uncorrupted, he exposed music to ruthless exploitation by successors less principled than himself.

Official stamp of the Nazi Chamber of Culture

CHAPTER 5

The Karajan Case

'The trouble with Karajan is that music was never enough for him.'
Zubin Mehta.

'German art of the next century will be heroic, steely-romantic, unsentimentally practical; it will be National with great pathos; it will be committed and bound to common interests – or it will not be at all.'
Josef Goebbels.

'I shall be a dictator.'
Herbert von Karajan, Salzburg 1955.

ON THE ICY Monday afternoon of 20 January 1946, a bespectacled, corpulent Englishman alighted from a first-class carriage in Vienna's western railway station. He carried false American papers procured in a Zurich hotel bar and spoke perfect, unaccented German. Bundled up in a baggy overcoat, a cigarette clenched between his lips and hundreds more buried in his baggage, he blended easily into the bomb-damaged streets and murky amorality captured in Graham Greene's screenplay *The Third Man*. Like Greene's hero, though less naïvely, he set off on a manhunt.

His name was Walter Legge and he was neither spy nor assassin but a British record producer masquerading as a Swiss businessman with the intent to commit a crime. Eight months after the War, it was highly illegal for Allied citizens to trade with the recent enemy. The law in this instance was no ass. Many of the demobbed soldiers and jobless bureaucrats milling around Vienna were accomplices in mass-murder. A process of 'denazification' had been set in motion to weed out the worst culprits. Although the procedure was flawed, fallible and confused, it gave reborn democracy in western Germany a breathing space to found a healthy society by barring known miscreants from public office, arts organizations and education. In Austria, by contrast, apart from a few well-publicized scapegoats, denazification was a farce.

Vienna in the early post-War period was an ideal haven for fugitive Nazis, offering them easy assimilation and, if required, ready access to escape routes. It was also a musical paradise. Three weeks after the surrender, the Vienna Opera was reinstated by order of the Soviet military commander with a *Marriage of Figaro* to celebrate May Day. Since Franz-Joseph's great opera house on the Ring was a mound of twisted rubble, the performance was given at the historic Theater an der Wien where Mozart first staged *The Magic Flute*. The conductor was Josef Krips, an accomplished Mozartian who had spent the war as an industrial clerk, having been sacked from the State Opera for being part-Jewish.

News of Vienna's musical renaissance flashed around ruined Germany and stars of the defunct Reich flocked to join the company. Its casts featured Maria Cebotari, darling of Hitler's Berlin, the intelligent tenor Julius Patzak, the superb bass-baritone Hans Hotter and Ljuba Welitsch, who stunned Richard Strauss with her Salomé on his eightieth birthday. Irmgard Seefried, Sena Jurinac and Hilde Gueden trilled secondary roles. The Vienna Philharmonic resumed its concerts in October 1945 under Krips' baton and the half-starved city once again had a full musical calendar that attracted worldwide attention.

Legge had not smuggled himself into the city to hear singers, though he signed up a dozen of the best and eventually married the beautiful, tough-minded Elisabeth Schwarzkopf who would dominate light soprano roles for the next twenty years. Nor was he much interested in the orchestra. He was searching for a conductor, a man who would direct the super-orchestra he was forming in London to mass-produce records that would secure his company dominance in the expanding post-War market.

Barely had he booked into a hotel than he bumped into Wilhelm Furtwängler in the blackout and bullied him into contract talks. But Furtwängler, enfeebled by years of conflict, was yearning to rejoin his Berlin Philharmonic. Legge needed a younger, leaner man who would impose his personality on London's unruly musicians and impress self-educated ex-servicemen into buying his records. Within four days he found his man at a Vienna Philharmonic rehearsal. 'I was absolutely astonished at what the fellow could do,' he noted. 'The enormous energy and vitality he had was hair-raising.'

Herbert von Karajan had turned up mysteriously in Vienna after vanishing in Italy towards the end of the War. The previous Saturday he gave a performance of Brahms' First Symphony with the Philharmonic that one American officer in the audience found 'unforgettable'. At the same time, he realized that 'we will have to blacklist him for a long time'. The conductor was a wanted man. He had been a cultural figurehead of Hitler's Germany, acclaimed in Goebbels' propaganda sheets as '*Das Wunder Karajan*' and paraded as a symbol of Aryan supremacy.

Hours before his next concert, Karajan was banned from conducting in public until his case was cleared. As soon as he heard the news, Legge came knocking at his door bearing gifts of whisky, sherry and sympathy:

He was living in the most uncomfortable conditions on the eighth floor of a block of flats, sharing a room with people he did not know. And we started to talk. I tried to make it a business conversation but he was obviously out for a real chat. He probably had not talked to anybody for a long time.

Karajan, in his account, made his situation seem less desperate:

My first meeting with Walter Legge was in Vienna in 1946 and took place under somewhat unusual circumstances. An exemption had been granted me by the American Occupation Forces to conduct a concert with the Vienna Philharmonic. For unexplained reasons [*sic*], the concert was abruptly cancelled half an hour before it was scheduled to begin.

At 4 o'clock that afternoon a Mr Legge was announced at my home, asking if we could talk. I told him about my situation at the time and he assured me that all that sort of thing would soon pass. What was most important, he said, was that the two of us would be able to make recordings together.

What was most important was that the two of us would be able to make recordings together. Legge's priority was undisguised. More important than politics or legality, than democracy or decency, than profitability or plain common sense, more important even than music itself, was his ambition to make good records. An autocrat and braggart, disliked within his own company as much as he was feared by rivals, Legge called himself the first professional producer and said his recordings would set the standards by which music is judged. On that frigid Friday in Vienna, his presumption struck a chord. 'One thing became quite clear from this first long conversation,' said Karajan, 'our way of thinking about music was in complete harmony.' Months later, 'defying the US and French military', Legge persuaded the British High Command that the Allied conducting ban did not preclude Karajan from recording. By the time he was finally cleared to give concerts, Karajan's records had made him world-famous.

'He, more than any conductor except perhaps Stokowski, was really made by gramophone recordings,' boasted Legge in his memoirs, though at the time he was worried enough about possible repercussions to ask the British cultural authorities whether they would allow Karajan records to go on sale. 'We're not denazifying in the UK,' he was bluntly informed, 'but as far as [the British zone of] Germany is concerned – not a hope.'

Legge transferred Karajan to London where, over the next decade, he made 150 recordings, among them electrifying cycles of Beethoven and Brahms, a dazzling *Rosenkavalier*, Mozart concertos, Bartók, Britten and Bruckner. The Philharmonia, EMI's all-star orchestra, emerged from the Abbey Road studios to set new standards of performance in the concert hall, just as Legge had predicted. With the advent of long-playing discs and stereophonic sound, records cemented their supremacy over live music. A mass medium had been born and Karajan was its kingpin.

In latter years he would belittle his recording orchestra, muttering that the Philharmonia played no better at concert than in rehearsal – 'just like a youth orchestra'. Unwilling to acknowledge anyone's assistance in this ascent, he showed no gratitude to his saviour. When Legge was sacked by EMI in 1963, a colleague found him moping outside Karajan's office in Vienna. '*Ich bin drei Tage ante-chambriert*,' he moaned, 'I've been kept waiting in the anteroom for three days.' Karajan, by now omnipotent in musical affairs, did not lift a finger to help him and Legge never worked again.

His role in Karajan's evolution had been doubly crucial. He taught him that the musical future lay in the record studio and that international law was no obstacle to artistic ambition. Legge was by no means the only hunter for Nazi talent. His competitors at Decca, through Maurice Rosengarten, an orthodox Swiss Jew, signed up the Vienna Philharmonic, some of whose players had recently worn swastika armbands and had stood by while six of their members were sent to the death camps. Deutsche Grammophon releases were seized upon by music-lovers while its parent company, Siemens, was facing charges for using slave labour at Auschwitz, Buchenwald and Ravensbrück. Legge could not care less whether an artist was a Quaker pacifist or SS torturer, so long as he made good records. Attacked by colleagues for dallying with ex-Nazis, he fired back a furious memo:

> The function of our company is to sell records. To dub an artist or member of the staff as a Nazi sympathizer is sabotage. These best-selling artists had no choice as to which side of the fence they should temporarily sit.

It was an argument he knew to be false. Every musician in Nazi Germany had a choice, perhaps the clearest moral decision that has ever confronted an artist. Many acted honourably and emigrated or refused to collaborate. Others built their careers on a bedrock of brutality.

* * *

The Third Reich seized control of music in two lightning moves. On 7 April 1933, its Civil Service Law sacked all Jews from state institutions. Thousands of salaried musicians, teachers and administrators were dismissed without compensation from opera houses, orchestras and music colleges. Arnold Schoenberg, a professor at Berlin's Academy of Arts, was left virtually penniless and fled abroad; others, less famous, were destitute and trapped. On 15 November 1933, Josef Goebbels announced that anyone wanting to work in the arts or broadcasting had to enrol with his Reich Chamber of Culture. This simple manoeuvre gave the regime control over artistic output in every genre. Without a Kulturkammer card, a German artist could not publish a poem, make a film, play in an orchestra or exhibit a picture.

By German standards the Chamber was 'a pretty chaotic outfit' and Goebbels finally turned it over to a ranking SS Gruppenführer, Hans Hinkel, who as State Commissioner for Music showed commendable zeal in scrutinizing the racial and ideological reliability of 'cultural personalities'. Hinkel kept 250,000 personnel files on artists in the Third Reich that fell intact into British hands – together with their commissioner, who was lucky to be let off as a 'minor criminal'. Musicians applying to the Kulturkammer had to fill in a questionnaire on their racial purity and professional status, naming two referees who could vouch for their competence (Richard Strauss wrote: 'Mozart and Wagner'). Jews and leftists were debarred, but most applicants were nodded through unless denounced by a colleague or neighbour. Given the mass exodus of artists in 1933, the Chamber could not be too choosy. Its card guaranteed employment rights and helped gain exemption from army service. No one *needed* to become a Nazi in order to work as a musician.

Joining the Party was a privilege, not an obligation. The conductor Hans Knappertsbusch was reported to Goebbels for mischievously asking a German diplomat in Holland if he was a Nazi and, if so, whether he was a *Muβ*-Nazi, an enforced member. 'There is no such thing,' retorted the outraged official. He informed Berlin that 'K. is no friend of the New Germany'. Knappertsbusch was duly sacked as music director of the Bavarian State Opera, although he continued to guest conduct.

Until the War, German musicians had multiple choice. They could either leave the country or remain; if they stayed, they could join the NSDAP or abstain. Most of the top names emigrated. Of the few who stayed put, none became Nazis. The composers Richard Strauss and Hans Pfitzner, initially well-disposed towards Hitlerism, stopped short of enlistment. Strauss was named President of the Kulturkammer, where his contribution was to demand fewer foreign operas and better playing at spa resorts; he was dismissed for corresponding with his exiled librettist, Stefan Zweig. Pfitzner, an ardent nationalist, was refused state honours after sardonically offering to compose a 'pimphony' for a Nazi leader.

The leading conductors Furtwängler, Knappertsbusch and Clemens Krauss stood aloof from the Party. Among the rising generation, Rudolf Kempe left his orchestra and joined the army rather than obey a Nazi order to dismiss his best violist. Eugen Jochum, aged 30 when Hitler came to power, became music director at Hamburg Opera in 1934 and remained there until 1949 without ever holding a Party card. His junior conductors Hans Swarowsky and Hans Schmidt-Isserstedt were not Nazis, nor were 87 per cent of his musical staff. 'It was a matter of supreme indifference [to Hitler] whether the artists he esteemed . . . belonged to the National Socialist Party,' wrote armaments minister Albert Speer, 'he regarded them one and all as politically feeble-minded.' Hitler told Speer: 'we should never judge artists by their political views. The imagination they need for their work deprives them of the ability to think in realistic terms.'

Those who joined the NSDAP did so either as fervent racists or frantic opportunists. In the former category were such peripheral composers as Paul Graener and Max Trapp, the music historian Hans Joachim Moser, the pioneering Liszt scholar Peter Raabe, the pianist Elly Ney and a clutch of singers and instrumentalists who crawled out of the woodwork in 1933 to take over institutions where they had long laboured anonymously. For ambitious and unprincipled musicians, party affiliation in 1933 offered a rapid route to the plum jobs suddenly vacated by Jewish outcasts. Thousands of positions were open and any pure German was eligible, but Party credentials might impress a prospective employer and Nazism had not yet committed unforgivable atrocities that might deter a sensitive soul. Many joined on the wave of euphoria that grips Germans at critical junctures in their history, though few failed to smell the smoke of burning books in the national *auto da fé* that took place in the square of every university town on 10 May that year.

Herbert von Karajan applied to join the Nazi Party while visiting his parents in Salzburg on 8 April, the day that Hitler's Civil Service Law was published in the press. His membership number was 1,607,525. Three weeks later, back in Germany, he rejoined at Ulm on 1 May. The date is noteworthy, for on that day the Party announced a freeze on new membership in order to halt a deluge of applications. Karajan was given a new number, 3,430,914. This dual affiliation caused clerical confusion and his highly-prized lower numeral was ultimately cancelled, perhaps as a punitive measure.* His Party card and file in NSDAP archives were captured by US forces and preserved at the Document Center of the US Mission in Berlin. They were reproduced in facsimile in 1982, despite legal threats by the conductor who claimed they were fake.

The controversy was not whether he joined the Party, but when. Karajan consistently maintained that he enlisted only in 1935 in order to become music director at Aachen. Three days before taking office, he was reminded of 'one last formality' by a friendly official. 'Before me

---

*Recent research indicates that the second (Ulm) number may have been backdated from the time of his Aachen appointment. It does not, however, dispute his earlier application at Salzburg.

was this paper which stood between me and almost limitless power . . .
so I said what the hell, and signed.' He compared it to joining an Alpine
club before being allowed to ski down a particularly inviting slope: a
trivial concession to secure a desired objective.

The discrepancy may never be satisfactorily resolved since those
involved are dead and the relevant documents at Aachen are protected
by stringent German regard for personal privacy. Karajan clearly tried
to portray himself as that mythical figure, the Muβ-Nazi, but there can
be little doubt that he applied in person at Salzburg in 1933, since proxy
nominations were not admitted. If, however, he joined in order to
advance his career, he was spectacularly unsuccessful. At the end of that
season he lost his contract at Ulm and spoke of suffering months of
unemployment in Berlin before he was talent-spotted by the Aachen
artistic director, Edgar Gross, an active SS man.

Karajan's movements in this period were left tantalizingly blank in the
methodically detailed curriculum vitae issued by his office. What was he
doing in Berlin and what did he say or do to convince the Nazi Gross of
his suitability? And how did he acquire a concert agent in Berlin who
was an SS Obersturmführer. If ever Karajan was involved in cloak-and-
dagger activities, as suggested after the War, it would have been in
1934–35 when he was 26 years old. It matters very little when he joined
the Party. What counts is what he got up to as a Nazi.

All that is known of his official involvement at this time is that on
1 June 1934 he applied to join the Reichsmusikkammer – which as an
Austrian he was not required to do – refusing to visit his sick grandmother
in order to secure his card. Clearly, this was a voluntary act, intended to
signal his political solidarity to the masters of German music. 'I would
have committed any crime to get that post,' he said of his appointment
to Aachen, the westernmost town in Germany with a millenium of musical
activity, a full-strength orchestra of seventy and an excellent operatic
ensemble. By some mysterious process, he had suddenly become one of
the hottest musical properties in the Reich, with both Karlsruhe and
Berlin bidding for his services. Rather than being forced to sign a com-
promising document to get the job, Karajan was able to dictate his own
terms, holding out for a salary that, he boasted, was higher than the
mayor's. Installed as opera conductor, he became general music director
for the entire town – at 27, the youngest GMD in the Reich. He did not
replace a refugee – Paul Pella having fled two years earlier to Portugal
– but ousted an arch-Nazi, the ideologue Peter Raabe, a mediocre performer who was compensated with the presidency of the Kulturkammer
when Strauss was disgraced.

Once in Aachen, Karajan's fame spread fast. By 1937 he was conducting *Tristan* at the Vienna State Opera; in April 1938 he made his Berlin

Philharmonic debut. On 30 September, while Hitler in Munich was sealing the fate of Czechoslovakia, Karajan led a hugely successful *Fidelio* at the Berlin State Opera. His *Tristan*, three weeks later, was acclaimed as nothing short of miraculous:

> *In der Staatsoper: Das Wunder Karajan*
> (In the State Opera, the Karajan Miracle)

bellowed the state-controlled *Berliner Zeitung am Mittag* in banner headlines over a review stating that certain fifty-year-old conductors could learn much from this young man.

The slur on Furtwängler was intentional. The State Opera was in the fiefdom of Hermann Goering, minister for Prussia, who was elated to have found a musician to challenge Furtwängler, protected by his enemy, Goebbels. He ordered his director of theatres, Heinz Tietjen, to advance the young contender swiftly. Karajan's agent, Obersturmführer Rudolf Vedder, provided additional support through his SS link to the dreaded Heinrich Himmler. Over the next four years, the Nazi leaders played high-powered games of poker with their pet conductors.

Karajan initially was everything they could desire: a talented and obedient musician who conducted tributes for Hitler's birthday, a special *Fidelio* to celebrate the *Anschluss* and odious works of musical propaganda such as Richard Trunk's *Celebration of the New Front*, whose choral finale was wound around the murderous *Horst Wessel Lied* in which 'Jewish blood spurts forth from our knives'. He was sent off to conduct opera at La Scala and concerts in Rome, the perfect cultural ambassador of one Fascist nation to another. In countries overrun by German forces he appeared with captive orchestras, making a fiery Strauss recording at the Concertgebouw, and performing the Wessel anthem in Paris.

Things started to turn sour in 1941. After the Allied bombing of the Berlin State Opera, Karajan found that one of his productions had been given to Furtwängler. Hitler, he was told, had formed 'a low opinion' of his work, allegedly objecting to his habit of conducting without a score, which Furtwängler said was impossible. Karajan went to the dentist and told the receptionist, who was Goebbels' niece, that he was joining the air force. Goebbels, anxious to conserve musical talent, stopped him. Furtwängler, meanwhile, continued moaning about Karajan's press coverage and the propaganda minister 'put a stop' to it. 'When all is said, he [Furtwängler] is our greatest conductor,' affirmed Goebbels. When the *'Wunder'* review author, Edwin van der Null, was sent to the front, Furtwängler was widely blamed for his death.

While conducting in Italy, Karajan learned that Aachen, dismayed by his absences, had given his job to a Dutchman. His attempt to succeed Karl Böhm at Dresden was stymied by the slippery Tietjen. Positions that he wanted became unattainable as the power pendulum swung against him. In 1942 he married Anita Gütermann, a wealthy woman with a Jewish grandparent. The NSDAP opened a file, which Goebbels quietly quashed. Karajan carried on guest conducting abroad, led a Bruckner ensemble in Hitler's birthplace, Linz, and gave Berlin concerts with the Staatskapelle, orchestra of the State Opera. In April 1944 he conducted the risqué première of Gottfried von Einem's Concerto for Orchestra, a jazz-riddled piece that was banned after one hearing. Its composer and his mother had previously been imprisoned by the Gestapo. Although Karajan was becoming a bit of a rebel, he still signed letters with 'Heil Hitler!' He was living at the Adlon Hotel, beside the Brandenburg Gate where, one August night in an air raid, a civil servant recognized him in the shelter. 'Karajan, usually so spic and span, was barefoot, in a trench coat, his hair standing on end.' Accustomed to comfort, he moved into the Swiss ambassador's peaceful country castle.

His Berlin concerts continued until February 1945, the penultimate event commemorating thousands of fellow-citizens killed in the Allied fire-raids on Dresden. Neither before nor after did he ever mourn the millions of his compatriots who were incinerated in the crematoria of Auschwitz. Six weeks before the fall of Berlin, having planned his escape for three months, he smuggled himself and Anita on to a plane bound for Milan, intending to move on to Switzerland or Spain. When fighting broke out between partisans and the retreating Wehrmacht he went into hiding in a friend's cottage beside Lake Como. While Allied investigators searched for him, he spent months by the lakeside teaching himself Italian.

* * *

In the weary confusion of defeat and victory, it was relatively easy for wanted Nazis to disappear in Europe, or emigrate with their families to a new life on another continent. Neither such course was open to a fugitive conductor. In an occupation that thrives on public attention, and with limited scope for self-fulfilment in South America or Syria, it was only a matter of months before all implicated conductors were accounted for. Karajan was the last to turn up. In September 1945 he was tracked down by the manager of the Trieste theatre, who sent a British Army major to fetch him to conduct concerts for the troops. He was given an identity card and free passage home to Salzburg, 'transported in lorries like beasts', he recalled. He lay low for the rest of the year at his parents' home; after conducting in Vienna, he was exhaustively interrogated.

The charges against him were the most serious facing any Nazi musician. In addition to playing a leading musical role in the evil empire, he was accused of having been a member of the Sicherheitsdienst (SD), the Nazi secret police, spying on fellow-musicians and exposing closet Jews and leftists. This suspicion was undocumented and eventually discarded. Karajan denied everything, admitting only to having joined the NSDAP in 1935 as a reluctant recruit.

'I was of the view,' he said later,

> that certain courts were preparing to act which had no right to pass judgement over me. There had been a war over which no-one could simply pass sentence. And those people whose job it was to decide whether I should conduct or not – those were people I knew too much about to be able to acknowledge them as competent authorities.

One investigator who pressed for an early reprieve was Otto de (von) Pasetti, a Viennese tenor who in 1933 had seduced Lotte Lenya away from Kurt Weill, then trailed the reunited couple to America. Pasetti was said to take pleasure in tormenting suspects with false promises that their restrictions were about to be lifted; he kept Karl Böhm on tenter-hooks for 18 months – sweet occupational revenge for an inconspicuous ex-singer. Another US interrogator, the former Austrian writer Ernst Lothar, called for a lengthy ban on Karajan. 'It seems absurd to assume that such an intelligent man should have become completely unaware of the meaning and consequences of becoming a Party member,' he argued.

While the Americans wrangled, the city fathers asked Karajan to organize the 1946 Salzburg Festival. He had assembled casts and started rehearsing three operas when US officers ordered him out of the Festspielhaus. Krips, Swarowsky and Felix Prohaska were brought in to conduct, while Karajan hid in the prompt box to help the singers along. Before his ban was revoked, he was engaged by the Lucerne Festival in neutral Switzerland and appointed artistic director for life by the Musikfreunde Society which runs Vienna's concert season.

In all, Karajan served thirty months of enforced unemployment, longer than any other musician. He would face demonstrations whenever he conducted in New York and in 1989 was the subject of a US Justice Department inquiry based on exactly the same charges that were tabled in 1946. If he had been personally involved in persecution or deportation, witnesses would certainly have come forward to testify in the decades of his fame, yet no evidence was ever presented. The long-running case against Karajan was evidently based on extraneous factors, inadmissible in a court of law.

Other musicians had much closer links with the Nazis, without actually joining the Party. Hans Pfitzner looked for protection to his namesake Hans Frank, Butcher of Poland, whose mistress was a famous post-War soprano. Richard Strauss relied on Baldur von Schirach, who hustled the

Jews of Vienna to the death camps and narrowly escaped the Nuremburg gallows. Heinz Tietjen, the sinister, half-English director of the Prussian theatres throughout the Weimar Republic and Third Reich, was responsible, together with the English-born Winifred Wagner, for restyling Wagner's operas to reflect Nazi ideology. Winifred was banned for life from running Bayreuth, but Tietjen was soon back in harness, taking over Berlin's city opera by 1948 and directing Wagner at Covent Garden two years later.

Then there was the curious case of Karl Böhm, who never joined the Party but was one of its earliest sympathizers. As a junior member of Bruno Walter's staff at Munich's national theatre, he broke off a rehearsal in November 1923 to watch Hitler's attempted *putsch*. When the marchers ran into a police fusillade, Böhm's heart went out to the wounded thugs.

In 1930, during the Frankfurt première of Schoenberg's opera *Von Heute auf Morgen*, he flew into a rage when his dark-haired wife, Thea, said she had been called a Jewess by brown-shirted demonstrators. 'I shall tell Hitler about this!' shouted her husband. There was an incredulous hush from his colleagues. 'You know Hitler?' demanded Carl Ebert, his stage director. 'Well, in Munich, everyone knew Hitler,' replied Böhm lightly. 'Anyway, the Nazis aren't so terrible – they want to eliminate women from politics.' There was a second shocked silence. 'Of course, not all women are worthless,' he went on obsequiously. 'Rainer *Maria* Rilke wrote some good poems . . .' Böhm's apparent ignorance of the great poet's gender, or his clumsy attempt at wit, shocked the sophisticated company even more than the disreputable acquaintance he had admitted.

As music director at Darmstadt and Hamburg, Böhm complained of 'too many Jews' in the company. His move to Dresden, where Fritz Busch had resigned over Nazi bullying, was among Hitler's first cultural appointments. Böhm maintained Dresden's sequence of Strauss premières, but stood discreetly aside when the composer got into trouble and did not object when Goebbels ordered *Die schweigsame Frau* to be cut to four performances. Böhm later boasted of his great friendship with Strauss.

Unable to join the Nazi Party while it was illegal in his native Austria, he repaired the omission by conducting at Party functions in Germany. Rushing home after the *Anschluss*, he greeted the Vienna Philharmonic audience with an outstretched Hitler salute, violating the rules of Nazi etiquette which stated that the 'German greeting' was not to be given at concerts. On the day Austrians voted to ratify the *Anschluss*, Böhm declared that 'anyone who does not approve this act of our Führer with a hundred-per cent YES, does not deserve to bear the honourable name of a German!' Appointed director of the Vienna Opera, he shed his only public tears of the era when the great edifice was bombed with his wife inside. Happily, Thea Böhm survived and fled with her family to the Salzkammergut before the Russians arrived. 'This was the beginning of a terrible time for me,' wrote Böhm, implying that the preceding tyranny had been quite tolerable.

He bitterly resented being unemployed, dependent on family handouts and the kindness of his former boss, Bruno Walter, who sent singing pupils to Thea Böhm. He wore the Austrian mantle of collective innocence as 'the first victim of Nazism' – an official fiction that conceals joyous pogroms and the gruesome statistic that Austrian SS guards in the death camps outnumbered Germans proportionally by five to one. Böhm's self-pity was still audible in a 1978 interview:

> I can clearly hear the question that English, Americans and Russians cheerfully asked me: 'If you were an opponent of Nazism, Herr Böhm, why didn't you emigrate?' They could well talk. I had a family to feed and no contacts with London or America. Where would I earn money there? The others, those who emigrated, had it much better than me, who stayed at home. They had no bombing raids to endure; they had work.

The 'others' had fled for their lives into abject poverty while Karl Böhm feathered his nest first under his Nazi friends, then in the reconstituted Austrian republic. When Vienna rebuilt its State Opera, he was named music director but withdrew within four months when the job began to interfere with his growing international career. He flitted lucratively among opera houses and orchestras, acquiring universal admiration for well-upholstered performances of Mozart and Schubert that were the antithesis of Karajan's disciplined executions. Dag Hammarskold asked him to direct the 1960 Human Rights Day Concert at the United Nations; Willy Brandt gave him a freedom medal in Berlin; the London Symphony Orchestra appointed him life-president. He was a stalwart of the Metropolitan Opera, and no-one was disturbed by his presence in New York. Only when Karajan came did tabloid newspapers insistently call for a boycott.

The smiling, soft-cheeked, home-loving Böhm could scarcely be associated with smokestacks and child slaughter, whereas Karajan, with his chiselled features, ruthless ambition and refusal ever to utter a word of regret for the atrocities, presented an entirely credible villain in the public mind. 'We were all Nazis – Furtwängler, Böhm, me . . .' he maintained, but he alone among conductors (along with soprano Elisabeth Schwarzkopf) was shut out from the Met by Rudolf Bing because he 'had been

Karl Böhm

described to me as having done more than was necessary' under the Nazis.

Bruno Walter generously exonerated his 'dear friend Böhm' and most Austrians of his aquaintance. Pablo Casals publicly pardoned his collaborationist French pianist, Alfred Cortot. Yehudi Menuhin campaigned to restore Furtwängler's good name. Karajan had no-one of stature to vouch for him and Furtwängler conspired relentlessly against him. At the mere suggestion that Karajan might conduct again at Salzburg,

> Furtwängler's face grew darker and darker. Finally he said, 'if that man K' – he would not take Karajan's name into his mouth – 'if that man K is there, I will give them a programme they will hate.'

If Karajan could be portrayed as a vigorous Nazi, Furtwängler would emerge a hero from their conflict and the Böhms of this world would appear less blameworthy. These internecine motives combined with his impeccable Aryan looks to malign Karajan in the public mind in the early post-War era. A deeper, subliminal perception, fuelled by his subsequent attitudes and ambitions, produced a lasting impression that Karajan was imposing himself on music as a kind of Führer-substitute. 'Unwittingly,' reflected his Decca producer John Culshaw,

> he filled the void left by the death of Hitler in that part of the German psyche which craves for a leader. His behaviour conformed to pattern. He was unpredictable, ruthless and outspoken. He was exceptionally intelligent and took great care of his appearance; in other words, there was an aura about him which, had it been a cultivated or calculated attribute, would have been repulsive.

Karajan shared distinctive traits with Hitler: remarkable powers of concentration, absolute dedication to long-term aims and an ascetic asexuality that attracted women and men alike. He was not much of a womanizer, though he married three times and was pursued, like pop stars, by a rash of opportunistic paternity suits. His American biographer relates an occasion when a rich man's gorgeous mistress entered her hotel room to find Karajan in the bed. He quickly got up and left. 'He was not interested in having sex with her. He said he could see her soul. She was a romantic ideal.'

This need for a glamorous 'loved one' was revealed in a set of love letters that were auctioned off at Sotheby's for £7,000 within a year of his death. They unveiled his passion for a *Vogue* journalist, Mary Roblee, who interviewed him before his first US tour in 1955, while married to his second wife. His Carnegie Hall concert, he said, was played solely for 'my darling Mary'. When she listened to his records, he felt like a god descended from Olympus to visit a nymph. They were alone together on a handful of occasions, but the letters contain not the faintest hint of carnal desire. His relationships with women were essentially sexless.

He surrounded himself with a coterie of gay men, headed by his long-serving 'secretary' André von Mattoni, a dignified and aristocratic former actor who, according to Culshaw, 'so far as we could tell did little work as such'. Their relationship was presumably companionable. Collaborators maintain that 'the homosexual part was very strong in Karajan, and

almost certainly active; you cannot begin to understand him without
appreciating that'.

There was a profound narcissism about his personal appearance. Sitting
in the front row of the Festspielhaus in Salzburg, you saw tell-tale stretch
marks behind his ears, betraying repeated face-lifts. In the opera house
and concert hall he orchestrated the applause, entering at the moment
of highest tension, departing in a flash before it began to fade. He
assumed in performance an expression of 'controlled ecstasy' – a trade-
mark so vivid that it became the title of a fawning Festschrift. At Bayreuth, he wanted to have a hole cut in the famous cowl so that the
audience could see the conductor. He employed his own photographers
and authorized every published image of himself, in action or repose.
Off the podium, he dressed impeccably in roll-necked sweaters that
exposed the minimum of bare flesh. The skin of his hands was scrubbed
to near-transparency; he was compulsively clean.

He resembled Hitler also in his detachment, the space he put between
himself and fellow-mortals. In a milieu where kisses and hugs are casual
pleasantries, Karajan stood inviolably apart. His eyes were icy blue and
his laughter uninfectious. Members of the Philharmonia found him
'remote and humourless' and felt his music lacked warmth. The Berlin
players revered his results but showed little fondness for the man, despite
the concern he devoted to their individual welfare, to the extent of
attending family occasions and arranging hospital treatment for ailing
wives and mothers. This solicitous tendency was integral to the Hitler
myth – 'der Führer, der für uns sorgt', the leader who cares, god-like, for
each and every citizen.

He gloried in his closeness to the orchestra he inherited from Furtwängler and directed until the year of his death. Berliners spoke of them as
being 'ein Herz und einer Seele' – one heart and one soul – but Karajan
had strange ways of illustrating unity. He told of a rehearsal in which
everything went wrong. 'Gentlemen, do you know what I'd like?' he
demanded. 'To tie a rope around all of you, pour gasoline on you and
set you on fire.' There was a dreadful silence until a player piped up,
'but then, you wouldn't have us'. 'Ah yes,' said Karajan, 'I forgot that.'
His remarks gained in horror for being uttered in the city that Hitler had
sought to immolate in his own Götterdämmerung. Yet Karajan preserved
the anecdote on film as a testament of intimacy.

The price of working with Karajan was to accept his absolute autocracy.
'I think what I resented most during the [1968 Met] Ring performances,'
said his Brünnhilde, Birgit Nilsson, 'was that we always had to be at his
disposal. We never knew what the rehearsal schedule was so that we
could plan our lives around it. We had to be there whenever he called
for us. We would wait hours for him sometimes. I suggested we leave . . .

but we were afraid of him.' He was, said Nilsson, 'just using us'. Agnes Baltsa walked out of his *Carmen*, tested beyond the limits of her Greek temperament. Young sopranos were stretched into huge roles, far beyond their tender capacity and sustainable only in the record studio. Exposed on the opera stage, Helga Dernesch, Katia Ricciarelli and others paid for his presumption with boos and vocal injury.

The strongest singers, who survived, were musically enriched. 'With Karajan, you suddenly experience music with new ears,' wrote Placido Domingo. 'His way of moulding an artist, of guiding a singer, is unsurpassed,' admitted Baltsa. 'As soon as he accepted you, he trusted you completely,' said Sena Jurinac. Even lifelong favourites, though, were prey to sudden attacks that sapped their self-confidence and left them quaking at his mercy. 'You have brown eyes, the eyes of a traitor,' he snapped unprovoked and in public at his set-designer, Günter Schneider-Siemssen. Never in 27 years did he address him with the familiar, friendly 'du'. Karajan, murmured his long-suffering orchestral manager, 'is like the weather'. He saw himself as a man of destiny, almost a force of nature. 'My time is sure to come, and I await it, calm and confident,' he wrote to a friend after the War.

'In his own mind, he *was* Hitler,' believes one record industry chief. 'There is no question,' says the American biographer whom he took to visit the Führer's lair at Berchtesgaden, 'that Karajan had great admiration for Hitler.' The *Führer Prinzip* was daily embodied by a musician who liked to be known as '*Der Chef*'. As he entered the Philharmonie building in Berlin, staff would stand to attention on the staircase, one on each step, proferring papers that he signed majestically as he ascended. His car had to be parked directly outside the artists' entrance, in defiance of police regulations. He would throw his coat to a record producer, underlining their master-servant relationship.

He shared with Hitler the chipped shoulder of an outsider, a provincial Austrian in cosmopolitan Germany – and not much of an Austrian at that. His paternal forebears were Greeks called Karajannis, his mother was Slovak. The aristocratic 'von' was a recent ennoblement by a minor court that became invalid in post-1918 Austria. He was baptised 'Heribert' but dropped the unheroic middle syllable at the onset of his public career. He later sued his elder brother to stop him flaunting their joint surname on a US tour with his organ ensemble. The world was meant to know only one Karajan.

He grew up in a mountain town where his father was chief surgeon. The musical spark that vanished when the Prince-Archbishop kicked out Mozart was being rekindled in summer festivals dominated by Max Reinhardt, Toscanini and Bruno Walter. As a child, Karajan crept into an organ loft to watch the Italian rehearse. He acknowledged all three as early influences, but his formative years as a conductor were spent in the Third Reich, where his boyhood idols were outcasts.

He was raised a Roman Catholic, buried by a village priest and eulogized by a Cardinal but – although he plastered Salzburg's shop windows at Festival time with pictures of his handshake with the Pope – he received no last rites. 'Music was for him a higher revelation than wisdom of philosophy,' said Cardinal Franz Koenig at his state requiem. He professed a fatalistic faith in Zen Buddhism and sought serenity in its meditative techniques and the promise of an unconditional after-life. His religious outlook was moulded by the pagan amorality of National Socialism and dazzled by its gleaming chalices of progressive technology. He worshipped fast machines and new inventions, flew his own jet and formed a deathbed axis with the masters of Japanese technocracy. He played with rich toys, he told a lover, to compensate for a deprived childhood.

Hitler and Karajan belonged to different social strata, generations and realms of experience: one starved in a garret and fought in the trenches, the other never knew a day's discomfort. Karajan received a streamlined musical training; Hitler was self-taught in the arts of life. Karajan was 24 when Hitler became Chancellor and just 37 when he fell. Practices and aspirations of the Third Reich took root in his personality and he proceeded to apply them vehemently to a vulnerable art.

The existence of a Nazi ideology is still a matter of academic dispute. Was there a coherent master-plan, or was it merely a rag-bag of assorted grievances welded together into a creed and implemented as opportunities arose? While it is easier to see what the Nazis did than what they stood for, some explicit policies are incontrovertible: subjugation and extinction of lesser races, continental conquest, industrial supremacy and the revival of a medieval concept of leadership. This *Führer Prinzip*, drawing on the darker recesses of folk-memory, was the subject of an admonitory sermon given on German radio two days after Hitler's accession by Pastor Dietrich Bonhoeffer. He was about to thunder against 'the leader who makes an idol of himself and his office and thus mocks God', when the last words of his broadcast were snipped off.

Hitler cultivated a Führer myth to bridge the gap between official optimism and brute reality. It exempted him in the minds of many Germans from their criticism of his regime. 'If the Führer only knew about this . . .' was a common lament when, often as not, the outrage was committed on his orders.

The extent to which Karajan exploited his role as leader can be seen in the hagiographies and record-sleeve hype that he invited. The 'extreme modesty' idealized by his copywriters co-existed with a visible hauteur and ubiquitous self-advertisement as 'the world's greatest conductor', as 'greatest exponent of Beethoven' and 'foremost interpreter of the music of Verdi and Puccini'. Only a ruthless man lacking in any sense of self-mockery could have authorized a book of glamour photographs whose preface proclaimed that 'it is hard to imagine anyone shyer of the camera . . .'. He learned the art of manipulating his own image from those who manufactured Hitler's. In Beethoven films that he produced with the Munich firm, Unitel, he had himself lit from above with spears of light reminiscent of the ones Speer invented to herald the Führer's entry to his Nuremburg rallies.

Another rule of governance he picked up from the Nazis was divide and conquer. He had only to observe how adroitly Hitler played off Goebbels against Goering, and both against Himmler, to understand survival technique at the very top. He invariably worked with at least two record companies and orchestras at one and the same time. 'No man had ever developed such finesse in the art of working off one party against another,' grudged Walter Legge. In studio, he would address technical questions to the producer and musical ones to the engineer, deliberately sowing resentment and confusion. 'By keeping everyone uncertain he was able to concentrate all solutions and power in himself,' says one producer. To show off his mastery to rehearsal guests he would provoke a burst of musical chaos from the orchestra. Then, with a wave of his stick he would magically restore harmony, manifesting his divine control of massed mortals. So long as he was alive, there was only one leader and one power-symbol in the musical world.

His Nazism did not extend to the dogmatic anti-semitism of *Der Stürmer*. His racism was couched in *echt*-Austrian euphemisms. In 1934, he declined a possible opening at the Volksoper in Vienna because 'all of Palestine' seemed to be gathered there, and he certainly would not want to mix with those people. Nevertheless, he took a part-Jewish wife, and, after the War hired a clutch of confidential aides who happened to be Jews. Among them were his Viennese agent Emil Jucker, personal secretary Rita Köhler, his intimate biographer Ernst Häussermann, his record associate, Michel Glotz, the Berlin concertmaster Michel Schwalbé and his conducting protégé, James Levine. But Karajan treated his Jews with particular condescension, reminding them regularly of their origins to keep them insecure. He shocked Giorgio Strehler with a casual tip he offered when the Italian director joined the Salzburg team. 'What you need more than anything else,' said Karajan, 'is a first-class private secretary. *Unfortunately*, the only one is a Jew.'

He controlled those around him so firmly that he never needed to lose his temper. 'If I don't raise my voice, they'll listen to what I say, and the less I speak, the more important each word is,' he explained. When he wanted someone fired, he did so out of the man's hearing. His breach with the Philharmonia came in a solicitor's letter; after quitting the Berlin Philharmonic, he refused to see a delegation of its oldest players and sent a minion to shoo them away. He shirked displays of emotion and was happiest alone in his air-conditioned underground bunker at home, playing omnipotently with his electronic controls.

He dreamed above all of world dominance, a Hitlerite ambition developed initially as a defensive response to the Furtwängler sanctions that excluded him from Austro-German and American summits but quickly becoming his primary motivation. 'He is a pathologically power-hungry individual,' says one of his biographers, 'his aim was to create a Reich of his own.' Once Berlin fell into his lap, the other citadels of music followed suit. He took over the Vienna State Opera in 1956 and was simultaneously head of German repertory at La Scala; he assumed control at Salzburg and had the pick of the orchestral dates in Vienna, London, Paris and almost anywhere else he cared to appear.

He talked of 'a long-cherished plan to amalgamate six major opera houses', rolling his own productions from one to the next in streamlined homogeneity. A Viennese joke of the time has him getting into a taxi and to the driver's question, 'where to?' replying 'it doesn't matter – I've got something going everywhere.' It is terrifying to contemplate how close he came around 1960 to achieving a total hegemony of world music.

His eight years at Vienna were the most prestigious since Mahler's, with glittering casts and a strong sense of purpose. What he lacked was Mahler's managerial flair and fervent dedication. He could not afford to spend much time conducting in Vienna and, in his absence, admitted that 'at least 100 performances every season were absolutely terrible.' His was not a golden age but a gold-plated imitation.

As a stage director he lacked imagination, commissioning imposing scenery to enliven static productions. His lighting was invariably dim, a deficiency copied slavishly by others; he had a lifelong fixation that singers should be spotlit with their mouths open and otherwise not seen at all. Every filament of his performances was beautifully presented but violent emotions were toned down. Stark tragedy was submerged in an overwhelming sheen of sound. The agony of Tristan and Isolde was subsumed in beauty. One emerged from a Karajan opera impressed but profoundly unshaken.

Harried by institutional incompetence, niggling critics and incessant government interference, he resigned after six years, was summoned back when staff walked out in sympathy and quit again two years later 'for health reasons' in a furore that involved the Austrian Cabinet – which vengefully sought to veto his appointment to the Salzburg board. He did not set foot again in the Staatsoper for thirteen years. His breach with

Italy was equally acrimonious. A quarter of a century later, when Zubin Mehta tried to get him to open the Maggio Musicale in Florence, Karajan confided that he had sworn never to return to the country after an enemy of his at La Scala had become head of state broadcasting and banned his records from the airwaves. He demanded an apology from the Italian government. Mehta procured an official note, delivered to his home by the Italian ambassador in Austria. Not enough, said Karajan. He wanted the Foreign Minister to apologize in person.

As a result of his feuds and foibles, the publicly funded cultural emblem of West Berlin did not set foot in Italy, Israel, Australia, South America, or anywhere in the Third World during his reign. He visited Japan every year, though, to promote record sales in his second-largest market. Karajan gave Berlin what Germans wanted, a brilliant icon that eclipsed anything the drab Communists could offer across the Wall. But he never lived in the city, never declared '*ich bin ein Berliner!*' He stayed in a penthouse suite at the Kempinski Hotel and ate like a tourist in its corner restaurant (his private redoubt was built at Anif, ten minutes' drive from Berchtesgaden). The sense of community and solidarity that Furtwängler had instilled in the Philharmonic was swept aside; it was now each man for himself. 'I play with an orchestra where every member hopes to outshine the others,' he proclaimed.

He kept the musicians happy by using rehearsals as commercial recording sessions, a clever wheeze that doubled their call-fees and kept down the production costs of his records. 'For years Karajan made it easy for this orchestra to follow him,' said a Berlin horn-player, 'it was a wonderful life.' On top of the professorial salaries they drew from the city, the musicians earned as much again from Karajan's enterprises. They drove Mercedes cars. Some bought second homes in the Salzburg Alps. Once, on an early US tour, they chided him over his $3,000 guest-conducting fee (it would multiply tenfold before he bowed out). He counter-sparred:

'Tell me, do you think the orchestra would be paid more if I took a lower honorarium?'

'No.'

'Who would gain if I got less?'

'The tour manager.'

'And whom do you begrudge the money most – me or the manager?'

Berlin and Salzburg were the twin fortresses of his empire, impregnably secured. He held out for an unbreachable lifelong contract with the Philharmonic, committing himself in return to just over half Furtwängler's concert schedule. It took eighteen months before the agreement was signed and Karajan never resigned himself to being denied Furtwängler's honorific title of *künstlerischer Leiter* (artistic leader). Berlin was content to bask in orchestral glory and advertised itself under the slogan '*Wie harmonisch Berlin ist.*'

Salzburg gave its native son a free hand to perform showpieces for the edification of well-heeled patrons in ball-gowns, dinner jackets and duelling scars who paid up to £250 for a seat and spent a fortune in its hotels and gift shops. Apart from four years as artistic director (1956–60) in which he blasted through the construction of a Grosses Festspielhaus into the mountainside (breaking, he bragged, 'all the windows of the old city'), he held no official position on the summer festival but, from a seat on its board, directed its operations for 35 years. Its opulent auditorium was created in his image: expensively tailored, electronically sophisticated and with a raised podium that made the conductor visible from every corner of the house.

To Salzburg's summer season, he added Easter and Whitsun Festivals in which his Berlin Philharmonic played and his record companies rolled their tape machines. These festivals were self-financed and totally autonomous of city and state. The *Ring* that launched the Easter event in 1967 was rehearsed at Deutsche Grammophon's expense and exported first to Geneva, then to the Met, where it was killed off by a strike after two episodes. It made a small profit and put a small town in a neutral nation of just seven million inhabitants at the epicentre of America's operatic perspectives.

For Salzburg, Karajan could do no wrong. When he needed extras for crowd scenes, the local army commander sent a platoon of conscripts. He packed cronies on to the summer festival board, from where his biographer Häussermann peddled influence and reputedly played Cupid between paunchy politicians and buxom young singers. A predominance of the performing contracts were assigned to Karajan's personal agents, Jucker, Glotz and especially his American manager Ronald Wilford. His connection with Jucker survived on an awareness of each other's Swiss bank accounts. It was alleged, though never documented, that he owned a slice of Wilford's company, CAMI. If this was so, he indirectly took a tiny cut from every CAMI singer, soloist and conductor who appeared in Salzburg and performed in Berlin.

Adversaries, real or imagined, were rigorously excluded. For years he kept Leonard Bernstein out of Berlin and sabotaged Georg Solti's recording sessions in Vienna by pre-booking the Philharmonic. Solti, who had never met him, knew no reason for his animus. Nikolaus Harnoncourt, the early music specialist and a professor at Salzburg's Mozarteum, was banned from the festival after critical remarks about Karajan were attributed to him in *Der Spiegel*. 'The whole of Salzburg knows about it,' said his wife after the edict had lasted almost twenty years, 'but there is nothing we or anyone else can do.'

Salzburg became Sleazeburg, a byword for greed and corruption. The artistic ideals of its founders were supplanted by media deals, mega-stars and a pervasive attention to the comforts of the ultra-rich. Bayreuth, Glyndebourne and the Rossini festival at Pesaro were equally dependent on wealthy patrons but none made mammon so flagrantly its motive as Salzburg under Karajan's direction. Only Karajan-linked record labels could buy advertising space in the town centre; only their artists featured in his festivals and received its prodigious fees.

While the rich enjoyed the music, musicians came to get rich. The inflationary scale of their payments, leaked to the fastidious German press, prompted the Minister of Culture in Vienna to set up an independent inquiry into the finances of a publicly accountable festival that somehow ran up a £600,000 overspend on lighting in 1988. The Berlin Senate was meanwhile investigating revelations that CAMI had tied a proposed Philharmonic tour to Taiwan to the sale of Karajan videos. For his eightieth birthday that year, CAMI made a fawning documentary called 'Karajan's Salzburg' and peddled it to gullible television networks around the world. The sceptical *Der Spiegel* featured him on its cover waving a dollar wand.

The scandals began to break only when Karajan was on his last legs (and were comparatively tame by Austrian standards of probity that allowed governments to survive the poisoning of wine exports and massive ministerial bribery over the Danube dam). Karajan, notwithstanding anecdotes of his avarice, kept his own fees at Berlin and Salzburg on a modest scale, or waived them altogether. He had no need to rifle the till when he owned the entire shop.

In the Third Reich, likewise, Goering plundered art collections and Himmler raided confiscated bank accounts while the Führer stood above it all, untouched by filthy lucre. Hitler's fortune was amassed in royalties from every German postal stamp that bore his picture and from his credo *Mein Kampf*, presented to every bridal couple. Karajan's wealth was similarly founded on royalties from almost 900 records, of which he sold 115 million copies, promoting Deutsche Grammophon to global market leader and accounting for one-third of its sales. He also dominated for a while at EMI, worked with Decca and flirted with CBS, cutting twice as many albums as any other conductor.

The rewards of his success were lavish. He piloted his own jet, parked a 77-foot racing yacht at St Tropez, drove outrageously fast cars and, when he wanted to please his coquettish third wife, the French fashion model Eliette Mouret, bought her 'first a Picasso, then a Renoir, then a Bellini – and the most beautiful jewels. Whatever I want,' she purred, 'my husband gives me.' Her amateur oil paintings decorate a DG edition of '100 Karajan masterpieces'. He retained the entourage of a heavyweight boxer, an 'imperial procession' of bodyguards and indefinable aides who trailed him everywhere. While such indulgences and pastimes were faintly ridiculous in a serious musician, they were not inherently sinister or demeaning. 'The fruits have been very great,' he once remarked of his recording career, adding hastily, 'I mean the spiritual ones, not the financial.'

The extent of his worldly fortune became glaringly apparent in the weeks after his death. His will, opened at Salzburg on 1 August 1989 by a Swiss attorney, Dr Werner Kupper, exposed the protruding tip of a well-stashed hoard. His business affairs had been discreetly funnelled through Switzerland ever since he visited the Lucerne Festival in 1947; his first lawyer was the Festival president, Dr Strebi, succeeded by a Dr Fischer of Geneva (shades of Graham Greene) and lastly by the tight-lipped Dr Kupper. His residence for tax purposes was in the uninquisitive canton of Graubünden; his house at Anif, one of four declared properties, was owned by Music International Establishment, a company registered in the *laissez-faire* haven of Liechtenstein. His films belonged to a firm he formed in Monaco. Depositing all his assets in tax shelters, he paid no death duties to the land where he was born and lived.

Kupper conservatively valued his estate at 500 million Deutschmarks (£163 million). The amount was incomprehensible. No musician had ever died a multi-millionaire, let alone a half-billionaire. It could not possibly have been amassed from half a century's concert fees and record royalties. As we have mentioned, Karajan's emoluments in Berlin and Salzburg were notably modest, never exceeding fifteen thousand Marks (£5,000) per concert, and for most of his life far less than that. He earned more on foreign tours, but was not a constant traveller. On record sales he received a royalty of below ten per cent, lowered below five by mutual consent with the lucrative advent of compact disc. In order to graft mega-millions from LPs he would have had to sell as heavily as the Beatles. Moreover, many of his record projects were expensive failures; he died owing EMI an estimated one million pounds (nearly two million dollars) in unearned advances.

If his fortune was not derived from the decimal points of royalties and the crumbs of his concert fees, where did it come from? Dismissing the possibility of embezzlement – and he was too well-advised to dabble in indictable crime – it can only have constituted the rewards of untrammelled power. He had ruled the world's greatest orchestra, richest festival and large sections of the record trade unhindered by external constraints. 'I shall be a dictator,' he warned Salzburg at the outset – and he was, more benign than political tyrants but no less autocratic, and ever alert to any financial advantage that might come his way. Absolute power was the ultimate lesson he learned in the Reich and it became the ultimate goal of his life. Once seized, the opportunities for enrichment and expansion through outright conquest and tactical alliances were limitless.

He had taken control of the record industry by the 1960s and was looking to gain access to wider means of production when he was introduced to Akio Morita, founder of Sony. Morita was a technical perfectionist, prepared to forgo commercial advantage for qualitative superiority. He would rather lose a market than compromise standards and would be beaten painfully in the videotape war by pitting the brilliance of his Beta system against JVC-Panasonic's dull but affordable VHS.

Morita was a classics fanatic who had to have music wherever he went. He ordered his engineers to design him a portable cassette player from a prototype they had made for a NASA space mission; he found the ensuing Walkman so indispensable that he put it on the production line and sold 100 million items. His deputy, Norio Ohga, had been a singing student in Berlin and remained an open-mouthed fan. Ohga's musicianship was sufficient for him to perform the baritone solo in Fauré's *Requiem* on a recording released by Sony. Both men became Karajan's guests at Salzburg and viewed him as their short-cut to Valhalla.

Fascinated by technology, he enjoyed being kept abreast of cutting-edge progress. Their interests came closer in the early 1970s, when audio sales of both hardware and software were squeezed by the oil-crisis recession and mounting customer resistance to clickety LPs, hissy tapes and the umpty-fourth version of Beethoven's Fifth. A US-led drive towards quadrophonic (four-speaker) sound flopped in a clamour of clashing formats, pulling down with it the last strongholds of American hi-fi. The time was ripe for the Japanese to advance with a new idea, but they had none yet in store.

The glint of a solution glimmered in Holland, where Philips engineers were converting sound particles into computer digits. This enabled them to record music and replay it without any intervening imperfection or degeneration. Digital sound was theoretically purer than spring water. Sony picked up the gist of this technique and wanted to forge ahead but were held back by Dutch caution. They took their case to Karajan, who was captivated. Calling a 1981 press conference with Morita, he endorsed digital sound with the words 'all else is gaslight' and exerted both public and private pressure on Philips, which partnered his DG label in the PolyGram group, to develop the process three years before they (or the technical means) were fully ready. DG spent a mint in setting up a CD-pressing plant at its Hanover base.

The outcome was a rapid audio revival as CD overtook the flawed LP. Ohga effusively offered 'special thanks to the Maestro who helped us develop digital recording' and equipped his Anif home with the latest gadgetry. Sony built a disc factory across the meadow with a twenty per cent subsidy that Karajan secured from the Austrian government. 'Professor von Karajan has been our economic and cultural attaché here,' announced the Japanese ambassador to Austria, Atsuhiko Yatabe.

Karajan, for his part, was able to record his favourite music all over again in digital sound. His connection with Morita became increasingly important to both septuagenarians; each carefully avoided mentioning the other in their autobiographies. As Karajan's influence increased over hardware development, Morita entered the software stakes by taking over CBS Records and Columbia Pictures. Together again, in perfect harmony, Morita and Karajan applied the CD formula to home-video, introducing a viewable disc called CD-Video or Laserdisc. 'I had goose-pimples all over on seeing it,' rasped the conductor.

The new medium was custom-built to fulfil his final dreams. Hampered by immobility and happy to spend his days before a bank of video screens, he had been devoting what proved to be his last decade to filming his core repertoire as a 'musical testament to the world'. Fascinated by movies, he had learned from some of the century's most ingenious directors, watching Max Reinhardt in Salzburg, conducting a Berlin *Zauberflöte* with Gustaf Gründgens, the serpentine Mephisto-figure in Klaus Mann's famous novel, and collaborating closely with Franco Zeffirelli and Jean-Pierre Ponelle. From 1940 on, he sought whenever possible to produce his own operas, on sternly traditional lines. 'The stage designers of today are either insane or idiots, or both,' he told Ingmar Bergman.

On film, his mid-career operas were most watchable when an independent director was involved – as in Zeffirelli's Unitel frisky version of *Cavalleria rusticana* – and least compelling when the staging was his own. His 1980 *Ring* folded three days after release in a Munich cinema. To counteract the visual limitations of players, instruments and conductor in Unitel's symphonic films, he arranged the orchestra in serried ranks like the stormtroopers in Leni Riefenstahl movies. In the final testament for his own company, Telemondial, he spared no expense and spent $20 million in search of an original image. Using fifteen cameras, he rehearsed all the angles with a student band before shooting film with the Berlin and Vienna Philharmonic orchestras. His ultimate hope was to replace the concert habit with a superior, cough-free musical experience. 'People who *really* want to concentrate will stay at home with the video,' he told an interviewer. To stay as close as possible to the music, he never let the cameras pull back more than five metres for a middle-distance or wide-angle shot. Lighting was progressively modulated to reflect changes of musical mood.

'It is my aim to show the work as it is constructed, the ebb and flow of tension, the musical line, the many voices . . .' he explained. The

Karakatures by Bernhard Leitner

central focus of attention was, of course, the conductor. 'In a music film you can finally show the conductor properly,' he said, 'In doing so, you not only fulfil a wish on the part of the audience but you also help their understanding of the music, as long, that is, as the images are correctly deployed.' In such febrile fantasies, he was no longer just the conductor of an orchestra, nor even *Generalmusikdirektor* of Europe, but orchestrator of the thoughts and feelings of the whole tele-viewing world.

He talked of filming eighty essential symphonies, loading them on to his Falcon jet and flying round the world to demonstrate their perfection. Editing obsessively, he was overtaken by death on the eve of the 1989 summer festival. Morita was mortified. Sony had been counting on him to lift off Laserdisc and convert viewers and broadcasters to its high-

definition 1125-line TV screens. Ohga, who was at Karajan's Anif home
the morning he died, collapsed two days later and was rushed into intensive care. Sony placed the largest wreath on his grave.

A bitter struggle broke out over his 43 finished videos. Sony, having
snapped up his DG producer, Günther Breest, to head its classical label,
heavily outbid DG to clinch a multi-million dollar deal with Dr Kupper;
it would need to sell twelve million copies to break even. The yellow
label struck back with a mass release of Karajan's older Unitel films.
Suddenly the market was awash with Karajan products on a medium that
had yet to win public confidence, and at a posthumous moment when
every reputation takes a dive. Two media groups went to war, each with
Karajan as its spearhead, blunting his impact and erasing the elitist appeal
of his output.

He had lived to see his empire crumble, its twin strongholds falling when
challenged from within. The first crack appeared in 1982 when the Berlin
Philharmonic rejected a female clarinettist whom Karajan hailed as a
genius. No-one doubted Sabine Meyer's excellence, but players said her
tone clashed with the rest of the section and her personality did not fit.

Although the orchestra had surrendered its autonomy in 1933 to
become salaried civil servants, it jealously controlled admission to its
ranks. Karajan had previously tried to force in new players but retreated
in the face of resistance. Neither side wanted to rock the luxury liner.
Now, tortured by a spinal disease and the onset of old age, he demanded,
as artistic director, the right to select players. Forget it, said the orchestra.
Furtwängler was *künstlerischer Leiter* and he never imposed a player on
us. You are merely chief conductor. Karajan responded with an open
letter agreeing 'to honour my Berlin obligation' but cancelling all tours,
recordings and Salzburg concerts. Typically, he had the Vienna Philharmonic standing by. He once likened his manipulation of the two orchestras to his preference for twin-engined planes: it made him feel doubly
safe.

While Miss Meyer played on a temporary contract and the orchestra
worked with conductors and record companies alien to Karajan, notably
the Israeli Daniel Barenboim, press acolytes painted Karajan as a champion of female rights in an all-male club. Public sympathy, however, was
generally with the musicians and his room for manoeuvre was constricted.
He still needed them to finish his all-important videos.

Conciliation was celebrated in a 1984 Bach B-minor Mass, after the
clarinettist resigned and the orchestra's general manager, Peter Girth,
was sacrificially sacked. To run the office and repair relations, the city
recalled the respected intendant, Wolfgang Stresemann, now over 80,
but he was unable to restore the old warmth. Karajan no longer attended

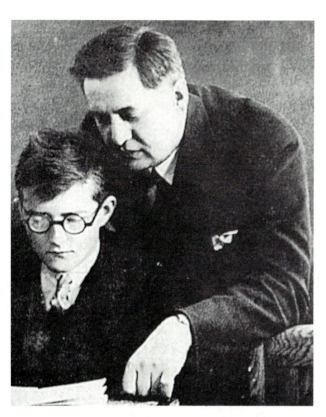

Vaclav Talich (*r.*) instructs the young Shostakovich. (The Lebrecht Collection)

Hans von Bülow made his Meiningen band stand up to play. (The Lebrecht Collection)

Handsome Felix Weingartner.
(The Lebrecht Collection)

'Hans himself' – the egregious
Richter. (The Lebrecht Collection)

Arthur Nikisch with the hypnotic eyes. (The Lebrecht Collection)

Willem Mengelberg, emperor of Amsterdam. (Philips Classics)

Otto Klemperer, granitic and indomitable. (Otto Klemperer Collection)

Bruno Walter, his amenable antithesis. (The Lebrecht Collection)

Arturo Toscanini at the helm in New York. (NY Public Library, Toscanini Archive)

Das Wunder Karajan – publicity portrait from 1938. (The Lebrecht Collection)

Wilhelm Furtwängler bows to (*l. to r.*) Goering, Hitler and Goebbels. (The Lebrecht Collection)

Man-made maestros Vladimir Ashkenazy (*l.*) and André Previn. (Royal Philharmonic Orchestra)

Barbirolli, one of four British batons honoured by H.M. postal service in 1972; the others were Sargent, Beecham and Wood. (The Lebrecht Collection)

Imperious Thomas Beecham.
(EMI Records)

George Solti, charming but
relentless. (Portrait by Sally
Soames)

Pierre Boulez, 'The Iceman Cometh'. (Portrait by Ward, *Sunday Times*)

Leonard Bernstein wringing the last drop of emotion.

players' weddings and funerals; the coronary attack that killed one violinist was attributed by his family to tension at work. The conductor was caustic in rehearsal, the players sullen and resentful. He demanded the dismissal of a quirky horn-player; the musicians reinstated him after court action. During the city's 750th anniversary year, he made just six appearances, pulling out of a concert for the head of state with 'gastric influenza' – a day before flying healthily to Japan. 'He is no longer chief conductor but a guest,' said Hellmut Stern, a front-desk violinist and leader of the anti-Karajan resistance.

There was only one prize he still wanted from Berlin: Furtwängler's title of artistic director and, with it, the right to name his successor. The honour was in the gift of the Christian Democrat city government, whose leaders Karajan had long cultivated. When they were routed in December 1989 by a coalition of socialists and Green environmentalists, he greeted the new cultural senator with a brusque letter of resignation.

His parting gambit was timed to favour his protégé, James Levine, who was about to begin an intensive period of work in Berlin. The orchestra was unimpressed. It waited the few months until his death, then elected a chief conductor as opposed to Karajan as he had differed from his predecessor. Claudio Abbado was in the Furtwängler mould: hesitant by inclination and a respecter of individual rights. Weeks later, the Berlin Wall burst open and the Philharmonic played under Barenboim and Bernstein for a reunified city. Karajan, a symbol of its former division, was relegated to distant memory. Two years after his death, the Philharmonie hall he helped design was eerily empty, shut down for restoration of its unexpectedly fragile fabric.

At Salzburg, too, rampant corruption resulted in the abolition of dictatorship. A three-man executive was installed to run the summer festival, headed by Dr Hans Landesmann, who had led the government investigation into its affairs. As artistic director he imported Gérard Mortier, of the Brussels opera house, who had openly attacked the 'mafia-like conditions' that prevailed under Karajan. In what became his final production, it would seem that the old maestro sensed something of the stagnation. At the close of *Don Giovanni*, surrounded by sycophants who outdid one another in effulgences of praise, an overhead microphone picked up the murmur he made to himself: 'Furtwängler would not have thought it was good.'

He liked to relate that when the Berlin Philharmonic informed him of Furtwängler's death and his election it was with the words: 'The king is dead. Long live the king!' Now, allies watched in amazement the swift dismemberment of his empire. 'The king is dead,' said Ronald Wilford sombrely. 'God save the republic.'

All that remained in permanence were the records, hundreds upon hundreds of indelible discs that would revolve and reverberate for as long as mankind listened to western music. On that frozen Friday in Vienna half a lifetime before, he was converted to Walter Legge's faith in the preeminence of recording and proceeded to propagate it with remorseless efficiency. Over the years he modified his musical style to conform to consumer requirements. The grit and fire of his early records, the wild attack that 'made the music sound dangerous', the surging energy of his first Beethoven cycle, were steadily smoothed down into a uniformity that became known as 'Karajan's beautiful sound'. People who listened in the comfort of their living-rooms or the driving-seat of their family four-seaters did not want danger with their music. They required a product without blemish or idiosyncracy, perpetual perfection for the price of a few pounds. Karajan was their guarantee of quality. His was the name they came to trust for the kind of technical reliability normally associated with German motor manufacture, supersmooth and trouble-free.

Riccardo Chailly, young Italian conductor of West Berlin's radio symphony orchestra, watched the meticulous detail that went into his rehearsals and records to the very end:

> The daily, thorough research of sound quality of an orchestra was most impressive. After nearly thirty years as chief conductor in Berlin he would treat groups of his orchestra like schoolchildren, fighting with all his energy to achieve a specific effect. He would not just let them play their own natural *Klang* but daily corrected them, manipulating and shaping the sound towards the effect he wanted. He would caress the air with the middle finger of his left hand to obtain smoothness, the texture of velour – and you heard it.
>
> When he recorded the Beethoven symphonies for the fourth time, after performing them around the whole world – bar by bar he rehearsed for accuracy and sparkle.

Musically, however, the outcome was less interesting than his previous cycles. Where late performances by Klemperer, Walter, Stokowski and other elder statesmen acquired dimensions of wisdom and grandeur, Karajan's recordings became shallow and insipid as he pursued continual refinement of the quality he perceived as beauty. 'Would you prefer them to be ugly?' he demanded when his interpretations were challenged.

Legge had been amazed at his ability to hit a quick fortissimo 'without the click of an attack: every phrase which can be begun beautifully is begun as beautifully as he knows how'. Not for him the shudder of a Furtwängler start, the lurch of a Klemperer adagio or the snap of a Nikisch allegro. He would complain that orchestral musicians 'play note by note' when what he needed on record was total sheen, an unserrated line. This picture-postcard concept of musical aesthetics – transposing in some way the matchless view from his Alpine windows – was most effective and least contentious in descriptive works such as Richard Strauss's tone poems and Gustav Holst's *The Planets*. It is hard to imagine a more gripping and glamorous account of Mussorgsky's *Pictures at an Exhibitiion* and Rimsky-Korsakov's *Shéhérezade*. These were occasions when, as one critic aptly put it, 'a work seems to be receiving its ultimate performance'.

He was unrivalled at making marginal composers sound like masters. Arthur Honegger owes his place in the concert repertoire, albeit at the fringes, to Karajan's stunning account of the *dona nobis pacem* resolution of his *Symphonie liturgique*. His interpretations of Slavonic and French music were often enchanting, lacking only the rough and piquant accents that distinguish them from all other music. Stravinsky ridiculed his 'tempo di hoochie-koochie' in the penultimate passage of the *Rite of Spring*; he never attempted the complex cross-rhythms of Janáček and Ives.

The smoothness he sought gave a numbing uniformity to his recordings. Vivaldi was performed by Karajan in much the same way as Mozart or Tchaikovsky. A best-selling album of popular baroque pieces amounts to a hilarious travesty, like plainchant sung by a pop group. He was inordinately proud of the sumptuousness he achieved in Schoenberg and Webern, even when the composer wrote in jagged lines. Yet he regarded himself as the acme of historic authenticity. 'I belong to a different age,' he reflected near the end of his life. 'And what I want to preserve for myself and posterity also belongs to a different age.'

It was in confronting tragic emotions that the Karajan approach came unstuck. In 1982, after surviving life-threatening surgery on his spine, he turned to Mahler's Ninth Symphony in which the composer confronted his own impending death. The interpretation was acclaimed as one of Karajan's finest achievements and, by the eminent critic Hans Heinz Stuckenschmidt, as the greatest performance of any music he had ever heard. The live recording won every imaginable record award that year. Those whose devotion to Mahler transcended their thanksgiving for Karajan's survival emerged deeply perplexed. Every note in the symphony was in its place and immaculately played, yet the performance was curiously hollow. It seemed to be demonstrating the proficiency of its participants rather than the symphony's anguish and anger. Andrew Porter, hearing the concert repeated in New York, felt the scherzo's horror and madness were being 'subordinated to a display of carefully equilibriated, highly wrought orchestral wizardry'. Peter Davis in *New York* magazine wrote of Karajan as 'master of the recorded cult which has purged the spirit from the music'.

This element of spirituality in Karajan's music is perpetually troublesome. What 'spirit' was evoked when an atheist performed a Mozart Mass, or an unrepentant Nazi conducted Mahler? In his trenchant Yale assessment of the philosopher Martin Heidegger, professor Richard Rorty argues that Heidegger's role in the Nazi era would no longer concern us 'were it not for his post-War silence about the Holocaust'. In Karajan's case, the silence was no less deafening and its persistence raises uncomfortable issues about the music he made. Music itself is amoral, of course, and personal flaws in a creative individual can sometimes be separated from the sublimity of his work. Wagner's music and Brecht's poems are infinitely more humane than their callous personalities. Karajan, however, was not creative, merely communicative. He was the channel through which music was funnelled. If that channel were bent or blocked by any impediment, grit or gold, whatever passed through would be affected by his own beliefs and personality – and this is the key to the Karajan question.

'The totalitarian element in Karajan's character manifested itself in the denial of contingency' – the elimination of chance and inspiration from music – wrote the Cambridge philosopher Michael Tanner. Everything he performed conformed to a pre-ordained pattern, and that pattern was set by ideals he absorbed in a dark era, and by commercial considerations. 'With Karajan, there is no struggle,' assessed the New York writer Edward Rothstein. 'Or, the struggle is already over by the time the music is heard. There is simply the presentation of the music by a man claiming the authority of absolute power.' Soloists were selected for their pliability. Only rarely did a pianist come out of his corner to fight, as Sviatoslav Richter did in the Tchaikovsky B flat minor concerto and Krystian Zimmerman in the Grieg. He was visibly happiest with young talent, like Anne-Sophie Mutter, who tended not to contradict.

'Like a dictator, he could not tolerate argument,' wrote the senior British critic David Cairns, 'but argument is the life-blood of Beethoven's symphonic thought. A Karajan performance of the *Eroica* . . . was a kind of cover-up.' Cairns admits to an 'active repugnance' for Karajan: 'Beauty without form, sound without meaning, power without reason, reason without soul – it is the deadly logic of hi-fi. Machines, we are told, will one day compose symphonies. At present they merely perform them.'

Those critics worshipful of Karajan were in the main – outside of Berlin and Vienna where he retained daily scribes of unswerving fidelity – dedicated record reviewers rather than music analysts. The distinction is significant for not only was their judgement swayed by audio-technical considerations that had no bearing on music but, in some cases, their very livelihood depended on an industry that viewed Karajan as its prime asset. The repeated assertion of such idolators that 'Karajan brought classical music to a hitherto inconceivably huge audience' is simply untenable. Many unrelated factors contributed to the post-War appetite for serious music and many other conductors would have found a wider audience had Karajan relaxed his aggressive monopoly.

That he should have been succeeded by a non-German was no surprise, for he had virtually obliterated the native species. So long as Karajan held sway, no German could make an international impression, apart from the uncontentious Böhm and the uncharismatic Schmidt-Isserstedt. He kept the rest in abeyance by privately denigrating old-school interpreters like Eugen Jochum and swamping the record catalogues with his own product. German conductors stood little chance of recording Beethoven symphonies when three Karajan versions were already in the shops.

The following generation was confined to provincial obscurity. Wolfgang Sawallisch and Christoph von Dohnányi were relatively little known beyond the state opera houses of Munich and Hamburg until Karajan went into terminal decline and their record careers finally took off. Dohnányi, son of one of Hitler's last martyrs and nephew of pastor Bonhoeffer, was alone among his colleagues in having the courage to confront the twin taboos of German music – Karajan's egotism and his commercialism – while the dictator was alive. Picking his words carefully, Dohnányi said: 'I don't think Karajan is in the German tradition at all. Karajan is a very special development. His abilities to get the results he wants are outstanding. You can question the results, of course, but this is not a German style of conducting. He is also the one who is in command of the commercial development of music business, the imperium of music, I would not consider this a specially German approach. This is an international flower.'

The kind of conductor Karajan cultivated were those who conformed to his overriding ideal of beautiful sound. Chief among them were James Levine of the Metropolitan Opera, who declared 'Karajan is my ideal'; and Seiji Ozawa of Boston, who made perennial pilgrimages to pay obeisance to his 'Maestro von Karajan' and was perceived by Berlin players as a sonic copy of the master-tape. Close your eyes and he could be Karajan, they quipped. While neither Ozawa nor Levine mimicked the old man's static podium posture, their tastes in music and the refinement they practised seemed to be modelled according to his particular preferences. Ozawa was an early graduate of Karajan's conducting course in Berlin, designed along with his conducting competitions to create a generation of mini-Karajans. Curiously, none of his prizewinners or graduates amounted to much. The names of Okko Kamu, Dmitri Kitaenko, Daniel Chmura, Emil Tchakarov and Daniel Oren languish in relative obscurity. The world, it seemed, had enough with one Karajan.

The unit he philanthropically endowed at Salzburg University to study the effect of physical stress on music-making was meant to discover why 'three of my colleagues [died], two at virtually the same place in Act III of *Tristan*'. Whatever his regrets for Felix Mottl and Joseph Keilberth, he was urgently interested in how to stay alive while conducting tense music. In this, as in almost every other initiative, his motive was self-centred. The rare gestures of generosity were tinged with ambiguity and self-glorification. Riccardo Chailly recalled that he was about to make his Berlin debut in 1980 with a visiting British orchestra when,

> five minutes before the beginning of the concert, a second door of the conductor's room opened and he appeared – like a vision of God. I said, Maestro, you want to make me feel dizzy. He said, in perfect Italian, I want to come and listen to you, what are you conducting tonight? I said, Maestro, I am doing a real Karajan favourite, Strauss *Don Juan*, please don't come. He said, I will listen backstage.
>
> When the attendants saw Karajan arriving, they opened a big double door on the left side of the stage – and the public saw him. There was big applause. He made a sign, and the door was closed. It was like the apparition of Banquo in *Macbeth*. I don't know where I found the courage to enter the hall and start.

He had placed the young conductor permanently in his debt and in his awe. Those players whom he helped in personal straits were expected to repay him with total loyalty. One hint of dissension and they were cast from his presence, their phone calls unanswered. His charm was considerable and seductive, but he turned it on and off at will and none were ever wholly secure in his affections. He wept copiously on the phone to Schwarzkopf on learning of Legge's death, having done nothing to keep him alive. Personal relations were, like all his prodigious gifts and possessions, permanently at the service of a higher cause – the pursuit of total and eternal power.

Autocratic politicians admired him unashamedly. 'This man has always fascinated me,' admitted Helmut Schmidt, the West German Chancellor. Margaret Thatcher, the British premier, told him she 'envied me my position, where people always did what I requested'. In Karajan's mind, however, the power and glory were never sufficiently secure. He had not become a household name like Toscanini, an intellectual icon like Furtwängler or a beloved idol like Nikisch. In America he was less famous than Leonard Bernstein, in France less than Pierre Boulez, in Britain less than Thomas Beecham, though he outsold all three put together. These shortcomings clearly irked him. 'When I am dead,' he said, justifying his video venture, 'people in the future will ask, what did he do? We can hear the music on record but what did he *do*? Now they will be able to see, if they want.'

It was the remark of a sad and defeated man. Mussolini, on the eve of his fall, said: 'Hitler and I have surrendered ourselves to our illusions like a couple of lunatics. We have only one hope left – to create an illusion.' Karajan created his illusion on records and films, and at his death he feared that it would not be enough, that he might disappear.

'For me,' said Christoph von Dohnányi, surveying the Karajan landscape with a cool gaze, 'a musician or politician is judged by results. It doesn't matter whether he learns a score in two minutes or two years. My main concern is what's the outcome. Look at Salzburg, look at Berlin. That's the result . . . There are many books about Karajan. There hasn't been one yet about a man who, in some way, jeopardized European music.'

CHAPTER 6

'A Starving Population and an Absentee Aristocracy'

KARAJAN CUT A further link with tradition by setting himself apart from the orchestra and the community it served. He never meant to belong anywhere, other than Salzburg; the unauthorized absences that got him the sack at Aachen were indicative of his future intentions. In Berlin he demanded to be made conductor for life but limited his contracted appearances in the city to twelve concerts a year, less than half Furtwängler's quota. As *Generalmusikdirektor* of all Europe, he demonstrated that it was technically possible in the jet age to be chief conductor in four places at once, earning four full salaries and the applause of an entire hemisphere. His immense fortune and flagrant ambition estranged him from orchestral musicians, whose resentment was compounded by his infrequent presence. He established precedents that enabled other conductors to whittle down their duties as music director. Where Mahler conducted 111 times in one season at the Vienna Opera, Claudio Abbado in the same office kept his commitment to just twenty performances. As music director of the London Symphony Orchestra, Abbado was not seen in its podium for nine months at a stretch, while gainfully occupied elsewhere. In some ways he personified the remote-control chief conductor of the post-Karajan epoch.

The principal victims of this phenomenon were leading American orchestras, which were obliged to abandon the benefits of a resident conductor in exchange for a highly paid fly-by-night with a day-job on another continent. In Philadelphia, Riccardo Muti drew a $400,000 music director's salary for sixteen weeks' attendance. His predecessor, Eugene Ormandy, hardly ever left the city boundaries in 44 years. Ormandy initially conducted 100 concerts for $50,000 a year and the plush Philadelphia sound was produced by his daily attention, and that of Leopold Stokowski, who had lived with the band for 26 years. Theirs was the real Philadelphia Story. Under Muti, the orchestra tended to sound like a dozen other top-flight orchestras in Europe or the United States.

When Robert Shaw retired in 1988 from the Atlanta Symphony Orchestra, it was noted as a sign of sad times that he was one of the last 'conductors of major orchestras whose principal residence was in the ensemble's home town'. In 21 years, Shaw had turned a semi-professional group of part-time insurance salesmen into a performing organization whose large-scale recordings were internationally welcomed.

The loss of a resident music director did not necessarily affect the technical level, however. Players simply became more adaptable through working with a gamut of guest conductors, but the coherent self-image of the orchestra was eroded. A new breed of arts managers took care of day-to-day business; and the music director became primarily a glamorous figurehead. His name on the press releases could exert enough box-office pressure to sustain a season of second-bests and keep the sponsors content. 'In American symphonic music,' writes the leading Chicago critic Robert C. Marsh, 'the first responsibility of a music director or general manager is to make his board look good.'

The American orchestra has been pronounced dead by one of its most respected administrators and its demise is openly discussed at annual conventions. Strikes, closures and falling subscriptions are symptomatic of lost principles and low morale. Most orchestras in America survive as museums of antiquated culture, with as much relevance to modern life and most of the populace as the municipal mausoleum.

Conductors have somehow escaped blame for a mess that is mostly of their making. Their collective responsibility becomes painfully apparent when the present malaise of mighty orchestras is compared, without nostalgia, with the not-so-distant time when a music director lived on the premises and ruled his institution with an omniscient eye.

The major orchestras in America were started by Germans who went west and stayed put wherever they collected an audience – men like Fritz Scheel who founded the Philadelphia Orchestra and the San Francisco Symphony, and Theodore Thomas who conducted the New York Philharmonic, set up the Brooklyn Philharmonic and finally formed the Chicago Symphony. Boston, the most cultured of US cities, was first conducted by a friend of Brahms, Georg Henschel, for whom an orchestra was assembled by a Civil War veteran, Major Henry Lee Higginson, in a hall built on the lines of the Leipzig Gewandhaus. Henschel was followed in short succession by fellow-Germans – Wilhelm Gericke, Nikisch, Emil Paur, Gericke again and Karl Muck, whose tenure was cut short by his wartime internment as a German spy. His musical scores were alleged to contain coded military information.

From 1881 until the philanthropic Higginson's death in 1919, the orchestra catered to reactionary tastes. 'Brahms was considered difficult,' relates the Bostonian composer Elliott Carter. 'When I was growing up, they used to say the EXIT signs in Symphony Hall meant, "this way in case of Brahms!" '

After the War, Boston flirted with Frenchmen. Henri Ribaud lasted a year, and Pierre Monteux was dismissed with an assurance that it was the orchestra's policy 'to change conductors every five years'. An amiable and accomplished musician, Monteux had steered a Paris orchestra serenely through the riots triggered by Stravinsky's *Rite of Spring*; as Diaghilev's staff conductor, he also premièred Debussy's ballet *Jeux* and Ravel's *Daphnis et Chloé*. In Boston, he imported European players and repertoire until forced out by a backlash from outraged local interests. The man who took his place was made of sterner stuff. He remained in Boston for a quarter of a century, making it a haven of modernism and creating the aristocrat of American orchestras.

Serge Koussevitsky owed his reputation to a self-financed concert series in Paris, where he usurped Diaghilev's mantle as purveyor of nouveau chic and took up a position on the fringes of the Stravinsky set. In the milieu of Russian exiles he was an anomaly, belonging neither to the dispossesed nobility nor to the conscientious anti-Communists. He had been a poverty-stricken double-bass player in the Bolshoi Opera orchestra when he captured the ear of Natalie Ushkov, daughter of Russia's richest tea merchant. Disposing hastily of a first wife and his Jewish origins (a distant cousin, Moshe, was a legendary synagogue cantor), he hung up his bull-fiddle and went to Berlin to take conducting lessons from Nikisch, whose gambling debts he paid off with his dowry. For their wedding present, Natalie asked her father to buy Serge an orchestra.

He made his conducting debut in Berlin and founded a publishing house there with Natalie's money to promote Russian composers, primarily the eccentric Skryabin. His later discoveries included Prokofiev, Stravinsky and Medtner. After the Revolution, he stayed in Petrograd for three years to conduct the state orchestra until collectivization convinced him to retreat with a diminished fortune to Paris, where he continued to play Maecenas to worthy composers. His expertise as midwife to new music would serve Boston in good stead. For the orchestra's 1931 jubilee he secured world premières of Prokofiev's Fourth Symphony, Honegger's First, Albert Roussel's Third and best, and Stravinsky's deathless Symphony of Psalms, 'composed for the glory of God and dedicated to the Boston Symphony Orchestra on the occasion of the 50th anniversary of its existence'. The rich creativity that he fertilized placed Boston firmly on the musical map. Koussevitsky, however, was unable to understand many of the scores and made composers play them to him on the piano until he grasped their meaning. Arnold Schoenberg accused him of 'general ignorance as a musician and as a man'. Stravinsky told a fellow-conductor:

Serge Koussevitsky. Caricature by his second wife

> Koussevitsky has no piano at his house(!). Do not be astonished at
> this, since this contrabassist never needs to play the piano, having
> become the American star purely through his conductor's baton. His
> genius frees him from the necessity of studying at the piano the scores
> that he deigns to conduct. For this inferior function, someone is
> always ready to play the music until this star has his ass full of it.

The underling assigned to this task was Nicolas Slonimsky, future doyen
of musical lexicography, who describes in his memoirs how, as he pounded out a symphony on the drawing-room keyboard, Koussevistky would
give baton cues to imaginary instruments. When he proved incapable of
catching the cross-rhythms of the *Rite of Spring*, his assistant rewrote the
music with new bar-lines to help him over tricky beats of 5/8 and 9/8 (this
simplified score was used in concerts by Koussevitsky's protégé, Leonard
Bernstein).

His competence as a conductor was open to question and he engaged
as guest conductors eminent composers who were unlikely to show up
his deficiencies – Ravel (whom he had previously paid to orchestrate

Mussorgsky's *Pictures at an Exhibition*), Glazunov, Respighi and Stravinsky. Monteux was never asked back to Boston while Koussevitsky was in command and the dazzling Dmitri Mitropoulos was banished after a brilliant triumph. Callous to his musicians and staff, whom he sacked without notice, Koussevitsky behaved tyrannically on the podium. 'Almost every rehearsal was a nightmare, every concert a thrilling experience,' wrote an assistant. 'There were in the BSO 105 players and 106 ulcers (one man had two).' In America's last non-union orchestra, men went to work with lumps in their stomachs and called their conductor 'the Tsar'.

Despairing of his audiences – 'the old ladies stopped their knitting,' he remarked to a soloist – he force-fed them a fresh diet of new music until they came to like it. No-one gave more support to composers exiled by the Nazis, winning popular acclaim for the elegant symphonies of Bohuslav Martinu and reviving Bartók's spirits sufficiently to inspire his Concerto for Orchestra. When Natalie died, he set up an enduring memorial foundation that paid Benjamin Britten to write his breakthrough opera, *Peter Grimes*, and still puts bread on the table of needy composers. Even Stravinsky, who called him a 'hypocrite, megalomaniac' and many worse epithets, remembered with reverence 'those things Serge Koussevitsky did for others without telling anyone . . . and for these secret things let him be rewarded infinitely'.

While he was at Boston, American composers like Roy Harris, Aaron Copland, William Schuman and Leonard Bernstein staked a strong claim to international attention. The summer school he founded at his Tanglewood estate has trained one in five of America's orchestral musicians; it has been the model for the Schleswig-Holstein and Pacific festivals in Germany and Japan. Bernstein unfailingly referred to him as 'my teacher and great friend'. Although Koussevitsky was arrogant and autocratic, ignorant of indigenous habits and unable to master the barest essentials of the English vernacular, he gave America a thriving heartland of musical creativity and an ensemble of which any European city could be proud.

His was an impossible act to follow. Boston replaced him with a mild-mannered Alsatian, Charles Münch, who conducted genially for thirteen years. It then applied martial law with two Germanic martinets who followed the Toscanini fashion, Erich Leinsdorf and William Steinberg. The nirvana of novelty gave way to numbing routine, broken only by Tanglewood's annual festival of youth. Hoping to restore lost sparkle, the board cast around for the most appealing of a younger breed of conductors.

Seiji Ozawa was a summer tutor at Tanglewood, where he had only lately been a mature student. He was 37 years old and music director in San Francisco. When Boston made him an offer, he decided to direct both orchestras at once, in addition to guest conducting in Europe and holding down a firm base in Japan. Ozawa sported a Beatle fringe, flowery shirts and cowboy boots, and wore a roll-necked sweater instead of a dress-shirt at concerts. His appointment was evidently aimed at rejuvenating the Symphony Hall subscription list. Oriental mysticism was all the rage among the East Coast college kids who escaped conscription to Vietnam; and Ozawa was, they said, *something else*. A native of Japanese-occupied Manchuria, where his father was a dentist, he was repatriated to Tokyo after the War and taken under the wing of Hideo Saito, a German-trained musician who was busily reviving the taste for symphonic music. (Back in the 1930s, a Tokyo ensemble under Prince Hidemaro Konoye had made the first recording of Mahler's Fourth Symphony, and Klaus Pringsheim, Mahler's repetiteur in Vienna, headed the Imperial Conservatory.)

Unable to afford tuition fees, Ozawa spent seven Jacobean years as a servant in Saito's house; in later years he formed an orchestra bearing his teacher's name. At 24 he was named by the NHK television network as the 'outstanding talent' in Japanese music, and was sponsored by a local company with the gift of a motor scooter. He phut-phutted off with a piano student riding pillion all the way to Paris, where he married his passenger (but not for long). He went in for a provincial conducting contest at Besançon and caught the ear of one of the judges, Charles Münch, who brought him to Tanglewood for the Koussevitsky Competition, which he duly won. Bernstein took him as his assistant to New York and he spent eight months in Berlin with Herbert von Karajan, who consigned him to the care of his powerful US manager, Ronald Wilford.

His talent was remarkable and his rise commensurately rapid. Within a decade he had ascended via the Toronto Symphony, Chicago's Ravinia Festival and San Francisco, to the summit of the Boston Symphony Orchestra. On the West Coast he had shown flair and determination, giving only three Beethoven symphonies in three years, but fourteen by Haydn, two by Ives and virtually everything Schoenberg had written for orchestra. At Boston, he blew in with a Koussevitsky special, Skryabin's *Poem of Fire*, in which all the house lights were extinguished and a galaxy of colours played upon the stage and ceiling. It was very Haight-Ashbury, very 1972. 'The audience loved looking at him,' said Marylou Speaker Churchill, principal second violinist, 'visually he's very satisfying.' The BSO launched an advertising campaign with the slogan: 'Put a little Ozawa in your life!'

For five years he shuttled between orchestras on opposite sides of America, giving neither more than a fragment of himself. 'Today we get the transient conductor,' grumbled San Francisco players to the *New*

York Times. 'They fly all over the country; they play here only ten or twelve weeks a year. They bring in all the stars they can, kick out anyone they want, and then, whoops, they are gone. A couple of years later they move on to bigger things and you are left with whatever is left, if you are left.' Shortly before he turned forty, Ozawa pulled out of San Francisco complaining of administrative overwork. Until then he had covered just ten of Boston's 22 subscription weeks, less than half the season. Although he now increased his participation by a few degrees, seeds of dissension had taken root and a hard-core opposition formed in the ranks. For more than a decade of his directorship, Boston was regularly rumoured to be seeking his successor. It was never a settled relationship.

Critics murmured that he became progressively less interesting and musicians accused him of everything from dullness to sexual discrimination. A leading music magazine demanded: 'When is Boston going to put its symphonic house in order?' and players lashed out against Ozawa in the Boston press. 'The orchestra is probably a collection of the finest instrumentalists in the world, but they sure don't sound like it,' said Jennie Shames, a violinist. 'We're desperate to have someone come and conduct us in the German literature, and be *inspired*,' carped Marylou Speaker Churchill. Another violinist, Cecylia Arzewski, said Ozawa spent too little time with the orchestra, and the quality of that time was inferior. 'He gets off the plane from Paris and starts to rehearse, and when he opens up the score of the symphony, he may not have looked at it since the last time he conducted it a year, or maybe four years, ago. Very often he repeats sections that don't need to be rehearsed because he wants to check out whether he's got it right. We call it panic time when he's around. His words of comfort to us when he's run out of time and the performance is the next day, you know what he says? "You be careful; I be careful." ' Arzewski quit soon afterwards. 'If those women said that,' Ozawa responded to the reported dissent, 'they are making their own graves.'

Players spoke out against what they saw as his indecision and insecurity. He appointed a principal trumpeter one year and fired him the next, only to have his writ overturned by arbitration. He auditioned interminably for new players, leaving important positions unfilled for a whole season. Some of the musicians' anger was kindled by his refusal to promote gifted women to principal positions. He blamed himself for being too democratic and too weak with musicians who had known him as a novice – 'I can't say "Cut off" because I was a student here.' His musicianship was meticulous but concerts and recordings of late romantic music seemed to lack total involvement. Fellow-stars admired his capacious memory and immaculate poise. 'He gives me a lot of inspiration in concert,' said the fastidious Polish pianist, Krystian Zimerman, 'and his firm conviction in what he can do impresses me greatly. I have great trust in his craftsmanship in a concert situation – he changes things from one concert to another without telling the orchestra, just knowing that he can show clearly what he wants. That's fantastic!'

His special efforts seemed to be reserved for gala occasions and for guest appearances in Europe. He gave a historic Paris première of Olivier Messiaen's only opera, *St François d'Assise*. By contrast, the works he commissioned for the BSO centenary in 1981 turned out to be insubstantial utterances by Americans, two unexceptional symphonies by British-based composers and an exotic oratorio by Michael Tippett that was conducted by his personal champion, Colin Davis. The pick of a poor pack was Leonard Bernstein's *Divertimento for Orchestra*.

The discrepancy with Koussevitsky's selection of masterpieces by the greatest living composers was instructive. Great music that Boston had brought to life – symphonies by Martinu, Honegger and Hindemith – vanished from its programmes under Ozawa, and Boston itself dropped out of the creative frontline. Unlike Koussevitsky, Ozawa never lived in Boston. He had a house on Stockbridge Mountain but this was simply a roof of convenience. His second wife, Vera, and their children remained in Japan and visited Boston only in school vacations. His salary, amounting to $381,000 in 1986, was paid into a company called Veroza (an amalgam of his wife's name) in a legal dodge aimed at paying less in taxes to Uncle Sam. After thirty years at the head of North American orchestras, his English is broken and barely functional.

All the while, his involvement with Japan has been continuous – despite a 1971 musicians' strike called against him for being 'disrespectful' to senior players. Japan has remained his power base, his greatest triumph as Boston's conductor was a 1979 Far East tour that took the first US orchestra to the People's Republic of China.

Ozawa denies being a 'jet-set conductor' and giving less than his full commitment to the orchestra at his command. Friends say he is a modest and engaging man who seeks neither enemies nor the obvious trappings of power. His peregrinations are the product of a phenomenal energy and physical fitness, though in 1990 he broke down with exhaustion and cancelled all engagements for three months. His artistic administrator in Boston confirmed that Ozawa travels more than any of his colleagues and is 'the only conductor of that level who lives in three places' – Asia, Europe and America. He is in many senses a child of his time, using information technology and the facilities of inter-continental travel for maximum personal advantage and job satisfaction. The benefits to music are less obviously discernible, whether on his own recordings or in the performing record of his orchestra.

Boston in the 1990s barely holds its place among the Big Five US orchestras. If Ozawa had applied himself monogamously to its interests, as Koussevitsky did, living close by and watching over its daily needs, his undoubted talent might have restored the orchestra to its former eminence. Equally, had he returned decisively to Japan, he could have established a bedrock of first-rate concert activity that would have liberated music lovers from dependence on expensively imported acts.

No-one ever accused Leopold Stokowski of stinting himself. At 94, after signing a new six-year record contract, he told reporters, 'I always want to be first. I'm what is known as egocentric.' Death took him by surprise soon afterwards, his ultimate ambition unfulfilled. In the longest of all podium careers, Stokowski deliberately put the con into conducting. Preoccupied by his public impact, he was part-showman, part-shaman, part-sham. Everything about him was fake: his age, his accent, his sexuality – everything, that is except his musicianship, which was so assured that few understood why he needed to raise a smokescreen of lies that obscured his genuinely momentous deeds.

Cockney born and bred, he spoke in an affected mid-European brogue and claimed to have been born in Krakow or somewhere in Pomerania at a date several years after his recorded birth in 1882 at Marylebone, London. He walked out of a BBC interview when confronted with the incontrovertible facts of his humble genesis: first-born son of a cabinetmaker of Polish descent and an illiterate Irish lass, who signed his birth certificate with an X. On one occasion he pretended that his father was a paleontologist; his countless falsehoods gave rise to widespread, though untrue, rumours that his real name was not Stokowski but Stokes.

As a boy he went to orchestral concerts, preferred Hans Richter to Arthur Nikisch, was admitted to the Royal College of Music precociously at 13 and found employment at twenty as organist at the fashionable and famous church of St James in Piccadilly, while living across the street above a Turkish bath of ill repute, among its 'men and wicked ladies', he related. His spiritual duties one Sunday so pleased the visiting rector of New York's central and chic St Bartholomew's that he was hired as director of music in the Manhattan church on a salary of $3,500 and a budget of $13,000 for staging Bach passions, which he directed impressively. The well-heeled congregation, whose founder was Cornelius Vanderbilt, contained a music-loving young socialite, Maria Dehon, who successively introduced Stokowski to his first two wives, the Texan pianist Olga Samaroff (born Lucie Hickenlooper) and the pharmaceutical heiress, Evangeline Brewster Johnson.

Endowed with a beauty that persisted into his eighties, Stokowski was irresistible to women. He was six foot tall with a slender figure, wavy hair, piercing blue eyes and an intense attentiveness to his prey. 'He subdues women with flattery and will chivalrously expend his most charming compliments, sometimes on the most unattractive; persuading each, whether she be princess or pariah, that for the moment at least she is the only existing female,' noted his record producer. Olga, whose Paris debut with Nikisch in 1908 set her on the road to stardom, was captivated by the would-be conductor and helped him arrange a Paris concert and acquire an orchestra in America. Mobilizing some influential cousins – General Alexander Hickenlooper, head of the Cincinnati gas and electric company, and Judge Smith Hickenlooper of the US district court – she enabled the 27-year-old neophyte to leapfrog over such favoured candidates as Bruno Walter to take charge of a reconstituted ensemble of German musicians in a state capital of considerable culture.

Stokovski – who spelt his name with a 'v' in Ohio for euphonic clarity – stayed in Cincinnati for three years and attracted national attention for the quality and content of his concerts, which included the US première of Elgar's second symphony (he maintained that the English composer divulged to him the amorous secret of his *Enigma Variations*). He formed an affinity with Rachmaninov and was featured in *Musical America* beneath the headline 'Leopold Stokovski – Thinker, Philosopher and Musician'; the adulatory profile was written by Arthur Judson, who became his concert agent and manager of his orchestra.

He did not get round to marrying the much-travelled Olga until April 1911, when America thrilled to news of their romance and the bride gushed to a St Louis reporter that 'Mr Stokowski is the greatest conductor in the world'. They honeymooned in Munich, where both liked to spend the summers, absorbing new currents of music. Olga gave up her international career at Stokowski's insistence to play the social role of conductor's wife and look after their daughter, Sonia. The marriage lasted twelve years and produced additional career advantages for the ambitious conductor.

Stokowski left Cincinnati in 1912 after a public brawl with the board and, heading for Europe, stopped in Philadelphia where Olga had connections and the orchestra was suffering under an abrasive and licentious German, Karl Pohlig. Stokowski took his job and Pohlig had to be paid off with a year's wages when he sued for breach of contract. The settlement was eased by a discreet contribution from Olga's friend, Miss Dehon. Cincinnati's offended manager, meanwhile, informed New York's senior music critic, Henry Edward Krehbiel, that Stokowski was 'a nervous, hysterical young fellow' of no great promise. Krehbiel, Mahler's chief tormentor, wrote off Stokowski as 'a young nincompoop'. Musical dialogue in turn-of-century America was conducted with bare knuckles. It was a Darwinian environment in which principled men perished and the morally flexible waxed exceedingly rich.

On arriving in Philadelphia, Stokowski adjusted his accent several degrees to the east and Olga prattled about 'the Slav in my husband'. He took over a demoralized ensemble and infused it with new players and strict discipline. Although too suave and self-conscious to stoop to outright brutality, he could be severe to the point of sadism. Mischa Mischakoff, who later led Toscanini's NBC orchestra, recalled how Stokowski, when unhappy with the timbre of the strings, would make each violinist play the passage on his own:

> No-one imagined that he would make the concertmaster play as well. That would be too humiliating. You couldn't take the chance that he would mess up the passage in front of the whole orchestra.
> He arrived at my chair and said: 'Mischakoff, I would like you to play.' I played perfectly, of course, and he turned back to the orchestra. I said, 'Excuse me Maestro, did you like the way I played this passage?' He said, 'Yes, it was fine, Mischakoff.' I said, 'I'm very glad you liked it, Maestro, because it's the last note you're every going to hear me play.' I packed my fiddle, walked out and left Philadelphia on the next train.

Within three years Stokowski had created an orchestra that was the envy of nearby New York. Its sound was rich and luxuriant, with the emphasis on an unbroken, continuously flowing musical line. He would go to the expense of hiring extra brass and wind players to cover passages where others had to breathe. However, he allowed fiddlers to bow as they pleased, rather than enforcing the uniform motion beloved by drillmasters. This freedom of expression, he said, released the fantasy and passion in his men.

Having improved the orchestra beyond recognition, he turned to the audiences and treated them to lectures on proper conduct and comportment at concerts. He began lacing their programmes with such novelties and oddities as Schoenberg's chamber symphony, Florent Schmitt's Viennese Rhapsody and Skryabin's Divine Poem, harbingers of his future schemes. At the unfamiliar emergence of Schoenberg's dissonances, there were disturbances in the hall. Stokowski stopped the music, walked off and, when silence was restored, returned to play the piece again from the beginning. His eye was ever on the press box.

In his self-absorption, he wanted more fame than music could provide. He had observed the American character and noticed its weakness for the spectacular. In March 1916 he launched a stunt of which Barnum himself would have been proud. Back in the summer of 1910 in Munich, he had watched the ailing Mahler score the triumph of his shortened life with the gargantuan eighth symphony, nicknamed the Symphony of a Thousand for its massed forces. Stokowski acquired rights for its first American performance and told his stunned paymasters in Philadelphia that he would conduct it three times there and a fourth in New York. It took six weeks to build a stage for his army and six months to rehearse the various choral sections. He brought together an orchestra of 110 players, three choral groups of 950 singers and eight vocal soloists – a symphony, in sum, of 1,068 participants. Advance publicity aroused a torrent of expectation and fifty-cent tickets changed hands at 200 times their face value. The number of performances was increased to nine and still demand was not sated.

At the première, there was a storm of approval. 'Every one of the thousands in the great building was standing, whistling, cheering and applauding, when Leopold Stokowski, his collar wilted, his right arm weary, but smiling his boyish smile, finally turned to the audience . . .' The acclaim in New York was equivalent. Reports of the concert blasted news of Verdun off the front pages and turned Stokowski into a national celebrity. He could have had any orchestra (or female music fan) in the land and was pursued by several, yet he remained loyal to Philadelphia (if not to Olga) for two decades and more.

He followed the triumph that same year with Richard Strauss's bloated Alpine Symphony, Mahler's *Das Lied von der Erde* and the first performance anywhere of Max Bruch's concerto for two pianos. He produced his own transcriptions of Bach pieces and popularized them with younger listeners. Before presenting Saint-Saëns' *Carnival des Animaux* at a children's concert, he led in, to squeals of delight, three live elephants, a donkey, three ponies and a camel. The conductor had turned circus-master for the afternoon.

But beyond his sensationalism and headline-seeking lay a missionary devotion to proselytizing classical music among new audiences, and new music among committed concertgoers. The catalogue of American and world premières given by Leopold Stokowski is unmatched by any conductor in history. It extends alphabetically from Amfiteatrov to Zemachson, and generationally from Sibelius symphonies to acrid poems by Henze. No conductor did more for his composing contemporaries. Stravinsky, living in poverty and exile, received three cheques of $1,000 each from Stokowski, purportedly acting on behalf of an anonymous benefactress. In this instance, Miss Dehon was not involved: the gift came out of his own pocket. When Andrzej Panufnik fled Stalinist Poland, Stokokwski sent an emissary to bring him to America and, although he declined, performed his music repeatedly. At 83 years old he unveiled Charles Ives' wild and wondrous fourth symphony, at 91 he introduced the 28th symphony by the reclusive Englishman, Havergal Brian. His curiosity about music was undiminished and his ability to attract public attention unquenched. Although he sought fame for its own sake, he shared it selflessly with the cause that lay closest to his heart. He shunned intimacy or conflict with colleagues and ended personal friendships abruptly when their usefulness expired. He was a loner. The greatest empathy he ever aroused within the profession came from Glenn Gould, the brilliant Canadian pianist who withdrew from concerts at an early age into nightbound studio isolation.

Stokowski's wives rarely knew where he was to be found. He hid from the world behind two Philadelphia females who became attached to him as teenaged groupies and guarded him to his death. Obsessed with public image, he was ruthlessly protective of his privacy and slept with two loaded Colt–45s by his bed. He arranged two of his divorces with extreme discretion and was visibly distressed at the messy tug-of love with his litigious third spouse, Gloria Vanderbilt (subject of a best-selling biography entitled *Poor Little Gloria, Happy at Last*). What the public saw, was a man apart. 'Leopold Stokowski was a demi-god in America,' noted the cellist Gregor Piatigorsky, and his very existence was an affront to Toscanini, who was the only God. The Italian resented his record and radio popularity and blocked him whenever an opportunity arose. So long as Stokowski remained in Philadelphia, however, he was invincible. What prompted him finally to leave was his unslaked thirst for fame and love. There were limits to the satisfactions a single city could bestow, even when he took its players on a trail-blazing trans-continental tour, the first by a US orchestra.

Having inaugurated modern opera in America with Berg's *Wozzeck* he tried to form an opera company but could not raise funds in the Great Depression. Orchestral backers were outraged when he taught junior audiences, organized into a Youth League, to chant the Communist hymn, the Internationale. One day in a central square he gave a concert of waltzes with two hundred unemployed musicians to advertise their desperate plight.

In 1936 he shared his podium with Eugene Ormandy and two years later yielded it forever as the lure of mass appeal beckoned. He made his film debut in a variety show, *The Big Broadcast of 1937*, followed it with an orchestral epic *100 Men and a Girl* and climaxed with Walt Disney's *Fantasia* in which Mickey Mouse cheekily tweaked the conductor's tails. Serious music had never been so attractively portrayed and untold youngsters were drawn to Beethoven, Tchaikovsky and Stravinsky by the snippets they heard in *Fantasia*.

Disney was finishing *Snow White and the Seven Dwarfs* when he recognized Stokowski in a Los Angeles restaurant and proposed collaboration. Given the gulf of intellect and taste that lay between them, their venture was surprisingly untroubled – thanks to Stokowski's saint-like forbearance at script conferences:

Disney: What does the Toccata and Fugue represent?
Stokowski: It is a motif or decorative pattern which gradually develops more and more. Finally it becomes perfectly free. The theme, which comes at the beginning, develops more and more, with more and more voices and instruments. It is a growth, like a tree growing from a seed.
Disney: We might use Stokowski's face . . . let the lighting effect and colour change as the music changes. I feel there is a theme in the background in the music, there, with something into the foreground and covering it up.
Stokowski: [No.] That is counterpoint . . .

When the movie was released in 1940, Stokowski made the cover of *Time* magazine for the second time in his career, the cartoon mogul made a fortune, while the ingrate Stravinsky grumbled of the 'execrable' perform-ance of his music and the 'unresisting imbecility' of the film. Half a century later, the playing and the sound quality in *Fantasia* still strike viewers as stunningly vivid.

Stokowski stayed in Hollywood to conduct concerts at the famous Bowl, including a Veterans' Night gala with Frank Sinatra, but had nothing to offer the movies beyond *Fantasia*. He had shot his bolt in a single epic and was, by all accounts, otherwise occupied. Screen fame was not the only bait that had drawn him to Tinsel Town. 'Stokowski had it in mind to have an affair with [Greta] Garbo, and that's why he went to the coast,' said the screenwriter Anita Loos, at whose house he met the frosty Swede, whom he had adored since seeing her first talkie. She now became the only woman he ever actively pursued.

Eleven years into his second marriage, Stokowski was forever besieged by female admirers to whom Evangeline sensibly turned a blind eye. When Garbo rumours sprouted in the gossip columns, she ignored them until one of their two young daughters came home saying, 'Who is Greta Garbo? Everybody at school says Daddy is having a romance with Greta Garbo.' Evangeline presented an ultimatum: keep it out of the news-papers until the children are grown up, or else. 'I can't do it,' replied Stokowski. 'All right, honey,' said his wife, 'then we're going to get a divorce and if I find someone who would be a good stepfather to them and all, I'll marry him.' In November 1937 she got a decree nisi in Reno on grounds of 'extreme cruelty'; two months later she wed a Russian prince and Stokowski was free to court Garbo. He was 55, she 32.

He sailed under a false identity for Rome, where he told the conductor Massimo Freccia that he was expecting 'a charming lady friend, Miss Gustafson'. Freccia did not recognize her until the newshounds converged in hot pursuit. The couple fled to a villa in Ravello where, guarded by savage dogs and Mussolini's police, they spent a month at bay. In the mornings they were overheard performing Swedish exercises to Garbo's command: 'Vun, two, vun, two, Mister Stokowski vy can't you keep

Leopold Stokowski by Raden

time?' To rid themselves of the rat-pack they called a press conference, each appearing separately. Stokowski denied plans of marriage. Garbo said: 'I wanted to see some of the beautiful things of life with my friend Mr Stokowski, who has been very much to me [sic].' No pictures were permitted. The only photograph of them together is a paparazzo shot showing Garbo bowed beneath a broad-brimmed hat with Stokowski trailing several paces behind. 'I only want to be let alone,' she repeated. After trips to Capri and Pompeii they shook off the press and vanished. Two months later a car smash in Sweden propelled them back into the headlines. Stokowski was driving, neither was badly hurt.

Stokowski returned to New York in August 1938, Garbo in October, each to a separate existence. Neither ever spoke of what passed between them. 'I never talk about personal things,' insisted the conductor in his many interviews; Garbo gave none. Friends said she was the only woman he ever loved. They shared a passion for self-exposure, expressed in nude sunbathing and the very nature of their professions; both, at the same time, yearned for privacy. Garbo hid in darkness for half her life. Stokowski sacked his most trusted manager for allowing an unauthorized camera into his rehearsals.

Everything about their affair, including its physicality, is uncertain. 'Garbo was a lesbian,' says Stokowski's friend and biographer, Oliver Daniel. 'I very much doubt that they were anything beyond good friends.' An orchestral manager, Jerome Toobin, asked Stokowski about Garbo and received the reply: 'Jerry, have you ever made love to a lesbian? It's wunnnderful . . .' Another biographer, Abram Chasins, sounded out Sigmund Freud on the subject. He concluded that Stokowski was unable to give or receive sexual satisfaction and probably never laid a finger on the forbidding Ice Queen. His successes with women, wrote another associate, were 'purely drawing-room conquests'. The sexual allure was simply another chimera behind which he could hide. In his eighties, Stokowski dined at Daniel's home, around the corner from Garbo's lair. 'After dinner I took him down to get a cab,' says Daniel. 'Just then, Garbo emerged from her apartment block. Neither of them even acknowledged the other.' In Garbo's life, the episode was a prelude to homebound reclusiveness; in Stokowski's, it marked the start of his wanderings.

The last third of his Methuselan existence was spent roaming from one orchestra and project to the next, pumping forth new music but somehow unable to settle or find contentment. He set up two new ensembles, using an incandescent performance of Mahler's Second to launch the American Symphony Orchestra in 1962. He was associated successively with the NBC Symphony, the New York Philharmonic, Houston Symphony and New York City Opera, before enjoying an Indian summer of concerts and recordings with the London Symphony Orchestra in the land of his birth, where he died in 1977 and was buried in the public cemetery of the parish of Marylebone.

'It seems doubtful to me,' wrote his record producer, 'that he has been happy at any time since he left the Philadelphia Orchestra.' The world looked upon him as an ageing playboy and Hollywood cast-off and his great achievement faded into distant memory. The critical verdict was tarred with elitist prejudice. 'Mr Stokowski's interpretations of classic works are occasionally superb,' wrote Virgil Thomson to a reader in 1940. 'One often has, nevertheless, the feeling of having been let down by him. Of having been sold second-class goods in a first-class box. I do not reproach him for letting me down, but I think I express the opinion of a large number of musicians and of disinterested music lovers when I say that his chief contributions to the musical tradition are all of a technical nature. I agree with you completely, of course, that his showmanship has served nobly toward the dissemination of whatever his contributions to our musical life has been.'

The new music he promoted made its mark in the performance of less colourful men, while his own première recordings lapsed into desuetude.

Stokowski's name is scarcely respectable nowadays among highbrows. Yet the orchestra he created survives as a pillar of musical America and his impact on America's musical climate has been irreversible. One of his favourite sayings was: 'there is good music and bad music, not old music or new music'. It became a cliché that helped soften the Toscanini-led resistance to novelty. Even Fiorello La Guardia – the Italian mayor of New York who whistled Puccini arias at his desk and conducted the national anthem at baseball games – was obliged to concur. 'Stokowski's right,' said La Guardia, 'quite right.'

*   *   *

The stigma of Hollywood attached itself to André Previn as a child and never really left him. A refugee from Hitler's Berlin, he fled to Paris and then to the West Coast, where his father, formerly a prosperous lawyer, was reduced to giving piano lessons. A second cousin, 'Uncle Charlie', was director of music at Universal Studios and found gainful employment for the gifted Andreas orchestrating scores for D-movies and occasionally conducting them. He took private lessons in composition and started writing his own scores; he went on to win four Academy Awards, most deservedly for *Irma La Douce* and *My Fair Lady*. He was also playing jazz in bars alongside Oscar Peterson, Dizzy Gillespie and Benny Goodman. He wrote arrangements for Frank Sinatra and Judy Garland and quirky, sub-Sondheim songs with his first wife, the jazz singer Betty Bennett and his second, the melancholy Dory Previn (who spilt the secrets of their divorce in a hit-ballad and autobiography).

Try as he might to put Europe behind him, he was dogged by childhood memories of Furtwängler and Berlin and impelled by an innate seriousness. He met Pierre Monteux while on army service in San Francisco and joined his conducting class. Many of the musicians he worked with in studio were former symphonic principals who had come to California for the sunshine and swimming pools. At weekends they played Mozart and Brahms in abandoned school halls and sometimes let Previn conduct them. He was heard by Schuyler Chapin, head of the CBS classics, and introduced to an astute agent, Ronald Wilford. Previn was now over thirty with a row of Oscars and enough royalties from his popular music to start a serious art collection. 'I can't say I regret working in films. What I'm sorry about is I spent so long at it,' he later reflected. 'It was a matter of getting back to what I was originally trained to do, and what my lifelong ambition was.'

Wilford offered to book him with 'every catgut orchestra in the country.' If he could make them sound better, he might have the makings of a conducting career. He sold Previn as a Hollywood star with a classical streak until, after seven lean years with the rough trade, he took over at the Houston Symphony. Having covered up his Europeanness in Holly-wood, he now had to play down his showbiz antecedents in the halls of high culture. Concerto recordings for CBS confirmed his pianistic skills. His conducting breakthrough came on RCA in Russian music recorded in London, union strictures having made US orchestras too costly for the record companies. With barely a year's experience as music director in Houston, Previn was named principal conductor of the London Symphony Orchestra.

He had a galvanizing effect on the LSO, which had fallen behind its sister London orchestras in the unofficial league table of artistic merit and monetary reward. It was always a headstrong band, whose members numbered such individualists as the future conductor Neville Marriner and soloists Barry Tuckwell and James Galway. It also exhibited a robust assertiveness, packing Josef Krips back to Austria with a punch in the teeth and cutting off its last conductor and record contract, Istvan Kertesz and Decca, in a blazing row over who picks the programmes. Ernest Fleischmann, mastermind of its commercial revival, was kicked out as manager in a boardroom coup.

The choice of a new conductor was dictated largely by the size of his record contract and his potential for generating publicity. As far as his concerts went, Previn's opening year was 'very shaky'. He commuted continually between Houston and London, learning symphonies on the red-eye flights and performing them the following night. What he lacked in musical perception, however, he made up in public image. London in 1968 was in its Swinging phase. It was 'cool' to be American, young-looking and married to a movie star, Mia Farrow. Previn was lionized by feature writers and television producers.

He got himself on to comedy shows with the fast-talking duo More-cambe and Wise and filmed series of populist musical pedagogy, modelled on Bernstein's proselytic lectures. He was dubbed 'Mr Preview' by the satirical magazine *Private Eye* and seemed more at home in front of a camera than anywhere else on earth. The flicker of a red light transformed his dull countenance into a sparkling fountain of wit and bonhomie. Previn was besotted with television, to the extent that he made thirty-second peak-time commercials selling 'the greatest television set in the world', which happened to be manufactured by the company that made his records, Thorn-EMI. 'Would you buy a second-hand symphony from this man?' headlined a Sunday newspaper. Many would: his records sold well.

The LSO revelled in his exposure and drew an appreciably younger audience. Musically, it cornered the market in symphonies by Russian and English romantics, every emotion worn on the sleeve. 'British music is a predilection I've had ever since I was a student; probably I have conducted as much of it as anyone alive,' Previn maintained. He was hailed by Little Englanders for making Vaughan Williams sound as profound as Tchaikovsky and, on tour in Russia, for restoring cuts in Rachmaninov's second symphony. 'One of the most unforgettable events of my musical life was seeing members of the Moscow audience openly and unabashedly weeping during the performance,' wrote Previn in a sleeve-note. 'It makes the symphony undeniably long but I feel that its honesty, its power, its heart-felt lyricism can stand it.'

Some critics dismissed him as a first-rate conductor of third-rate music, but he won the uncritical allegiance of the leading record reviewer and none could cavil at the way he had boosted morale in the LSO. In England, said a TV producer, 'Previn *is* music.' He quit Houston and bought a home in the Surrey stockbroker belt, modulating his vowels to leave barely a trace of American argot. He even assimilated English musical terminology, speaking of bars rather than measures, and semi-quavers in place of the more explicit sixteenth-notes. He invaded Europe with the LSO, giving the Austrian première of Shostakovich's eighth symphony at the 1973 Salzburg Festival and taking up guest dates with major continental orchestras, notably the Vienna Philharmonic which commissioned him to compose something for them. His best friend was the solemn ex-Soviet pianist, Vladimir Ashkenazy.

What turned the tide against Previn was the parallel rise on the South Bank of the River Thames of the London Philharmonic under Bernard Haitink and the Philharmonia with Riccardo Muti, both giving Beethoven and Brahms performances of an integrity that the LSO could not match. Previn was now so busily airborne that he admitted to giving just ten concerts a season in London and not seeing his orchestra for months on end. The LSO felt that it needed a conductor of greater depth in romantic repertoire and in 1975 its ruling members resolved to get rid of Previn, underestimating his resilience. Learning that his contract was being terminated, he summoned a players' revolt that sacked the manager and elected a new board of Previn loyalists. This sweeping counter-coup kept him safe for four more years when, having served longer than any other LSO conductor, he was elegantly retired, to be replaced by Claudio Abbado. At around the same time he lost Mia Farrow, who went off to live with Woody Allen, but rebuilt his life with the Pittsburgh Symphony and an English wife, Heather.

His nine-year tenure in Pittsburgh was respectable. The PBS television hook-up that sweetened his contract ran out after eight broadcasts and Previn was consigned to a dreary food industry town and its picayune politics. He fell out with a new manager and pulled out two years early on learning that he had approached Lorin Maazel, whose family lived in the city. The affair was discreetly glossed over. 'To lose a job is one thing,' he said, 'but to keep your manners has to be done at the same time.'

Previn was evidently relieved to be extricated from Pittsburgh and to swing back simultaneously to the twin poles of his magnetic compass, London and Los Angeles. In a deal with his London manager, Jasper Parrott, the Royal Philharmonic, Beecham's last orchestra, named him music director with authority over all its activities, whether concerts or recording commercial jingles. In Los Angeles he rejoined Ernest Fleischmann, the manager who provided his first LSO dates, in a Philharmonic homecoming that would snuff out the last sneers at his lowbrow Hollywood pedigree. Previn was pushing sixty, an age to stamp his mark on musical culture. He had refrained from recording the Beethoven symphonies, saying, 'If someone goes into a record shop and asks for the *Eroica* and he is then given a list of everyone since Nikisch [*sic*] who recorded it, why wouldn't he pick some gigantic interpretation?' Now he was ready to face the summits and aspire, from the podium of two fine orchestras, to establish enduring credentials as a 'Great Conductor'.

His failure was apparent within two years and an embarrassment after five, by which time he had vacated both positions. The débâcle was public and, in personal aspects, perplexing. Previn was a gifted musician, much liked by fellow professionals. If he had brought just a glimmer of his LSO fire to the two orchestras, he could have sustained the myth he had worked so indefatigably to create. But the Previn that returned to Los Angeles and London was listless, lacklustre and limping along with arthritis. 'He's not physically strong,' said Fleischmann, 'we've had to protect him.' Conductors have performed brilliantly on far greater disabilities. The problem with Previn seemed moral rather than physical: he sounded like a burnt-out case. In an Elgar concert of the kind he used to swagger through, a *Times* critic wrote that he 'merely travelled blandly through the town like a hansom cab with the blinds down'. His digital re-recordings of Rachmaninov paled in comparison with the glowing LSO originals. London players said he was paying the price for overwork and excess travel. Learning scores at high speed had left him low in musical reserves when his physical strength faltered. He latterly claimed to 'spend about a month studying a score' before conducting it. 'I walk in the woods here but that's just to go over the lines – to make sure I know the words . . . When it's something I've done a lot of times before, I try to think if there's a new way of doing it.' The extra effort and imagination provided no appreciable enhancement to the music.

The tragedy of Previn, for tragedy it certainly was, saddened and mystified his former players. One of the more perceptive LSO string players concluded that the flaw lay in his personal makeup. 'André is one of the most talented musicians I have known,' said the player, who wishes to remain anonymous. 'The trouble is, he was too easily satisfied. He would work with us on a piece and we'd get to a certain point and give a really good performance. Then we'd come back to do it again and he was not interested in going any further. Among conductors, the great ones are always dissatisfied, always trying to go beyond. André, once he had done a piece, he had done it. That, for me, explains his decline. He had nothing to drive him on, so he became weary and limp.'

Leaving aside any possible medical cause, the collapse of Previn was indicative of a malaise that has decimated his profession. No matter how high his media profile, he never gave much of himself to an orchestra or public. In London it was as little as ten concerts a year, in Pittsburgh never more than 16 weeks, broken by frequent flits home. Los Angeles did not thrill to his presence, since his presence was so insubstantial. A year after joining the Royal Philharmonic, he surrendered the role of music director to Ashkenazy and settled for the lesser position of principal conductor. 'I didn't want to get into an uproar every time I saw on the schedule a conductor or soloist who, quite frankly, should not be allowed to grace our platform,' he explained, admitting his inability to control the orchestra's operations. He promised that his duo with Ashkenazy would invoke 'a new era in the London musical scene', a prognosis that failed to materialize.

In Los Angeles, he fell into a reverse trap when a strong manager relieved him of responsibility for decision-making. Fleischmann was a former conductor whom Previn called 'the best idea man and programme maker I have ever come across. He knows every arcane piece of music. He knows whether it will work and in conjunction with what.' Finding that Fleischmann was appointing guest conductors without consulting him, Previn avoided a showdown and watched the situation deteriorate until the manager killed off his contract. 'Ernest,' said Previn in an extraordinary outburst, 'is an untrustworthy, scheming bastard.'

'It didn't work out for the orchestra,' said Fleischmann. 'Here is this amazing musician, gifted in all kinds of directions. He earns the respect of musicians everywhere. Yet he always had something holding him back. I had hoped that bringing him back here would unlock that special spark.' The double release left Previn in limbo, guest conducting and recording as much as ever before but jobless and bypassed by head-hunters. 'He would like to be an elder statesman,' say friends, advancing various explanations for his early burnout.

The damage done to orchestras by absentee music directors may take longer to show through given the astonishing competence of professional musicians, who can get by with almost anyone on the podium. It is to conductors that the breach has proved most disastrous. Previn and Ozawa are cases of music fatigue. Less visible are the younger casualties who drop out from overwork and lose their bearings before they attain prominence. The umbilical cord that Karajan cut between a music director and his orchestra has snarled up and started to strangle the conducting profession.

CHAPTER 7

The Gremlin in the Garden

'IT IS ALL very well to say, "conductors are born not made" – but have we ever seriously attempted to make them?' This complaint by Edward Elgar in 1905 came as English music emerged from a 200-year creative desert to find itself leaderless. At symphony concerts, pompous professors would hack their way through Brahms like beaters on a grouse-shoot; the visits of Nikisch and Richter were islands of clarity in a mud-bath. There was no tradition, no soil, in which a native conductor might grow. After Mendelssohn's death and Berlioz's departure, British concert life was commanded by Jullien-type entertainers or glorified bandmasters. Singers were the star attraction at both opera and concerts; the quality of accompaniment was of marginal consequence. Only in Manchester, where Charles Hallé set up an eponymous orchestra for a community of German expatriates, did symphonic music receive its due. Hallé himself hailed from Westphalia and when he retired after half a century the orchestra experimented briefly with an Englishman before turning for security to Richter. Local talent was conspicuously lacking.

It was therefore nothing short of a miracle that thirty years later Britain boasted four conductors of world renown and several more of recognized ability. The seed of this fecundity was sown by the record industry, which set up studios in London while Victoria was still on the throne and exported its discs through the city's global trade routes. An infrastructure of concert-giving evolved around this activity, whether in preparation for an incipient recording or as live advertisements for the finished product. British conductors became household names in Europe and America, admired for their panache and versatility.

Open conflict between them was avoided by invisible demarcation lines of individual propensities. Thomas Beecham held sway over Haydn and Mozart, and the French and Russian repertoire, Henry Wood over late romantics and early moderns, Adrian Boult tackled Brahms, modern British music and Bergian brain-teasers, while John Barbirolli held sway in Italian opera and English pastoralism. Yet beneath this apparently civilized arrangement bubbled a cauldron of resentments, stirred by one man's determination to dominate all forms of music-making in the imperial capital.

Beecham's was not a violent tyranny like Toscanini's, nor a Mahlerian pursuit of unattainable perfection, but a very English autocracy that governed by patrician charm and bared its teeth only when thwarted. As a dictator, Thomas Beecham was benign, benevolent and, in most respects, beneficial to music. He was, however, unquestionably a dictator and long after his death, his mischievous goatee still wags a capricious influence over London's profusion of concerts and the fading fortunes of its premier opera house.

When Beecham bowed in, opera was strictly a seasonal pastime and the only concert series was the summer Proms, conducted in their entirety by Henry Wood, who ran them on minimal morning rehearsals. There was one central concert venue, Queen's Hall on Upper Regent Street, and two orchestras: the resident Queen's Hall ensemble and its offshoot, the London Symphony Orchestra, a bunch of rebels who balked at Wood's understandable demand to see the same players in concert as he had rehearsed that morning. London musicians were proficient, poorly paid and fiercely protective of their time-honoured liberties.

Beecham, in the course of half a century, introduced four additional orchestras and countless opera ventures. By the time of his last concert London was styling itself music capital of the world and boasted a richer year-round musical offering than any metropolis on earth. That was Beecham's bounty. There was also an equal measure of blight, the legacy of a capricious personality who crushed any competition and abandoned his orchestra and country at their hour of need. 'He is a music-maker who bows the knee to none,' wrote a sympathetic string-player, 'and whom all must serve who wish to work with him.'

Born into privilege – his father manufactured a popular laxative pill and was Mayor of the Lancashire town of St Helen's – he faced his first orchestra when the Hallé turned up for the mayoral investiture without its venerable Richter. Young Beecham, an aspiring pianist, volunteered to conduct. 'I have drifted into conducting because I am fond of it. It is by far the most enjoyable branch of music to me. I detest solo playing,' he told the local press. London presented a tougher obstacle. Unable to win the confidence of promoters, he booked a debut with the Queen's Hall orchestra, whose players were in playful mood that night and wilfully sabotaged his efforts. At the next attempt, he formed his own New Symphony Orchestra.

It was assumed that he was being bankrolled by the paternal pill-pusher, whose annual personal income was estimated at £85,000 (well over three million pounds in today's terms), but Beecham had fallen out with his father for committing his mother, who suffered from 'nervous attacks', to a lunatic asylum. Fighting through the courts for her release and divorce, he was cut off with the proverbial shilling and forced to seek finance from other sources. He moved in with wealthy American diplomats in Kensington and in 1903 married their daughter, Utica. Eight years later, after siring two sons and being cited as co-respondent in a high society sex scandal, he left her. They were not divorced for three decades when, in order to remarry, he applied for a quickie US decree on grounds of her 'extreme cruelty'. Utica said: 'I am the unhappiest woman in England. And the happiest. This is what it means to have been married to Thomas Beecham.'

For the misdemeanours of his first marriage he atoned with a tender devotion to his young second wife, the pianist Betty Humby, who became hooked on drugs and suffered a horrible personality change. To appease her irrational and often racist demands, he sacked loyal players and was alienated from old friends but, whatever Betty did, he would not repeat his father's crime. 'Sir Thomas resisted all attempts to put her away,' relates an assistant. 'She died climbing the walls in a hotel room in Buenos Aires. Only after she was gone could he finish the epic recording of *Carmen*, in which she had driven off the diva, Victoria de Los Angeles.' In his final years, he was cared for by a third wife, Shirley Hudson, who had been working for his orchestra in the accounts department.

If his marital record was unconventional, he was equally inconsistent with mistresses. Even as his messy affair with Mrs Maud Christian Foster, flirtatious American wife of a property developer (there was much inter-marriage at that time between the British and US moneyed classes), was being exposed in court and reported down to the last trivial detail in the popular press, he made an important new conquest in Emerald, Lady Cunard, wife of the shipping magnate and 'one of the most amusing women in London'. Emerald was eight years his senior, almost forty and, once again, American; he obviously feared English ladies and felt confident in the easier manners of Edith Wharton's *Age of Innocence*.

For thirty years he was true to Emerald after his fashion and she, in return, provided financial and social support for his schemes. They were discreet in company, never addressing one another by first names, but were patently close. Emerald was devastated in 1943 to learn of his secretive second marriage from the newspapers; it was the only time her daughter ever saw her weep.

Beecham affected to despise women – none, he said, 'was worth the loss of a night's sleep' – and was contemptuous of Americans. He plainly needed both species more than he cared to admit; and with both he experienced rare failure. His 1930 advent at a New York Philharmonic concert turned into an embarrassing débâcle as his fellow-debutant, the Russian pianist Vladimir Horowitz, took an entirely different tempo in the Tchaikovsky concerto from the one his conductor was beating. American players did not take Beecham to their unionized hearts, journalists did not appreciate his jokes and the only job he ever landed was with an orchestra in unsalubrious Seattle. 'Many musicians recognize his gifts as conspicuous but distinctly limited . . . "a talented amateur",' reported a senior US record producer. 'As for any real *culture*,' sneered Beecham on his return home, 'it will take them fifty years to discover what the word means and probably another fifty to absorb what Europe has had to bequeath them in that respect.'

Among British musicians, on the other hand, he could do no wrong. They had never known a conductor who treated them as equals, played schoolboy pranks, paid them out of his own pocket and excused his periodic shortage of funds with treasurable wit. 'Now then, gentlemen, do your *worst!*' he would urge as the baton came down, and the response was invariably spirited. 'In this piece,' he warned before confronting the delicate textures of Sibelius's tone poem *Lemminkaïnen*, 'you may find it a matter of some difficulty to keep your places. I think you might do well to imagine yourselves disporting in some hair-raising form of locomotion . . . My advice to you is merely, Hold tight, and do not let yourselves fall off. I cannot guarantee to help you on again.' By evoking an air of shared adventure, he put players on their highest mettle and won their affection and fidelity; such gambits fell flat with rigorously disciplined American orchestras.

'He aroused that excitement, that shiver down the backbone, that a hardened orchestral player gets less and less as he gets older. I always got that with him right up to the end,' recalled one of his veterans. In the music that lay closest to his heart – Haydn, Mozart, Strauss, Sibelius and the French – he would arrive at rehearsal meticulously prepared and players found their parts liberally amended to his specification. In less favoured works, his performance could be perfunctory. 'Well, at least we finished together, dear boy!' he loudly consoled his soloist, William Primrose, after completely losing him in the Walton viola concerto. Elgar protested publicly on being informed that Beecham was steadily shortening his First Symphony as he took it around the nation, shedding more than a fifth of the score before he was forcibly stopped.

He led his players inebriately around Liverpool's finest hotel one night, collecting its light-bulbs and dropping them from a great height down the elevator shaft. He tormented tenors – one found himself walking around with a placard 'I am a tenor' on his back – and submitted good-looking soloists to torrents of sexual innuendo, but his respect for orchestral musicians was conspicuous and lavishly reciprocated. They might be kept waiting weeks for wages, but many were discreetly helped when they fell on hard times. It is inadvisable to speak ill of 'Tommy' among men whose loyalty he commanded and who followed him to the ends of the land as he assembled and activated orchestras.

He filled less than one-third of Queen's Hall with the New Symphony Orchestra's opening programme of unfamiliar French works, but among the sparse attendance was the composer Frederick Delius, who hired the orchestra to perform his own music and invested its conductor with a unique authority. 'The simple fact is that Delius's music was written for one man only to create,' observed a player. Another composer drawn to Beecham's concerts was Ethel Smyth, a militant, mannish suffragette and intimate friend of royalty. 'Never in England,' she noted, 'indeed only in Vienna under Mahler, had I heard music rehearsed to such a pitch of perfection.' She persuaded him to conduct her opera *The Wreckers* and, by presenting Beecham's father to King Edward VII after curtain-fall, restored the conductor to paternal favour and fortune.

Beecham could now afford to hire the finest players and promptly forsook his NSO – 'he was something of a will-of-the-wisp', wrote its next conductor – to form an eponymous Beecham Symphony Orchestra that became renowned as the 'fireworks orchestra' for its incandescent cocktail of colour and noise. He could always get the best players, he boasted, 'and for a very good reason: they are *bored to death* where they are'.

The fireworks orchestra was extinguished in the course of his new-found enthusiasm for opera and he did not pick up another orchestra until mid-war, when he donated money to save the Hallé and the LSO, mistakenly assuming that he had earned the right to dictate their future. With the advent of institutional broadcasting, he made a bid for the BBC's salaried symphony orchestra, but lost out to the phlegmatic Birmingham conductor, Adrian Boult. Beecham, incensed, retaliated by creating the London Philharmonic with top players from the LSO, the Hallé and the BBC itself. 'Nothing so electrifying has been heard in a London concert room for years,' wrote the leading critic Ernest Newman of its opening concert.

Boult's ensemble, though, proved to be its equal and, when Toscanini came to town, it was the BBC he chose to conduct. Beecham scorned the Italian and allied with his antipode, Wilhelm Furtwängler, to earn himself occasional dates with the Berlin Philharmonic. He hired Furtwängler's exiled aide, Berta Geissmar, and piqued the Nazis by bringing her to Germany when he took the London Philharmonic to play for Hitler. He kept the orchestra busy for seven fat years by linking up with the Royal Philharmonic Society and engaging it for his own opera seasons at Covent Garden. At the outbreak of war he loftily disbanded the company

– which reformed independently – and announced his departure for America and Australia.

'My country declared a state of emergency,' he quipped, 'so I emerged.' Other artists were excoriated for abandoning the besieged island but Beecham escaped his share of opprobrium. History has been unnaturally kind to him and he was frequently mentioned in the same breath as the war-leader, though one saved the nation and the other merely his skin. 'I have in my lifetime seen two really great men,' said a trumpeter, 'one was Churchill and the other was Beecham.'

When he crept home in 1944, however, Beecham found himself unwanted. The London Philharmonic would not have him back and, at the Hallé where he retained an honorary presidency, John Barbirolli was implacable. 'If you let that man near my orchestra, you won't see my arse for dust,' he warned. Beecham was 65, broke and bitter. His former opera assistant, Walter Legge, asked him to inaugurate EMI's Philharmonia orchestra but swiftly disengaged when Beecham tried to alter its name and take control. Determined to have his own way, Beecham formed another orchestra, this time with patronage from Buckingham Palace. The Royal Philharmonic was his last creation and he directed it to the end of his days. In one way or another, he had been involved with all of London's five surviving orchestras and left the city with more music than it could sensibly sustain. The back-biting that persists between the orchestras is his undying legacy. Any well-meaning attempt to rationalize their industry has been dashed on the rocks of an immutable rivalry that Beecham engendered.

Away from the messes he made in London, he held on to strongholds in the cities of his native north-west. 'It was an unwritten law in Liverpool that the first choice of dates offered to guest conductors was given to Beecham,' confessed an orchestral manager. In Manchester, he 'shot down every candidate who was considered for the post of permanent conductor; meanwhile he conducted the Hallé himself'. He was outraged to lose the Hallé to 'that upstart Barbirolli', whom he had once employed, first as a cellist then as a junior opera conductor.

Beecham could not abide the success of a British colleague. Early on, he provoked the unflappable Henry Wood and was banned from the Proms, which he conducted only once while Wood was alive. Neither of these pioneers of British conducting mentioned the other by name in their respective autobiographies. The deceptively reserved Adrian Boult was not deemed worthy of his acid wit, which was increasingly kept for Malcolm Sargent, a showman whom he nicknamed 'Flash Harry' but cleverly deployed as a decoy. Sargent, a dandified womanizer who committed more public offences against living composers than any recent practitioner of comparable eminence, was a tacit ally of Beecham's and was promoted with his approval. Installed at the BBC in place of Boult, Sargent almost wrecked its orchestra. With Beecham, he remained on the best of terms and dined weekly at his flat.

Barbirolli was clearly a class apart; and when the Cockney ex-cellist succeeded Toscanini at the New York Philharmonic, where his own shortcomings were warmly remembered, Beecham's bile knew no bounds. He fired off libellous letters to the manager, Arthur Judson, and, on a celebrated Sunday in 1942, conducted the New York City Symphony at Carnegie Hall directly after Barbirolli's afternoon concert with the Philharmonic. Besieged by Toscanini diehards on his board, and fighting for a share of media attention against the NBC orchestra, Barbirolli felt doubly betrayed by a former friend and fellow-countryman. 'He is even a dirtier dog than I thought,' he told his wife.

By 1942 Barbirolli had run into trouble with New York critics and was being pressed by the musicians union to accept US citizenship. Desperately homesick, he obtained special permission from Churchill to sail in a convoy of 75 ships, of which 32 were sunk, and give a month of 32 morale-boosting concerts with the LSO and London Philharmonic. The Los Angeles Philharmonic made him a lucrative offer, but he opted for England and a vacant, poorly paid podium at the Hallé.

He arrived in Manchester to find a bankrupt organization with hardly any players, the rest having been mobilized into the forces or taken safe jobs with the BBC northern orchestra. Returning from the world's richest concert institution, he rolled up his sleeves and held daily auditions. 'It didn't matter if they had flat feet, as long as they had straight fingers,' he joked. Most nights he sat up bowing parts for the strings. Within weeks he had put together a new ensemble with a highly visible component of young women. In a matter of months the resurrected orchestra was a legend whose abilities were broadcast across the free world. As the Germans mounted their last-ditch offensive in the Ardennes, he took the Hallé to the Belgian battlefront and performed for the troops, playing twelve hours a day; 'and at night Barbirolli would not go to his billet until he had seen all his orchestra safely in their quarters'.

A steadfast and decent man – he broke with Toscanini after hearing him insult Bruno Walter – he fostered a family spirit and remained with the Hallé for the rest of his life, another 27 years. His rehearsals were intensive and highly detailed, which some attributed to a deep-seated insecurity, others to a virtuosic need to practise upon his instrument, the orchestra. He might abuse the players in rehearsal – 'most of you seem *incretinated* this morning' – but would join them for coffee in the break and offer the offenders a lift home in his car. Players were encouraged to bring him their talented children, whose musical education he would supervise before taking them into his orchestra. Michael Davis, the present concertmaster, is the son of a Hallé violinist; he cannot reminisce about 'JB' without tears welling in his eyes. Rodney Friend, another Mancunian discovery, went on to become concertmaster of the New York Philharmonic.

Belying the provincial location of his orchestra, his programmes were cosmopolitan and continually varied, as befitted a Londoner of French and Italian parentage with a penchant for culture of all kinds, not least culinary. He tended to prefer rich sauces and textures, arraying Elgar and Vaughan Williams against Beecham's Delius and weighing in with Debussy's *La Mer* instead of the French fripperies of his antagonist. Beecham longed to get his hands again on the Hallé, but Barbirolli barred him for life.

He was the only British conductor who matched Beecham in his impact on audiences and players – and not only in his own country. At the Berlin Philharmonic, senior musicians still carry the sound of Barbirolli's Mahler Ninth in their ears, no matter how many conductors have performed it since. A latecomer to Mahler, Barbirolli devoted almost fifty hours of rehearsal to the Ninth when he performed it with the Hallé and was amazed to find in 1964 that the Berliners had not played it since before the Hitler era. The response was overwhelming.

He gave more than 70 concerts in West Berlin in the 1960s, the first and only British conductor to impose his personality on the Philharmonic. 'John Barbirolli lived for music alone,' said its manager.

'This man whatever he touched, he was blessed by God,' says the Italian conductor Ricardo Chailly. 'In 1970 I had the fortune of hearing all the Barbirolli rehearsals of Mahler 7th at La Scala. I was too young to understand how great this man was, but the warmth, the humanity, were unique. He was going to record it in Berlin but died soon afterwards. This was his last Mahler performance. I looked everywhere at La Scala for a tape of these rehearsals but no-one can find one.'

Somehow, Barbirolli never attained Beecham's popularity or his aura of personal magic. He lacked the aristocratic mien, the flashing wit and certainly the moral laxity of his compatriot; perhaps also the crude ambition. He was a gentle, often melancholy, man: modest, home-loving and temperamentally monogamous. The street vendor who sold flowers from a stall beneath his window and exchanged a cheery greeting with him each morning was among the friends who gathered around his death-bed. He was very much a man of the people. Vaughan Williams called him 'Glorious John' for the splendour of his performances, but the man himself was mildly unassuming and widely underrated. He shied away from the larger-than-life glamour that opera, in particular, bestows upon its heroes and that Beecham acquired in such over-abundance.

* * *

Opera in England, insofar as it existed at all, was intended for the ultra-rich. It was staged by wily impresarios for wealthy afficionados at the height of the London season, when the landed gentry presented their daughters at court and hobnobbed with their peers. The crowning glory was a priceless migrant nightingale called Nilsson or Patti whom everyone flocked to hear. German and French opera gained a following of sorts around the turn of the century but attempts to impose on Covent Garden the kind of artistic coherence that existed in Vienna and Milan was resisted by their Ladyships who ran the house committee. The so-called 'golden age of opera' that is alleged to have flourished before the First War amounted to an uncoordinated succession of singing stars – Caruso, Melba, Destinn, Tetrazzini – who happened to be alive at the same time, and in London between the months of May and July.

Beecham broke this restrictive cartel wide open. In February 1910, with his father's backing, he presented Richard Strauss's year-old *Elektra*, bowdlerized of its Biblical affinities by the Lord Chamberlain, and then kept going until New Year's Eve with 190 performances of more than thirty operas to complete the first full operatic year the country had ever experienced. Strauss and Bruno Walter were his fellow conductors, and the venture cost a mint, but it had the effect of making Beecham and opera inseparable fixtures in British social life. The prime minister, Lord Asquith, was personally involved in partially relaxing censorship for *Salomé*, and the composer Ethel Smyth made sure that royalty turned up for galas. The productions were rickety and many of the works were poorly performed. 'I lacked the experience or inexperience to gauge the capacities or incapacities of my artists,' Beecham admitted, 'and frequently mounted operas more for the purpose of hearing the music myself than for giving pleasure to the public.'

Nevertheless, Oscar Hammerstein of New York was impressed by the potential audience and built an opera house of his own within mezzo-forte cry of Covent Garden. It folded in eight months with losses of a million dollars. 'Where Oscar Hammerstein failed, Thomas Beecham is succeeding,' opined a conductor. 'He has proved in his latest venture that opera can be made a paying proposition.' Well, almost.

Unable to afford another full year's worth, Beecham brought over the brilliant Diaghilev Ballet from Paris, then took his orchestra to accompany their appearances in Berlin. The climax of their co-operation came in 1913 with the second production of Stravinsky's *Rite of Spring*, received in London with respectful bewilderment rather than the reactionary uproar it faced in Paris. He introduced *Der Rosenkavalier* at Covent Garden and, finding its governing Syndicate insufficiently appreciative, set up *Ariadne auf Naxos* and a Russian season at the Theatre Royal,

Drury Lane. Rescuing a poverty-stricken opera company in the provinces, he ran a *Ring* around the country.

The early summer of 1914 was the ultimate round of his Russian roulette – three operas featuring the astounding bass Feodor Chaliapin, and no fewer than fifteen ballets. 'It was not the first season of its kind but it marked an apogee,' wrote a young chap about town.

> Never had London known anything more brilliant: Chaliapin at his best, the ballet at its best, a wonderful chorus, and a superb orchestra (Beecham's own), with scenery and costumes that were the talk of the whole country. Everybody, [ourselves] included, poured out money to buy tickets; the auditorium was a sight unparalleled in Europe; the hostesses of London, great and small, kept well-nigh open houses. It was as if we divided unconsciously the end of an era. For, after a short entracte in July, the stage was set in August for the insane tragedy . . .

During the First War, with Covent Garden requisitioned for use as a furniture warehouse (in the Second it served as a dance-hall), Beecham toured his company in thirty operas around the land. After a grand finale at Covent Garden in 1919–20 with premières by Ravel, Puccini and Massenet, his entire enterprise collapsed under a mass of debt and legal complications arising from the death of Beecham senior and the suicide of a business partner. Threatened with bankruptcy and summoned by the Official Receiver, the conductor solemnly intoned: 'and for what He is about to Receive, may the Lord make him truly thankful'.

A British National Opera Company took over the props and persisted with his productions but was evicted from Covent Garden and replaced by short seasons of German opera conducted by Bruno Walter. Beecham, bouncing back, formed a short-lived Imperial League of Opera with funds from Lady Cunard and friends before returning to run Covent Garden's international seasons in the 1930s with his London Philharmonic Orchestra in the pit. In addition to two *Ring* cycles, much Mozart and memorable Rossini, he experimented with indigenous operas by Delius, Eugene Goossens and George Lloyd and hired the cream of continental conductors: Furtwängler, Weingartner, Erich Kleiber, Reiner and Knappertsbusch. Strauss came with the Dresden Opera to perform *Ariadne auf Naxos*, at which the German ambassador, Joachim von Ribbentrop, gave the Hitler salute in the Royal Box. Beecham turned a Nelsonian blind eye to political imbroglios, ignoring the ugly tensions between German refugees in his company and the Nazi singers he regularly brought over.

Covent Garden once again became the focus of cultural attention, despite concurrent initiatives at Sadlers Wells and Glyndebourne, and Beecham was unquestionably the engineer of its revival. 'On a hundred occasions I have been tempted to stand up and thank Providence for

Beecham,' wrote Ernest Newman, 'and probably would have done so, could I have been sure I was addressing my thanks for so demoniac a phenomenon to the right quarter!' For all its glitter, though, opera was strictly a seasonal attraction, sustained by upper-class whim rather than widespread demand. It did not become a year-round fixture until after the War, when the economist Maynard Keynes proposed state support of the arts to a Labour government otherwise committed to stringent austerity. A department store executive, David Webster, was installed as manager at Covent Garden with a brief to build up a company of British singers, chorus, orchestra and production staff entirely from scratch. Although the governing board remained essentially plutocratic, with a sprinkling of Oxbridge dons – high society, high finance and High Table – its aims were determinedly populist and proselytic: opera sung in English at a price the general public could afford.

Covent Garden could have had Bruno Walter or George Szell as music director, but wanted to avoid another power-broker in the pit. Instead Webster picked Karl Rankl, a former Schoenberg pupil and Klemperer aide of solid operatic experience and no discernible brilliance who would get down to the business of training players and singers without indulging in ego fantasies. Over the next five years Rankl's workmanship created a British company that rose, on its night, to international standard. Almost everything was sung in English, even by foreign guests of the calibre of Kirsten Flagstad and Elisabeth Schwarzkopf. The precocious Peter Brook became director of productions, Salvador Dali designed *Salomé* and Tyrone Guthrie directed *La Traviata*. It was a remarkably promising beginning, with more than a little glamour, assembled on a shoestring subsidy of £120,000.

'It was Rankl who established the musical side of the company,' confirms one of his singers, 'Rankl who breathed life into it and created a musical organism that wasn't going to wither.' Sadly, his conducting was not of the same durability. As pressures mounted, it became scrappy and hysterical, mirroring an insecure and humourless personality. 'What does it take to wake you up this morning?' he growled at the leader of his orchestra. 'Beecham's Pills,' retorted the player cruelly.

Rankl's achievements were at once underlined and overshadowed by the arrival of Erich Kleiber, who demonstrated that Covent Garden was now capable of an outstanding *Rosenkavalier* and *Wozzeck* – given the right conductor. Kleiber himself demanded too much money for the job and there was a three-year interlude while Rankl was sent shamefully packing to Scotland (and later Australia) and Barbirolli, Rudolf Kempe and Benjamin Britten were considered as potential successors. Webster kept the show on the road and in the 1954–55 winter staged three major premières: Michael Tippett's first opera, *A Midsummer Marriage*,

Britten's *Turn of the Screw* and William Walton's *Troilus and Cressida*, the last ruined by Malcolm Sargent's indolent lack of preparation. Britain's composers were now gaining credibility and its young singers were heard around the world, objectives that had always eluded Beecham. Not the man to applaud when others attained where he had merely aspired, he carped to the foreign press: 'there can be no national opera in England when there are no composers and no singers. To talk of national British opera is pure humbug.' Beecham's war on the rebuilders of Covent Garden revealed the coarser aspects of his machiavellian nature. Denied a role at the house he once half-owned, he first issued a writ for the return of his stage sets. Lawyers assured the company it owed him nothing and the litigant withdrew.

His next assaults were more insidious. He began alleging corruption at Covent Garden by a pederastic clique, led by Webster whom he described as 'that homosexual haberdasher' – each of the ten syllables drawled with malice. The house had become 'a bugger's opera' and 'Twilight of the Sods'. Britten, its outstanding composer, was 'homo, sweet homo' and other reckless epithets. His slanders were not just intemperate but downright dangerous. Homosexual conduct was as much an imprisonable offence as it had been when Oscar Wilde was sent to Reading Gaol; liberalization was some years hence. Webster, who lived in placid domicility with a lifelong partner, was questioned by his board and obliged to assure them of his propriety. One of the Covent Garden directors later resigned, promising to uproot unnatural vice in the opera house. Beecham's witch-hunt had begun to work.

The other flank of his offensive was xenophobic. Having once done so much to popularize French, Russian and German art, he now resorted to the rhetoric of small-minded chauvinism. 'I say the Italians, the French, the Germans and other countries would not dare to put a foreigner in charge of a national institution. We put them in everywhere and not a voice is raised,' he told a London literary luncheon. 'We proclaimed to the world that we could not govern our national institutions. Covent Garden is the laughing-stock of the world!' At the 1949 conference of the Incorporated Society of Musicians he railed against 'the strange and un-English way of doing things' at Covent Garden, adding 'I don't think the word "racket" is out of place.'

With some sympathy for his genuine grievance at being shut out – 'they never came near me!' he moaned – and with astute timing, Webster offered him the olive branch of a *Meistersinger* and the opera of his choice for the 1951 Festival of Britain. Beecham picked Michael Balfe's *Bohemian Girl*, a long-forgotten and swiftly forgettable nineteenth-century hit. He was out of tune with the times.

His outrage was assuaged temporarily until Covent Garden installed yet another foreigner as music director. Rafael Kubelik, the outstanding Czech conductor, had emigrated after the Communist putsch and sought refuge in London. Idealistic to the point of naïvety and gifted beyond measure – as befitted a son of the dazzling but improvident violinist Jan Kubelik – he was a man of principle and a stranger to compromise. 'If a musician doesn't fight for freedom,' he once said, 'he is a coward and a deserter to the human family. Music is a force for good. Mahler had a mission to fight for the good in mankind. I play only what I feel is important to society, to the community.' He passed up a chance to fill Boult's shoes at the BBC in favour of a finer orchestra in Chicago – only to endure three years of strife with the city's omnipotent music critic, Claudia Cassidy, who abominated his attachment to new music.

Back in London, his performance of *Katya Kabanova* at Sadler's Wells brought Janáček into the British repertory and won him the confidence of Covent Garden, though some feared he was too guileless and too good to last. On Rankl's foundations and with Kempe and Giulini as guest conductors, he brought the house to a consistent international standard, comparable to the Met. 'Rafael Kubelik was responsible for an *Otello* during autumn 1955 which caused virtually a change of mind in public and critics about the possibilities of the young company,' wrote an insider. He had the confidence to sack Tito Gobbi from *Otello* when the Italian star turned up late and to promote in-house talent, giving Joan Sutherland her first major role in Poulenc's *Dialogue of the Carmelites*. His production of *The Trojans*, the first integral performance of Berlioz's masterpiece, won acclaim for the Canadian tenor Jon Vickers alongside a local soprano, Amy Shuard.

Kubelik was weak when it came to decision-making – described as 'the velvet hand in the velvet glove' – and hyper-sensitive to external criticism. Beecham waited until his Achilles heel was exposed, then struck with wicked precision.

Press coverage of the company's first ten-year report had stung Kubelik into issuing an unnecessary reply in *The Times*, calling on critics to 'ignore the snobs and instead fight for communion between the British public and British composers and singers'. His challenge gave Beecham the opening to write to the newspaper, like the crustiest of retired colonels, with a virulence he had stored for a decade.

'In defiance of all common sense [Covent Garden] engaged as musical director a foreigner,' he began, harking back to Rankl. 'After the departure of this gentleman from the London scene there followed an interregnum during which the misguided directors had plenty of time and opportunity to select some Englishman of musical attainment and general culture to meet this supreme need. Now we have another foreigner in charge . . .'

Kubelik, deeply hurt, shot off a resignation letter to Covent Garden and *The Times*: 'I learned that my status as a foreigner might be regarded as a handicap to creating a British national opera. Feeling that my person could be a serious obstacle to the successful achievement of this noble goal, I prefer to resign as musical director.' A statement of support from the board stayed his hand and the letter never appeared, but Beecham's skulduggery had soured his enthusiasm and he refused to renew his contract. 'I don't remember why I left,' he said years later. 'Perhaps I made a mistake. Fate is strange.'

He went on to run an excellent orchestra at Bavarian Radio and briefly enter the Met as music director in 1973. In latter years he became one of the most beloved of guest conductors until arthritis and heart disease forced him to retire at 70. 'Let me back, I want to die out there!' he begged as they carried him from the Munich podium after he collapsed in a Bruckner Ninth. Vaclav Havel's 'velvet revolution' brought him bounding out of invalidity to conduct an emotional account of Smetana's *Ma Vlast* in the centre of Prague on the day of the first free election. 'Only conscience,' he once said, 'can produce great art.'

With typical gaiety, Beecham offered to take over *The Trojans* after Kubelik had left and, with hypocritical alacrity, was welcomed back by the directors. He was nearing the end and ready to mend fences. At an eightieth birthday lunch, Webster was chosen to read out congratulatory telegrams from artists and grateful composers. 'What, nothing from Mozart?' said Beecham drily.

His last words to his wife, on the night he died, were, 'never forget me'. At Covent Garden he lives on, his bearded bust pointing out over the crush bar, a permanent reminder at every interval of evanescent glories and present shortcomings. Having finally attained world status, Covent Garden might have afforded to forget the flickering memories of his transient seasons and address itself to the future. Yet the more it flourished as an international house, the greater were its difficulties in a society unwilling to lavish large amounts of tax revenue on the performing arts. By 1990 Covent Garden was collaring one-tenth of the national arts budget, and stridently demanding more. The cost of star-studded opera had run riotously out of reason.

'Would the Royal Opera work better if it were to return to a limited season of international opera each year?' asked an editorial in *Opera* magazine, uttering the hitherto unthinkable as opera in London faced its bleakest winters since the War. Closure at Covent Garden was imminent and a sense of regression was inescapable. Thirty years after Beecham's death the old reprobate's shimmering pipe-dream of a national opera house of international standing remained elusive as Covent Garden sank ever deeper into a mire that was still partly of his making.

* * *

Kubelik's successor as music director at Covent Garden was a fierce taskmaster whom musicians nicknamed the Screaming Skull. He dispelled the dream of opera in English, matched his singers against the best in the world and brought about the supreme decade in the company's life – and his own.

Georg Solti never wanted the job. He had been running opera houses in Munich and Frankfurt for 15 years and was about to start a well-paid symphonic career with the Los Angeles Philharmonic. Arriving on the West Coast, however, he found that the board had appointed an associate conductor, Zubin Mehta, without consulting him and instantly resigned. Before returning to Europe he paid a courtesy call on the octogenarian Bruno Walter, who virtually ordered him back to opera. 'You have to do it,' said Walter. 'If a generation drops out after ours, the opera tradition won't be kept. You must do it.'

The sense of duty that took him to Covent Garden was outraged by the easy-going ambience he found there. 'I came from the German theatre where the *Generalmusikdirektor* is a Tsar,' he recalled. 'No-one said to me, No. I came here and suddenly you can't do this, you can't do that. I wanted discipline, precision. Opera is a military operation. They called me "the Prussian" – me, a Hungarian Jew.' They called him other, less complimentary names. A cabbage was thrown on to the stage one night painted with the words 'Solti must go!' The same slogan was daubed on the windscreen of his car. There were anti-semites about who wished him harm; the mild-mannered staff conductor Reginald Goodall was a Mosleyite Fascist and had to be moved.

Solti felt ill at ease with the English upper classes who ran the opera house and was coached by his Swiss wife, Hedi, on how to take tea with them. For all his outward assertiveness, he needed constant reassurance from the chairman, Lord Drogheda, a newspaper publisher whose wife was a piano pupil of one of his Hungarian friends. Drogheda championed his cause against Webster's indifference and the grumbles of his staff. 'There may be a few bloody noses from time to time,' said the chairman, 'but I would rather that, than everything being slightly or more than slightly below par.'

'My English life is entirely Lord Drogheda's making,' confirmed Solti. Only the chairman's determination stopped him from leaving after three years, unhappy at the lack of facilities, the hostile atmosphere and a feeling that Covent Garden was not doing enough to promote his name. He was unsettled by the nagging insecurity of the permanently homeless.

His life had been a sequence of nomadic vicissitudes, with a few lucky breaks. A penniless pianist at Budapest Opera, he turned up at Salzburg in 1937 in the middle of a flu epidemic with a letter for Toscanini. 'Do you know *Magic Flute*?' demanded Maestro, sitting him at the piano and conducting him with a single finger. After a while, he said '*Bene*' and Solti was up and running.

Months later, in the second act of his operatic debut in *The Marriage of Figaro*, he realized he had lost the attention of his Budapest audience; news had just broken that Hitler was marching into neighbouring Austria. Sacked by Admiral Horthy's racist laws, he went to Switzerland just before the war to ask Toscanini for a job and was trapped there for the duration. A tenor named Max Hirzel, 'let me come to his house to coach him in the role of Tristan and I stayed there for a year and a half. He saved my life. I learned Tristan, he didn't.' Swiss police ordered him back to Hungary but he could not get a transit visa across Germany and managed to win a Geneva piano competition and gain a work permit. 'This was the ultimate humiliation – they allowed me to teach *five* pupils, not one more. I managed to survive on a bare minimum. As a musician, I had the advantage of speaking a universal language.' He kept up his pianism – just in case – long after he became a conductor, and in his seventies returned to the keyboard to play public Mozart duos with Murray Perahia. 'Sir Georg underestimates his technical facility,' said Perahia. 'He plays very well. He's very brave.'

The war over, he learned that an ex-Hungarian, Edward Kilenyi, was in charge of music for the US occupation forces in Bavaria and applied to him to become chief conductor at the bombed-out state opera in Munich. He omitted to mention that he had only ever conducted one opera, the distracted Budapest *Figaro*. 'It was not for several years that Munich discovered I was conducting everything for the first time,' he laughed. Richard Strauss watched him rehearse *Rosenkavalier* and offered some professional advice. 'You enjoy it too much,' he warned, 'let *them* enjoy, not you.' Conserve energy, said Strauss, take it easy. 'Why do you conduct with *both* hands all the time?' Solti, a late starter in his mid-thirties, was in too much of a hurry to pay heed. He drove himself, and the music, relentlessly hard, his bullet-head thrust forward in the pit like a battering ram.

Christoph von Dohnányi, who played piano at his Munich rehearsals and rejoined him as a conductor in Frankfurt, remembers Solti as 'a very clear and straightforward man, uncompromising, tough. Solti was a great boss. He was strict, he was demanding, he was working very hard. You never had the feeling he would ask you something he wouldn't do himself.' 'I can think of no conductor in my lifetime who has *worked* harder than Solti to win the plaudits of maturity, and who deserves them more,' endorsed his record producer. Gustav Mahler was fond of saying: 'An artist who is a Jew is like a swimmer with one short arm – he has to swim twice as hard to reach the shore.'

Introduced to Decca as a piano accompanist, Solti demanded

recognition as a conductor and in a decade was presiding over a complete *Ring* recording, a grail that had eluded all of the great conductors. Solti repaid Decca's faith with a lifelong fidelity, remaining with the label in an unbroken partnership unique in the annals of recording. His name was made by records, and his records in turn, revolutionized the state of live performance. 'Because of gramophone records – not only mine but many of my colleagues' – you were suddenly able to hear a cast that was so good that *even in Crefeld* they could not do every night a different [unrehearsed] cast any more. It became a sort of catalizator that one had to do better-prepared, kept-together performances.'

At Covent Garden, he established a rigorous professionalism. 'Whatever one may think of Solti as an interpreter,' said a repetiteur, Richard Armstrong, 'one thing is unarguable: he was a fantastic opera house musical director. He knew all the tricks, what the priorities were.' As head of Welsh National Opera, Armstrong would apply Soltian principles. 'What was most heartwarming in my time,' said Solti, 'was that a new generation of English stars came on to the international scene, from Joan Sutherland to Gwyneth Jones, all my children. If I had any merit in this house it was this: at first the public wouldn't pay any price for an English singer. Very slowly we changed that, because it turned out that the young English generation were as good as any on the continent, or better. In the last 25 years England and America have produced almost all the best singers.'

Several of his vocalists had advanced under Kubelik, and Sutherland was, in any event, Australian; but Solti imbued the cast with his own confidence and encouraged them to shine. Bounced by Beecham from his big-band *Messiah* recording, Sutherland settled with Solti's record company and, when not conducted by her own husband, Richard Bonynge, recorded happily with her music director, making a cameo appearance as the Woodbird in his *Ring*.

Bewildered at first by his bluntness and barbaric accent, the singers gradually softened him up with their drollery. 'John, dear, I beat twelve here,' he reminded John Lanigan in rehearsal. 'Don't worry, Maestro,' said the Australian tenor, 'I never look.' On another joker, Solti avenged himself on tour in Tel Aviv, by having a rabbi thank the panic-stricken singer for having agreed to sing his part in Hebrew. A touching humanity counterpointed the relentless ferocity of his music-making. He could never resist the cry of a musician in need and many found personal cheques in the post when sick or disabled. He did not forget what it meant to be desperate.

'There was about Solti a streak of magnificent selfishness,' wrote one of his singers. 'Nothing else mattered to him except his performances and everything else took second place to them.' If it could not be done perfectly, he would rather cancel than compromise. He called off a high-profile recording of *Un ballo in maschera* after Jussi Björling refused to be corrected, telling the conductor, 'you go home and study your part – I know mine'.

Only a letter from the philosopher Isaiah Berlin induced him to continue with Schoenberg's *Moses und Aron*, which turned into one of the triumphs of the epoch. Its stark-naked orgy around the Golden Calf, directed by Peter Hall, provoked widespread ribaldry, and a shout of 'filthy brutes!' from the philanderous old publisher, Victor Gollancz. Solti was himself fond of female company. His first marriage ended in London and he remarried – after 'a violent affair' – Valerie Pitts, a BBC girl who came to interview him, and stayed. He was 52 years old, she 27.

His homelessness came to an end in a rambling house in Hampstead, where the centrepiece of his trophy cabinet was a framed letter from a minor civil servant removing restrictions on his continued residence in the United Kingdom. In 1971, the prime minister, Edward Heath, attended his valedictory *Tristan* and presented him afterwards with the insignia of his knighthood. The conductor who had made Covent Garden cosmopolitan had paradoxically become an Englishman. His account of Elgar's second symphony, recorded in a single take, was cherished by its concertmaster as the 'most immaculate' he ever played. On leaving the opera house, Solti took up with the London Philharmonic.

His primary attachment, though, for the next twenty years was to the Chicago Symphony Orchestra, which he forged into the most powerful instrument in America, giving more than 900 public concerts and making well over one hundred recordings. He earned a record 29 Grammy awards and auditioned tirelessly for new players, yet did not spend one night more than absolutely necessary in Chicago, where a suite was kept for him in the 'super-deluxe' Mayfair-Regent Hotel. He cut short one season to catch his daughter's birthday party in London and cut down his commitment to a mere six weeks in the orchestra's centennial year. Solti was no shirker, but his personal priorities were always uppermost. 'They need me – I don't need them,' was his feeling about Chicago. *Time* magazine put him on its cover as 'the fastest baton in the West'.

'The important thing is money,' he said, when asked for the formula of his success. 'Our musicians here are very well paid. *Very* well.' Solti became a millionaire and played the stock markets with virtuosic flair. His music-making mellowed, though his ambition remained keen. At an age when even conductors think of slowing down, he became actively involved with reform-minded Hungary and, the ultimate satisfaction, grabbed a share of Karajan's mantle at Salzburg after rescuing the festival in the summer his rival died.

His short-arm energy remained prodigious as he neared eighty years

old. The man who once impaled himself on his baton while rehearsing
Parsifal still tore into studying a score with such force that it had to be
sent to the binders after a few days. In Vienna he began recording the
most expensive opera ever made, a stellar cast in *Die Frau ohne Schatten*;
in Salzburg and Chicago he took dates for the end of the century; and
at Covent Garden he returned frequently to conduct a new production,
and testify to the summit of his achievement.

He had told the company on arrival, 'I have only one desire: to make
Covent Garden the best opera house in the world.' When he left ten
years later, the promise had been fulfilled beyond anyone's expectations.
With Vienna in disarray after Karajan's era, La Scala anxiously seeking
a saviour and the Met in a fiscal mess, Covent Garden could justifiably
claim to be the world's leading opera house. It had the singers, the self-
assurance and the ingenuity to create outstanding productions at regular
intervals. It was riding a crest in the inventiveness of British theatre and
borrowed its finest talents, appointing Peter Hall of the Royal Shakespeare Company as artistic director. It seemed to be on the brink of a
long-heralded golden era when Beecham's ghost began to walk again,
malevolently, across its stage.

'We all felt that we must appoint a British conductor,' decided the Covent
Garden chairman on Solti's departure. 'If we appointed a fourth [fore-
igner], it would be tantamount to saying that despite all the years of
operatic experience gained since the war there was no native-born conductor worthy of the job.' The insular seed that Beecham planted was
about to flower and in 1971 an Englishman was made music director,
regardless of whether he was the best man for the job.

Five contenders were considered. Goodall was ruled out on personal
grounds. Edward Downes, a hard-working house conductor, was felt to
lack charisma and went instead to Sydney to lead, unhappily, its new
opera house. Charles Mackerras, an Australian who earned his spurs in
the contrasting worlds of Janáček and Gilbert and Sullivan, was too
closely bound with the Sadler's Wells company (soon to become English
National Opera). John Pritchard, a gay favourite of Webster's, was content with his position at Glyndebourne. That left Colin Davis, hailed as
'the best we have produced since Beecham' when he took over a 1959
Don Giovanni on little rehearsal. Married to the soprano April Cantelo,
he joined Sadler's Wells and became music director. Then he hit the first
of several personal crises: 'I decided I didn't like anything in my life. So
I stood back and smashed it all up,' he said.

He fell for the Persian girl who looked after his children and suffered
torments while the Iranians blocked her return. The London Symphony
Orchestra took him on Asian tour, meaning to appoint him chief
conductor. Davis performed poorly and received only six votes in their

ballot. A happy second marriage and the support of the BBC's head of music, William Glock, restored him to the rails. He picked up the baton at the radio orchestra with sufficient flair to propel himself on a long recording career with Philips. Many still found him abrasive but Covent Garden, which had co-opted Glock on to its board, was confident that his personal foibles could be kept in check while his talent flourished.

Davis, now 44, confounded his supporters by trying to resign almost immediately. He had become mesmerized by Peter Hall and was distraught when his partner pulled out to run the National Theatre. He was subsequently bewitched, and similarly abandoned, by the German director, Götz Friedrich. A lowly bank clerk's son from the London dormitory belt, Davis was ill-matched with Webster's successor, John Tooley, a patrician operator with connections in the business and political sectors. Tooley was often called upon to smooth over Davis' differences with the Covent Garden board, cosseting the irascible music director through a 15-year tenure, the longest and least edifying in Covent Garden's modern history.

His reaction to press coverage could be highly emotional. 'Are they out to destroy me?' he wailed on reading early reviews and sobbed loudly down the phone at the author of a Sunday newspaper profile. At his annual press conference, he would sit with his back half-turned away from Tooley and let fly at innocuous questions. 'Why don't you take this job for six months and see if you can criticize afterwards?' he snapped. When a friendly writer summed up a season containing the complete *Lulu*, as 'something old/ something new/ something borrowed/ something blue,' Davis snarled: 'Are you accusing us of pornography?'

Mystic, intellectual, reclusive and self-absorbed, he was a misfit in an increasingly problematic pit. The orchestra, relieved of Solti's rigours, took life much easier with Davis. His authority was greatest in Berlioz and Tippett, whom he twinned ill-advisedly to open the Barbican, London's second concert centre. Box-office receipts were so meagre that the LSO spent the next five years fighting off bankruptcy. In the opera house, Davis got respectably to grips with a *Ring* cycle and in 1972 was invited to Bayreuth, the first British conductor to appear there. He was never asked back. In America, he became principal guest with Ozawa's Boston Symphony, where players admired his ability for getting the sound he wanted 'without insulting our intelligence'.

Conducting, he said, is like 'holding the bird of life in your hand: hold it too tight and it dies, hold it too lightly and it flies away'. So delicate and nebulous an approach to life was ill-suited to the hurly-burly of the opera house. Although one commentator hyperbolically wrote of the Davis era as 'the finest since Mahler's in Vienna', Covent Garden lost its bearings during his long tenure and fell victim to the tyranny of singers and producers. A succession of star vehicles formed the pillars of its planning and the house spirit evaporated. Morale sank and the orchestra went on strike.

Davis was disappointed not to have his contract renewed. The house meanwhile had lost its allure, and the position carried less clout and cash than La Scala, Vienna or the Met. Nine names, including Abbado, Muti and Barenboim, were apprehensively approached, and bluntly refused. Bernard Haitink declined three times before succumbing to appeals to his better nature. 'I did not think I was the man for it,'' said the Dutchman. 'It would drive me mad, it was a tremendous risk. But I was 55, and it could be my last challenge.'

A native of opera-free Amsterdam, Haitink never saw an opera as a child nor conducted one till he was past forty. He had spent his life at the Concertgebouw, transfixed by its sound from the age of nine and appointed principal conductor at 31. When a cost-paring government sought to cut its playing staff, Haitink threatened to leave Holland if so much as one musician was sacked. 'The Concertgebouw is a family,' he said, 'you cannot cut off an arm or a leg.' He led the orchestra for 25 years until falling out with a new manager and leaving in a huff.

In the early 1960s he also took on the London Philharmonic and for eleven years 'was the catalyst that changed the orchestra's fortunes', in the words of its vice-chairman. He was a familiar figure in London, though never a shooting star, and much liked by musicians. 'When he first did *Heldenleben* I adored working with him in the solo role,' recalled the London Philharmonic leader, Rodney Friend. 'Then one of the men in the orchestra told me had just recorded it with the Concertgebouw. I was terribly jealous. After the concert, I was sitting with some colleagues when Bernard came in. I jumped up and made some half-joking remark about the recording. He was so upset. The next week I looked at the schedule and saw we were down to record [Rimsky-Korsakov's] *Sheherezade*. He had never conducted it before but put it in as a compensation because he knew that I was hurt.'

What made Haitink the most effective of recording conductors was his utter dependability. Every performance was well-crafted and polished. The records can be replayed without irritating the listener with interpretative idiosyncrasies or flashy gestures. He tended to understate emotions, particularly in Mahler, but his level-headedness proved invaluable in reassessing Shostakovich, whose music had suffered the personal and political fantasies of previous conductors. Despite his workmanlike attitude and matter-of-fact remarks, his music-making was at times surprisingly passionate. 'He doesn't realize,' said Friend, 'just how good he is.'

Haitink underwent his baptism in opera at Glyndebourne in 1972 and became its music director alongside Peter Hall in a secure and strife-free environment. The rolling landscape and social exclusivity of the Sussex country house festival were no preparation for the dingy office and stingy paymasters he would find at Covent Garden. Friends warned he could be digging his professional grave. This may have helped make up his mind: Haitink does not lack moral courage. He arrived at Covent Garden shaken by his Concertgebouw rift and the ending of a long marriage. His message to the company was forthright. He would ban fly-by-night stars and base new productions on 'a family of singers and producers who enjoy working here and are willing to rehearse'.

He wanted to democratize the audience, provide more affordable seats, make opera accessible: 'It is against my nature to charge people *anything* to listen to music.' He signalled a return to founding values and opened with a *Jenufa*, staged by the Russian director Yuri Lyubimov, that was sung in Czech but carried supertitles above the stage so that everyone could understand what was going on. Only a few fuddy-duddies objected to the innovation.

Lyubimov was hired to produce a new *Ring* that would be toured around the country, but dropped out after a disappointing *Rheingold*. From that point on, the Haitink regime seemed to lose heart. Götz Friedrich was called back to restore the *Ring*, a safety-first option that promised few excitements. The new general director, Jeremy Isaacs, a television executive, was closeted in his office wrestling with negative balance sheets.

Instead of sacking the stars, Covent Garden blazoned the return of Pavarotti as the high point of a bleak season. Junior conductors performed without rehearsal. Seat prices shot up to £120; in 1949 the most expensive ticket had been nineteen shillings (90 pence). The 140-fold increase, compared to an average twelvefold inflation over the forty years, was attributable to the exorbitant fees of guest singers, designers, producers – and conductors, who earned almost one hundred times more per night at Covent Garden than they had in Rankl's day.

Haitink's dissatisfaction was observed in tetchy behaviour and rumours abounded of his imminent departure. He was among the contenders to follow Karajan in Berlin and took up a role with the Rotterdam Philharmonic, the leading rival in Holland to the Concertgebouw. As he helped plan a three-year closure while Covent Garden was reconstructed, doubts were expressed if it would ever open again as a year-round operation. The company had strayed too far from founding principles, and Haitink lacked the fire to inspire another miraculous revival.

Georg Solti was notably keen to exonerate his successors from any shadow of blame for the collapse. 'It's much more difficult today to lead an opera house than it was in my time,' he said. 'It's hard to get really first-class singers. Also, there are so few operatic conductors – ten at most in the top class – and never in history has opera been played in so many places. I am very happy that I don't lead an opera house today,' he said.

While the malaise was not confined to Covent Garden alone, it was proving critical in a company where resources were limited. In the hope of raising more money, the Keynesian vision of opera for all had been suspended and the stalls were reserved for a circle of highly affluent sponsors and their business guests, who were attracted purely by the promise of vocal display – the same audience that flocked to hear Caruso and Melba before Beecham began his revolution at the turn of the century.

Beecham had vacillated opportunistically between international and English opera, alternating in tune with public sentiment and the funds available. Committing himself firmly to neither, he left behind no substance for the future, merely the hint of occasional pleasures. A British opera of international calibre, the dream of post-war idealists, was reduced to beggary. Covent Garden had become its charnel house and young musicians looked elsewhere in the quest for creative satisfaction.

CHAPTER 8

Collapse of the Conducting Composer

COMPOSERS DROPPED OUT of the music director bracket early in the century as the two occupations drifted inexorably apart. One was perceived as spiritual and other-worldly, the other belonged all too obviously to the material world of power and wealth. The priestly part of the podium function, inasmuch as it survived, resembled the posturing of Sunday-morning televangelists, who preached saintliness while reeking of riches and, periodically, of vice.

Composers were permitted to conduct on ceremonial occasions and when they were stony broke or creatively fallow. Rachmaninov and Hindemith, Stravinsky and Britten, commanded respect with a baton without ever achieving positions of authority. The composer-conductor as a joint vocation expired with Mahler and Strauss. A handful of music directors plugged away at composing but neither Furtwängler nor De Sabata, Kubelik nor Previn, was remotely as interesting on paper as they were on the podium. It had become untenable for a musician to run a company by day, direct the show at night and husband his creative urges for the summer recess. Summer was now taken up by festivals where maestros earned their highest fees. Music had become a business whose directors were obliged to subjugate creative fantasies to fiscal reality.

Paradoxically, it was within earshot of Wall Street that the composer-conductor made his last stand before extinction. New York became, for the only time in its history, a mecca for serious musicians between 1958 and 1977 as two creators tested their radical theories on a willing public. One believed fervently that everyone could be made to love music – that is, to love him. The other held with equal force that intelligent people could be weaned from an addiction to melody and persuaded to accept an ascetic rulership – his own. Both left an indelible imprint on a new generation of listeners, and both ultimately quit on discovering that being a music director was snuffing out their precious muse.

America's oldest orchestra, the New York Philharmonic never held the nation's attention for long. Episodes of glory with Mahler and Toscanini were evanescent, and swiftly succeeded by longueurs with lame conductors. The Philharmonic held its place among the 'Big Five' orchestras on grounds of corporate magnitude rather than artistic merit.

From 1922 to 1956, it was managed by America's leading concert agent and used as a showcase for his soloists and conductors. Arthur Judson took a ten or fifteen per cent cut from most of the artists he engaged for the Philharmonic – on top of his managerial salary. From 1915 to 1935, Judson also ran Stokowski's Philadelphia Orchestra. He moved into media as co-founder and second largest shareholder in the Columbia Broadcasting System (CBS), where he steered music programmes towards the interests of his clients. It took a trust-busting investigation in Washington to loosen Judson's stranglehold on the music America was allowed to hear.

Players in the New York Philharmonic had no say in what they performed and with whom. Decisions were taken by a board of dilettantes and implemented by their administrator. Frustrated to the point of sporadic violence, the musicians earned a fearsome reputation for slaughtering soft-skinned conductors. 'They have more nerve than Europeans do to expose mediocrity,' understated a recent concertmaster. Along with the half-baked and the merely hopeful, several fine conductors were brutally treated and others took heed and kept clear of Manhattan. John Barbirolli was given so rough a ride that he risked the real danger of U-boats to regain the relative tranquillity of bomb-blitzed Britain. The choleric Artur Rodzinski sacked fourteen players on arrival and was reputed to carry a revolver in his back pocket at all times; he was sent packing after wrecking Judson's office, not without provocation. Otto Klemperer was crushed; Bruno Walter ran off to the West Coast; Dmitri Mitropoulos was harried to an early grave.

Manhattan's ghetto of high culture, protected by armed guards from its populace, came to regard the orchestra – along with the tuxedo-thronged Metropolitan Opera – as culturally irrelevant. The Philharmonic, said the composer-critic Virgil Thomson, was 'not at the centre of intellectual life'. In almost 120 years of existence, it had never appointed an American conductor, nor sought to broaden its pinhead base among the melting-pot cultures that make up New York.

By 1957 it was disintegrating as a playing unit and losing large tranches of audience. Desperate measures were called for, and the board went haring downtown to search for star appeal. The target was a youthful polymath they had once pushed out of the Philharmonic for personal reasons. Leonard Bernstein was now a box-office hit on Broadway. He had scored heavily with *On the Town* and bombed with *Candide*, but was about to break all records with *West Side Story*, transplanting Romeo and Juliet among street gangs of Hispanic immigrants, to whom Carnegie Hall seemed remoter than the moon. His own ambitions, however, remained highbrow and when the Philharmonic directors came up with an offer while he was still on the road with *West Side Story*, he jumped at it. 'For the first time in our history we've got a solid bridge between the young people around the country and the Philharmonic,' rejoiced an orchestral violist.

Thirty-nine years old and elegantly dressed, Bernstein was fast becoming a television personality chatting about music in the simplest of terms; but his orchestral experience was minuscule. He had spent isolated seasons with the New York City Symphony and the war-torn Israel Philharmonic and guest conducted here and there, yet could not hold down a steady job. Raised by the rigid hands of Reiner and Koussevitsky, he came onto the market during the McCarthy witch-hunt when his leftist sympathies, homoerotic inclinations and racial origins rendered him virtually unemployable in America. Koussevitsky implored him to change his name, get baptized and married and clean up his act, but Bernstein went his own way and his openness cost him any chance of inheriting the Boston Symphony, or advancing beyond his pupillage at the New York Philharmonic.

Bernstein was a product of the Manhattan era that brought forth the novels of Normal Mailer and Gore Vidal, the paintings of Mark Rothko and Jackson Pollock, the theatre of Tennessee Williams and the concert works of Aaron Copland and Samuel Barber. 'Lenny was part of a New York generation that believed everything in the world was going to turn out well,' assessed his disciple, Michael Tilson Thomas. Although Massachussetts-born, he was generically New York Jewish: ebullient, generous, effusive, coarse, and as mordantly funny as Woody Allen.

'He identifies himself with New York,' said Yehudi Menuhin. 'Lenny is the embodiment, the crystallization of much of the life of New York, not only the Jewish expression but the various bases and the quality of the town itself.' He had after all, written its theme song, 'New York, New York, it's a wonderful town!'

He had burst on to the front page of the *New York Times* at 25 years old by stepping in unrehearsed, as a junior staffer, to replace the flu-stricken Bruno Walter in a national Sunday-afternoon broadcast on 14 November 1943. 'Mr Bernstein had to have something approaching genius to make full use of his opportunity,' averred a *New York Times* editorial, and he was swamped with media coverage. But almost fifteen insecure years would pass before he got an orchestra of his own – the selfsame New York Philharmonic.

Its players knew him as 'Lenny', the lowly assistant who struck lucky, and he would have to lead them by consensus and conviction, rather than by force. 'I don't know of any other conductor who has been called by his first name – and a diminutive thereof to boot,' he remarked. 'Of course . . . it has absolutely no tone of denigration. People don't understand this, because it sounds disrespectful, as if the musicians are not taking me seriously. But if that were true, how could we have lasted for more than one season?'

His guileless informality affronted traditional concertgoers who liked to cloak their maestros in mystery. They hated his high jumps on stage and his prefatory pre-concert comments. Harold Schonberg, urbane chief critic of the *New York Times*, faulted him repeatedly on points of technique, especially when Bernstein led concertos from the piano, an instrument on which Schonberg was a noted authority. He reflected that

> at the beginning of his career with the Philharmonic it could, with a great deal of truth, have been said that nobody loved him but the public. Mr Bernstein did not seem to be able to get good reviews. [His] extravagant podium mannerisms were derided. His interpretations were often called vulgar. He was accused of going in for cheap, external effects.

Learning symphonies as he performed them, his interpretations were showy and superficial – and young people adored them. The Philharmonic tripled its subscriptions under Bernstein. He was energetic, glamorous, good-looking, garrulous and rich, the kind of man you read about in glossy magazines and saw on the Johnny Carson show. He had acquired respectability by marrying an award-winning, faintly exotic actress, Felicia Montealgre Cohn, and raising a model family of three. He was the idol of professional young couples pushing their way up the greasy career pole.

He flung open his general rehearsals to the public and plugged local composers, himself especially. 'There was no audience-orchestra relationship when I arrived,' he said. 'The audience felt remote and left out.' In his Young People's Concerts, televised by CBS from Carnegie Hall, he cast himself in the role of proselytic teacher, a familiar figure from Jewish mythology where God's unwritten laws were passed from mouth to ear by successive venerated sages. His style, though, was anti-scholastic. To elucidate sonata form, he croaked out a Beatles song; pitch relations were explained in baseball metaphors; music was made accessible to everyone. Bernstein maintained he was sustaining a tradition he had received from Koussevitsky, who had studied with Nikisch, who in turn had played, under Wagner's baton, the Ninth Symphony of Beethoven. No higher legitimacy was attainable by a musician, whatever his methods. 'Nikisch is my musical grandfather,' he told a mystified Russian audience.

Americans who discovered Beethoven by way of Stokowski's Disney cartoons now watched their children turning on to classics by way of Bernstein's televized elucidations. His weekly audience was estimated at ten million. 'We don't always realize how important teachers are,' he began one broadcast, 'in music or in anything else. Teaching is probably the noblest profession in the world – the most unselfish, difficult and honourable profession. It is also the most unappreciated, underrated, underpaid and underpraised profession.' The pedagogic approach extended to his orchestra. 'Teaching is perhaps the essence of my function as a conductor,' he said. 'I share whatever I know and whatever I feel about the music. I try to make the orchestra feel it, know it and understand it, too . . . the whole joy of conducting for me is that we breathe together. It's like a love experience.'

This symbiosis of intellectual and emotional insemination defined his relations with musicians, few of whom would emerge untouched from his rehearsals. In the ecstasy of achievement, he kissed players of both sexes on the lips and wielded his sexual attraction to bend them to his musical will. He thrived on contact with students, returned perennially to teach at Tanglewood and founded sister-festivals in Germany and Japan. 'You make old guys like me feel young again,' he told the young players at Sapporo. 'I don't care who he sleeps with, how he dresses or how he talks,' said a Tanglewood alumnus. 'When he gets up on the podium, he makes me remember why I wanted to become a musician.'

For the hard-bitten professionals of the New York Philharmonic, Bernstein made music come alive again. 'I remember going on tour and doing Mahler One, a pain in the neck to take on tour – you don't get to the restaurant till half-past ten. But each night when Lenny did that piece, you wanted it to go on and on and on and on . . .' said a concertmaster.

Their confidence rising, the players came out twice on strike in support of higher wages and job security. Bernstein personally won them an extra $1,000 a year in guaranteed record royalties. In the course of eleven years with the Philharmonic, his technical deficiencies were steadily repaired or ignored as he matured into a conductor of imposing stature. Schonberg finally forced himself to acknowledge that 'without losing his natural flamboyance' Bernstein had begun to conduct big works 'in performances that had shape as well as colour, structural integrity as well as freedom within the phrase'. Stravinsky gave a 'Wow!' on hearing the *Rite of Spring*, and Bernstein eased the reprobate's return to Russia by performing the *Rite* in Moscow for the first time in thirty years.

He embraced Mahler's music with the force of self-discovery, befriending the composer's widow, recording the first complete symphonic cycle and painting immodest parallels between himself and a dead titan whose time had come at last. 'Mahler was split right down the middle,' he wrote in a hi-fi magazine, 'with the curious result that whatever quality is perceptible and definable in his music the diametrically opposite quality is equally so.' Of Bernstein, a Boston companion said: 'Almost anything one could say of him would be true.'

He was sensual and cerebral, moralist and hedonist, humble and vain, American and cosmopolitan, loving and narcissistic. He exhibited an 'intense love of life and disgust with life', a dichotomy he attributed equally to Mahler. 'I began to feel myself in direct contact with Mahler's message,' he announced, and the affinity began to assume the dimensions of hyperbolic self-delusion. Asked by a fellow-conductor for advice about Mahler's Ninth, Bernstein opened his performing score to reveal pages criss-crossed with his own markings and alterations. 'Mahler was a great conductor who performed eight of his symphonies and showed us how they were to be done,' he explained. 'The Ninth he did not live to conduct. This one,' said Leonard Bernstein, 'he wrote for *me*.'

Mahler, in the image created by Bernstein for his 1973 Harvard lectures, was a visionary who fought against humanity's rush to self-destruction. 'Ours is a century of death and Mahler is its musical prophet,' he proclaimed, seeking to find himself a similar role. He failed, however, to become a courtier at John Kennedy's Camelot, after causing a small scandal by kissing the immaculate First Lady while drenched in post-concert perspiration; he mourned the slain brothers extravagantly. Upon Robert Kennedy's assassination, he fruitlessly endorsed Eugene McCarthy's anti-war ticket for the White House and sniped at Richard Nixon's regime in his *Mass*, composed to inaugurate Washington's Kennedy Center. For his 65th birthday, he sent a strip of sky-blue cloth to friends around the world, asking them to wear it to show their love for him and their support for 'a mutual and verifiable nuclear weapons freeze'. Movie stars, bell-boys, beach bums and an entire Hungarian orchestra sported the blue armband.

Other causes he championed were Amnesty's campaign on behalf of political prisoners and the State of Israel's right to survive; yet he was not troubled by the plight of Palestinian detainees in Israeli prisons. He supported civil rights in the segregated American south and abominated the apartheid regime in South Africa, but appointed only one black musician in the Philharmonic. Whatever quality was 'perceptible and definable' in Bernstein, its opposite was equally apparent.

His social conscience took a battering after a cocktail party he and Felicia threw in their Park Avenue apartment one January night in 1970. The guests of honour were Black Panthers, ghetto organizers who preached liberationist violence, supported Mao, Castro and the PLO, and raised funds mainly by strong-arming white and Jewish shopkeepers in their neighbourhood. At the Bernsteins they collected thousand-dollar donations from movie-makers, furriers and trend-setters; the conductor pledged his next fee. This pleasant gathering was lucklessly infiltrated by the social commentator, Tom Wolfe, whose report in the *New York Times* coined the term 'radical chic' for rich people who got kicks from mixing with rough trade.

The *New York Times* went straight for the jugular in its editorial:

> The group therapy plus fund-raising soirée at the home of Leonard Bernstein, as reported in this newspaper yesterday, represents the sort of elegant slumming that degrades patrons and patronized alike. It might be dismissed as guilt-relieving fun spiked with social consciousness, except for its impact on those blacks and whites seriously working for complete equality and social justice. It mocked the memory of Martin Luther King Jr. whose birthday was solemnly observed throughout the nation yesterday. Black Panthers on a Park Avenue pedestal create one more distortion of the Negro image.

Bernstein, beleaguered by angry Americans of every shade and race, first blamed the Panthers for being irresponsible, then denied that the party had ever taken place: it had been a civil liberties meeting. Ten years later he named the real culprit:

> I have substantial evidence now available to all that the FBI conspired to foment hatred and violent dissent among blacks, among Jews and between blacks and Jews. My late wife and I were among many foils used for this purpose in the context of a so-called 'party' for the Panthers in 1970 . . . The ensuing FBI-inspired harassment ranged from floods of hate letters sent to me over what are now clearly fictitious signatures, thinly veiled threats couched in anonymous letters to magazines and newspapers, editorial and reportorial diatribes in the *New York Times*, attempts to injure my long-standing relationship with the State of Israel, plus innumerable other dirty tricks.

As America turned against him, he resolved to quit. Disillusion, says Michael Tilson Thomas who became his confidant at this time, 'set in when John Kennedy was murdered. That was followed by Martin Luther King and Robert Kennedy, Vietnam and the rise of right-wing ideologies in America.' The optimism of the 1945 generation had been sadly confounded.

He gave various reasons for leaving the New York Philharmonic. He could not face firing older players; he was running out of causes. 'I lack somebody to champion,' he complained. 'When I think back on the years of Koussevitsky, who proudly brought forth one Copland symphony after another, Roy Harris, Bill Schuman, Prokofiev, Stravinsky! He had all these glorious pieces. That period is over. When I came to the Philharmonic, I was expecting something like that to happen, and I find it so terribly disappointing that it hasn't – not really. I don't have anybody to champion – a movement, a group of composers, a school.'

He neglected to mention the most significant disappointment, in himself. As a composer he had ground to a standstill while conducting the New York Philharmonic. In 1965 he took a creative sabbatical and emerged with the Chichester Psalms, the most innocent and widely sung of his choral works. Bernstein felt obliged to defend its simple harmonic idiom in a mawkish poem that he published in the *New York Times*. He had failed to keep pace with the avant-garde, and frustratedly turned out twelve-tone rows to show that he could write them as well as any so-called modernist. Self-doubt is evident in all his work. Perpetually dissatisfied, he talked longingly of devoting his whole time to writing music that would outlast him, symphonies like Mahler's that would 'embrace the whole world' and change the way it thought.

Another nagging frustration was a persistent lack of recognition in Mahler's continent, Europe. He yearned to conquer the Old Country. With these aims in mind, he brought to an end, on the anniversary of Mahler's death in 1969, the longest music directorship in the annals of the New York Philharmonic. They gave him a motor boat as a farewell gift, but he never really sailed away. He still lived on Park Avenue and kept coming back to conduct. When the orchestra went looking for a music director twenty years later, Bernstein's was the first door they tried.

To follow Bernstein, the New York Philharmonic chose his opposite. No two musicians were more unalike than the sensual, extrovert Bernstein and the ascetic Pierre Boulez whose compositions and personality appeared austere and monochrome by comparison. One was voluble, the other soft-spoken; one fastidious, the other feverish; one conducted with his entire body, the other with the tips of his fingers. Bernstein revelled in big tunes, Boulez scorned them as 'nostalgia'. You had only to look at their scores to spot the difference. Bernstein sprawled all over the page, scribbling, inserting, erasing in a huge scrawl; Boulez wrote between the staves in a minuscule, meticulous script.

All they had in common was an aspiration to compose, conduct and instruct, an irresistible charisma and an intellect that ranged formidably across the woof and warp of western thought. Both could discourse compellingly on Schopenhauer and Kandinsky, Plato and Edgar Allen Poe. Bernstein was inclined to name-drop a catalogue of formative influences who meant nothing to his bedazzled audience. Boulez, according to an adoring assistant, 'knows more about art than an artist, more about literature than a writer'. Both were cultural omnivores who raided other disciplines to construct their most ambitious compositions, Boulez dipping into contemporary art and poetry, Bernstein into philosophy and pop-song.

After the sweaty embrace of Bernstein's gregariousness, New York readied itself for the aloof, balding Boulez, who kissed no-one and kept inscrutably apart. 'The Iceman Conducteth,' warned the *New York Times*. His warmer side was seen only by orchestral musicians, whose prowess he quietly praised. He was at his most convivial during rehearsal breaks, trading gossip over plastic cups of coffee. He was a good raconteur but lacked much humour and rarely laughed out loud from deep within. 'I don't think he has any close friends,' said one of his oldest associates. He never married. He had an Austrian companion, Hans Messmer, who occupied a separate apartment in the same block and was sometimes introduced as his valet.

In the podium, he was revered for an ear that could pinpoint a single false intonation in a hundred-piece chord. No less a rigorist than George Szell recommended him to the Philharmonic, while Otto Klemperer regarded him as 'the only man of his generation who is an outstanding conductor *and* musician'. Boulez conducted with merciless precision; under his command the Philharmonic played with enhanced clarity. 'What is important in the masterpiece is to take away the dirt,' he liked to say. He was the ideal elucidator of modernism and the orchestra acquired proficiency, and even a liking, for the shimmering sonorities of Debussy and the bewildering nebulae of Varèse. The wild abandon of Bernstein's Stravinsky concerts gave way to disciplined demonstrations by Boulez of a modern master's rhythmic ingenuity.

Bernstein's fans walked out on Boulez, along with many senior subscribers. They were replaced by long-haired Woodstock types who thronged to his question-and-answer 'rug concerts' at Greenwich Village and asked him about the meaning of life. He talked of reshaping the Philharmonic's programmes along the lines of Manhattan's fabulous Museum of Modern Art (MOMA), where Picasso's *Guernica* was a starting point for exploration rather than the end of figurative art as we know it. 'We changed the audience,' said Boulez happily. 'I wanted people interested in concerts, not only in social life.'

He refused to conduct Tchaikovsky, dismissed Brahms as 'bourgeois and complacent', derided Prokofiev as 'a very small talent', and banned Britten and Shostakovich as unforgivably 'conservative'. Any composer who had not 'felt the necessity' of Schoenberg's twelve-tone system was simply 'superfluous'. In Boulez's outlook, the main stream of music ran from Bach through Beethoven, to Wagner and Mahler, then to Schoenberg and Webern and, finally, himself. Yet he refrained from exploiting his position to perform his own music, conducting only two works in six New York seasons, while at the same time making few concessions to local interests.

'They have no-one in America as good as Hans Werner Henze,' he declared, 'and that is not setting your sights very high. A composer the stature of Stockhausen, they have not.' Such arrogant assumptions – modified later on encountering the high-minded music of Elliott Carter – counterpointed a deep-seated humility that was expressed in selfless devotion to an ideal. Boulez never sought stardom. His aim in becoming music director was not to gain glory but to advance a revolution. 'In politics you call this "entryism",' he explained. 'You cannot forever bark outside like a dog. So I progressively accepted positions of responsibility, to change not the whole world but part of it.' He called it 'changing the threshold of our period'.

He had begun the insurrection directly after the War, erupting on to the Paris scene by disrupting a Stravinsky concert with a noisy pro-Schoenberg demonstration. He then outraged the other flank of modernism by burying Caesar instead of praising him in a heartless eulogy entitled, 'SCHOENBERG IS DEAD'. He sought his own voice among the dreaded young devils of Darmstadt who conspired to change the language of music, which they felt was inextricably implicated in Europe's lapse into totalitarianism. The music of the future was being redesigned along the lines of Webern's serial codes by the likes of Karlheinz Stockhausen and the Italians Bruno Maderna, Luigi Nono and Luciano Berio. Boulez shared their aims and wrote his early sonatas under the additional strict aegis of the doctrinaire Catholic, Olivier Messiaen.

He worked as director of music for a small theatre company that had broken away from the Comédie Française and in 1954 started the Domaine Musicale series of new music concerts, directed mainly by foreigners. 'You think my idea was always to conduct?' he demands. 'Not at all. I discovered it of necessity because all the people conducting contemporary music were German first – [Hans] Rosbaud and [Hermann] Scherchen – and were of the older generation. For the music of my generation, we wanted somebody directly connected with us, so I began to conduct.'

He was over thirty before he performed outside Paris, replacing the dying Rosbaud at the Donaueschingen festival. At Baden-Baden in 1958 he directed, together with the composer and Bruno Maderna, the première of Stockhausen's ultimate Darmstadt creation, *Gruppen*, requiring three conductors for its separate orchestras. Although he accepted a position with the local radio orchestra, he denied being a conductor, never used a baton – 'it would freeze my hands' – and always worked with an open score, which he left clean of any personal markings.

Back home, he remained the *enfant terrible*, calling for the Mona Lisa to be smashed and the Opéra to be burned – metaphorically, he maintained. Burying his *bourgeois* origins, he wrote articles in the un-capitalized, unpunctuated style of the American poet e e cummings whose name he cited in the title of one of his works. Every word uttered in this mode carried equal weight, just as every note was equal in Webern's twelve-tone scale and all men were equal according to Marx and Engels. Such orthodoxies were far too ardent for most avant-gardists who, like the Greek partisan Iannis Xenakis, rejected the laws of Darmstadt as 'a kind of fascism'. French politicians would soon accuse Boulez of using '*Führer*-like methods' in his attempt to subvert democratic authority.

Having stormed the Opéra with *Wozzeck*, he was asked to submit a plan for reforming French music to André Malraux, the Gaullist minister of culture, who considered music a 'secondary art'. Lobbied heavily by the old guard, Malraux threw out his scheme and placed in charge of musical affairs the composer Marcel Landowski – 'a dim, inconsistent individual', according to Boulez. He had argued strenuously against entrusting the administration of music to any composer – meaning, any composer other than himself – and retaliated by going 'on strike against the whole of French musical officialdom'. He published a repudiatory diatribe, '*Pourquoi je dis non à Malraux*', cancelled all his concerts, forbade French orchestras to play his music and made his home in Baden-Baden among the Germans, whose language he spoke faultlessly.

Ten years of exile were spent expanding his performing repertoire and pursuing entryist opportunities. The editor who published his anti-Schoenberg obituary, William Glock, had risen to controller of music at the BBC; and in 1969 Glock appointed Boulez principal conductor of its symphony orchestra. He was the first foreigner ever to conduct at the Promenade concerts and drew crowds of youngsters to a disused railway shed in Camden Town where he performed the latest dissonances and discussed them with his audience late into the night. A wave of British composers, led by Harrison Birtwistle, Peter Maxwell Davies and Alexander Goehr, received a terrific fillip from Boulez's support and the climate he created.

He conducted *Parsifal* at Bayreuth and was picked by Wieland Wagner to lead the centenary *Ring*, in a formal renunciation of Wagner's Francophobia. The 1976 cycle, in a spare setting by Patrice Chéreau, was serialized on televison in weekly parts like soap opera, attracting Wagner's largest global audience. George Szell, who heard him in Baden-Baden, brought Boulez to Cleveland as his putative heir and introduced him to New York. Glock was dismayed when he took a second orchestra and Klemperer was scornful, but there was no stopping Boulez once he saw an opportunity to command the twin capitals of the English-speaking world. In retrospect, he failed: both London and New York reverted to traditional diets as soon as he was gone. Boulez, however, believed he had left his mark, 'like a trace of poison in your food', and returned at regular intervals to add another dash. Orchestras would always welcome a 'Boulez servicing' to brush the cobwebs from their ears.

By the time he reached America, his attention was engaged elsewhere ('in 1970 I already knew that I would be leaving New York in 1976') in plans to fulfil his paramount purpose. Serialism had got stuck in a rut and the language of music failed to advance appreciably beyond its Darmstadt vocabulary. Boulez was becoming convinced that the solution lay in computerized wizardry that could create an electronic soundscape to augment existing tones. 'A knowledge of how the computer works is as necessary to the composer today as knowing fugue and counterpoint,' he declared. 'I don't see any other way forward.'

He was unimpressed by Stockhausen's scratchy electronics and believed what was needed was a mainframe computer of such magnitude that it could crack the conundrum he had wrestled with all his working life. He dreamed a Wagnerian dream of a castle in which musicians and scientists worked together to forge the key-ring to the future. A prototype institute of this kind was being planned in Munich but Boulez needed one close at hand to realize his musical ideas before they ran out.

While on holiday in 1969 at his sister's home in Provence, Boulez was called to the phone. 'It's the Elysée Palace,' she said. 'Take the number and tell Howard I'll call him back,' said Boulez, thinking it was a practical joke by his English agent. When the phone rang again, he found himself invited to dine with Georges Pompidou. The president wanted to know what it would take to bring Boulez back to France. He outlined his castle in the air and Pompidou promptly authorized it, at a construction cost of ninety million francs. The *Institut de recherche et coordination acoustique/musique*, known as IRCAM, was dug underground beside the cultural complex that would bear Pompidou's name in the former market quarter of Les Halles.

Just as Bayreuth preoccupied Wagner from the day of its conception, so IRCAM accompanied Boulez in his thoughts wherever he went in the early 1970s. He was plainly relieved to leave America and face the future head-on in his high-tech bunker, insulated from natural air, light, sound and the infection of dissident thought.

He avoided Bernstein in New York and ever after (though they fell prey there to the same prurient biographer), yet the pair would go down together in history as instigators of the Philharmonic's most illustrious epoch. Their achievement has been viewed in some quarters as a triumph for the creative artist who, when so minded, could still re-establish his God-given primacy over mere interpreters. This, however, is a romantic fallacy that fails to take account of the price both composers paid for venturing into conducting. It may be too soon for an objective assessment of their complete output but, as they approach the end of a composer's fertile years, it is beginning to look as if becoming music director robbed Boulez and Bernstein of the fullness of their creative potential.

Both were reluctant maestros, by their own admission. Boulez said: 'I am not a professional conductor. I do it always with a purpose and always with the desire to return to composing.' Glock felt 'guilty about making him conduct' and Klemperer warned that 'what is important for him, in my opinion, is to develop as a composer. That he conducts splendidly – my goodness, that shouldn't be so terribly important.'

His priority was to compose, yet the chronological list of his works shows a steep decline once he began to conduct. Almost all his important pieces were written before he went to the BBC. Even Boulez, an obsessive reviser, has not tinkered with *Le marteau sans maître* (1955) and *Pli selon pli* (1962), the orchestral music that made his name and will preserve it. Works of comparable individualism are rare in his later *oeuvre*. Only the *Rituel*, wrenched from his soul in memory of the short-lived Maderna, and *Répons*, written on his massive computer to rebut criticism of IRCAM's sterility, possess such vitality. At IRCAM Boulez was given conditions and equipment to his own specification to create the music of the future. It was, literally, a dream come true. But all that has emerged so far is the thrice-revised *Répons*, which is so wedded to his massive 4X mainframe that it can hardly ever be performed outside the bunker. Despite designing an ideal environment for himself, Boulez has complained that administrative and official burdens are blocking his progress. He has talked of resigning as director to compose in peace, but dares not walk away until his experiment starts to vindicate its expensive existence.

Resentment has been rising at the fifteen million francs spent each year to subsidise its stark concerts and staff of sixty. IRCAM swallows half the national subsidy for new compositions and its resident Ensemble Intercontemporain takes three-quarters of the funds for contemporary concerts. So far, few composers of note have found inspiration within its subterranean labyrinth – apart from Birtwistle, who applied its electronics in his opera *Mask of Orpheus*. IRCAM is under siege and the tide is running heavily against the toneless avant-gardism that it represents. Baffled by its problems and blocked in his own scores, Boulez has latterly increased his international appearances as guest conductor, the last refuge of an embattled reputation. 'You must not be influenced by them,' he says of the unbelievers. 'If you have something to say, say it in spite of everything. If you reach an audience, well, that's better; but if you don't immediately reach an audience, you must wait and be patient. The integrity of the message, to tell, is much more important than to be understood immediately.'

In France, his whim is still law and his opera house with an electronic-

ally adjustable acoustic may yet come to fruition in the smaller hall of
the Bastille. President Mitterrand is building him a new concert hall and
he dominates the reformist agenda at the conservatories. 'Of course, he's
got too much power,' admits an associate, 'but who else is there?' After
Boulez, there will be no deluge in France, but a desert.

Bernstein never sought to change the landscape in that way. His aims
were more modest and, simultaneously, more vain. 'I am not always a
very good conductor,' he admitted when introducing an edition of his
recordings, 'not even always a good conductor. "Great" is a word too
abused and universally misused for me ever to call upon it in a serious
statement. The truth is that I am a Musician, who performs various
musical functions from composing to teaching, among them what is
known in the commercial world of recording as *conducting*.'

Once he had mastered the repertory, he stamped his style on it by
distending symphonies beyond their normal dimensions. His DG recording of Tchaikovsky's *Pathétique* ran half as long again as anyone else's;
his *Enigma Variations* seemed endless; his third Mahler cycle was more
wilful than ever before. 'Perhaps the fact of being myself a composer,
who works very hard (and in various styles), gives me the advantageous
opportunity to identify more closely with the Mozarts, Beethovens, Mah-
lers, and Stravinskys of this world, so that I can at certain points (usually
of intense solitary study) feel that I have *become* whoever is my alter ego
that day or week,' he maintained. 'At least I can occasionally reach one
or the other on our private Hot Line.'

Musicians were prepared to indulge his composer's prerogative, par-
ticularly in performances of his own music. The Polish pianist Krystian
Zimerman recalled playing the solo part in his Second Symphony, *The
Age of Anxiety*:

> One night he came into my dressing room and said, 'Kennedy died
> 25 years ago tonight. Oh God, I'm so depressed.' We went on stage
> and he started *The Age of Anxiety* at about half the speed we had
> rehearsed it! That was a genuine response to a deep-felt emotional
> need. That's what makes an honest musician.

It did not, however, make an indelible composer. His popular career
ended with *West Side Story* in the month he accepted the Philharmonic,
and the music he wrote after quitting the orchestra persistently missed
its mark. Following the deplorable *Kaddish* for John F. Kennedy, he
produced a semi-staged mass that offended Catholics as much for its
banality as its sacrilegious assertion that all you needed was love and
peace; the Beatles had said it more cogently. Bernstein atoned by giving
a Vatican concert for Pope Paul VI.

Except for the ballet *Dybbuk* and the short opera, *A Quiet Place*, a sequel to his earlier *Trouble in Tahiti*, his output consisted of breezy overtures and bitty movements. Two vocal cycles – the *Songfest* for America's 1976 bicentennial and *Arias and Barcarolles*- reflected mounting disillusionment with his country and himself, the lament of an aging insomniac. '*Arias and Barcarolles* is about all the things he worries about in the night when he can't sleep, about self-doubt,' confirmed Tilson Thomas. Its themes range from Schubert pastiche (*Nachspiel*) to the kind of marital dialogue that Stephen Sondheim handled more deftly; other composers had, yet again, covered the ground ahead of him.

He left his wife to carouse with his own sex, returning home in 1978 to nurse her through terminal cancer and himself through public remorse. The less he managed to compose, the more he waved the baton. Afterwards he would spend hours, whisky tumbler and cigarette in hand, signing records and pressing flesh. Bernstein was never happier than after a concert among his adoring fans.

He hungered not for power but for love: which he pursued with the obsessiveness that Karajan applied to power. 'The trouble with you and me, Ned,' he told the composer Ned Rorem, 'is that we want everyone in the world to personally love us. And of course that's impossible: you just don't *meet* everyone in the world.' He persisted in trying, though, both in person and through the media. His contract with Deutsche Grammophon stipulated an unbreachable 'guarantee to give Leonard Bernstein absolute star treatment . . . top advertising and promotion'. He had press coverage monitored like a movie starlet. Copies of every article that appeared anywhere in the world were sent to Bernstein's private company, Amberson Enterprises, where staff kept a 'shitlist' of disrespectful writers, who were denied subsequent access to him.

The other manifestation of public love was measured in money. Bernstein commanded the highest conducting fee in the world, a basic DM 40,000 (£13,000) per night. The cheque itself counted little to a multi-millionaire who often gave his fee to charity and had enough stashed away to keep his children comfortable in perpetuity. What mattered was not the money but the sentiment it signified. If Bernstein was the highest paid conductor, then the world obviously loved and desired him more than any other.

This Bernstein of the vanities was mobbed by adulators wherever he went. Groupies thronged his green room and kings and presidents asked him to dinner. To the man in the street, he was the most famous living musician. In New York and Jerusalem, he was a living god. To the record industry he was the sage and prowhead of the post-Karajan era. He had everything a musician could want, except recognition for the serious music he had written. He roved the world performing it himself, sometimes making his appearance conditional on its inclusion. Yet, in his sleepless nights and shortening days, he was tormented by naked fears that the applause and fame were due to his conducting and to *West Side Story*, while the serious works he had wanted to give the world remained stunted, silent or forever unwritten. His death, at the age of 72, was received with stunned incredulity wherever music is played. Despite violating every rule of self-preservation – smoking like a steelworks, drinking Scotch by the vat and sleeping with whoever took his fancy of either sex – Bernstein seemed immune to mortal perils. The cancer that killed him did its sordid deed swiftly and privately, and the response was a widespread outburst of grief. When Karajan died the year before, corporations mourned. When Bernstein went, men and women wept in every western metropolis as they recalled his extravagances and whistled tunes from *West Side Story*. 'He had first to die for his work to become free,' it was said of Mahler; and the musical perspective began to alter before his corpse was cold.

Alive, Bernstein had courted ridicule by flagrantly exposing his faults in an insatiable pursuit of public attention. Dubbing himself 'the greatest success since Jesus Christ', he deprived eulogists of the chance to praise and made debunking a facile task. Dead, he acquired a halo of martyrdom as critics realized that, in concentrating on his obvious shortcomings, they had overlooked the magnitude of the man. Players from his orchestras in New York, London, Vienna, Amsterdam and Rome came together to render a black-tie valediction in Carnegie Hall, where the podium seemed empty and sombre as never before. Bernstein in the flesh had been irresistible and intolerable at one and the same time. Bernstein departed was about to be canonized as the last of the conducting titans, leaving behind a colourless and unconvincing succession.

CHAPTER 9

Strange Tales from the Vienna Woods

THE VIENNA PHILHARMONIC is a law unto itself. Its course over a century and a half is littered with decisions and indecisions, both artistic and executive, of the kind that consigned the brontosaurus to remorseful extinction. The orchestra, however, survives with its greatest asset intact: a continuous playing tradition that somehow withstood the collapse of two empires and the loss of the Transylvanian and Czech hinterlands from which its finest players came.

Assembled by Otto Nicolai from members of the opera house ensemble, the Vienna Philharmonic was created to earn the underpaid players extra income on their nights off. The first six concerts netted a small fortune of eight thousand florins and the Philharmonic became a seasonal fixture at the ornate and acoustically perfect Musikvereinsaal. Its reputation grew with the calibre of players who passed through the ranks, among them the conductors Richter and Nikisch and the composer Franz Schmidt. More recent graduates include the virtuoso violinist Wolfgang Schneiderhan and the conductor Walter Weller. Other members formed renowned string quartets and taught at Vienna's conservatories. Principal positions and traditions in the orchestra passed from father to son.

'The Vienna Philharmonic had a special etiquette for all they did,' noted a tour manager in 1930. 'The superb self-assurance of every member of the orchestra and their ostentatious pride in belonging to this famous body of players was quite unique. As a matter of fact, every member of the Vienna Philharmonic feels himself to be a god, and expects to be treated like one.'

This was the orchestra that worked with Brahms, Bruckner and Richard Strauss (not to mention Johann). It aimed to please the public and make a profit, but was not averse to sentimental condescension and overwhelmed Bruckner by letting him conduct. (The symphonist stood on the podium beaming and motionless for several minutes. 'We are quite ready, Herr Bruckner, do begin,' nudged the young concertmaster,

Arnold Rosé. 'Oh no,' said Bruckner, 'after *you*, gentlemen.') Such support for living creators dwindled in the present century and the orchestra's last gesture was to retrieve the octogenarian Hans Pfitzner from post-War penury and settle him in a Salzburg old-age home. So far as musical content went, concerts by the Vienna Philharmonic became the most conservative in Europe, albeit the best played.

This was the same orchestra that sacked Gustav Mahler as conductor when he was seriously ill, and sent the largest wreath of all to his funeral. Rosé, its first violinist for 57 years, was thrown to the wolves in 1938 and narrowly escaped with his life. Six other players died in concentration camps as the orchestra donned swastika armbands to signal its enthusiasm for Nazism, surrendering its autonomy by offering itself to Hitler as 'the most beautiful gift of the Ostmark province to the greater German Reich'.

None of this greatly affected playing standards or working practices, which remained constant whatever the regime or the conductor. Typical of the Vienna Philharmonic was a player's reply to a friend who asked what the visiting Maestro would be conducting tonight: 'I don't know what he's conducting. *We're* playing the *Pastoral*.' Discipline was evident only in performance. Furtwängler once walked out in high dudgeon when a front-desk cellist who had lunched rather too well loosened his trousers for comfort and, leaning forward to turn a page, exposed himself shamelessly to the podium. Otto Klemperer, who liked the Viennese better than the Berlin Philharmonic, conceded that 'individual members can be very disagreeable'.

When engaging conductors, the players preferred proficient mediocrity to manic mastery. Rigorists like Klemperer were rarely invited and newcomers had to get by on minimal rehearsal – or none at all, as Herbert von Karajan found to his dismay. After the stock market crash of 1929 flattened the box-office, the title of *Ständiger Dirigent* (permanent conductor) was dropped and the balance-sheet repaired by assembling an all-star line-up of conductors, each of whom could guarantee a sellout. The chosen few included Furtwängler, Knappertsbusch, Walter and Strauss, who declared: 'only he who has conducted the Vienna Philharmonic players knows what they are – and that will remain our secret!'

Recovering rapidly from war and occupation, the Philharmonic grew rich on an exclusive recording contract with Decca, which had previously struck a sweetener deal with the Vienna Octet, whose leader happened to be chairman of the orchestra. The arrangement gave the Philharmonic a royalty on every record sold, while other orchestras were paid a flat fee for their sessions and derived no profit from sales. As for the much-trumpeted exclusivity, this did not prevent the Vienna Philharmonic from appearing, under its own name and various pseudonyms, with rival labels and their luminaries.

Its closest contacts were with Karajan and Karl Böhm, whose concert availability was limited, so it continued to divide the playing season of some sixty concerts among up to a dozen guests. This power of patronage gave the players a useful lever over their bosses at the state opera – for every conductor wanted the honour of appearing at the Philharmonic concerts – but cut no ice with record companies. The orchestra made no secret of its dislike for the tough-minded Georg Solti, whom Decca installed for a Beethoven cycle and the complete *Ring*, and was dismissive of his fellow-Hungarians Ferenc Fricsay and Istvan Kertesz. It had, complained a record producer, 'little time for any conductors, except those who were either dead or half-dead'.

During the Salzburg summer of 1988 the orchestra went on strike against the young Italian Riccardo Chailly, who had ventured to criticize its ways. Visitors were expected to flatter the Philharmonic if they wanted to be asked back. Zubin Mehta, a perennial guest, knows how: 'When one thinks of music, one thinks of Vienna,' he tells the local press. 'Any principal conductor from any orchestra wants to get from his musicians the same quality of music that the Vienna Philharmonic produces.' Mehta was awarded the 1990 New Year's Day concert, a globally televised confection of Strauss waltzes that the Philharmonic used to play under its own concertmaster until 1979, when it realized that a big-name maestro would bring in more money. Its choice of conductors is governed by a delicate balance of fiscal reality and personal favouritism. Money alone cannot buy a date with the Vienna Philharmonic, nor is musical magic enough if unsugared by commercial prospects. Compatibility is required in both respects if a conductor is going to get on with the Vienna Philharmonic.

There is, however, a striking anomaly in the orchestra's much-hyped 'love affairs' with three current conductors whose foremost attributes offend the very bedrock of Viennese taste. All three are American, Jewish, intense and uncompromising. Each possesses something of the qualities that provoked Mahler's dismissal and Solti's disfavour. As a phenomenon, their relationship with Vienna seems inexplicable on either side. Yet beneath the alliance lies a shrewd strategy of mutual self-interest. At the bottom line, the orchestra is bent on expanding its markets and improving its international image, the conductors on promoting a personal mythology by entering a rostrum graced by the immortals. The Vienna Philharmonic counts in dollars and yen, the conductors in Freudian dreams.

* * *

Of all the legends ever invented about Leonard Bernstein and Vienna, the most pervasive is this:

> The story of how Leonard Bernstein opened the Book of Revelation
> for the Vienna Philharmonic Orchestra is well-known. Quite simply,
> these players never performed Mahler until Bernstein persuaded
> them that his music was not all that bad. Now they do, wonderfully.

This paragraph is not a piece of record-sleeve flummery, but the opening
of a concert review in *The Times* of London. It went on to relate that
the orchestra's principal clarinettist, Peter Schmidl, occupied the same
seat as his father and grandfather before him, the earliest Schmidl having
been appointed by Mahler himself. By mixing factoid with historical fact,
the critic reinforced the fantasy to read: 'The Vienna Philharmonic,
Mahler's own orchestra, was unable and unwilling to play his music until
Mahler-incarnate came from America to show them how to do it.'

Bernstein has gone out of his way to give credence to this *canard*,
supported by the players themselves. Surrounded by members of the
orchestra while on tour in Israel, he told Austrian television: 'I feel a bit
responsible for Mahler. Before I came, they (the Philharmonic) couldn't
play a page of his music.' 'There is one person responsible for the worldwide recognition of Mahler, and that is Bernstein,' confirmed the orchestra's chairman.

Beyond mere hyperbole, this was so patently untrue that the motives
for making it up need to be carefully examined. Mahler never suffered
from unfamiliarity or incomprehension in Vienna, rather the reverse.
Until January 1938 his music was performed by the Vienna Philharmonic
on many occasions, and historic first recordings were made of *Das Lied
von der Erde* and the Ninth Symphony, both under Bruno Walter. Attitudes to the symphonies were ambivalent, sometimes violently so.

During the seven years of Hitlerism, Mahler's music was banned and
between 1945 and 1960 it fell out of vogue around the world, promoted
only by such isolated enthusiasts as Zdenek Nejedly, the Stalinist Minister
of Culture in Prague, and the aging loyalists Klemperer and Walter. At
this time, though, many of the premier Mahler recordings were being
made in Vienna, where sessions were cheap and the music was well
known. Walter brought Kathleen Ferrier to record *Kindertotenlieder* and
Das Lied with the Philharmonic, for extra authenticity. The orchestra
also taped the First Symphony with Rafael Kubelik and two cycles of the
Lieder eines fahrenden Gesellen with Dietrich Fischer-Dieskau and Kirsten Flagstad. Hermann Scherchen recorded four symphonies with the
State Opera Orchestra – the Philharmonic by another name – and F.
Charles Adler conducted three others with the Philharmonia Orchestra
of Vienna, another obvious pseudonym.

The quality of these recordings refutes any suggestion that the Vienna
Philharmonic, pre-Bernstein, was unable to play 'a page' of Mahler.
Walter, for his farewell to the Philharmonic, gave a poignant account of

the Fourth Symphony and Klemperer conducted them in the Ninth. By the time Bernstein arrived in the mid-sixties, Mahler featured in every Philharmonic season (see the chart overleaf). Abbado, Mehta and others of the next generation performed Mahler in the Musikverein before him. He was a parvenu, not a pioneer. 'He came to Vienna with a T-shirt saying "I love Mahler",' recalled one player. His Mahler breakthrough, the *Resurrection* Symphony in June 1967, was momentous mainly for being performed on the State Opera stage, and for all involved donating their fees to Israel, during the Six-Day War.

The need to see himself as Mahler reborn was a leitmotiv for much of Bernstein's life that reached a climax when he confronted his idol's orchestra, just as he completed in New York the first symphonic cycle on record. These were justifiable causes for pride; but to insist that he had single-handedly restored Mahler to the Vienna Philharmonic was an outrageous exaggeration that stemmed less from misplaced vanity than from a bottomless pit of unresolved guilt.

No musician knew better than Leonard Bernstein what had happened to his people in Europe, and how his profession had performed under Hitler. In 1948 he conducted in Munich and Vienna and swore never to return. Georg Solti at the Bavarian Opera had fixed a date for him, he related,

> to conduct this all-Nazi orchestra . . . at the first rehearsal they wouldn't even look up from their music. But after half an hour they were licking my shoes and holding my coat and lighting my cigarette – it was, you know, such a revelation about the German character, the two sides of the coin, the slave and the master.

Some days later he conducted an ensemble of Dachau survivors at a displaced persons camp. 'When I was telling them I was going [on] to Israel, they were screaming "take us with you! take us with you!" ' He did not face an orchestra again in Germany until 1976 when he returned to Munich with Claudio Arrau for an Amnesty International fund-raising.

When he met the Vienna Symphony Orchestra, they wanted him to perform a Bartók piece that had resulted in failure for Herbert von Karajan and the rival Philharmonic. Bernstein demurred: 'I didn't go back. I hated the whole spirit of intrigue.' He left behind his marked-up score of Mahler's ninth symphony which, he told a biographer, was then handed over to 'the other conductor' who used it for concerts and a recording. This was pure fantasy: Karajan did not conduct Mahler's ninth for another thirty years.

By 1966, nearing the end of his tether with the New York Philharmonic and an unappreciative press, Bernstein was anxious to extend his reputation. He was pushing fifty, the age Mahler died, and was known only

Mahler Concerts by the Vienna Philharmonic 1945–70

1945	First Symphony	cond. Fanta
	Kindertotenlieder	Joseph Krips (3 performances)
1947	Fourth Symphony	Rudolf Moralt (x 2)
	ditto	Otto Klemperer
	Das Lied von der Erde	Bruno Walter
1948	Second Symphony	Walter (x 2)
	Lieder eines fahrenden Gesellen	Krips
1949	*Das Lied von der Erde*	Walter
1950	Fourth Symphony	Walter
1951	First Symphony	Moralt
	Gesellen	Wilhelm Furtwängler
1952	Fifth Symphony	Rafael Kubelik
	Das Lied	Walter
	Kindertotenlieder	Clemens Krauss
	Gesellen	Furtwängler (x 2)
1955	First Symphony	Kubelik (x 2)
	Fourth Symphony	Walter (x 2)
1957	Second Symphony	Kubelik
	Sixth Symphony	Dmitri Mitropoulos (x 2)
	Ninth Symphony	Kubelik (x 2)
	Kindertotenlieder	Karl Böhm (x 3)
1959	*Das Lied*	Kubelik
1960	Fourth Symphony	Walters
	Seventh Symphony	Kubelik (x 2)
	Eighth Symphony	Mitropoulos
	Ninth Symphony	Mitropoulos (x 3)
	Das Lied	Herbert von Karajan (x 3)
1963	Second Symphony	Klemperer
1964	First Symphony	Georg Solti
1965	Second Symphony	Claudio Abbado
1966	First Symphony	Zubin Mehta
	Das Lied von der Erde	Leonard Bernstein (x 3)
1967	*Kindertotenlieder*	Böhm (x 3)
	Second Symphony	Bernstein (x 3)
1968	Ninth Symphony	Klemperer
1969	*Gesellen*	Böhm
1970	Second Symphony	Abbado (x 2)

Between the war and Bernstein's debut, the Vienna Philharmonic gave 47 Mahler concerts – as well as 'numerous' performances of individual *Rückert Lieder* and *Wunderhorn* songs.

In the 1970s, when Bernstein was supposedly teaching them how to play Mahler, the Vienna Philharmonic gave 20 Mahler concerts under Bernstein and an almost equivalent tally, 19, with Claudio Abbado.

as a Broadway composer and the conductor of an American orchestra. His record sales in Europe were puny and he was shut out, partly by Karajan's animosity, from the vital markets of Austro-Germany.

Swallowing the contempt he continued to express privately for Germans, he leaped at an invitation to conduct *Falstaff* in Vienna. 'Since the departure of Herbert von Karajan from the Vienna State Opera no conductor has been so extolled in this house,' reported the *New York Times* of his instant triumph; indeed, no comparable *Falstaff* had been seen there 'since the already legendary performances under Toscanini'. Bernstein also gained the confidence of the Vienna Philharmonic in Mozart concerts they gave together and wounded his New York players by telling them how inferior they were to the Viennese.

Vienna next assigned him its most cherished opera, *Der Rosenkavalier*. 'When I asked for ten rehearsals, they were absolutely horrified and said that they were born already knowing every note and word of this opera,' he related. 'Basically, they have no idea how waltzes are played in Vienna, or rather they have not one but a hundred different ideas . . . I listened to everybody very carefully and even followed around some of those quartets who play waltzes in the pub but who also have disagreements and just do it the way they feel. So in the end I went ahead and did it my way.'

'The audience went completely wild; the final ovations lasted twenty minutes, with 48 curtain-calls,' noted *Die Presse*. 'A great deal of poetry unfolded in such places where, after decades of sloppiness, nothing remained but the so-called "mood".'

Days after leaving the New York Philharmonic in May 1969 he turned up in Vienna to perform Beethoven's *Missa Solemnis* for the hundredth anniversary of the opera house. The following year he conducted *Fidelio* for Beethoven's bi-centennial. Neither Karajan nor Böhm nor any other Austrian was considered worthy for these sacramental national occasions. Bernstein, the American Jew who spoke more Yiddish than German, had become Vienna's favourite son and gained himself a passport to the German *Heimat*. He was financed by a Munich company, Unitel, to film television documentaries and symphonies with the Vienna Philharmonic, and signed an exclusive record contract with Deutsche Grammophon which scored heavily with a remake of *West Side Story* but saw no profit from his other compositions. After 16 years working together, the yellow label reaped the whirlwind when Bernstein replaced Karajan in the mystic role of leader-priest. When the Berlin Wall came crashing down, it was Bernstein who appeared on the scene on Christmas Day to direct the orchestral ceremonies in a unified German performance of Beethoven's Ninth. In the pragmatic view of the DG president, he had become the 'repeated bearer of good fortune' for the German record industry and the Vienna Philharmonic in particular.

What was in it for the orchestra? At first blush, an overwhelming musical experience that liberated players from legacies of inhibition with a conductor who danced like a dervish and kissed them on the mouth. 'We feel his love, his own enthusiasm for music,' said the concertmaster, Hans Novak. 'Bernstein opened all doors with us because he had the courage to translate all his feelings into movements without restraint.'

Those doors were not only metaphorical. Bernstein introduced CBS Records to Vienna, giving the Philharmonic a significant American outlet. For its next US tour, he marshalled public sympathy by having them give a benefit concert for the New York Philharmonic pension fund, orchestra to orchestra, all men are brothers . . . He took the Vienna Opera on its first American visit in 1979 with a *Fidelio* that Andrew Porter described as 'a company love-in, rather than a serious account of Beethoven's opera'. On the second holiest night of the Jewish calendar, he conducted the Vienna Philharmonic in Mahler at Carnegie Hall. Bernstein may not have restored Mahler to the Vienna Philharmonic, but he certainly cleaned up Vienna's image in America.

The act of reconciliation he performed in Israel was no less meaningful. Austria, unlike Germany, had refused to acknowledge its Nazi crimes or pay reparations to the victims. It remained anathema to many Jews and elected as president a former Nazi, Kurt Waldheim, who was shunned by every civilized government. Israel itself was a small nation of little commercial or diplomatic significance, but the opinion of Jewish musicians, managers and audiences around the world was of major concern to any musical organization and might be swayed by a rapprochment with the Jewish state. There were only twelve million Jews left in the world but an awful lot of them were culturally active. The Vienna Philharmonic wanted their approval and Bernstein was the man to procure it. To celebrate his own seventieth birthday and the state's fortieth anniversary, he took the orchestra to Israel in September 1988 to plant six trees for its Nazi martyrs and play Mahler's pessimistic Sixth Symphony to ecstatic audiences. 'You can't separate music and humanity,' he told Israelis, 'we're all flesh and blood.'

The moral rehabilitation of Vienna was accomplished by a conductor who abominated their society at first sight and swore to boycott it. The price for his retraction was psychological, an exacerbation of the guilt feelings that Bernstein was prone to suffer and, being Bernstein, took no trouble to conceal. 'I was entitled to my guilt,' he said after his wife's death. 'And I can't tell you what havoc guilt can cause. You can't know.'

Bernstein was the most Jewish of all musicians, by ancestry, upbringing and inclination. He took pride in speaking and studying Biblical Hebrew. The self-wrestling rhetoric of his essays and lectures is rooted in Talmudic argumentation and many of his favourite phrases are not English, but Yiddish. He once described Mahler as standing 'in the position of Amen-sayer to symphonic music', a term unrecognized by the OED but familiar to Yiddishists as *Omenzogger*, an individual devoted to repeating ritual responses during communal prayers. Bernstein was steeped in Judaism at every level of his consciousness. 'It is perverse that Lenny should have this love affair with the most anti-semitic of cities,' said Gunter Schuller, an American composer of non-Jewish German origins. 'For Lenny to go back to that city and make believe these are wonderful people is hard for me to comprehend.'

He need not have gone to Vienna if all he needed was international credibility. That could have been granted by other great orchestras. But Bernstein wanted more: he wanted the Austro-Germans to love him, to become their acceptable Jew, to succeed where other Jews since Mahler had failed. Above all, he longed to conquer the city that had expelled Mahler, to avenge the insult, and triumph where his father-figure had been vanquished, the aspiration of every Oedipal son.

No praise touched him more deeply than the approval of Karl Böhm, the unrepentant Viennese Nazi. In a letter to the dying Böhm he wrote of being 'amazed at the warmth and musical closeness of our relationship'. With the imprimatur of Böhm and his kind, Bernstein's position 'in the kingdom of European music was, so to speak, that of an adopted son'. The guilt he felt for the betrayals involved in this process found public expression in televised meditations on Mahler and Wagner, shot in Vienna, in which Bernstein expatiated on Mahler's 'shame of being ashamed to be Jewish', of anti-semitism and of father-son relations – straying far from any relevance to his topic, or to documented fact. Bernstein was, as ever, talking about himself, talking himself out of the moral dilemma in which he was trapped.

Expiation could be obtained only if the end justified his questionable means. The myth that depicts Bernstein as the apostle who converted Mahler's enemies to his gospels was the process by which the conductor aimed to evade the moral consequences of his compromises. In the official Philharmonic version: 'Mahler wrote music as he felt it as a Jew, and

Leonard Bernstein is deeply convincing as a musician and as a Jew when he comes to us and says, 'Gentlemen, this is what Mahler must have meant.' It is a powerful piece of public imagery, a tale that involves just enough recognizable elements for critics to give it unthinking credence.

* * *

Anyone watching Lorin Maazel record the Mahler symphonies in the Musikvereinsaal with the Vienna Philharmonic might have shut his eyes and imagined that the composer himself was in charge. Conductor and orchestra understood one another without having to say very much. Long stretches of music flowed uninterrupted, underpinned by a current of mutual respect and the faintest hint of steel. 'I'm not a disciplinarian,' said Maazel. 'I'm not interested in power. We're just colleagues working together. They play the instruments, I provide the structure, the order.'

Maazel was another conductor who imagined himself in Mahler's position. He came to Vienna as director of the state opera in 1982 and lasted three years before he was driven out for jeopardizing its cosy status quo. 'I was not brought in to improve efficiency,' he admitted, wearing a three-piece business suit, 'It just happened that way. I'm a good manager. I plan programmes well in advance, so we no longer pay singers to fly in and out for one performance. Everyone sings several nights at a time. That way, we save money, the cast get to know one another better and the standard improves.'

His cardinal offence was to cut the number of different operas staged each month from twenty-odd to as few as seven. This meant that the Viennese might have to wait months between *Magic Flute*s, but that every production was properly rehearsed by the full cast, rather than cobbled together with whoever was around on the day. He invoked an overtime ban, negotiated job losses with the crustiest of unions and demanded that everyone, but everyone, fulfil their contracts. 'We no longer have a situation where you pay a star for twenty performances and he only sings thirteen,' he said drily. Pavarotti, Domingo and friends swallowed the medicine and came back for more.

Maazel claimed that his measures saved the taxpayer half a million dollars a year and brought in an extra quarter-million at the box office. 'All I'm doing,' he maintained, 'is applying modern business techniques.' The company was in dire need of revitalization, having languished without musical leadership since Karajan's angry departure almost two decades earlier. 'The opera has always had its best periods when a musician was director,' reflected a senior official and there was talk of a Mahlerian spring in the air while Maazel imposed his reforms. He performed heroically in the pit, coping with a *Tannhäuser* in which the tenor lost his voice after ten minutes, his understudy was found absent in Berlin and an unrehearsed novice, Spas Wenkoff, had to be nursed attentively through the opera by the unflappable music director. No-one could have coped better than Maazel did on opening night. 'He walked on casually, conducted without a score and gave a performance that was traditional but full of conviction,' said an expert witness who joined the roar of applause.

Born in France, raised in America, Maazel read philosophy and mathematics at university and spoke fluent French, German, Russian and Italian. He played the violin virtuosically and wrote his own film scripts and novels. He was alternately charming and arrogant, ultimately elusive. He belonged nowhere and was at home everywhere. As a conductor he was the most naturally gifted of his generation, a man who assimilated scores on sight and directed them as if it were the easiest thing in the world. He had been allowed to conduct Toscanini's orchestra at the age of eleven and was the youngest man, and first American, ever to lead an opera at Bayreuth. In his late thirties he was Karajan's counter-foil in Berlin, running the Deutsche Oper and radio orchestra at one and the same time and carving out a name for himself on record.

He was given the Viennese job on the strength of his Berlin achievement but made a fatal error in failing to fawn upon politicians of the tiny state and to flatter its minnowy music critics. Franz Endler, chief critic on *Die Presse*, Hanslick's shrunken organ, felt 'personally grieved that Maazel did not seek his support when he arrived'. He formed an alliance of wounded writers who attacked Maazel in their columns and fed inside information to Helmut Zilk, the ambitious but musically inexpert minister of culture in a notoriously corrupt socialist cabinet. Zilk saw himself as the next foreign minister and launched his bid by bearing down on the foreigner at the Opera.

Maazel gave ammunition to both sets of enemies by referring to himself as the second most important man in Austria after the chancellor, and promising to make every night a gala. When his aim fell short, as it invariably must, he was pounded by a conspiracy of critics. Zilk accused him publicly of using untested singers – they turned out to be international performers – and demanded a review of Maazel's contract, worth half a million dollars a year, tax-free. When the director wrote to five newspapers rebutting the charges against him, only the Salzburg daily printed his open letter. Anti-Maazel leaflets fluttered around the auditorium at the opening of a starry *Turandot*, staged by Broadway's Hal Prince, and the embers of residual xenophobia were vigorously fanned by the intriguers. 'Maazel is everything the Viennese don't like,' noted a resident diplomat. 'He prefers Italian opera to German; he is unemotional; he doesn't care for *schmalz*; he's American and he is a Jew.' 'I hate him, detest him, can't wait for him to go,' spluttered an opera-going civil servant who, on reflection, was unable to define what she found so offensive.

Zilk and his hacks turned to attack Maazel's conducting trips abroad; Mahler had been similarly assailed. Maazel announced an extension of his contract on improved terms, only for Zilk to issue a public denial, stipulating that he was being made to conduct more in Vienna, an extra 15 performances. 'I love to conduct,' protested Maazel, 'but as a form of recreation. I can't see it that way if I'm grinding out eleven operas in fifteen nights. I'm not born to be a hack, even a very talented hack. I like to have time to work out every detail and I like to have the energy and freedom from other musical cares: go down the pit and conduct *Tosca*, with no other notes in my mind.' He was working forty nights in Vienna, 85 elsewhere.

Next came the affair of the national treasures. Priceless paintings, it was reported, had been removed from the Kunsthistorisches Museum to decorate the mansion that Maazel rented in the leafy suburb of Grinzing. 'I was asked by the museum director if I would agree to hang a few paintings,' explained Maazel wearily, 'to be seen by important artists and foreign guests who sometimes visit me. I am still waiting for my own paintings to arrive from New York.' His reception room, built above a full-length indoor swimming pool, was dominated by four huge canvases, one of them an odious olive-green study of demons frolicking around a fetid pond. He lived alone, separated from his second wife, the pianist Israela Margalit. Paparazzi snapped him escorting a German film starlet, scandalizing Catholic Austria. Opening the 1984 season, he had to lean against the rear wall of the pit to get through a performance, and collapsed afterwards. Doctors diagnosed a middle-ear infection and prescribed prolonged rest but Maazel rushed back, knowing that if his next production failed his neck was on the block.

He was given the Vienna première of the complete *Lulu*, long resisted in Alban Berg's native city for its dodecatonal dissonanaces and explicit sexuality. The full three-act version, premièred by Pierre Boulez, had taken five years to reach the Ringstrasse. Maazel had wanted to use an American director, Joseph Losey, but was forced to accept a staff producer, having assigned the title role to another American, Julia Migenes. 'Lulu is a creature of our own times,' said Maazel, 'drifting rudderless through a changing world, surrounded by things she doesn't understand.' This comment could equally have referred to himself.

Half the cabinet turned out for the opening and dissent was anticipated as the grey-faced director entered the pit. The reception that greeted him was surprisingly sympathetic, the worst reactionaries having stayed away to protect the sanctity of their eardrums. 'Thank God there were no demonstrations,' sighed an aide at a post-curtain supper thrown by the US ambassador at the Hotel Astoria, where Maazel turned up in the company of his eldest daughter, visibly relieved. It was merely a temporary reprieve, however, and on the last night of the season his antagonists clinked champagne glasses in victory in the very same hotel. Maazel departed in less than two years, but left his mark on the political and operatic map. Zilk was denied the foreign ministry and demoted in the next reshuffle to the mayoralty of Vienna. The critics had their ticket allocation cut and the opera schedules in Vienna would never return to their former anarchy. Maazel's successor, Claudio Abbado, committed himself to half as many performances and avoided any administrative involvement.

In the two years until Abbado was freed from La Scala, the state opera reverted to Maazel's predecessor, Egon Seefehlner, a dour administrator who saw its function as 'a museum of opera, in which the objects do not have to mean anything'. Seefehlner had scores of his own to settle with Maazel: 'I brought him first to Berlin, then here, but he attacked me as a dilettante who left the house in chaos. I could now say the same. For me, he remains a very good conductor and I would have been happy to remain his friend, but you can't speak about the Minister in the way he did.' The official opera yearbook omitted his photograph and pretended he had never existed. Maazel denied that personal animosities or anti-semitism had fuelled the conflict. Jewishness was peripheral to his concern; he felt closer to Zen Buddhism. 'I had to resign,' he insisted, 'to draw attention to the fact that what was happening here was a violation of a director's prerogative.'

All the while his relations with the Vienna Philharmonic were relatively unruffled. The players had disliked him as a young man 'because he made them rethink repertoire which they considered their own property', but Maazel mellowed in middle age and the orchestra warmed to his perceptible empathy. 'What a conductor is doing,' he maintained, 'is to provide a frame, setting the tempo and then giving plenty of room for each musician to express himself, making him feel comfortable, being encouraging and supportive.' A Sibelius cycle he recorded for Decca was a revelation to musicians who had previously considered the Finnish symphonist too bleak for their palate (Bernstein subsequently claimed to have introduced Sibelius to Vienna). An integral Tchaikovsky set had similar resonance with an orchestra that knew only the popular fourth and fifth symphonies and the *Pathétique*. A mutual respect blossomed between the Vienna Philharmonic and Maazel. They did not 'love' him as they loved Bernstein but they liked the sound he made and they positively doted on the princely dimensions of his recording contract.

In Vienna Maazel was given a free hand by Decca and negotiated his own deals, toughing it out for half the night in smoke-filled rooms over half a point of a putative royalty. (He switched from Decca to CBS on succeeding George Szell at Cleveland, where he produced a Beethoven cycle of such perversity that it became a collector's item.) He built a studio within the Vienna opera house to make live recordings of his best shows – in the event, only *Turandot* got on to record – and delighted the orchestra by providing bonus record payments for performing their statutory nightly duties. Standing as he did in Mahler's shoes, it was inevitable that Maazel should record his symphonies. The Philharmonic, despite Bernstein's incursions, had never attempted a complete cycle. This venture was destined to drag on for five unhappy years after Maazel's removal from the opera and its stability was fatally undermined by the upheaval. Interpretatively, Maazel's approach became more and more aloof, almost to the point of distraction, and while the orchestra played with refinement, it gave none of the blood-and-guts commitment that Bernstein drew. Only the first and fourth symphonies, the earliest recorded, impressed.

Maazel, though he compared himself loosely to Mahler, evinced no special sentiment for his precursor. He lived across the road from the cemetery where Mahler lay buried but did not bother to visit the grave until the day Lord Snowdon offered to photograph him beside it. In his battle within the opera house, the Vienna Philharmonic supported him until the moment his position looked untenable, then adroitly switched horses. They, too, could be unsentimental about a former director.

In his final months in Vienna, Maazel talked of taking a long break from conducting. 'Right now I need more time to spend with my children, to write a couple of books and maybe some music, climb a mountain in Kashmir, to do the things I want to do before I'm too old.' Days after his resignation, he was on the phone to orchestras, asking for dates. And over the next two years he gave more than 250 concerts in both hemispheres, rarely spending a week in one spot. In London, he performed all nine Beethoven symphonies in a single day with three alternating orchestras, wearing training shoes with his formal tails. 'This is going to test my theory,' he said, 'that conducting is, among other things, a sport. You've got to be fit to conduct. And if you haven't learned to conserve your energies in concert, you're in the wrong profession.'

He took a part-time post with the Orchestre National de France and resisted the vacancy at La Scala but was unable to return to the top in America, where the Cleveland decade weighed heavily against him. Only a highly skilled conductor could have so thoroughly dismantled George Szell's shining instrument, which Christoph von Dohnányi was labouring to restore. In the end, Maazel reluctantly returned to Pittsburgh, the grimy town in which he grew up and where his parents still lived, his father working as an actor in B-movies, his mother as a music teacher. Maazel had played in the orchestra under Fritz Reiner, 'an unpleasant, portentous person', and inherited it from the dishevelled André Previn. He 'sort of backed into it', taking four years to be sweet-talked into the music director's role. 'The chairman of the board came to me and said, "what's the matter? don't you like it here? don't you want to see your parents more often? aren't you happy with us?" and I realized that I had no good reasons except that I didn't want another job.'

This was not entirely accurate. There was one job that Maazel desired, a perch from which he could crow loudly over Vienna. In the ulterior music capital of Berlin, Herbert von Karajan's days were numbered and Maazel determined to succeed him at the Philharmonic. Backed by a solid record of activity in the city, he cultivated ties with the orchestra's business managers and encouraged CBS, now under Japanese ownership, to replace DG as its single largest record contractor. When Karajan died, he was so certain of success that his aides persuaded the *New York Times* to publish his profile on election day and faxed invitations to the world's press to attend a Maazel press conference the following day in Berlin. Little did he imagine that his name would not even crop up in the electoral college. 'The trouble with Lorin,' explained one player, 'is that he is fantastic in rehearsal but he gets bored by the time the concert comes around.'

Maazel's response was petulant. He sent a letter to every member of the Berlin Philharmonic announcing his immediate withdrawal from all future work. At the excruciating press conference Maazel, freshly arrived from a Russian tour with the Pittsburghers, said he would dedicate himself entirely to the 'city of Pittsburgh and its wonderful orchestra'. The price of his devotion was reputedly a million-dollar salary, the first seven-figure conductorship in history.

Disillusioned, and with his sixtieth birthday now behind him, Maazel pulled out of Europe completely. Those who know him say he will be back. There are few enough living conductors of his calibre for orchestras to forget his phone number, and Maazel keeps in touch with their managers. His failures have been ascribed by colleagues to visible flaws in a gifted personality exposed at too tender an age to the unforgiving glare of publicity. The wounds he suffered as a *Wunderkind* have left scars on his character; a tendency to superciliousness has made him needless enemies. But the blow that brought him down was the same that toppled Mahler 75 years before, the insidious hostility of a city that supposedly lives for its music. The Vienna Philharmonic has asked him back to give concerts, but Maazel has so far failed to respond. If ever a surgeon has to fit the marathon-running Maazel with a transistorized pacemaker, he will probably find the word Vienna engraved upon his heart.

*   *   *

An American of the next generation was plunged into mid-life crisis by the Berlin verdict. James Levine, Karajan's protégé, had expected to inherit his kingdom. Managers warned him that feelings were running high against his mentor and he would face the backlash, but Levine was too convinced of his destiny to pay heed. He had constructed his career circumspectly, avoiding all but the most innocuous of press interviews, and setting up his stall at the Metropolitan Opera and in Karajan's domains. He sought no reputation in western or eastern Europe, was not seen in London or Moscow from one decade to the next. Every effort had been directed to capturing the centre, working each summer at Bayreuth and Salzburg and gaining recognition for his conscientious rehearsals, a red towel slung permanently over his shoulder to mop the flowing perspiration. He was corpulent, curly-haired, comradely and competent in everything he touched. He was 'Jimmy' or 'Big Jim' to everyone.

Karajan's death came at the worst possible moment for Levine. He was closely identified with Karajan's American agency, CAMI, which had fallen out with the orchestra over touring terms. Then, in the week before the players went into electoral conclave, his German agent, Karen Wylach, was accused of losing the orchestra part of a European tour by making substantial financial demands on his behalf. Levine seemed tinged with the tawdriness of the Karajan era and his name did not come into the reckoning for the succession. When Berlin spurned him and Salzburg was handed to a man the Austrian government had appointed to investigate Karajan's nepotism, the American went into a painful depression. A life's hopes had been dashed, and he was still only 45. But happily for the Met director, an equal opportunity was close at hand. 'When we asked the Vienna Philharmonic with which conductor they would like to record Mozart – the last one was Karl Böhm – they replied unanimously: James Levine,' related the DG president, Andreas Holschneider. The Viennese players had enjoyed his company at Salzburg and were now delighted to have a collaborator of his stature to flaunt at Berlin.

Levine was known as a sensitive accompanist and an immaculate judge of voice. He had learned orchestral conducting the hard way, under George Szell's severe tutelage at Cleveland, and spent 15 years hauling the Met out of a slough of artistic and financial despond; but his prime achievement had been to nurture a succession of fine singers in a world bereft of vocal talent. By some freak of nature, or economic prosperity, Italy had stopped producing Puccini voices and Germany was clean out of Heldentenors. When Bayreuth needed a Wotan and Milan a Mimi, they came rummaging in Levine's American closets. He turned out the Wotan of the nineties, James Morris, whose singularity was such that he sang the role both on Levine's DG *Ring* and in the concurrent EMI recording with Bernard Haitink. Kathleen Battle, another Levine discovery, was soon able to name her own fee in Mozart and Strauss parts. The up-and-coming Aida was Aprile Millo, groomed at the Met. Maria Ewing, a captivating Carmen and Salome, had been spotted by Levine at a Cleveland audition where Pierre Bernac gave her the thumbs down. 'Bernac didn't think I would project [vocally],' she remembers, 'but Jimmy didn't care about that. He was interested in the style and expression.' He kept an eye on her tuition and gave her breaks at the Met until a rupture with her husband, the director Peter Hall, severed their tie.

Levine's singers did not possess the enormous voices and personalities traditionally associated with opera stars. He admitted that a well-cast *Butterfly*, which could be taken for granted in the 1950s, had now become 'the exception rather than the rule', but in his Metropolitan Opera, there were fewer black holes in the casting department than at Covent Garden, Dresden or Rome. In an era of vocal austerity, Levine's little-leaguers filled the gaps adequately. 'He can make you better than you are,' admitted Battle. 'This is a terrible period for opera,' said Levine. 'Maybe someday they'll think I was crazy, putting all this work and energy into an art form in decline. Frankly, I'm not at all sure that it isn't a losing battle.'

In addition to developing singers, Levine worked wonders with the troublesome orchestra, never one of the Met's glories. In the course of seventeen years he rehearsed insistently and steadily replaced players until just 39 veterans were left and the remainder were fiery youngsters who knew no other master. Levine rewarded their confidence in him by taking the orchestra to perform at Carnegie Hall and winning them the highest salaries in America, starting at $1,084 a week in 1990 and swelling regularly with broadcast and record emoluments.

'The crowning achievement of James Levine's tenure at the Met,' opined the *New York Times* on the front of its arts section, 'is the playing of the orchestra: its night-to-night standards, its steady and remarkable improvement over the last twenty years, its peak accomplishments of rare excellence. This is the one facet of the vast Met enterprise that supporters and detractors agree in finding positive.' On the reverse side of this Sunday morning accolade was a full-page advertisement for seats at the Met. New Yorkers dearly wanted to believe in their opera house and the artistic facts for once sustained their faith. The two leading record companies were fighting for its productions, while conductors like Carlos Kleiber had nice things to say about the musicianship.

All this achievement was directly attributable to Levine, who had entered the company at the age of 28 and became music director just four years later when the Met was on the brink of bankruptcy at the close of Rudolf Bing's free-spending epoch. Rafael Kubelik resigned almost before he took office, and Levine replaced him in a triumvirate partnership with executive director Anthony Bliss and John Dexter, brought over from London's National Theatre to enliven the stage direction. His task was to breathe life into a stagnant musical atmosphere, which he attacked with a 'visible, fully communicated delight in making music'. Levine gave himself fully to the Met, working in residence right through the season from August to May and conducting a high proportion of the performances himself. 'He really does put the Met first – and that's so rare among today's conductors,' said a colleague. He took over repertory planning, casting and direction until in 1985 the *New York Times* affirmed 'it's Levine's Met now'. He had total control. 'What Jimmy wants, Jimmy gets,' was the motto. General managers came and went, but Levine ruled on unhindered.

He lived on the premises and let in no intruders. He claimed to know 75 operas. When Levine was not conducting, the standard was deplorable. Nonentities and no-hopers took the baton and third-raters were allowed on stage. 'James Levine makes sure that he gets the singers he wants for his own performances and leaves Mr Friend (artistic administrator) to improvise the remainder of the season,' charged the *New York Times*.

Levine defended himself against accusations of selfishness and protectionism by saying that his critics wanted to have it both ways. 'Everybody agrees about the continuous improvement of the orchestra, and nobody has written about how you can't have that and a guest conductors' showcase at the same time,' he replied. It was also the case that the Met could not afford to keep a top conductor for four weeks of rehearsal when he could earn a fortune nightly on the concert circuit.

Joan Sutherland and Marilyn Horne complained of being barred from the Met by Levine's lack of sympathy for the *bel canto* operas in which they excelled. Gabriela Benačková, the foremost Jenufa, was offered Carmen and Butterfly at the Met, when she wanted to sing Janáček, which Levine apparently did not know. His limitations could have been camouflaged by close advisers and conducting colleagues, but Levine had none. He was a loner, recruiting his brother as a bodyguard and turning for counsel only to Karajan and their common manager, Ronald Wilford.

His taste in production was moulded by Karajan's monumental antediluvianism. He recruited directors from Salzburg – Jean-Pierre Ponnelle, Franco Zeffirelli and Otto Schenk – and had his *Ring* designed by Karajan's aide Günther Schneider-Siemssen. It was critically slammed as 'stillborn', derided by one Wagnerian for its 'devastating lack of theatricality' and lampooned by a cartoonist as 'the oldest new production I've seen'. Levine's conducting came in for less criticism, though he seemed distracted at some performances, preoccupied it was said by news of Karajan's Berlin resignation.

The extent of his conservatism provoked a storm at Bayreuth, where Levine abandoned his customary discretion at the *Parsifal* press conference in 1989 to attack the seasoned German producer Götz Freidrich for 'going too far'. He had conducted Friedrich's staging for six successive summers without uttering a word against it. 'In all our work over the years,' said the producer, 'he never communicated his reservations to me.' Levine denied that he was reactionary, pointing to his conducting of works by Schoenberg and Berg – which, like Karajan, he performed opulently, minimizing the music's inherent dissonance. At Bayreuth he was one of a clutch of Jewish conductors, along with Maazel, Solti and Barenboim, whom Wolfgang Wagner employed to lay the ghosts of its past. At Salzburg, he performed inoffensively under Karajan's aegis from 1976, making a mark in his own right in 1988 with Ponnelle's provocative staging of Schoenberg's *Moses und Aron*, set in a desecrated Jewish cemetery thronged with extras clad in the prayer shawls and phylacteries of orthodox Jews.

'Picturing the Jewish race in Schoenberg's *Moses und Aron* in simplified terms close to a Nazi caricature has a disturbing flavour in President Waldheim's Austria,' noted a British observer. There was an unscripted pogrom, and Jews wearing the Nazi-enforced yellow star were depicted bowing to the monetary god of the golden calf instead of joining in a sexual orgy, reinforcing the racist smear that Jews cared more for money than physical pleasures. These glosses on the score could not, obviously, have been intended anti-semitically since the production was 'warmly backed by a conductor Jewish to the core, James Levine, for years now a favourite son in Salzburg'. The production was greeted with perceptible unease and scattered walkouts. Levine, typically enigmatic, did not clarify his involvement. Was he seeking to taunt ex-Nazis with their crimes? Merely partnering a display of bad taste? Or, as seemed likeliest, helping to sanitize history at the scene of its excrescence, where half a century earlier synagogues were vandalized and Jews killed on the streets? All that could be ascertained from his musical interpretation was that Levine rid Schoenberg's score of its rough edges and presented it as a rich essay in late romanticism.

The Vienna Philharmonic played beautifully under his baton and, in the spring of 1990, set off with him on an American tour. They liked Levine for his collegial attitude and receptive nature. 'I don't get any satisfaction from telling an orchestra to do something that they don't feel for themselves,' he said. 'Obviously not every member of an orchestra can agree with everything I'm asking them to do; but what *is* possible is to work on the music rather in the way one works on chamber music, so that the players can digest it and communicate that to the listener without the conductor having to act as middleman. And that's very different from doing something because someone tells you to, or because you'll be fired if you don't. In that sense, it's very chamber-like.'

He enjoyed playing chamber music with members of the orchestra; from smaller works they graduated to a Mozart symphonic enterprise for DG. Levine was not troubled by the arguments for playing Mozart at authentic pitch and on period instruments. 'It's very important to understand that all classical composers tried to imitate the voice . . . its natural vibrato, its tendency to express individual emotions, its tendency to tension in extreme registers' – qualities that were best produced by modern instruments in the polished playing of the Vienna Philharmonic.

His attraction to the orchestra lay in practical compatibility and in his commercial connection with the leading classical label. His Jewishness was also more an asset than a hindrance. The Vienna Philharmonic, which saw itself as an ambassador for its society, was eager to appease the Jewish people for past misdeeds. On a visit to Israel, its chairman said: 'To this day, we have people asking questions about why we hire so many Jewish conductors and soloists, and my answer to them is that we do not hire Jews: we hire the best musicians.'

Mahler, weary of Vienna. Sketch: Hans Vindloff

CHAPTER 10

Formula Uno

No ONE WAS more astonished than Claudio Abbado when the Berlin Philharmonic emerged from its post-Karajan conclave on a sunny Sunday in October 1989 and declared him the new chief conductor. The Italian had not thought he was in the running. At 55 his career seemed stagnant, even in decline. He had recently been beaten by Daniel Barenboim in the contest to succeed Georg Solti at Chicago and renewed his own contract at the Vienna State Opera on vastly inferior terms. The day before Berlin made its decision, he was negotiating to become conductor of the New York Philharmonic, a rebellious orchestra plainly unsuited to his quiet temperament but offering high rewards in cash and kudos and a bolt-hole for the day Vienna became altogether untenable. His life and the political map of the musical world were now transformed over-night. The music industry had serenely expected the Berlin players to plump for business as usual and pick the conductor with the best financial credentials: Lorin Maazel, Riccardo Muti and James Levine were hot favourites. When Muti withdrew with four days to go, the Sony-backed Maazel was so confident of election that he set up a press conference in Berlin for the following afternoon. It backfired horribly. Instead of pop-ping champagne, the angry American plucked the grapes of wrath.

The depths of the orchestra's resentment at Karajan's industrialization of music had surfaced with a vengeance. Most musicians were determined not to elect another empire builder and wanted to reclaim the autonomy stolen from them by Hitler and Karajan. Although their deliberations were kept strictly secret, it is understood that the meeting, at a country house belonging to the Siemens family, opened with a resolution: given that all the candidates were commercially solid, the debate would focus exclusively on artistic merit. They spent the next six hours comparing the relative values of the least oppressive nominees, Barenboim, Haitink and the previously untipped Abbado. When the puff of smoke went up, it was seen as evidence of divine inspiration and hosannahed by musicians the world around.

Abbado is the antithesis of Karajan and all he stood for. His best is imprecise but expressive; he hates to be called 'Maestro'. Politically, he lines up with the left and his musical culture is modernist; friends include the highbrow pianist Maurizio Pollini and the Communist composer, Luigi Nono, Schoenberg's son-in-law. He selected for his inaugural Berlin concert as chief conductor two symphonies by Schubert and Mahler, separated by an abstract *Dämmerung (Twilight)* by the 37-year-old German, Wolfgang Rihm. He announced plans to use the smaller Philharmonie hall for experimental music. He was artistically open-minded, and both public and performers felt refreshed by his presence. 'Abbado is good for business and also for new sounds,' headlined a Berlin daily.

The money men were appalled. 'This has gotta be some kind of joke,' said the concert agent Ronald Wilford, who represented most of the front-runners including, curiously, Abbado himself. The Philharmonic's general manager, who had been stubbornly resisting dismissal as a Karajan relic, abruptly resigned. The Berlin government sent its cultural senator to Vienna to negotiate Abbado's release from part of his operatic commitment. 'We are delighted that a man with such close connections with Austria has been appointed in Berlin,' purred Hans Landesmann, reformist finance director of the Salzburg Festival and Abbado's long-term confidant. 'The bonds between Vienna, Salzburg and Berlin are going to be *very* strong.'

Any parallel, however, with Karajan's mastery of the triple summits was misplaced. Abbado was merely an employee in Vienna, answerable to an ex-baritone, Eberhard Waechter, who had been appointed over his head as artistic director. At Salzburg he is an honoured guest among many, while in Berlin he urgently sought to placate rival conductors and secure their continued co-operation, in stark contrast to Karajan's vendettas. In many musical and personal respects he resembles Wilhelm Furtwängler, setting himself above material concerns on a cloud of intellectual vagaries. His arrival turned the clock back in the city to an era of lost idealism, before the onset of power politics.

It also tolled a requiem for the Austro-German succession that had ruled Berlin since Bülow's day. Karajan had left no heirs of his own race. Not only did the Philharmonie fall to a Milanese who owed him few favours, but the radio orchestra was run by a second Milanese, Riccardo Chailly, and the Deutsche Oper installed a controversial Venetian, Giuseppe Sinopoli. Riccardo Muti of La Scala was a popular seasonal visitor. The capital of German music had fallen to Italians, for the first time since Toscanini's all-conquering tours in the 1920s.

Had the new rulers shared a common sense of purpose, they might have shifted the centre of musical gravity decisively southwards. Being Italians, however, they are divided by regional and political antagonisms that preclude any possibility of collaboration. The legacy they inherited from Toscanini, and indirectly from Garibaldi, was inherently divisive.

The conductor who safeguarded La Scala for quarter of a century after Toscanini's departure was Victor de Sabata, a musician whose mild manners turned to raging fury whenever he took stick in hand. De Sabata was an underrated composer who preached an uncompromising dogma of textual integrity. 'I have in my mind a million notes,' he said, 'and every one which is not perfect makes me mad.' Human fallibility left him frustrated and unfulfilled. Admired in both operatic and orchestral repertoire, he gave his last performance at Toscanini's funeral and promptly retired, at the early age of 65. De Sabata had sustained La Scala as the premier shrine of Italian opera against Mussolini's ambition to transfer its glories to Rome and against the meddling of post-War politicians. He had call upon the considerable conducting skills of younger contemporaries, Tullio Serafin and Vittorio Gui, both renowned for their vocal expertise, and it was their unbending tradition and dedication that underpinned Milan's magnificent operatic era of Callas and Tebaldi.

After the War there emerged from hiding the brilliant Carlo-Maria Giulini, who led the return to concert normality as conductor of the Rome and Milan radio orchestras, having previously played the viola under the visiting batons of Walter, Furtwängler and Klemperer. Giulini longed to meet Toscanini, who lived next to his Milan studio, but lacked the effrontery to knock at his door. It was the old man who, on hearing his broadcast of Haydn's forgotten opera, *Il mondo della luna*, sent his daughter to congratulate the young conductor and invite him home, where an enlightening friendship ensued. He went to work with De Sabata at La Scala before gravitating to a peripatetic existence with remarkably few long-term commitments.

If Giulini has failed to fulfil the high career expectations generated by his 1950s and early 1960s Mozart and Verdi recordings, it is a tribute to his beatific nature. It pains him to be paid for the privilege of making music; his wife saw to it that he was remunerated, handsomely. He has enjoyed a lifelong marriage and his loyalty to friends has been unblemished; he left the Royal Philharmonic when it dismissed his ally Peter Diamond and abandoned Los Angeles when his wife fell ill. 'We called him Saint Sebastian for the agonized look that appeared on his face when he conducted a Mass,' relates Elisabeth Schwarzkopf. Back from holiday on a primitive Greek island, he regretted that he could not have stayed on as a hermit. 'To live there,' he told a Philharmonia player, 'one would have to be very simple, which I am not, or a saint, which again I am not.' The musician disagreed: 'In my view he is nearer the latter than nearly all the other conductors . . .' Giulini has proceeded through musical life without making an enemy, or stamping his mark upon history. He has even avoided the mantle of elder statesman.

Toscanini, in his dotage, became an irresistible magnet for Italian musicians, an oracular force and the last living link with Verdi. Claudio Abbado, at 18, was among the elect who were summoned to make music in his parlour, playing a Bach concerto and conducting a chamber orchestra. It is not an experience he greatly relished. As a child he had watched Toscanini rehearse the Scala orchestra, aghast that any man could treat musicians so brutally. Then he heard Furtwängler: and resolved to be a conductor. He shared with the revelatory German a richly cultured upbringing. His ancestry could be traced to a 12th-century Arab warrior, Abbad, who built the Alcazar at Seville and etched his name indelibly in its wall. His father, Michelangelo Abbado, was a concert violinist, teacher and musicologist at the Verdi conservatory; his Sicilian mother published children's stories and during the War was tortured and imprisoned for hiding a Jewish child. Claudio, her middle son, born in 1933, scrawled 'Viva Bartók!' on public buildings as a token of dissent.

His political and artistic orientation was conditioned by the family's resistance to Fascism. He has been an unwavering supporter of the Italian Communist Party and a pioneer of dangerous and 'decadent' music in some of the most sedate institutions in Europe. After tuition in Milan, where he played in a student orchestra under the much-admired Giulini, he went to Austria to work with the eccentric pianist Friedrich Gulda and the austere conductor Hans Swarowsky, a Schoenberg pupil. This education was supplemented by watching Walter and Böhm at rehearsal and singing in a chorus under Herbert von Karajan in Beethoven's *Missa Solemnis*. Although Karajan later engaged him for Berlin and Salzburg, their relations were distant and wary. Abbado, in a tribute solicited by his record company for *Der Chef*'s eightieth birthday, wrote: 'Herbert von Karajan has created an orchestral sound that is closely linked with his own personality, and unique in our century.' It would be his unexpected privilege to dismantle that sound.

Abbado enjoyed Vienna and treasures fond memories of pranks he got up to with a fellow-student, Zubin Mehta. Both attended the opera nightly and Abbado admitted a Mahlerian ambition to direct it. This wish, too, would be magically fulfilled. He beat Mehta at the Koussevitsky competition but fell behind on the career ladder and was still entering contests when the Indian was music director in Montreal. Winning the 1963 Mitropoulos Prize got him nowhere, nor did a year's assistantship with the New York Philharmonic. Then a concert with the radio orchestra in Berlin caught the ear of Karajan, who offered him a Cherubini Mass at Salzburg. Abbado stuck out for Mahler's *Resurrection* symphony, never performed before at the festival, and scored a tremendous triumph. La Scala took note. He made his home debut in a Bellini opera and in 1968 became principal conductor of the orchestra, which had degenerated since De Sabata's departure. Abbado polished up playing standards by introducing a sprinkling of foreign players.

His political affiliation and local links served him well in Milan, where the trade unions were all-powerful and his brother, Marcello, was head of the conservatory. The retirement of the veteran *sovrintendente*, Antonio Ghiringelli, left La Scala open for a 1972 takeover by Abbado and two like-minded radicals, Paolo Grassi and Massimo Bogianckino. The time was over-ripe for change. Wealthy patrons turning out for gala nights were pelted with rotten vegetables by the hoi polloi who could not afford seats, nor wanted to see much of the stale stuff within. Morale was low and morality laughable. Abbado, over the next 14 years, revitalized both the spirit and the substance of the opera house. He lengthened the season, cut seat prices, gave performances for workers and students and took casts out to perform in factories. In the six-week summer recess, he kept La Scala open to show opera movies free of charge. He played inside-right for the company football team and wore the colours of the city's champions.

His Verdi cast was recorded by DG to international acclaim and his Rossini comedies were captured memorably on film. At the same time he pushed through a contemporary programme that would have brought down any other operatic regime in the world. He gave a famous *Wozzeck* with forty rehearsals, inaugurated Stockhausen's *Licht* cycle and performed new pieces by Ligeti, Penderecki, Berio and Nono. The outstanding younger conductors came to La Scala: his Vienna friends Mehta and Barenboim, Maazel and Ozawa, and the elusive Carlos Kleiber, whose sister was Abbado's secretary.

All this was achieved against a lowering background of political instability, flecked with kidnappings, strikes and government collapses. Italy in the 1970s seemed on the brink of revolution. The northern bourgeoisie flocked across the Swiss frontier at weekends to put their jewels in safe keeping; terrorism was rife. State subsidies vanished at the last moment, productions and tours had to be cancelled and Abbado's partners lost heart and departed. He quit twice, rescinded his resignations on receiving huge votes of confidence from the authorities, the intelligentsia, and junior staff who adulated him. The Amsterdam-based conductor Riccardo Chailly, son of a Milanese composer, 'grew up with the style of Claudio Abbado and was a complete fanatic for him! I still believe he is one of the greatest living conductors, with great sophistication, culture, finesse, and never with the tendency to search for an effect.'

Reticent and awkward in social intercourse, especially with foreigners, Abbado displayed a rare aptitude for communicating with young people. He led a European Community Youth Orchestra (which grew up into the Chamber Orchestra of Europe) and formed a Gustav Mahler Ensemble with music students from the composer's homelands on both sides of the East-West divide. The teenagers, coached by players from his professional orchestras, gave sparkling performances and Abbado devoted himself unsparingly to their physical welfare during the long, hot summers they worked and travelled together across Europe.

Away from La Scala, he conducted *Don Carlos* at the Met in 1968, complained of not getting the singers he was promised and never returned; at Covent Garden he is remembered for an awesome *Boris Godunov*. But the cream of his energies were invested in Milan, where locals marvelled at his ability to cope with an administrative structure devised by Mussolini and a legalistic chaos that could land directors in jail for doing their job. Thirty operatic officials were imprisoned in 1978 for violating a new law that forbade dealings with artists' agents – but how else was a cast of singers to be assembled? Conductors who worked abroad were forbidden to hold credit cards and obliged to repatriate their earnings. Film stars were arrested in front of the news cameras for alleged tax evasion, *pour encourager les autres*.

Abbado's patience finally came to an end in 1986, and La Scala replaced him with Riccardo Muti, his arch-rival. His departure has never been fully explained and appears to have been induced by a combination of fatigue and the lure of the only other opera house that ever occupied his dreams: 'Vienna was the job he wanted ever since his student days there,' says an orchestral friend. To avoid the full burden of responsibility, he demanded the appointment of Claus-Helmut Drese, a Swiss opera chief, as his artistic director. Initially, Austria welcomed them with open arms. The rediscovery of Rossini delighted audiences and the rigours of *Wozzeck* and *Pelléas* were, for Vienna, bravely borne. The Janáček tragedies were reintroduced and minor Mozart took its place beside major. Abbado was dubbed a *'Schatzgräber'* – finder of lost treasures – and commended as a public educator when he reinstated the Schubert opera, *Fierrabras*.

It took two seasons for the grumbles to surface. Vienna likes to have popular operas on tap, but had to wait weeks between one Puccini night and the next. When did Pavarotti last sing? Where is all the public money going? The newspapers, scenting operatic scandal, began baying for a sacrifice. Abbado was too precious to throw to the wolves, so the government sacked his cohort, Drese. An ex-singer and a concert agent took over the management of the opera house on greatly reduced budgets. Abbado was backed by the orchestra and urged to make a stand. He protested at Drese's sacking but, asked if he would resign, murmured, 'no, not as far as that'. Knowing he could not return to Muti's Milan, he could not risk losing Vienna and tamely extended his contract to 1997, on demoted conditions. He had swallowed his pride in exchange for job security. Months later, Berlin beckoned and his prospects rose again, like mercury in an invalid's thermometer.

On paper, West Berlin could hardly have picked a less suitable chief. Abbado had never held office in Germany, and was associated by training, temperament and contractual obligation with Berlin's cultural antipode, the city of Vienna. The onus of his professional occupation was biased towards opera and his relations with orchestras, where conductor and conducted face each other naked without scenic or dramatic encumbrance, had been limited. Apart from his youth ensembles, he had been principal guest at the Chicago Symphony for a couple of years and was a fixture in the Vienna Philharmonic calendar. His sole experience of leading a concert organization was eight years with the crisis-ridden London Symphony Orchestra; and his achievements and disasters in London provide intriguing pointers for the future of the Berlin Philharmonic and the music industry that hangs upon it.

He was brought to the LSO to add a touch of class after a razzle-dazzle decade with André Previn that created a boom in recording and television activity but a loss of confidence in mainstream symphonic repertoire. The LSO needed a long immersion in Brahms and Beethoven. It was about to take an expensive leap into the dark by leaving the concert epicentre on the South Bank and moving into a new hall on the edge of the City's financial district, which turns into a ghost town nightly at six o'clock. The LSO, and its Barbican neighbour the Royal Shakespeare Company, would have to put on programmes of sufficient compulsion to convince commuters to miss the 6.22 from Waterloo and stay for the show.

Its opening gambit, a Berlioz-Tippett season with Colin Davis, turned out to be so calamitous that the oboist-chairman Anthony Camden had to take a month off work and go round City boardrooms with a begging bowl to stave off bankruptcy. The musicians worked seventy-hour weeks to pay off their deficit. They would arrive at concerts after putting in a ten-hour day recording jingles for television adverts. 'I can't tell you the number of times I have started a session with Abbado when I was already feeling weary,' confessed the concertmaster, Michael Davis.

Abbado disliked the high-tech Barbican hall, demanded more wooden cladding to embellish the sound, and never really came to terms with its ambience. He was unhappy at finding the players so overworked but admired their ferocious independence and pledged to help them survive. He proposed a centenary series of all the music of Anton von Webern. Nothing seemed more certain to wipe out what remained of their audience but it signalled a turning point in the orchestra's troubled fortunes. Playing his Italian card for all it was worth, Abbado raised capital from the office-manufacturers Olivetti, scored a critical and popular triumph and repeated the concerts in Vienna and Paris. Two years later he gave a 'Mahler, Vienna and the Twentieth Century' season that introduced to London the art of thematic programming. A slow learner, he had mastered fewer than half of the Mahler symphonies himself and modestly called in senior conductors to add lustre and authority to the cycle. In addition to modernism and innovation, he performed the desired Beethoven cycle, complete with the piano concertos played by his friend Pollini.

For Michael Davis, working with Abbado was 'the most challenging and important and artistically satisfying experience of my life'. Although rehearsals were detailed to the point of narcolepsy and what little the conductor said was uttered in fractured English, in concert 'the man seemed to throw his reserve aside and go 150 per cent all out for the music'. His relations with the players were convivial and he became particularly close to the players' chairman, Anthony Camden.

The harmony was disrupted when the LSO learned from press reports that it was getting a raw deal on records. Abbado had contracted to record a Beethoven cycle in Vienna and Tchaikovsky symphonies with Chicago, saving for his own orchestra the more meagre pickings of Mendelssohn and Ravel. When reproached, he smiled sadly and said, 'it's not my fault – DG insisted'. Matters came to a head with a 1987 performance of Mahler's Ninth Symphony that none who played in it will ever forget. Abbado had taken a six-month sabbatical to learn the score, alone in his Alpine chalet. He took the LSO in mid-winter to the Canary Islands and spent a week rehearsing the symphony bar for bar. His Barbican concerts were epic and the performance was toured continentally to huge acclaim. After the last concert, Abbado disclosed that he was about to record the symphony with the Vienna Philharmonic. He later told players that his DG recording fell short of their live accounts, but this was small consolation. 'He learnt that symphony with us, and recorded it with them,' growls one musician. 'It rankled,' mutters another.

A tiny incident in the rehearsals illustrates his frailty in handling human situations of his own making. Christine Pendrell, a splendid cor anglais player, had joined the LSO from Muti's Philharmonia specifically because she wanted to play for Abbado. In Mahler's Ninth, where her instrument has little to do, Abbado asked her to take over the lower reaches of the oboe part. Fine, said Pendrell, 'and you'll tell Tony (Camden)?' 'No, you tell him,' said the conductor, walking away. 'Just a minute,' said the player firmly. 'I like this orchestra and want to stay in it. This is your decision, your responsibility.' Abbado gazed at her uncomprehendingly.

It was an unpleasant duty and he meant to escape it. If his friend Tony was about to be hurt, he would rather someone else did the hurting.

His decision to move to Vienna was imparted to the orchestra at second hand and Camden's appeal to him to retain links with the LSO went unheard. His farewell concert was magnificent but the manner of his departure left a bitter residue. Rich Italians who had fawned on the LSO during his residence vanished overnight. Abbado had spoken of London as his second home but would absent himself for nine months at a stretch and easily pulled up roots. His second marriage ended at this time, as he took up with the Soviet defector, violinist Viktoria Mullova.

Abbado has relied heavily on surrogates, delegating the details of his concert series to a Viennese concert manager, Hans Landesmann, and his recordings to a DG producer, Rainer Brock. Behind a Furtwänglerian aura of indecision, he made sure his interests were looked after by some of the sharpest minds in the industry. The contradictions in his conduct were exposed in contact with orchestral musicians, who felt he was trying to be all things to all men. He is a Communist sympathizer who cultivates a fan-club of businessmen; a cerebralist who loves *Carmen*; an Italian who longs to be cosmopolitan. 'Claudio's a great musician, but a feeble human being,' concluded one LSO principal. 'He has a knack for leaving other people holding his problems,' said an orchestral manager. 'But the most important lesson I learned from Claudio was, in artistic matters, you never compromise.'

He shies away from the public gaze and left his Berlin signing ceremony without uttering a word in reply to the welcoming speeches. Those who have penetrated his barriers of shyness and motherly secretaries bring back reports of a warm, gentle and somewhat confused man who is happiest when tending his rooftop garden and secure only in the realm of his art. He lives modestly in a downtown Viennese penthouse, watching old British film comedies for diversion. He skis in winter and suns himself in July in a Sardinian summer home. In most respects, Abbado seems unambitious. Only when he mounts Karajan's rostra does he reveal a determination to change the world, uprooting the artificially 'beautiful sound' and replacing it with a timbre that is distinctly his own.

Unlike Karajan, he did not haggle over a lifelong appointment in Berlin but settled for a seven-year contract with a three-year renewal option that will see out the century. His salary was a mere DM 140,000 (£50,000) with a fee of DM 24,000 (£8,000) for a minimum of 24 concerts a year. He was not aiming to be unutterably rich, and told his record company to forget about making videos of his concerts. He does not get a kick out of seeing himself conduct. His concern, he said, is to modernize the repertoire and democratize the orchestra.

These have been halcyon days for Abbado, unexpectedly finding himself at the head of his profession, his future secure until retirement. But Berlin is a brash and brutal city and the tensions of its unification are certain to spill over into the Philharmonie. If things go wrong in Berlin, as they did in Vienna, he cannot expect salvation from another quarter. Once the honeymoon is over, he will have to prove himself continually against the mutterings of Karajan loyalists and arch-conservatives. And waiting at his shoulder, ready to pounce, will be the rival he least wants to let in.

Of all the contenders for Karajan's crown, Riccardo Muti was the most devastated at the way the empire crumbled. He had often said he wanted to succeed Kajaran's successor, standing by while the interim heir was consumed by the players' pent-up frustration, before riding in on a white charger to pick up the pieces. Abbado's accession in Berlin and Landesmann's in Salzburg amounted to the worst possible scenario for Muti. If the Milanese made a reasonable impression, he could expect to remain in Berlin for a decade at least. If he failed, they would not want another Italian. Landesmann's plans at Salzburg involved a massive increase of modern repertoire, in which Muti wanted no part.

The origins and extent of his enmity with Abbado have been concealed by both parties, though neither denies its existence. Like fighting cocks, they occupy segregated cages. Abbado's friends are not Muti's, and vice-versa. Star conductors who flocked to La Scala while Abbado was in charge avoided it once Muti arrived; his regime has been propped up principally by the power of his own performances. 'I was tied up to the Abbado era,' explains Riccardo Chailly when asked why he left his home town. 'When era changed, many things changed. It's self-explanatory to say that.'

Muti will not mention Abbado by name, speaking only of 'my predecessor'. He used to denounce him in public but acquired discretion on coming to Milan, where the Abbado clan is strong. 'I never judge the work of others,' he hedged, faced with a direct question about standards at La Scala. 'When I improve the orchestra, it is not a criticism of my predecessor. My position in going to La Scala is not to follow someone else, but to bring my own personality and ideas. This will create, of course, a change.'

What befell La Scala was more like a revolution: political, stylistic and ideological. Where Abbado had been bashful, Muti was brash; pragmatic centrism replaced leftist chic; and precedence was restored to the literalist doctrines of Toscanini and De Sabata. His era opened with Verdi's revivalist *Nabucco* in which he played down the *Va, pensiero* slaves' chorus, *sotto voce*, exactly as written in the score. Although the tune has the status of a national anthem, he would not let Verdi be used for rabble-rousing, nor would he permit a repeat of the chorus. He spoke of music as 'a communion' between performer and public. Any intrusion would be sacrilegious. Abbado was never given to such sweeping sentiments or flamboyant gestures. He survived at La Scala by quiet diplomacy and backroom deals; Muti seemingly set out his stall in the open. 'The conductor,' he said, 'cannot be a slave.' He was less beholden to politicians and vested interests than any maestro since Toscanini.

Muti styled himself 'a man without compromise'. At 29 he had stormed out of his first general rehearsal at La Scala after failing to get his own way. 'One of the best decisions I ever made,' he calls it. He boycotted Milan for ten years until he was guaranteed artistic control of any opera he conducted. For his comeback, he hand-picked a happy *Marriage of Figaro*. On Abbado's departure, he rebuffed approaches from the Scala management, responding instead to an approach from the musicians. 'The orchestra and chorus,' he announced, 'feel I am the right person at this moment to help them improve.'

If Abbado gazed progressively ahead, Muti placed his priorities firmly in the past. 'I want to get back to the days when Karajan, Serafin, De Sabata and others were making great recordings at La Scala. Also in the theatre I want to create a team around me of young musicians, in the way that Toscanini had.' He revived long-unseen Wagner operas and produced Rossini's uncut *William Tell* in a five-and-a-half-hour marathon to open his third season. 'Here, we will avoid the cheap things that are heard in some opera houses where singers or conductors have no respect for the text. *Rigoletto, Traviata, Trovatore* have been massacred far too long. We will go back to what Verdi wrote,' he declared.

'There is general agreement that he has had a galvanizing effect on the orchestra; there has also been a welcome stabilization of the Scala's finances,' wrote a veteran observer. The change was particularly noticeable in the character of his opening night audience, which grew increasingly fashionable – film stars, company directors, junior ministers – and impossibly rowdy. EMI had to postpone live recordings to later performances in which the patrons were less ostentatiously partisan. Amid the mayhem Muti would stand aloof, curling his Neapolitan lip in disgust at northern incivilities.

His roots are in the deep south, his mother a girl from Naples, his father a doctor in the Apulian town of Molfetta, where Riccardo grew up in an almost African landscape, the women clad from head to toe in dusty black. 'Until television came, it was like living in ancient Greece,' he recounts. 'The classical *liceo* (secondary school) was very strong, and we had little money. So we spent our time like Aristotle and Plato, teachers and students, discussing politics, history and philosophy.' He played violin and piano at home and was 15 before he heard an orchestra, taken to a school-hall concert in the provincial capital, Bari, by Nino Rota, composer of Fellini's film scores. There was no blinding flash of light: he cannot remember what was played. When the family returned to Naples in 1958, the seventeen-year-old Riccardo entered the conservatory as a pianist on Rota's recommendation.

> One day the director of the *conservatorio* called me into his office. They needed someone to conduct the end-of-year concert. Generally they used a conducting student, but that year the class consisted of a monk, a priest and a woman. He asked me: 'Are you ready to conduct tomorrow?' That afternoon, a teacher showed me how to beat in four, in three and in two – and once in six.
>
> Next day I went in front of the student orchestra to rehearse a Bach concerto. I gave the first downbeat – a strange feeling, everyone should experience it – you give a gesture in the air and the sound comes out. After two minutes, the teacher telephoned the director and said: 'A conductor is born.' I felt it, too. Immediately.

He transferred to the Verdi conservatory in Milan with special permission from the Minister of Education to take a ten-year composition course in five. 'Never for a moment was I tempted to write a phrase that would remain for posterity,' he says. He earned spending money by accompanying students in Maria Carbone's singing class, where he met and, after a four-year courtship, married a graduate mezzo from Ravenna.

Cristina Muti has taken on the duties of an Italian wife. She stays at home with the children while Riccardo is out conducting but all the while manages his affairs and keeps his diary. He has no other personal or managerial assistant and hardly any confidants in the musical world. There are, says a friend 'few musicians whom Muti likes or respects'. In southern fashion, he has built his life around an extended family. 'I am a citizen of the world when I conduct,' he says, 'but here is my house where I can be a normal, simple person with my family, a few friends, where we can enjoy life. This has been the secret of my professional relationships.' His walled-off two-storey house at the bottom of a cul-de-sac in central Ravenna, not far from Dante's tomb, is three hours' drive from La Scala. Here, he roams the streets unnoticed licking an ice cream, fetches the groceries on his bike and swims in the sea. Chickens peck and cackle in his well-tended garden, a rural counterpoint to his cosmopolitan existence.

Of Cristina he says: 'Musically we have basically the same outlook: we had the same teachers, breathed the same air. I ask her opinion, but my decisions do not depend on her. I like to discuss things with her, as I did from the beginning when we were students. She is my greatest critic; many times from seeing her face I understand that she has not liked at all what I have done. She is not a judge, but a companion.' His domestic inviolability is a tremendous source of strength, enabling him to keep his plans secret until the moment is right. Muti is known for springing surprises. It gives him the power of unpredictability and an aura of fear. He rarely has to ask for anything twice.

He won a conducting competition in 1967 and made his debut at the Maggio Musicale, the Florentine May festival, in a programme of Mozart and Britten. He was appointed permanent conductor and remained 12 years in Florence, gaining an enviable reputation for obduracy. He once told the tenor Luciano Pavarotti, 'either sing what Bellini wrote or find yourself a new conductor'. Saddled with an artistic director whose prime qualification was his party card, he quit and brought out the orchestra, chorus and ballet on a three-month strike until the dilettante was sacked. 'Political problems arise only when things don't go well artistically,' he laughs. 'Politically,' says a colleague, 'he is a brilliant operator. He can get anything he wants.' By the age of thirty he was conducting the Berlin Philharmonic and the following year made his London debut with the (New) Philharmonia Orchestra. Six days later he became its principal conductor.

The orchestra was in a state of collapse, desperately seeking a successor to the 86-year-old Otto Klemperer and almost out of funds. A merger was being contemplated with the London Philharmonic and the playing had become so scrappy that a visiting conductor asked, 'are they professional?' Muti turned the orchestra around and made it into London's finest. He auditioned a bright young set of principal players and restored the finances with a heavy schedule of EMI recordings. In the late 1970s when Abbado joined the LSO, it was Muti's Philharmonia that set the tone. He was also the sexiest conductor in town, with razor-sharp tails and a shiny black head of hair atop a sultry face. Speaking few words of English, he made himself unmistakably understood in body language. The tantrums he would throw in Italy – spontaneous rehearsal combustions that reminded witnesses of Toscanini – gave way to quiet chats in the corridor with his English players, to whom he remains quite attached. After a big recording he would take the crew to dinner, spouting lewd jokes and musical gossip while preserving a certain distance. 'Riccardo might slap you on the back,' says a record producer, 'but you would never slap him first.'

He left London in 1980 to inherit the Philadelphia Orchestra from Eugene Ormandy who had headed it for 44 years. Again, his impact was immediate, stripping down the plummy sound to a clean-edged tone more acceptable to record companies. He was attacked by loyalists for making Philadelphia indistinguishable from any other ensemble but retorted that he wanted a distinctive sound for each composer and style, rather than the blanket glow the orchestra would indiscriminately bestow on whatever it played. Philadelphia emerged as the most impressive orchestra in America, with the possible exception of Solti's Chicago Symphony. 'Muti,' said his concertmaster, 'has been touched by God.' He attracted a younger audience, was the envy of nearby New York and pressured the city fathers into building him a $100 million concert hall. 'I am a serious person,' he liked to say and had little enough to laugh about in the 16 weeks of the year he spent alone in a hotel suite in the dreary industrial city. 'Don't tell them in Philadelphia you saw Muti smile,' he begged his hostess after a relaxed weekend. His sobriety was seriously rewarded: almost half a million dollars for four months' work.

When Karajan died, he was in pole position for the race to succeed. He had impressed Berlin recently with a Brahms cycle and the players with his low-key approach; he was admired in Salzburg for his Mozart operas. Secure at La Scala, he had performed wonders with tough US and British orchestras. His relations with the late potentate had been friendly enough to ease his path yet independent enough to avoid charges of cronyism. 'I know him well, he knows me well,' he said of Karajan. 'He has invited me every year since 1972 to Berlin, so I believe that he has a not-terribly-bad opinion of me.'

Abbado's victory left him dumbfounded. He pulled out of the running on the eve of the election, knowing his support was insufficient and expecting to benefit from neutrality. With his enemy in power, his hopes were dashed and he retreated in disarray. Weeks later he jacked in his Philadelphia job in an emotional outburst. 'I have felt under a great deal of pressure and stress in my life. It is time for me, who has been taking care of musicians for more than twenty years, to take care of myself, to find myself – not that I am lost – to think, to read, to have a real life,' he told a press conference. He said he had not taken a vacation for twenty years nor walked since 1978 on the beach at Marina di Ravenna. His announcement was greeted 'with shock and deep regret' by the board and with tears from some players. While not unconnected to squabbles over the $100 million hall ('Now no-one will be able to say that I wanted this hall built for me,' he said), it was symptomatic of a mid-life crisis in which he saw long-desired goals snatched permanently from his grasp.

Muti withdrew to regroup and reconsider. 'Everything a musician does is political,' he once said; he needed to form fresh alliances and strategies. He was both young enough and resilient enough to mount a fresh challenge but was forced into the uneasy position of awaiting an opportunity, rather than creating one. Moreover, he was not the only Italian who was waiting in the wings for Abbado to come unstuck.

*   *   *

Just to mention the name of Giuseppe Sinopoli is enough to make other conductors foam at the mouth and players throw up their hands in anguish. Not that he has done them any harm. On the contrary, Sinopoli has performed many acts of selfless generosity and is one of the most accommodating of colleagues. He is a man of intelligence and intellect, widely read and well-spoken. His compositions are accomplished, his lifestyle unexceptional. What incenses musicians about Sinopoli is what he does to the music he conducts.

The product of an unmusical household, he was sent to medical school at Padua and studied music in secret. He qualified as a doctor in 1971 but never practised medicine, slipping away to Vienna where he joined the last conducting classes of Hans Swarowsky, Abbado's teacher. He formed a Bruno Maderna Ensemble to perform new Italian works and was himself endorsed as a composer by cognoscenti of the avant-garde. In 1981, aged 35, he gained a wider public with an opera staged at Munich by the most influential of German producers, Götz Friedrich. Its subject and title was the evanescent twentieth-century figure of *Lou Salomé*, who denied herself to ardent and eminent admirers, from the philosopher Nietzsche to the poet Rilke, before losing her inhibitions to Sigmund Freud and surrendering her virginity at forty years old. The opera was moderately well-received, though modernists condemned it as a betrayal. 'He used to be a composer, now he has become a romantic,' sneered Pierre Boulez.

His first recordings won him Artist of the Year award from the Deutsche Phono-Akademie and his career was set for lift-off. He switched agents from a small Paris office to a mighty New York manipulator, affected a broad-brimmed Borsalino hat and succeeded Muti as conductor of the Philharmonia, whose players he overwhelmed with a lucrative touring schedule and DG record contract. Artistically, it was a disastrous move for the orchestra, costing the services of Vladimir Ashkenazy and Simon Rattle and provoking Muti to threaten legal action if it so much as retained his name in concert programmes. 'My love for the orchestra is unchanged,' insisted Muti; he could not bear to see what had become of it.

London's critics, a fair-minded clique of individualists as a whole, tend to give a new conductor a sporting chance. When Sinopoli arrived, their horror was instant, unanimous and uniformly sustained. The lone exception to the chorus of dismay was a leading record reviewer who hates to say anything bad about anyone and managed to find some words of praise for Sinopoli's 'quiet authority'. Londoners became accustomed to reading notices of Sinopoli concerts at which the critic was evidently present under duress. 'What an infuriating and unpredictable conductor Giuseppe

Sinopoli is!' wrote a Wagnerian in *The Times*. 'One approaches his concerts with the Philharmonia with a considerable degree of trepidation. Will he vulgarize yet another masterpiece? Will he show it in such strikingly new light that it will never be the same again? Will he be able to start it together?' A gentler critic reported her 'sense of regret and a slight sinking of the stomach at the end of the evening'.

'It is hard to know what to make of a Bruckner performance where the basic necessities – or at least what one had always taken to be the basic necessities – are so conspicuously lacking,' wrote *The Times*'s chief critic, accusing the conductor of 'inadequacy'. The common tone of these reviews is of mystified unease, rather than vindictive vituperation. London critics prefer their orchestras to do well and greatly regretted the decline of Klemperer's ensemble.

'Sinopoli has done a hell of a lot for the orchestra,' defended the Philharmonia's principal trumpeter, John Wallace. 'He tries to improve conditions all the time. The contract with Deutsche Grammophon is fantastic and we do a lot of touring through that because he's very big on the continent.'

Critics in other countries were certainly more accommodating, but the musicians were no less scathing of Sinopoli. The Berlin Philharmonic took the extraordinary step of revoking his record contract after a concert in which players were convinced he had lost his place in the score. 'A record is the document of good collaboration,' said the orchestra's business manager. 'That did not exist with Sinopoli.' The Vienna Philharmonic refused to work with him. He became a fixture with the troubled New York Philharmonic but was not considered a potential music director. Only in Japan was Sinopoli an unqualified hero.

He proved significantly less contentious in opera and was genuinely popular with vocalists, who found him supportive. 'It is getting to be very rare these days that you find an experienced conductor who knows how to work with singers,' said Mirella Freni. 'Giuseppe loves music – and loves opera; and he conveys this to all those who work with him.' His accounts of Verdi and Puccini were generally satisfying, both live and on record. Such was the conviction of his backers that Sinopoli made his Wagner debut at the shrine itself, in Bayreuth, and was appointed music director by Friedrich at his Deutsche Oper in Berlin.

The ingredient of his operatic success was equally the seed of his symphonic calamities. Sinopoli studied psychology during his medical studies and applied post-Freudian analysis to character development and interaction in musical drama. Beside the astonishing liberties taken by dominant opera producers who transplanted works to different societies and locations, his scenic interventions were insignificant and sometimes insightful. In concert, they were laughable.

'Sinopoli is, in fact, a composer first and foremost,' wrote an adherent.

> Music is for him a path towards representing, openly and logically,
> the contradictions of existence, the labyrinths of the mind. Thus,
> when he interprets the music of other composers, he sets out from
> the evidence of the finished form and descends into the labyrinths,
> into the psychological contradictions that drove the composer to gen-
> erate that form. For Sinopoli, there is a link, born of necessity,
> between musical form and psychological ferment . . .
>
> There is a deviation, an illness, a neurosis that forces the artist to
> transform his own sensibility into form; in this manner the artist,
> rather than remaining a prisoner of his neurosis, liberates it and
> liberates himself from it . . .

In the theatre, such utterances are readily mistaken for wisdom. Applied
to abstract music, they amounted to psycho-babble. When Sinopoli
sought to interpret Schumann's second symphony purely as a function of
the composer's obsessional neurosis (in diagnostic reality, a clinical form
of manic depression) the results were risible. His approach to Mahler was
wilfully deconstructionist, ridding the second symphony of its resurrective
uplift and the sixth of its ominous prophecy – 'mannered, lacking in
emotional power', noted Andrew Porter of Sinopoli's performance. 'If
Mahler had wanted his Fourth Symphony to last more than an hour, he
would have written a great many more notes,' objected a *Times* critic.
Sinopoli's description of the First Symphony was in direct conflict with
biographical and musical fact:

> The Mahler First is about the loss of nature [he told the *New York
> Times*]. In Mahler, there is a feeling of nature as the moment in
> childhood where everything is in order, and the feeling of loss because
> as life progresses it moves farther and farther from that natural state.
> Once you begin to stray, the conflicts begin. And what Mahler is
> saying here is, Come back.

Mahler offered various explanations of the symphony, which he performed more than any other. None conformed with simplistic nature
worship. His work protested against infant mortality, mourned the loss
of his own siblings and applied a caustically original irony to the natural
elements of bird cries and folksong. He once said: 'the First has not yet
been grasped by anyone who has not lived with me,' indicating its profoundly personal character and refuting any attempt to present it as a
celebration of the countryside.

Sinopoli, in his self-image as 'a modern, probing interpreter' assumed
a licence to extrapolate and create his own version of a masterpiece. In
this, he was not alone. Leonard Bernstein, in his latter-day vanities,
departed far from the spirit and letter of the scores he performed.
Bernstein's musical authority, however, was never questioned by fellow-

maestros; Sinopoli's, on the other hand, was never acknowledged. 'Most of us are prepared to recognize the other leading conductors and help them out where necessary,' said one maestro, insisting on anonymity. 'We are, after all, in the same profession. But this *person* is not one of us.'

Nevertheless, Sinopoli has continued to rise, boosted by commercial acceptability in Japan, the world's most profitable and least critical market for classical music. He took the Bayreuth company there in 1989 on its first venture outside Germany, and attracted patrons who paid three times the top ticket price in Vienna. He was photographed in traditional Japanese robes and made himself amenable to local media. In Japan, he *looked* the part of the great conductor and that seemed to suffice. The lure of the yen and the glitter of DG's golden contract induced the Philharmonia to extend his contract into the nineties, though players muttered against him and the manager talked as if he were gone.

Sinopoli also took on the newly democratized Staatskapelle of Dresden, Europe's oldest orchestra, a useful acquisition since his job at the Deutsche Oper blew up before it began in a spectacular 'crisis of confidence' with Götz Friedrich. Sinopoli, according to the intendant, wanted the last word in every decision. Success, it was suggested, had gone to his head – along with a ridiculous salary of seven hundred thousand Deutschmarks (£250,000) for conducting only two productions a year. Friedrich, a wily campaigner, came out on top but Sinopoli gave no sign of having taken a beating. He may lack the professional credentials of Abbado and Muti but he is not short of self-confidence. He has let it be known that he is aiming for the very top. Colleagues, amazed at how far he has got, are unwilling to predict how much further he might rise. In a world short of conductors, he may yet become the conductor of the future.

CHAPTER ELEVEN

The Mavericks

BURN-OUT IS UNCOMMON among conductors. As a breed, they are survivors who outlast their partners, attaining a longevity that keeps them physically active at four-score years and more. Those who fly dangerously close to the flame are stigmatized as 'unreliable' in an industry that prizes perseverance and productivity above incandescence. A principled tendency to cancel concerts will weigh heavily against a man's career prospects. Temperament is tolerated in a conductor, as in a politician, only once he has attained the very highest rank and can no longer be crossed.

Refusal to compromise cost Jacha Horenstein his livelihood. One of the century's outstanding interpreters, assistant to Furtwängler in Berlin and first performer of Berg's Lyric Suite, he came to grief on the rise of Nazism and the rocks of his own intransigence. Fleeing the black shirts in Düsseldorf, he made such perfectionist demands on foreign orchestras that they never asked him back. He ended up half-starved in America, conducting a New Deal workers' band. 'The family was supported for a number of years largely by private assistance from friends and by my mother who put her former opera career to use as a voice teacher, acting coach and stage director,' recalled his son, Peter. After the War, Horenstein gave Paris its first *Wozzeck* and recorded a heart-stopping Mahler ninth in Vienna but was bypassed by top orchestras and forced to ply his trade at far-flung festivals.

He was about to pull out of a defective Mahler second in Johannesburg when the festival director, Ernest Fleischmann, himself a former conductor, sat up all night persuading him to stay. Horenstein relented, conducted the performance and was invited to London when Fleischmann became manager of the LSO. His 1959 Royal Albert Hall concert of Mahler's eighth symphony marked the starting point of the British Mahler revival – and belatedly of his own. Over the next decade, working with a small label, he made remarkable recordings of a wide-ranging repertoire, from Nielsen to Hindemith, authentic Bach (with Nikolaus Harnoncourt on viola da gamba) to Panufnik.

'He was the first to admit he had been his own worst enemy,' recalls his record producer; but recognition came too late for him to reap its rewards. 'One of the greatest regrets in dying,' Horenstein is supposed to have said on his deathbed, 'is that I shall never again be able to hear *Das Lied von der Erde.*'

Admirers of the Romanian iconoclast Sergiù Celibidache revere him as an idiosyncratic idealist, almost a musical saint. 'Celi' has certainly bucked the system, but doubts remain about his motivation. A music and philosophy student in Berlin in the last years of the Reich, he became last-ditch conductor of the Philharmonic when a wayward sentry shot and killed its interim leader, the unfortunate Leo Borchard; months earlier, the orchestra had called him a 'filthy Romanian'.

An untainted neutral citizen, Celi held the reins until Furtwängler was allowed back and worked harmoniously with him up to his death. 'I didn't want to be Furtwängler's successor,' he has insisted, 'no-one could be.' But when Berlin voted overwhelmingly for Herbert von Karajan, he announced a lifelong boycott of the Philharmonic and vanished from public life for seven years. Through a German guru he had become a Zen Buddhist and, in the years of his disappearance, is alleged to have scoured the orient in search of eternal truth. This mystique is somewhat dispelled by the facts of his continuing work with a south-west German orchestra and an Israeli ensemble in Haifa, and a tour he undertook in Latin America. He had to eat, after all. He returned to routine as conductor of the Swedish Radio orchestra in 1961. As the odious Wall went up in Berlin, he launched a fierce attack on West German society in a Danish paper and provocatively began collaborating with the Communist authorities in East Germany. He eventually came to terms with western materialism and returned to the federal Republic to take on orchestras in Stuttgart, Bamberg and, finally, the Munich Philharmonic which he made into an impressive instrument. He demanded huge fees and extravagant rehearsals, adopted expansive tempi and produced remarkably delicate textures. Other orchestras would book him as a tonic against routine playing but his conduct was ever unpredictable and the LSO dropped him smartly after he bawled out their wind-players in front of TV cameras. He loves television and his Munich concerts are among the most widely screened in Europe.

The cult of Celibidache is founded on his romantic peregrinations – the middle syllables of his name have justifiably libidinous connotations – and his absolute refusal after 1950 to make commercial recordings. He abhors discs as ersatz obscenities and said listening to them is like fornicating with a photograph of Brigitte Bardot. Pirate tapes of his concerts fetch black-market prices and their scarcity has helped fuel his celebrity, particularly in the United States, where he did not appear until 1983.

The advent of video brought a change in his attitude. Celibidache filmed Bruckner's fourth symphony for release on Laserdisc, on condition that there would be no separate audio record. This curious distinction undermined his previous stance: if a record is a poor substitute for the excitement and high frequencies of live performance, then video is infinitely less satisfactory, with its artificial lighting, distorted camera angles and relentless focus on the movements of the conductor. That did not bother Celibidache. He despised records, its seems, not for their ersatz quality but because they concealed the soundless personality of the conductor – and he never wanted to be anonymous. Some worship him as a Furtwängler-figure but the truth about Celi is less unsullied. He is a showman, plain and simple, with an eccentric, though effective, mode of self-projection.

The two genuine misfits in conductors' tails need no such gimmickry. They are identified by an obsessive determination that borders on the suicidal, and an infuriating disregard for contracts and social norms. Carlos Kleiber and Klaus Tennstedt have little else in common beyond their age and national origin. Kleiber is a reclusive, polyglot intellectual, Tennstedt a congenial man of simple tastes. Kleiber commands universal respect from orchestras; Tennstedt is viewed with anything from affection to outright derision. Kleiber is outwardly serene, Tennstedt transparently vulnerable. Both are one-offs, inimitable, uncontrollable and breaking every sensible rule of musical survival.

Carlos Kleiber is an enigma, perhaps even to himself. He was intended for a safer scientific occupation by his father, Erich, who endured a dozen desperate years in South America after leaving the Berlin State Opera in a clash with the Nazis. Contrary to legend, Erich applauded his son's musical gifts. When the boy was 21 his father told a colleague: 'He has got very good ears and at the moment he is studying the timpani – he wants to do it all from scratch.'

The elder Kleiber was an autocratic perfectionist who entered the record books by demanding 34 full orchestral rehearsals for the inaugural *Wozzeck*. He was forever threatening to walk out if he did not get his way – 'well then I am going back to South America!' – and was inclined to double his fee from one season to the next. 'When there is no trouble in the theatre, I make it!' he would growl; his American wife, Ruth, had a knack for finding something to raise his temperature. Warning him that the Covent Garden pit was too cold, he refused to rehearse until shown a thermometer in which the mercury rose to a satisfactory level. Administrators were petrified of him but musicians warmly appreciated his concern for their welfare – 'always he was on *our* side', said one player.

Post-war morale at Covent Garden shot up on his arrival. In 1950 he was asked to be music director in London and at the Met – and refused both. He briefly returned to East Berlin but could not stomach the Communist regime and resumed his wanderings, unable to settle, 'an enemy of compromise'. Some saw in him the Mahlerian ideal of an artist 'who bangs his head against the wall until he makes a hole'.

He was unusually considerate of singers. 'Go on tonight and do not worry, all the mistakes tonight are mine' he told them before a first-night curtain. 'If anything goes wrong, look at me and it will all come right.' Equally, he was utterly unforgiving of slackness and remembered a player's error with undiminished anger after twenty years. On several public occasions, he subjected his son to scathing outbursts of humiliating criticism. He died in 1956, just as Carlos was beginning his apprenticeship in German opera houses. Their complex relationship has overshadowed his son's entire controversial career.

Carlos Kleiber advanced quietly through Duisburg and Düsseldorf to Zurich. He became music director at Stuttgart at the age of 36, quit after two years and has never held another post. He shunned approaches from record companies until 1973; he was 57 before he made his Met debut and almost sixty when he conducted the Berlin Philharmonic. Having first acquired a rich repertoire, he whittled it down to a bare handful of favourite operas – *Wozzeck, Bohème, Otello, Rosenkavalier, Elektra, Fledermaus, Traviata* and *Tristan* – and a similarly limited selection of symphonies. All are works that his father excelled in.

His conduct became increasingly erratic. Hypersensitive to criticism, he would head for the nearest airport at the slightest hint of dissent, inducing promoters to panic that someone might inadvertently say or write something to offend him. London concert managers have not forgiven the critics whose reviews of a 1980 concert provoked an enduring boycott. When he undertakes an opera, he does not require a new production but demands three weeks of rehearsal for a hardy perennial like *Bohème*. The uncertainty that envelops his every appearance generates high tension among the performers, who are then pleasantly surprised to find him unfailingly helpful and approachable, with the most explicit and visible beat of any living conductor. 'Don't worry,' he assured Placido Domingo's late replacement in a celebrated Covent Garden *Otello*, 'I'll follow you.' He can be impossibly intense. 'How could he keep that up? It would kill him,' say players. Riccardo Chailly remembers his La Scala *Otello* as 'the greatest performance I've ever seen in my life'. He refused to record the opera because he disliked the available Desdemonas. At his New York *Bohème*, both orchestra and singers stood in a spontaneous ovation at his first rehearsal break. 'I have never seen conducting like this, so supple, so versatile,' said one of the players. The chairman of the Metropolitan Opera crept stealthily into his box to watch; if he had been spotted, Kleiber might have walked out.

He has cancelled more recordings than the few he has released. For *Wozzeck* in Dresden, he insisted that EMI recover all of the orchestral parts that his father prepared for the 1951 British première and copy them for the German players. At considerable trouble and expense, the parts were meticulously prepared and driven across Europe. Came the morning of the recording and Carlos Kleiber quit without explanation.

Many of these extreme reactions are his father's attitudes writ large. The spectre of Erich is reflected in his tenderness with musicians and his obduracy with the commercial establishment. It also haunts his performances. Erich Kleiber conducted a Beethoven Fifth for Decca that has long been regarded as perhaps the most trenchant on record. Carlos twenty years later performed the symphony for DG in an astonishingly intense account that was arguably finer even than his father's. Such comparisons infuriate him. An unmistakable ambivalence towards his unsparing parent lies at the root of the Carlos Kleiber conundrum. Old colleagues of Erich are careful to avoid his son, fearing his hair-trigger response. 'The problem with Carlos,' says a veteran record producer, 'is that once Erich was dead, he saw the entire musical world as a surrogate. When he cancels a concert he is killing his father, when he conducts a great performance he is identifying with him.'

This perfect conductor has repeatedly professed his hatred for conducting. 'I only conduct when I am hungry,' he told Herbert von Karajan. 'I want to be a vegetable,' he told Leonard Bernstein. 'I want to grow in a garden, sit in the sun, eat, drink, sleep, make love, and that's it.' He is ferociously protective of his privacy, living on a mountain outside Munich with his Yugoslav wife, Stanka; they have a son and daughter. He has never given an interview but has amused himself with pseudonymous letters to the press, including an attack in *Der Spiegel* on Sergiu Celibidache. But his abstracted mien and otherworldly outlook conceal a shrewd business brain and a precise valuation of his own worth. He negotiates his own contracts whenever he makes a record. When the Vienna Philharmonic convinced him to give the 1989 New Year's Day concert, Kleiber conducted a three-way telephone auction for his tapes with DG, EMI and Sony-owned CBS. Bidding started at DM 300,000 (£120,000) with Kleiber demanding precise details of each label's marketing plans. Sony's enthusiasm pushed the price up to a record half a million Deutschmarks, whereupon Kleiber called the other two bidders and conveyed his regrets. 'I hope this won't affect our relations in future, but Günter [Breest of Sony] is so keen on this,' he apologized – and covered himself by granting video rights to DG. Promoted by two major labels, each aiming to outdo the other, his record became an instant best-seller.

Kleiber is among the foremost living conductors and was the first to be approached by the Berlin Philharmonic, in vain hope rather than expectation, on Karajan's death. He can be endearingly modest – waving a *Tristan* score at a passing record producer in Bayreuth with the appeal, 'what am I to do with this? can you give me any insights?' – and has a handful of loyal conductor friends. But the tiny sum of his achievements is disproportionate to his capabilities, and Kleiber still shows no sign of letting the world have more than a glimpse of his genius. He has preserved the gritty independence he inherited from Erich and turned it into a barrier against the extraneous forces that control musical activity. But the price of his resistance has been the burying of his gifts. Unless his attitude undergoes a late upheaval, Carlos Kleiber will, like his father, fail to attain his rightful place in posterity.

*   *   *

In all the performing arts, one or two talents in each generation are too wayward to handle. Theirs is what is commonly called genius. Untrained and untamed, it cannot be funnelled down conventional channels. It balks and it bridles. It bites the hand that would feed it and the mouth that pouts to be kissed. It is subversive and pervasive, undermining the tidy routines of a system that has the power to confer greatness upon mediocrity, but cannot harness the wilder gifts of God. Marilyn Monroe, Billie Holiday and Maria Callas were such creatures. They were consumed too soon, while the sensible Jane Fondas and Joan Sutherlands survived. Dylan Thomas burned out, Ted Hughes burbles on; Shelley drowned, Tennyson trod water. Whatever Mozart died of, it was not a surfeit of caution.

Klaus Tennstedt is a living affront to the modern conducting machine, a musician whose nervous intensity sears all around him. 'I have never seen a conductor give so much at rehearsal,' said one veteran London player. At the end of a Bartók concerto, he is wearier than his soloist; after a Mahler symphony he is utterly spent, his face has an alarming pallor, his spidery legs are barely able to bring him back to receive the applause. Exhaustion befits Tennstedt as mourning becomes Electra.

Sensible people warned from the outset that Tennstedt could not last; Tennstedt has no truck with sensible people. Conductors contemplated him with frank alarm. Some began whispering that he was 'a fraud'. Tennstedt didn't notice; his mind was on the next concert. Perhaps this was his secret, the sensation that each performance could be his last. Each event was both an undreamed privilege and an act of desperation, the fulfilment of a lifelong ambition and a confrontation with naked fear. 'When Tennstedt comes on stage,' said a colleague, 'neither you nor he knows for sure that he will reach the podium without tripping over, or that he will manage to conduct a whole movement. Then he does it, so brilliantly that you wonder how you – or he – ever doubted him.'

Not since Furtwängler has a conductor approached his task with such trepidation. There are similarities in their willowy physiques and vague waves of the baton, to which Tennstedt has added a comic mannerism of bending at the knees before a big crescendo – 'like a demented stork', wrote one critic. There, however, the parallels end. Tennstedt lacks Furtwängler's indomitable confidence, his sense of being part of a history and a tradition. Tennstedt came from nowhere and had nothing behind him but frustration.

His life began when he fled East Germany; he cannot remember the exact date. He had planned his escape for two years, resigning from the opera at Schwerin to pick up freelance work in Berlin while awaiting his chance. In twenty years as an opera conductor he had not once faced a first-rate orchestra nor made a recording. He was not a Party member and had not been trusted to travel, except in eastern Europe and Venezuela. He longed to prove his worth and knew that his only hope lay abroad. Luckily, a radio concert of his from Berlin was picked up in Sweden and he was offered a date by the Gothenburg Symphony Orchestra. Greedy for hard currency, the authorities let him go. After the concert, in March 1971, Tennstedt requested asylum. His defection passed almost unnoticed. Aged 45, he was completely unknown this side of the Wall.

For nine months, he freelanced around Sweden and West Germany until his wife, Inge, escaped on a false passport and he opted for financial security as director of opera at Kiel, on the Baltic coast, some seventy miles from his former home in Schwerin. Outwardly, his life had altered very little except in a degree of affluence. The beer he drank tasted the same, he still went sailing on Sundays and rode his bicycle around the same shoreline. It was a pleasant existence, the ambition restored to ice. 'I thought maybe I'd get asked one day to Mannheim or Wiesbaden,' said Tennstedt, 'but never to Hamburg or Munich.' He once phoned a senior DG producer to point out glaring errors in a prestige recording of a Strauss opera, only to be brushed aside like a country bumpkin. A musician from Kiel – *um Gottes willen!* – daring to fault the judgement of a great conductor. It so happened that his father, leader of the second violins in Halle, had played the music with its composer.

Then, a chain of events in 1974 transformed Tennstedt into the most sought-after conductor on earth. It began with the death of the diabetic Czech conductor, Karel Ancerl, leaving the Toronto Symphony with a sheaf of vacant dates. Its manager, Walter Homburger, flew to Europe on a listening trip. A shrewd judge of talent, Homburger had discovered the young Glenn Gould and promoted both Zubin Mehta and Seiji

Ozawa. While in Hamburg, he heard of a Bruckner Seventh being played two hours up the autobahn in Kiel. One symphony was all it took for him to engage Tennstedt to perform a Beethoven concerto with Itzhak Perlman. Following up his own hunch, Homburger advised a leading agent to be present. Next day Tennstedt was approached by Ozawa's Boston Symphony. 'What would you like to conduct?' he was asked. 'You mean I get to choose?' he replied.

He chose Bruckner's Eighth, the ninety-minute 'nightmarish hangover' that Hanslick had despised and few conductors can bring off without concentration lapses. As he entered the rehearsal, his first with a famous orchestra, Tennstedt was seized by self-doubt. 'I was scared,' he admitted. 'Music is an abstract art. Every musician when he comes into rehearsal has his own special conception. The oboe knows what tempo he thinks is right in the first theme of the scherzo, so does the second flute. Along comes the conductor and has to unify the ideas of 100 or 120 individuals. In a provincial orchestra that's no problem. But with top musicians it's a great art to persuade them of your conception. That, for me, was going to be very difficult. I was sure of the rightness of my conception, but I was never sure that I could convince them.'

He grabbed a telephone and called Kiel. 'I can't do it,' he cried, 'I am coming home.' 'Are you crazy?' shouted Inge. 'Go in there and conduct. *So, bitte!*' – and cut him off. At the first coffee break, the players rose to their feet and banged the stands in acclamation. Tennstedt was amazed. The concert itself was a revelation. He treasures a banner headline in the *Globe*:

Bruckner – Tennstedt – BSO – Once in a lifetime.

'America is a musical village,' he discovered. 'When someone succeeds in one big city, the whole continent knows about it next day.' Before the week was out he was offered concerts with the top orchestras – and like a boy in a sweetshop took them all, shuttling around America's Big Five, across the Atlantic to the London Symphony Orchestra, to Amsterdam's Concertgebouw, the Vienna Philharmonic, even to Karajan's Berlin. EMI gave him a carte blanche recording contract.

'Tennstedt is the world's great guest conductor,' says Simon Rattle. 'He has the effect of energizing an orchestra in his own way quicker than almost anybody.' But every time he faced a new orchestra, his anxiety redoubled. A less sensitive man would have basked in the adulation and banked the fees. Tennstedt kept asking himself, 'who am I, a provincial musician, to direct these fine performers, players who work only with the very greatest?' At every rehearsal, he recalls, 'I had to begin anew with all the energy I could summon.'

In Philadelphia he dissolved in tears, telling the orchestra how his father had taken the gramophone and some contraband foreign records into their bed during the War and, huddled beneath a heavy eiderdown, asked: 'Want to hear the finest orchestra in the world?' Now he was standing in its rostrum. At each rehearsal he had to crank up his courage afresh, until the effort became too great and he broke down after a US tour. He calls this crisis his '*Zäsur*', the crack between his former obscurity and sudden celebrity. All he had ever wanted lay outstretched before him, yet he dared not reach out and grasp it. He felt unworthy.

'This *Zäsur* was a terribly tough time,' he confessed. 'It was then that my love for Gustav Mahler began.' At home in his apartment overlooking the Bay of Kiel he studied symphonic scores that he had never heard performed and, in Mahler's intimate torments, found a mirror of his own. 'I, too,' he said, 'had led a complicated life.'

Past tragedies were marked on his flesh. An inoperable growth on his left hand had ended his career as a concert violinist and pushed him, after a year's homebound depression, onto the podium*. He left behind in the east a personal bereavement so intimate that he cannot yet bear to discuss it. He began to perform Mahler's symphonies as if they were a matter of life and death, as indeed they were. 'For a conductor, the relationship to Mahler *must* be the best,' he told a German journalist. 'We will always have to conduct composers we're not so keen on – you may like Grieg or Tchaikovsky, or Saint-Saëns, or whoever – but for one composer this will not do. It will not do for Mahler. One must *believe in* Mahler, wholeheartedly proclaim one's allegiance, to be able to interpret him.'

This kind of fanaticism was deeply suspect to Germans accustomed to Karajan's unruffled blanket of beautiful sound and he was ejected from the Berlin Philharmonic. Tennstedt longed to convince his own people but never quite succeeded, his anxiety increasing each time he performed for them. A Brahms *German Requiem* that brought a London audience to its feet drew puzzled grimaces from Germans. It was not seemly to make music like that. He found his favourite public in London, where luridly coiffed punks stood motionless in the bearpit of the Royal Albert Hall through his ninety minute performance of Mahler's Sixth. 'Mahler was a prophet,' said Tennstedt, 'writing not for his own time but for our own.' The London Philharmonic devoted itself unreservedly to his passions. 'Every player wonders sometimes what a conductor does,' said one rank-and-file violinist. 'With Tennstedt you don't wonder. You *know*.'

*At about the same time in Dresden, Herbert Kegel learned that a hand injury sustained during military service spelled the end of his ambitions as a pianist. He went on to become a successful conductor, with a recorded Beethoven cycle to his credit.

Midway through their first US tour, the principal percussionist, Alan Cumberland, broke his ankle, but rather than abandon his conductor and colleagues to a substitute, pedalled through Mahler's Fifth with one foot in a plaster cast. The orchestra gave 18 concerts coast to coast in twenty days, Tennstedt flogging himself to the point of exhaustion. Neither his confidence nor his constitution could stand the pace. He smoked heavily, one cigarette every six minutes, and drank steadily. The greater his success, the more insecure he became and the more dependent on his patient wife, a retired mezzo who travelled with him as a totem of reassurance. At the end of the tour he collapsed and doctors ordered him to take three months rest. He re-emerged at Easter 1985 in Salzburg, where his Bruckner Fourth was critically abused for emotional excesses. In a huff, he called off the summer's *Capriccio*.

Fidgeting away at home, he agreed to an extended interview with the present author for the *Sunday Times*. 'I must be fit for my London season,' he insisted, rattling the tankards on the table of his balcony. He pulled out a sheaf of letters imploring him to take on work he could not handle. Rolf Liebermann at Hamburg Opera offered Strauss operas, Levine at the Met wanted a *Salome*; he would have leaped at the chance of a *Ring*. Forbidden to work, he was unable to relax. He had few hobbies or extra-musical interests apart from ballooning in the Canadian Rockies, playing chess and sailing on the Bay below. He read little except scores. It was as if he feared that any slackening of concentration would jeopardize his music. Watching him pose for glamour photographs was painful; in every position he seemed angular and awkward. Only when he conducted did Tennstedt look animated.

My article concluded with an uneasy prediction:

> If he manages to balance the need for self-preservation against the demands of his uncompromising intensity, Tennstedt stands to win all the glittering prizes in the musical storehouse.

Three months later the hopes were dashed. Halfway through his London season, he went to the United States for his winter's round of the Big Five orchestras. While conducting Barber's Adagio for Strings in Philadelphia, he felt a tickle in his throat. A doctor who called at the green room examined him at his surgery next day and diagnosed cancer of the vocal cords. He flew home to undergo emergency surgery, followed by 30 days of radiation treatments. He sounded hopeful on the phone – 'I must get well, I must win' – but began to worry that his voice might fail him if ever he managed to stand again before an orchestra. He returned to give an awesome Mahler Sixth at the Royal Festival Hall that left many in tears, and five further concerts passed without mishap. The danger seemed to be over.

In June 1986 he celebrated his sixtieth birthday among friends in Israel, the first post-War German to conduct there freely, without the faintest taint of Nazism in his family. It was a heart-warming occasion with a tinge of soul-searching. He resumed smoking. The two Beethoven concerts he conducted in London that autumn were indelible. Not since Klemperer had the seventh symphony sounded so momentous. He cancelled his next date but recovered to give two galas at which he was presented to the Prince and Princess of Wales. He revelled in royal approval. He flew back to the States and broke down in Boston. He was getting a reputation for cancelling. To the discomfiture of his own orchestra, he withdrew at the last moment from a tour of Italy and Germany. After two months of recuperation, he returned to America, and lasted a fortnight. This time, doctors told him to take a year's rest. Haitink and Solti took over the LSO's spring season.

The end, when it came, was banal. He had planned a comeback with Brahms' fourth symphony, Barber's *Adagio* and Mahler's *Kindertoten-lieder* at the Proms, his favourite setting, on 25 August 1987. The Tennstedt trauma had aroused German interest and *Der Stern* sent a star reporter to the event. The BBC was televising the concert. He was going to be famous, at last.

At five o'clock in the morning, before leaving Kiel, Inge Tennstedt telephoned the London Philharmonic to say Klaus could not stomach a press conference. Not to worry, came the reply, the concert was all that mattered. On arrival in London he said he was not sure that he could face the orchestra. His fears were brushed aside; they had become part of the pre-concert routine. Driving to the rehearsal, he was tetchy and uncooperative. To the orchestra's rousing welcome as he entered Watford Town Hall, he announced that he was performing under severe strain.

The first movement of the Brahms went, despite his dread, superbly. The fervour was there for all to feel. As the orchestra heaved a sigh of relief and appreciation, the conductor went off to his green room for a coffee. Fifteen minutes later he refused to re-emerge. 'I am too ill: I just can't do it,' he told the orchestra's manager, John Willan. Singly and severally, his closest friends begged him to continue. 'Just go and stand out there, and we'll do the rest for you,' implored one player. Willan and his chairman, David Marcou, warned him of the inevitable consequences. Even the German journalist volunteered a desperate appeal. Inge Tennstedt wept on Willan's shoulder.

A joint statement was agreed by which Tennstedt 'resigned' forthwith as music director of the London Philharmonic on grounds of ill health. No orchestra could live with his terminal uncertainty. There seemed to have been no physical cause for his collapse. The doctors had given him a green light, he looked fit and had stopped a course of anti-cancer medication that made him nauseous. What cracked in Klaus Tennstedt that summer morning was his fragile self-belief. He lacked either the background or the guile to cope with a system that, like a suburban bank manager, values dependability over inspiration and a solid appearance above all else. The myth of the great conductor demanded that he should appear at all times to be in total control. Tennstedt, each time he raised a baton, walked a tightrope over an alligator swamp, exposed his terrors to all who cared to see. Ever superstitious, he blamed the final disaster on Barber's *Adagio*, the piece he had been performing when his cancer was first diagnosed.

By an effort of will and the threat of poverty, he struggled back on to the international circuit six months later with a Mahler symphony that stunned Philadelphia and New York. 'The Ninth has rarely seen such a unity,' wrote one critic, 'One suspects that Mahler would have been pleased.' Walking off the Carnegie Hall stage he stumbled, broke an arm, and conducted the next concert single-handed. Luck was never his friend. In London, 'welcome back, Klaus!' banners were unfurled whenever he entered the Festival Hall and his performances were invariably packed out. He gave a Mahler Fifth with the longest, most breathtaking Adagietto anyone could remember and seemed to be return-ing to full form. Just as the orchestra was debating his reinstatement as principal conductor, he broke a hip and cancelled six months' worth of engagements.

Like the accident-prone Otto Klemperer, Klaus Tennstedt may yet rise again. He may even discover hidden resources to overcome self-doubt and feel comfortable with his unquestioned abilities. He will not, how-ever, take another job or seek a prime position in a world he cannot understand. Outside Britain and the United States he remains unappreci-ated, denigrated in Germany, unheard in France, obscured by far smaller talents in Japan.

When the borders came down between the two Germanies there was an outpouring of invitations from the eastern sector to the finest musician who had emerged – and been submerged – in the forty years of their republic. Tennstedt delayed his return concert, uncertain of his welcome. He survives, in Simon Rattle's accurate assessment, as 'the world's great guest conductor', gracing one podium after the next, never able to settle or find his place in a musical economy that tolerates nothing less than bankable dependability.

CHAPTER 12

Insider Dealing

AT THE END of a concert by the *second* orchestra in one of America's great cities, an exuberant visitor bursts into the green room. 'Magnificent, maestro!' he gushes, introducing himself as principal conductor in a historic university town. 'When are you coming to work with my orchestra?'

'Whenever you like,' replies the weary performer, whose best efforts are forever being obscured by the local mega-band and its $500,000 a year podium star. The campus concert could be a useful break. If he plays an interesting programme, one of the music professors might review it in a scholarly journal and earn him some much-needed brownie points. He buys his new friend a few beers and drives home in his battered Chevvy, humming *Gaudeamus Igitur*.

Months later, he bumps into his acquaintance at a symphony league convention.

'I haven't yet been offered a date,' he nudges gently.

'And I am waiting for you to give *me* one,' is the frigid reply.

'I don't get it,' says the musician from the metropolis. 'I thought you enjoyed my concert and wanted me to guest-conduct your orchestra. I never realized there were strings attached.'

'Where were you born?' says the college conductor pityingly, and in words of two syllables explains that there are no free rides on the podium. In return for letting a fellow-struggler loose on musty musicologists, he expects to be rewarded with a concert in a metropolis that will look good on his own threadbare C.V.

This exchange, reported to me by the injured party, is typical of a barter system operated by music directors at every level. The top names do not stoop to such crude quid-pro-quos. They play monopoly with multinational software contracts and 'friendly gestures' – a euphemism for aggressive insider trading by the most secretive of concert parties. Music directors get ahead and stay there by means of reciprocal favours. Behind closed doors, they strike deals that determine the musical diets of Stockholm and San Francisco five years ahead, perpetuating their common prosperity. 'If you conduct two concerts for me, I'll bring a big soprano to your orchestra at half her usual price; do me an unpleasant choral modernism by a native composer and I'll throw in a Berlioz *Requiem* with television.' A music director can, if so minded, pack his season with cronies and business partners. So long as the concerts are proficient and well-attended, no-one will protest.

Thankfully, the conducting world is not a closed shop. Clashing egos and ideals create healthy competition, so that a newcomer who fails to penetrate the most powerful clique can always infiltrate another. He might join the Abbado circle, for example, by volunteering to coach one of the Italian's beloved youth orchestras. He will need, of course, to be eligible in terms of musical competence, pay certain social dues and respect club rules and historic animosities. A member of the Muti set is careful not to flirt with an Abbado loyalist, just as a Furtwängler follower would not have praised Herbert von Karajan.

Furtwängler went to vast lengths to shut Karajan out of his sphere of influence. Karajan, when his turn came, operated a watertight veto. 'The [Berlin] Senate can say Bernstein will conduct: they have the right – they would never dare do this,' he once boasted. Bernstein and Solti were past 70 before they crossed Berlin's Checkpoint Herbie. Eugene Ormandy, who snubbed the ex-Nazi on his 1955 US tour, was shut out for life from an entire continent. 'Mr Ormandy would like to conduct in Europe where I have influence that he does not,' gloated Karajan. Nikolaus Harnoncourt, the early music specialist, was permanently barred from the tax-funded Salzburg Festival, where Karajan violently resisted the concept of Mozart played in his home town on instruments the composer would have recognized. 'Authentic' Mozart performances would challenge the ersatz product peddled by Karajan and his accomplices.

Such abuses of power by the so-called 'music director of the world' are unusual only in their scale and malevolence. Antagonisms have flourished between music directors of unequal temperaments from Bach's day onwards. The difference nowadays is that conductors counter-balance their enmities with mutually supportive friendships, exactly as businessmen behave during a takeover battle. The conductor is no longer a lonely, Olympian figure but a card-carrying member of a cabal. When artists detest and strike sparks off one another, there can be creative benefits. Nothing spiritual, however, can arise from cosy collusions formed to fortify an established power structure.

'In my time,' growled Otto Klemperer at Daniel Barenboim and his back-slapping chums, 'Furtwängler, Bruno Walter and I used to *hate* each other.' This was not entirely true, for the three had shared bursts of wary esteem, punctured by interpretational and ideological differences.

Nevertheless, Klemperer's concern was well-founded. Praise by his friends can do more damage to a musician's mental balance than biased criticism. Solidarities founded on personal affection and communal self-interest are bound to undermine professional standards. Old Otto's warnings went unheeded. The young generation, blithely confident in their collective strength, leaped lemming-like into a confrontation they could never hope to win.

*   *   *

Daniel Barenboim was the brains of a brilliant group that blossomed in the 1960s and came snapping at both of Karajan's Achilles heels. Overtly Jewish and loudly lauding the lamented Furtwängler, they bonded into a defensive formation when Karajan blocked their path to Berlin. Informal, outspoken and attractive to younger record-buyers, they came together as a group in Christopher Nupen's 1969 film of Schubert's *Trout* quintet, with Barenboim at the piano, his fellow-Israelis Itzhak Perlman and Pinchas Zuckerman playing violin and viola, his wife Jacqueline du Pré as cellist and Zubin Mehta plucking the double-bass. Colleagues called them 'the Kosher Nostra', a nickname redolent of racial and mafiose incestuousness.

Mehta was the odd man out. Bombay-born scion of Zoroastrian fire-worshippers, he learned enough Hebrew and Yiddish in the Israel Philharmonic podium to fool the officiating rabbi by masquerading as a Jew at the wedding of Barenboim and du Pré, where he stood witness beneath the canopy. He had been Barenboim's closest friend since the pianist was a chubby wonder-child in short pants, brought to Europe by ambitious parents, fresh from his barmitzvah. At summer school in Siena he was taken under wing by Hans Swarowsky's star students, Mehta, then 20, and Abbado, 23. The affable Indian heaved the over-serious kid on to his shoulders, melting his grim determination with mischief and laughter.

Metha was on the brink of a flying start. After an unhappy spell in Liverpool, where he encountered racism, he passed through Montreal to take over, at 26, the world-class, well-run Los Angeles Philharmonic, remaining for fifteen years. A happy debut around the same time with the Israel Philharmonic developed into a parallel tie. When the Jewish state was besieged by Arab armies in June 1967, Mehta flew in to encourage the troops and lead the victory concert on Jerusalem's Mount Scopus. In the same heady week, he conducted performances by Barenboim and Du Pré on their wedding night.

Barenboim's aspiration to conduct had been delayed while he attained celebrity at the keyboard with Beethoven sonata cycles in London, New York and on record – a cerebral feast normally reserved for interpreters advanced in age and sagacity. His intellect was formidable; older musicians already turned to him for enlightenment. His wife, by contrast, had an instinctive gift, her world-weary account with Barbirolli of Elgar's cello concerto stunning listeners with its intuitive evocation of an old man's regrets. Curiously, when she re-recorded the concerto with her husband as conductor, her attack lost its bite.

Though Barenboim had led Australian orchestras on a tour in 1962, his breakthrough came a few years later, when a cycle of Mozart piano concertos with the English Chamber Orchestra, directed from the keyboard, brought offers pouring in from bigger ensembles. A 1968 London Symphony Orchestra concert in New York prompted Harold Schonberg to confirm in the *New York Times* that 'Mr Barenboim is a born conductor, and doubtless will develop into a major one'. Most of those he worked with belonged to his close-knit crowd. At his New York conducting debut, the soloist was the like-minded Russian exile, Vladimir Ashkenazy. Following friend Barenboim's route he began leading Mozart from the keyboard, gradually moving up to Tchaikovsky and Sibelius symphonies. After spells with the Philharmonia and Cleveland, he became music director of the Royal Philharmonic Orchestra in 1986 and of Berlin's Radio Symphony Orchestra four years later.

Furtwängler was uppermost in Ashkenazy's mind when he prepared a Beethoven symphony – 'I used to accept everything he did as perfect . . . now I am also open to Klemperer.' The old waverer had risen as oracle to the new generation. For Abbado he was 'the greatest model'. 'I can truly say that not a day passes when I don't think, "I wonder what Furtwängler would think about this," ' said Barenboim, whose interpretations were often frankly imitative.

The young lions were emerging as a force of musical destiny. As they hurtled around the globe, they kept in touch by playing Furtwängler tapes to one another over long-distance telephone calls. With Zuckerman also attracted by the baton, the clique now numbered four conductors, the rising violinist and cellist, and a host of sympathizers who included the sybaritic pianist Arthur Rubinstein, the German baritone, Dietrich Fischer-Dieskau, and most of the ECO's star guests and discoveries. Andrew Davis, an English conductor who understudied Barenboim on a Far East ECO tour, was quickly passed on to Mehta.

For fatherly guidance the group would turn to Isaac Stern, fiery New York violinist and passionate supporter of Israel. Fiscally shrewd and politically astute, Stern led the 1960 campaign to save Carnegie Hall and remains president of its proprietorial non-profit corporation. His former secretary, Lee Lamont, runs ICM, the New York concert agency that represents the leading string soloists. A man of high principles, eloquent and intellectually arrogant, Stern has been accused of keeping his adversaries out of Carnegie. He is the dominant personality in New York music, nurturing close ties with Leonard Bernstein and other influential US brokers. Barenboim's Kosher Nostra were given a second nickname, 'the Stern Gang', recalling the Jewish terrorist underground in pre-independence Palestine.

Stern's hand was sensed in Mehta's selection to succeed Pierre Boulez at the New York Philharmonic. New York was looking to turn the clock back to late romanticism and lazy listening, wooing wealthy patrons who had been scared off by the asperities of contemporary music. Sir Georg Solti was the obvious choice; other runners were Maazel, Ozawa and Haitink. Mehta, however, had friends in high places. Stern said: 'He's the right guy in the right place at the right time.' Solti, who had not forgiven the Indian for displacing him in Los Angeles, was furious at being thwarted.

Once Mehta was installed in New York, Barenboim released his American agent. 'Zubin is my manager,' he said simply, 'and I am his.' Friends were there to help one another, weren't they? His own progress as conductor had solidified with his installation in 1975 at the Orchestre de Paris in place of the ubiquitous Solti. American orchestras wanted him but Barenboim was tragically no longer available to them. His wife, the most passionate of cellists, had been struck down by a wasting disease, multiple sclerosis, and was confined to their London home under round-the-clock care. He elected to remain nearby, commuting from Paris to be with her most weekends. Still only in his early thirties, he watched her subside slowly into incoherence. Du Pré had tickled him out of his single-mindedsolemnity; he, in return, had brought her stability and serenity. Theirs was a rare union in which both partners were enhanced humanly and artistically.

Barenboim acted impeccably during 14 years of torment, though resentment and frustration periodically threatened to derail him. He found consolation in hard work, loyal friends and, after a long interval, discreetly in Elena, wife of the Russian violinist Gidon Kremer, with whom he set up home and had two children. The entire musical community, journalists included, conspired to keep his Parisian ménage secret from Du Pré until her merciful death in 1987.

Paris kept his mind fully occupied. Its orchestra presented a colossal challenge, one that had previously defeated both Solti and Karajan. Discipline was lax, training was perfunctory and the repertoire had holes in it the size of lunar craters. Brahms was booed as too German, Mahler was misunderstood and the new music director had the dubious distinction of giving the French première of Bruckner's ninth symphony, a mere eighty years after it was composed. 'France is not a musical nation,' declared the novelist André Malraux, De Gaulle's minister of culture. Barenboim set out to prove him wrong. He ordered German instruments to replace the wobbly French brass and invoked a harmonic homogeneity indistinguishable from the timbre of other European orchestras. Within eight years he had doubled the audience Karajan had attracted. 'We aimed to educate the old public and create a new one,' he said. 'Since they are not steeped in the conventional repertoire, we have been free to experiment.'

The Salle Pleyel buzzed with novelty. Lutosławski concerts that played to half-empty houses in London sold out in Paris, where the new was always chic. Composers conducted their own music – 'they need less rehearsal than anyone else,' calculated Barenboim – and a vital strand was added to his web of alliances when Pierre Boulez returned home to found IRCAM, his ultra-experimental sound laboratory. The two had shared a Berlin debut twenty years before, Boulez conducting Barenboim in a Bartók concerto; now Barenboim premièred Boulez's *Notations* and the composer responded by conducting the Orchestre de Paris and assisting in its rehabilitation. 'Boulez is one of the truly great conductors,' said Barenboim, 'yet I have never met anyone so devoid of personal vanity. He'd say to me: "You fix up your new season with all the other guests – when you have a gap, come to me, and I'll fill it." '

Their amity bore fruit when François Mitterrand, in the time-honoured fashion of French Presidents, began monumentally planning his own immortality. For the bicentenary of the French Revolution he would erect a £300 million ($600m) opera house on the very spot of the Bastille prison which irate paupers had stormed in 1789. His Opéra Bastille would finally give Paris an international house to match Vienna, La Scala and Covent Garden. Paternalistic hoardings around the building site proclaimed: 'Ici, l'état investit pour votre avenir' – 'Here the State invests in your future.' The people were, of course, not consulted. Boulez was. France's pre-eminent composer proposed the construction of a futuristic *salle modulable* – an alternative hall in which the acoustic could be adjusted electronically – and the appointment of his *cher collègue* M. Barenboim as musical and artistic director.

The less controversial of his two recommendations went through on the nod. Only afterwards did anyone point out that the *chef* of the country's top orchestra knew next to nothing about opera. Apart from a few festival Mozart and Wagner stagings, none of them particularly distinguished, Barenboim had devoted all his attention to mastering symphonic literature. He commanded a bare handful of operas and knew nothing of stagecraft. He was, however, a rapid learner – ECO players once saw him assimilate over a cup of tea a score he performed that night

– and had at his side the veteran administrator Peter Diamand, who had given the Holland and Edinburgh Festivals their operatic base. For the initial seasons, Barenboim played to personal strengths. The music director would conduct three Mozart and two Wagner operas in elaborate stagings by Patrice Chéreau and Harry Kupfer. For the rest, he called on the services of his very good friends. Boulez would come out of his lightless IRCAM dungeon to dazzle the world with Debussy's *Pelléas et Mélisande* and Schoenberg's *Moses und Aron*, Solti would cover Strauss and Mehta was ideal for Verdi. What more could an opera house ask for?

Something French was missing. *Carmen* and *Pelléas* apart, the Opéra Bastille contained none of the nation's glories, no Lully or Rameau, Gounod or Saint-Saëns, not even *Guillaume Tell* and *Don Carlos*, the great French operas of Rossini and Verdi. It was an ill-prepared, insensitive menu, to say the least, but Barenboim was deaf to chauvinist suggestions. 'The foundation of the repertoire is Mozart, Verdi, Wagner,' he insisted.

A friendly word from Mehta might have softened his stance. Unlike the ex-pianist, Mehta had been immersed in opera since his student days in Vienna and won his spurs with a 1969 *Entführung aus dem Serail* in Salzburg that prompted the veteran Mozartian Josef Krips to exclaim, 'The next Toscanini has been born!' Triumphs followed at Vienna, Milan and the Met, though not at Covent Garden, where he was haughty with the press and was attacked for glibness. Otherwise, he got on famously in hyper-sensitive opera circles – even Karajan liked him. Mehta's horizons were as broad as his ambitions were limited. He was everyone's friend, and a threat to no-one. He would come in useful to Barenboim when the tumbrils started rolling.

Things began going wrong at the Bastille before the first pane of glass was set in its concrete exterior. Cash was squandered on aborted designs, ministers kept changing their minds. The role of the existing opera houses was undefined. Mitterrand's brief was a contradiction in terms, an international opera house with high-gloss productions that would also be an 'opera for the people'. Ancillary leisure facilities were proposed, a swimming pool was contemplated. Barenboim wanted a new orchestra, musicians in the old Opéra threatened to strike. Ten experienced opera administrators refused the post of chief executive before Barenboim enticed Pierre Vozlinsky, manager of the Orchestre de Paris. The conservative prime minister, Jacques Chirac, hovered between scrapping the project and turning it into a high-culture showpiece. His government was routed at the polls.

A year after his appointment Barenboim was conducting a flaccid *Götterdämmerung* at Bayreuth when the new socialist minister of culture,

Jack Lang, walked into his dressing room during an interval, accompanied by a superbly tailored gentleman whom he presented as the saviour of the Bastille. Pierre Bergé was the legendary lover and manager of Yves Saint-Laurent, frail genius of French fashion. A brilliant entrepreneur with an explosive temper, he had built a business that sells £250 million worth of fashion accessories each year. With the rewards, he had bought himself a restaurant on the Champs Elysées and a chic theatre where he staged Monday-night lieder recitals by Caballé, Te Kanawa and Domingo. He and Yves owned a house in the high-class homosexual resort of Marrakech, a villa in Deauville and shared a country cottage outside Paris with the Langs. The self-made clothing merchant loaned the socialists his private plane during the elections. Soon afterwards he was made president of all the Paris opera houses, with a particular brief to sort out the Bastille crisis. His immediate task was to find an administrator, for Vozlinsky had quickly scuttled back to his placid orchestra. Finding potential successors deterred by Barenboim's total artistic and musical discretion, he eventually installed a Communist organizer of public entertainments, one René Gonzalez. Although pledged to support the music director, Bergé profoundly disliked his plans and personality.

Barenboim returned from Bayreuth professionally battered and publicly embattled. He had mishandled the *Ring*, parroting Furtwängler's conception and tempi without matching his penetration. Critics of several nations and varying outlooks agreed that his casting had been inept and his conducting impossibly fidgety, unsettling singers and audience alike. Barenboim brushed off criticism – 'I have received good notices for far too many bad concerts to allow my judgement to be influenced by press reviews,' he liked to say – but his inviolability was damaged and he was running out of luck. Awaiting Daniel in Paris, at the high noon of hallowed lunchtime, was a ravenous lions' den.

President Mitterrand greeted him with the Legion of Honour and a kiss on both cheeks, the Judas touch. As relations with Bergé, Gonzalez and the musicians union degenerated, they orchestrated a press campaign against Barenboim. The veteran administrator and composer Marcel Landowski, led the charge in *Le Figaro*, calling the music director an absentee landlord and claiming he would spend less than four months a year at his post. Confidential details of his contract were mysteriously leaked to the press. He was reported to be earning seven million francs a year (£700,000/$1.1m), of which £250,000 was paid salary and £20,000 ($30,000) for every performance he conducted – almost twice as much as Abbado and Maazel received in Vienna. As a foreigner, he got the first million francs tax-free.

Money, though, was never the issue. Paris traditionally rewards its artists better than most European capitals, and no-one ever criticized the millionaire Bergé for paying singers over the odds at his own theatre. At stake was not cash but clout. It was a question of who ruled France's operatic citadel, and how. In the eyes of Bergé and his glitzy, gay companions, Barenboim was an insensitive, foreign *petit bourgeois*. The conductor considered his antagonists philistines, social butterflies and xenophobes. A whiff of anti-semitism invaded his ethnic consciousness as excessive public emphasis was laid on his monetary ambitions.

While Patrice Chéreau sprang to his defence, accusing the socialists of sabotaging the opera, Barenboim remained tight-lipped. 'If I stay alive in Paris, it's because I have always stayed out of politics' was his motto, but the lack of political support proved his undoing. On Friday 13 January 1989, Bergé delivered the *coup de grâce*. He called a press conference to declare the post of Bastille music director vacant, having learned to his delight that the Chirac government had neglected to sign Barenboim's contract, negotiated in its dying days.

At the Salle Pleyel that night there were tears and cheers of sympathy as Barenboim led the Orchestre de Paris in the second act of *Tristan*. His friends rallied round within hours, sending a telegram to Mitterrand, Lang and the prime minister Michel Rocard, with copies to the news agencies, annoucing that they would not work at the Bastille until Barenboim was reinstated. The cable was signed by the soprano Jessye Norman, the producers Chéreau, Kupfer and Peter Stein and five conductors responsible for key Bastille productions: Solti, Mehta, Boulez, Carlo-Maria Giulini and Christoph von Dohnányi.

A sixth conductor, not directly involved, added his signature unprompted to the list, Herbert von Karajan, who had opposed Barenboim at every musical turn, was outraged at his treatment and realized its potential implications for every music director. On a matter of principle and a test of strength, he buried personal animosities and put his prestige behind the Bastille boycott. 'Suddenly he's my best friend,' Barenboim told intimates, 'he's calling me up every day from Austria with advice.' The scene was set for a full-scale showdown between maestros united and the might of the modern state.

Barenboim, at his own press conference the following Monday, gave the performance of his life, tackling every issue note by note and rebutting each of Bergè's charges. He was legally entitled to seek the best deal for himself and, to appease the new regime, had volunteered to cut his salary by one fifth and his fees by half. He flourished a diary showing he was spending longer than four months of the year in Paris. He denied elitist slanders. 'It is abhorrent to me that I am forced to treat a cultural programme as political, and that the future of a major cultural institution is lowered to a personality conflict,' he ebulliently declared. 'He has got them on the run,' rejoiced a supporter.

His magnificent counter-attack rocked the government and left its bicentennial plans in ruins. No conductor of quality would enter the Bastille, warned off either by Barenboim's gang, or Karajan's. When Giulini seemed to hesitate, unwilling to disappoint friends on either side of the barricade, heavy persuasion was brought to bear. Mehta, everyone's friend, co-ordinated the resistance. But just as it seemed that the solidarity of musicians might prevail over politicians, Barenboim punctured his own cause. Three weeks after the Bastille beheading, he gratefully inherited the Chicago Symphony Orchestra, worth around $700,000 a year. from the retiring Solti. He had obviously intended to hold both jobs at once, with a total income of well over a million pounds ($2m). 'It may be true that the money that musicians earn is staggering and probably far too high,' he told an interviewer. 'I don't for one minute disagree with that. But fortunately or unfortunately we live in a world, in our profession, where there is a kind of market and there are kind of accepted norms and known salaries, and I don't think that mine was out of proportion.'

What was disproportionate was his determination to hold two overpaid directorships at one and the same time. Had Barenboim, in his sudden insecurity, not rushed to claim Chicago, he would have retained public sympathy in France, and perhaps eventually regained the Bastille. By grabbing greenbacks, he confirmed in French minds everything Bergé had insinuated. His sacking was no longer a matter of principle but of expedience.

Nevertheless, conductors continued to stand firm against Bergé's increasingly desperate overtures. Sir Charles Mackerras, an eminent Australian outside the senior cliques, wanted nothing to do with the Bastille. Loners like Lorin Maazel, Charles Dutoit and Sergiu Celibidache failed to respond. Marek Janowski, Polish conductor of the Radio France orchestra, imposed impossible conditions. Bergé was descending further and further into an abyss of nonentities when Stern's friend Leonard Bernstein volunteered his multi-national youth orchestra from the Schleswig-Holstein Festival ('I don't understand him,' muttered Mehta, 'I just don't understand'). In the event Georges Prêtre, a Frenchman 'who has presided time out of mind over displays of musical mediocrity such as Paris is famous for', led a Bastille Day opening for world leaders and Jessye Norman, wrapped in a sheet of red, white and blue, sang the climactic *Marseillaise*.

Bergé had by now found an outsider who was prepared to bust the boycott. Myung Whun Chung, aged 36, had one thing in common with Barenboim: neither had conducted much opera. The Korean, younger brother of the flowing violinist Kyung Wha Chung, had deputised in a

Lorin Maazel at his youthful Bayreth debut. (Festspielung Bayreuth)

James Levine, red towel slung typically over left shoulder. (Deutsche Grammophon)

Claudio Abbado, astonished in victory. (Deutsche Grammophon)

Riccardo Muti, dumbfounded in defeat. (Philadelphia Orchestra)

Giuseppe Sinopoli: the face of things to come? (Deutsche Grammophon)

Indivisible Kleibers: Erich (*left*), Carlos (*right*). (Sony Classical)

Fragile Klaus Tennstedt. (London Philharmonic Orchestra)

The shadow of Mitropoulos, sketch by Eugen Spiro. (courtesy of Peter Spiro)

Daniel Barenboim, acknowledged ringleader. (Clive Barda)

Zubin Mehta, his trusted ally. (Clive Barda)

Sian Edwards, beating a path for women.

Neville Marriner, risen from the ranks. (BBC)

DG chief Andreas Holschneider, flanked by his early music partners John Eliot Gardiner (*l.*) and pianist Malcolm Bilson. (Deutsche Grammophon)

Esa-Pekka Salonen, fast risen from Finland. (Clive Barda)

Hard-headed Simon Rattle inspects his Birmingham concert hall. (Birmingham City Council)

Ronald Wilford, the power behind the podium. (The Lebrecht Collection)

Levine production at the Met and done enough in Verdi at Florence to become principal guest at the Teatro Communale. In the week of his Bastille appointment, he was conducting Mozart's *Idomeneo* there with a sound that was 'hard-driven, top heavy and subject to eruptions of furious snappy energy'.

Like Barenboim, Chung started out as a pianist, taking second prize at the 1974 Tchaikovsky competition in Moscow before raising his sights to the rostrum with an apprenticeship under Giulini at Los Angeles. His ascent stopped dead with a German radio ensemble in Saarbrücken. He got some second-rate dates with metropolitan orchestras but no-one left his concerts shrieking 'Eureka!' and he did not come into anyone's reckoning for a major position until the moment of his Parisian assumption. Speaking no French, he explained in Asian-accented English that he took the job 'because the reward justifies it – on a musical and personal level'. In a city with no recent record of operatic excellence, his innocence and enthusiasm will suffice until, in due course, time, tact and Lutecian temptations whittle away the Bastille blockade.

The Barenboim débâcle was a sobering setback for conductors. The two most powerful alliances of podium dictators had pitted their combined strength against blundering bureaucrats – and lost. In terms of real power, they learned, a music director might talk tough but he wields a pathetically small stick. At the place where the French nobility were forced to give up their hegemony, the conductor cabals were challenged head-on, and routed. Only Karajan came out of the crunch with any credit, burying an unnecessary hatchet with unusual grace while effortlessly extending his influence. An excess of pride, greed and myopia had brought the wrath of state on to Barenboim's head. He lost both his job and a country he loved dearly in circumstances close to disgrace. His friends had stood by him unthinkingly, without weighing the issues or opening his eyes to impending danger.

Perhaps they had no more help to give. 'I love Zubin's friends,' said Mehta's second wife soon after their marriage. 'I really love them. I just wish they would love other things as much as their music. It's all they ever talk about. I can't help thinking that a group of brick-layers or orthodontists or football players would have something else in common that they could talk about besides their work.'

Nancy Mehta had unwittingly pinpointed the group's vital strength and frailty. A preoccupation with musical politics had closed their minds to the wider world. They had become ill-informed and unadvised. An inflated collective confidence that excluded and scorned non-musicians left them isolated when power-brokers closed in for the kill. They had built themselves a musical ghetto. When its walls were breached, they were left looking helpless and dismayed.

Defeat at the Bastille stripped the last shreds of lustre from Barenboim's charmed circle. Du Pré was dead, Ashkenazy's Russian soul had turned to perestroika, Zuckerman was stuck irresolutely in the American mid-West and Perlman seemed intent on breaking world fee and sponsorship records. The fiddler had quit Stern's ICM and hitched up with Mark McCormack's tennis-starred IMG in pursuit of earthly wealth and glory. The onus rested heavily on Mehta and Barenboim to rescue the gang's collective reputation and their extraordinary God-given talent.

In January 1988 Mehta gave a moving eulogy at a London memorial service for Jacqueline du Pré. He recalled performing the Elgar concerto with Jackie and rehearsing it recently with a world-famous soloist who, seeing tears streaking the conductor's cheeks, said brutally, 'You've thinking of *her*, aren't you?' Mehta told him: 'I shall never perform this music again.'

He went straight from the service to give his first concert for 15 years with a London orchestra, conducting Strauss's sprawling *Symphonia Domestica* and Schubert's sixth symphony with such raw emotion that the London Philharmonic were swept off their seats and spontaneously asked him to become music director. Mehta mulled it over. London had always given him a poor press and he liked the idea of conquering the capital of the former empire in which he was raised. Yet, after being told by impartial critics that his credit had improved with them, he finally declined. 'I have been a music director most of my life,' he told the orchestra, 'let someone else have the headaches. I'll come back as a guest.'

He was reaching the end of his tenure with the New York Philharmonic, the longest in its history and not the most distinguished. Two years after his arrival, the orchestra lost its CBS recording contract and all but vanished from the global scene. The players broke into bitter squabbles. 'Put a hundred Italians and Jews and Scandinavians and Poles and Americans on one stage, and you're bound to have tantrums,' said a concertmaster who departed early in the Mehta era. 'There were difficult moments when the whole orchestra threw a tantrum.' Mehta seduced wealthy donors, filling the orchestral coffers and most of the seats, but whenever the Philadelphia came to Carnegie Hall with Muti, or the Chicago Symphony with Solti, he heard his orchestra comprehensively eclipsed. In a beauty contest put together by *Time* magazine, it no longer ranked among the Big Five bands, outplayed by the likes of Leonard Slatkin's St Louis Symphony. 'The music generally seemed sodden and lifeless, missing a sense of line and balance and purpose,' noted a seasoned New York observer.

The Israel Philharmonic subsided into parallel paralysis under its once-dashing director. During the 1950s and 1960s the refugee ensemble had sustained musical standards out of all proportion to its scarce funding and remote location. Bernstein, Solti, Barenboim, William Steinberg and the mercurial Sergiu Celibidache gave it high international profile and Decca regularly flew out to make records. The best players gradually grew old or trickled back to Europe and their replacements, sabras and Russian immigrants, were not always up to scratch. The Israelis probably had more problems than Mehta could overcome, but he did little for orchestral proficiency or morale. He was accused in 1987 at a Tel Aviv industrial tribunal of 'terrorizing' musicians and giving them heart attacks, after demoting a viola player with 43 years' service. To his credit, he never pandered to local sensibilities or politicians. He persistently sought to play Wagner, banned in Israel for his virulent anti-semitism, and planned to give peace concerts in Egypt long before diplomatic niceties were fulfilled. In the final analysis, though, Mehta presided over the decline of two great orchestras.

His conducting ability is incontestable, repeatedly proven with the Berlin and Vienna Philharmonic orchestras who blaze away for him in symphonic show-stoppers. 'To play with Mehta was always a feast,' said Arthur Rubinstein of his concerto partner. He is intelligent, literate, gregarious, caring. Perhaps he was just not cut out to be a music director.

In both New York and Tel Aviv, his seasons were stacked with soloists swapped with Barenboim and friends. A fresh crop of fiddlers, nurtured at New York's Juilliard School by Isaac Stern's friends Ivan Galamian and Dorothy DeLay and agented by his ex-assistant at ICM, were passed from stage to stage. They included the Japanese prodigy Midori, who cut her debut records with Zuckerman and Mehta, and the Israelis Shlomo Mintz, Gil Shaham and Matt Haimovitz. Joan Rodgers, an English soprano groomed by Barenboim for his recorded cycle of Mozart operas, received concert dates with Mehta. Despite disasters, the gang was still recruiting.

Barenboim, post-Bastille, faced fresh resistance in Chicago. He had won the orchestral vote narrowly ahead of Abbado, Solti's candidate, and in the teeth of an 'Anybody but Barenboim' campaign emblazoned across the Chicago *Sun-Times*. Musicians wondered why no American had been considered for the job. 'There are a lot of really fine conductors out there, but they are not the ones who can talk their way into a career,' muttered Jay Friedman, Chicago's veteran trombonist, implying that Barenboim owed his ascent to astute negotiating skills rather than any depth of musical interpretation. His US tour shortly afterwards with the Orchestre de Paris reinforced these prejudices in notices of unprecedented venom. *Newsday*'s Tim Page dismissed him as 'a fourth-rate conductor' and the *New York Times* called his *Tristan* 'most disappointing'.

He was also coming under fire in Israel, where he had refused to perform for troops during the Lebanon war and publicly condemned the continuing West Bank occupation. His comments in a 1989 newspaper interview nettled the dovish mayor of Jerusalem, Teddy Kollek, who sent him a cable saying don't bother to come home. The Tel Aviv daily *Ma'ariv* trumpeted his disaffection in an editorial headlined 'A conditional Israeli'. Barenboim denied any disloyalty and was soon welcomed back, though not with the same warmth. Israel was vital to his emotional stability and social conditioning. 'There was a quality of life there in the 1950s that I have never found anywhere since,' he reflects. 'We were all committed to an idealism, to building a new country, a new society. We would laugh at girls in our class who wore makeup or high heels: it seemed irrelevant and decadent. Much of my self-confidence stems from that childhood in Israel.'

Where was Barenboim's idealism when he stuck out for millions of francs? How could events have turned so sour for a musician of his supreme capabilities? Human pressures had clearly taken a toll: the parental push that dominated his childhood, the trans-global capers – playing the *Hammerklavier* sonata at Carnegie Hall within hours of landing at Kennedy – the dreadful death of his domestic bliss, the siege of Paris.

Behind these personal problems lay an older conundrum. Many brilliant instrumentalists before Barenboim had mounted the podium, but none seemed ever to translate the fullness of their playing insight to the baton. Neither Pablo Casals nor Mstislav Rostropovich, immortal cellists both, joined the front rank of conductors. Rostropovich, the acme of elegance on his cello, flails about tubbily when working the Washington rostrum. Yehudi Menuhin and David Oistrakh, violinists of singular eloquence, have been little better than adequate time-beaters. Fischer-Dieskau and Placido Domingo, deeply thoughtful singers, are superficial with stick in hand. They all turned to conducting not for cash, for they could earn twice as much as a soloist, nor out of power-lust but in the conviction that they could conjure from the orchestra the special timbre that sang so naturally out of their instrument. 'I always think in terms of orchestral colour when I play the piano,' said Ashkenazy, who progressed steadily as a concert maestro, studiously avoiding the rocks of opera on which his friend came to grief.

No-one will dispute Barenboim's capacity to captivate musicians. 'If he composed, he would be another Mozart,' said one Berlin player, 'there's nothing he cannot do.' Thwarted in Paris, he sought an opera house in Berlin and was seen at Bayreuth head-to-head with the city's cultural senator. Both the Staatsoper in the eastern sector and the Deutsche Opera in the west were going begging, and Barenboim was keenly interested – if the money was right.

His prime challenge, though, was Chicago, where the press were ready to taint him with nepotism and the orchestra were plainly unenthused. In the Windy City, there were no friends to offer solace; he stood alone between the shoreline and the stinking slaughterhouses. Chicago is an unsentimental city, merciless to weak musicians. It will make or break Daniel Barenboim's long-term prospects as an international conductor.

CHAPTER 13

Left Outside

EVEN AT THIS late stage in the emancipation of races and sexes, women and blacks are barred from conducting top orchestras and gay conductors are obliged to disguise their lifestyle. In enlightened societies where discrimination has been outlawed, concert platforms remain above the law, bastions of masculine, Caucasian supremacy. A woman may be elected prime minister. She may administer justice in the High Courts and the sacraments in church, but she cannot be trusted with a symphony orchestra for a couple of hours.

The anomalies in this situation are ubiquitous. The cabinet ministers who appointed Claudio Abbado at the Vienna State Opera and Berlin Philharmonic were both women: yet no woman has ever conducted either institution, nor has any female been admitted to the Vienna Philharmonic. In the major American orchestras, several of the top managers and many of the board members are women. None has dared to instal a female conductor. A girl can become a star singer or instrumentalist, but she need not apply to become concertmaster of the Boston Symphony Orchestra, let alone its conductor.

A similar double vision affects racial minorities. While Jessye Norman can boom her way to glory on the operatic stage, black conductors are stuck on the starting-block. There are no blacks at the head of major orchestras because none has got over impossible obstacles at ground level. The gay dilemma is more opaque, clouded by a conspiratorial silence. Against repeated allegations that certain opera houses, notably Covent Garden and the Met, have been dominated by homosexual cliques, gay conductors have learned to lie if they want to live. Opera may thrive on gay support in the upper galleries, but woe betide the gay musician who gets exposed.

Around the time Oscar Wilde was bunged into Reading Gaol, the foremost baritone in Europe was Theodor Reichmann, an imposing figure of a man who had sung Amfortas in the first *Parsifal* and Wotan in the inaugural Covent Garden *Ring*. He was a mainstay of the Vienna Opera until the day Gustav Mahler entered his green room without knocking to find him ramming a fellow from the chorus. Reichmann was dismissed from the company and died within months, broken-hearted, at the age of 54. The affair was hushed up and survives only in oral tradition. Mahler, normally well-disposed towards oppressed minorities, had acted out of strict self-preservation. Sexually insecure, he had been shrilly accused of vice by sopranos who had attempted unsuccessfully to seduce him. Had word leaked of Reichmann's impropriety, Mahler himself might have been implicated and forced to resign.

While every imaginable hetero act has been committed or simulated in the opera house, pederasty was beyond the pale. Britten and Copland, both gifted conductors, were tormented by social prejudice and, while welcomed as guest conductors, neither was put in charge of a significant musical institution. A musical director was expected to personify a myth of male potency. Any divergence from this norm risked the fate of Dmitri Mitropoulos, 'a fine, decent, altruistic man' who was hounded to an early death by the jackals of New York.

An austere idealist, Mitropoulos had been raised for the priesthood by two uncles in the monastery on top of Mount Athos after his father lost his life saving refugees from Turkish massacres at Smyrna. Deflected from a contemplative calling by his musical gifts, he composed the first modern Greek opera, *Sister Beatrice*, at 23 and was helped by Camille Saint-Saëns to win a travel scholarship to Berlin, where he studied with Ferruccio Busoni and became Erich Kleiber's assistant at the State Opera. Shunning the cosmopolitan temptations, he returned home to work at building up the Athens orchestra. Six years later, invited to conduct the Berlin Philharmonic, he found that his pianist was sick and calmly walked out to play Prokofiev's third concerto himself, directing from the keyboard. Not since Bülow's displays had Berlin heard the like. Mitropoulos was an instant sensation, showered with invitations to France, England, Italy and the Soviet Union. He persisted with his Greek orchestra and spent his guest fees on buying them new instruments.

Looming war clouds in Europe finally lured him to America. After a debut in Boston in January 1936, he moved on to Minneapolis, where 'an audience that is considered one of the calmest and coldest-handed in the country became an excited mob that staged the nearest thing to a riot ever seen in Twin Cities concert halls'. German-populated Minneapolis had lost Eugene Ormandy to Philadelphia and needed a chief conductor. News that Mitropoulos would take the job was greeted by cries of 'yippee' from the city's music critics.

A tall, bald, brawny man, his hands while conducting 'resembled those of Muhammad Ali fighting for a world title'. On the podium, 'he started punching the air bare-handed, unleashing a weird repertoire of frenzied gestures and scowls and grimaces that registered every emotion from terror to ecstasy'. Once he dug fingernails so deeply into his palms that players watched aghast as blood dripped on to the floor. He had no use for stick or score. Conducting with a baton, he said, 'is like playing the piano with gloves on'. As for a score – 'Hamlet doesn't walk on stage reading his part. Why should I?' His memory was the envy of every conductor but Mitropoulos never boasted of it. His sole vanity was reserved for his magnificent physique, which he advertised by training spotlights on himself during concerts.

A progressive in both politics and art, Mitropoulos commissioned works by Hindemith, Bloch, Nabokov, Milhaud and Copland and Krenek. He picked as concertmaster Louis Krasner, who had premièred the Alban Berg concerto, and gave with him 'the most astringent evening in Minneapolis music history', a performance of Arnold Schoenberg's violin concerto. In a middle-American industrial town he performed half of Mahler's output – music unknown in New York and *verboten* in Vienna – and made an electrifying première recording of the first symphony. In twelve years he turned a proficient, provincial ensemble into a world-beater and enjoyed the applause of the entire city. It left him totally unprepared for the lynch awaiting him in Manhattan.

After a rapturous New York debut in 1940, he was implored to replace the beleaguered John Barbirolli but by the time he consented, ten years later, veneration had turned to venom. Olin Downes, music editor of the *New York Times*, warned publicly that he regarded music as a religion and reserved 'the right to be intolerant against a believer of a different faith' – meaning Mitropoulos, whose modernism was not to his taste. Lesser critics took their cue from Downes and used the Greek giant for target practice. They attacked the kind of music he performed and its supposedly debilitating effect on his orchestra. Something in the critical tone suggests that he was being attacked not for his devotion to new music but for a different kind of love that dared not speak its name. 'Oversensitive, overweening, over-brutal, over-intelligent, underconfident and wholly without ease,' sniped Virgil Thomson with nudge-wink adjectives.

As the innuendos mounted, hagiographers were enlisted to repair his image. 'He has never married,' wrote the obsequious David Ewen, 'because he did not wish anyone or anything to divert him from his complete absorption in music!' He supposedly never touched hard liquor, was 'a disciplined smoker' and ate vegetarian food for 14 days at a stretch, allowing himself a little chicken on the 15th; in fact, he regularly patronized hamburger joints.

Foolishly, he let himself be photographed in swimming trunks for *Life* magazine and received guests in his green room naked from the waist up. 'The lonely, wifeless conductor,' noted one reporter, 'often used sexual analogies to express his ideas about the conductor's role.' Conductor and orchestra, explained Mitropoulos, were joined mystically at rehearsal in an act of intercourse that produced its 'child' in the evening performance. This kind of talk struck a low note with red-necks in the New York Philharmonic. Despising his sexual orientation and detesting the discordances he made them play, they rode roughshod over his mild attempts to impose discipline. 'He was a gentle, sweet man,' wrote Harold Schonberg, 'and that was one of his troubles.'

When Downes died in August 1955 his job went to Howard Taubman, a Toscanini cheer-leader who weighed into Mitropoulos with a full-page exposé, headlined:

The Philharmonic – What's Wrong with It – and Why.

All blame was laid at the conductor's door. Within months, Mitropoulos was forced to suggest to the Philharmonic 'that my colleague Leonard Bernstein will be invited to work with me, and I am sure that together we will be able to prepare a very sound and stimulating season'. Bernstein was hot stuff on Broadway and, to all appearances, sexually straight. The fact that he had once enjoyed an erotic connection with the Greek, who 'laid some kind of conductorial passion and groundwork in my psyche', was known only to a handful of intimates. He was now respectably married and, compared to the humiliated Mitropoulos, had the makings of a winner. At the end of the season, Bernstein ousted his sometime lover and took command of the Philharmonic.

Mitropoulos moved to the Met, where he gave its first world première for 25 years with Samuel Barber's *Vanessa* and enjoyed a warm relationship with the orchestra and directors. Two years later he was dead, felled at 64 by a heart attack while rehearsing Mahler's third symphony for a concert at La Scala. The second bassoonist drew a cross in his score at bar 86 and wrote a note at the side saying: 'Maestro Dmitri Mitropoulos died at this point of the symphony on the morning of November 2nd 1960.' He had always been a physically fit man who climbed mountains in summer. He was also a thoroughly decent human being who gave away 'most of his possessions and all of his money, mainly to needy musicians and music students'. He wilted under the savagery of New York's press and players and somehow lost his will to live. Mitropoulos was crucified for his sexuality rather than his musicality. His name has been expunged from music's hall of fame, his records are rarely reissued and his sole legacy is an international conductors' competition whose winners have included Claudio Abbado and Edo de Waart.

* * *

The orchestral homophobia Mitropoulos endured has diminished over the years as gay musicians came out of the closet and tolerance increased. However, other factors that contributed to his downfall remain unchanged. While tennis stars can titillate breakfast-time televiewers with lesbian revelations and playwrights play openly with once-forbidden fruit, conductors are required to maintain a façade of sexual 'normality'. Elaborate deceptions are contrived to fool the public. One American maestro travels with a 'live-in girl-friend' on his arm while his aides comb the streets for potential male lovers. His arrest for 'cottaging' – picking up men at a public lavatory – was shushed up by his board of management. A German conductor would frolic with his pianist boyfriend in Chancellor Helmut Schmidt's drawing room but concealed the liaison from his fans. A London music director devised a variety of euphemisms to introduce his gay companion. No matter how committed they are privately to gay pride and Aids charities, homosexual conductors are forced by the music industry to dissimulate in public.

A notable exception is Jeffrey Tate, principal conductor at Covent Garden and the Rotterdam Philharmonic, who has posed in a Sunday newspaper with his German lover, Klaus Kuhlemann, and confessed that

> . . . true love comes only after a long time of knowing someone, and has a strong element of companionship in it. I live with Klaus and I've lived with so much more fulfilment as a result of these ten years together. I now have a stable base to my life to which I can always return.

Tate's candour was conditioned by his circumstances. Cruelly disabled by spina bifida, he is immune to cheap jibes and can break down in tears during a difficult rehearsal without fearing assaults on his masculinity. He is virtually alone in his openness. Even Leonard Bernstein, who conceded nothing of himself, took umbrage at reports and books that publicized his sexual proclivities, and various protégés prudently denied any intimate connection with him.

These public constraints are imposed on gay conductors by two deep-seated pockets of intolerance. Every musician for the past century and more has known that, if he wants to be rich and famous, he has to make it in America. Half the world's professional orchestras are in the United States, funded mainly by private donations and run by committees that are dominated by women, usually the wives of leading citizens and sponsors. Lesser local ladies provide ancillary support, licking envelopes and raising funds at garage sales, fashion shows and $250-a-plate dinners. 'We women can make the difference between public apathy and an expanded market for musical services,' urges one activist.

Their reward is glamour – the privilege of socializing with the spruce figure who, nightly at their behest, bends the city's orchestra to his will. The strain of sexual fantasy and sublimation in this relationship is undeniable, and sometimes encouraged. A macho maestro in the prime of life is a powerfully attractive figure. If he is homosexual, his appeal to the lady activists of middle America will diminish.

A second pressure is exerted by record companies, whose classical consumers are predominantly male, middle-class and middle-aged. One British survey shows that two out of three buyers of classical CDs are men over the age of 35. Enter any record store on a weekday evening and you will find suburban fathers and husbands standing shoulder to shoulder at the racks of new releases, as if at a urinal. Some secretly wave their arms in front of the living-room speakers, indulging in an innocent dream of podium power.

This need for vicarious identification with musicians on record is a curious impulse that has generated a mass pastime in the Far East, where weary executives flock nightly to *karaoke* bars to sing their hearts out against pre-recorded backing, in desperate imitation of western vocalists. One in ten Japanese homes has acquired sing-along equipment intended to *'fulfil every tantalizing fantasy of stardom'*. Walter Mitty dreams are equally common in classical music and to harness them the record trade has concentrated consumer fantasies on the carefully manicured image of the conductor. On the sleeves of his discs and the windows of record stores, the maestro is made to look like everything the average record-buyer longs to be: sexually attractive to women, dominant and spiritually aloof. In a word, not gay.

Conducting careers rely on the effectiveness of record company publicity. To be a star, a conductor must conform to a preset mould, from which little deviation is permitted. Record companies require conductors to look like immaculate leader-figures – *Führerpersönlichkeiten*. Conductors who reject the essentials of this uniform image can forget fame and fortune. Seemingly all-powerful on the podium, music directors live in thrall to commercial taste. Gay conductors, victims of corporate cowardice, are advised to hide their presumed vice as timidly as any country vicar.

* * *

The podium ban on women has been blurred by marginal concessions but remains solid in the places where it counts. No substantial orchestra or opera house has appointed a woman musical director; no large record label has put its faith in a female conductor.

'There is no occupation concerned with the management of social affairs that belongs either to women or to men, as such,' wrote Plato two millennia ago; yet the idea of a woman managing the performance of

music remains anathema even in societies where women have achieved
the highest office. Committee wives in middle America are said to abhor
the notion of a female incumbent, while male commuters want the symphonies they hear while driving to work to be conducted by one of their
own.

Whether they act tough or soft, women conductors have been given a
hard time by male-dominated orchestras. Women politicians can get away
with wheedling and posturing, but conductors, whose appeal to fellow-
musicians is instinctive, are dismissed as frauds once they seem to act out
of character. Unable to play a role and unable to be herself, a woman
conductor has still to find her natural place in the podium.

In orchestral society as a whole, women are relative newcomers. The
first female musicians in London were engaged in 1913 by Henry Wood,
who was frankly amazed that his men 'took kindly to the innovation'.
Adrian Boult filled a quarter of his BBC Symphony Orchestra with girls,
but would not let them into the cello section, where their posture might
provoke lascivious distraction. Musicians' unions in America refused to
admit any women until 1904 and two further decades passed before the
sex barrier was broken in a major orchestra, when Alfred Hertz hired
five girls at the San Francisco Symphony. The New York Philharmonic
held out against women until 1966. Leopold Stokowski, whose preference
for female companionship was widely reported, refused to have women
in his Philadelphia Orchestra. Thirty years later, Stokowski underwent a
Pauline conversion and threw his prestige behind the conducting aspirations of his secretary, Beatrice Brown, who ran an orchestra in Scranton,
Pennsylvania. 'Why should there not be women conductors?' mused
Stokowski. 'Perhaps at the beginning there will be prejudice . . . but if
she is a good conductor the public will come to accept her.' He took on
Judith Somogi to train his American Symphony Orchestra and she went
on to become *Kapellmeister* at Frankfurt Opera under Michael Gielen's
liberal regime. 'What we need now is a whole army of women pursuing
conducting careers,' urged Somogi shortly before her early death of
cancer, but Europe was unmoved and the Berlin Philharmonic was still
kicking up a ruckus over Karajan's introduction of a woman clarinettist.

For many years, the only option for a woman conductor was to start
a single-sex orchestra, a questionable entertainment offering high culture
with a hint of naughtiness. The high-minded Vienna Ladies Orchestra
ended up playing in American beer gardens. Mahler's niece, Alma Rosé,
daughter of the Vienna Philharmonic concertmaster, directed her Wiener
Walzer Mädeln until a tragic romance led to her incarceration in Auschwitz where she conducted a women's ensemble that played for the SS
guards, until they murdered her.

In France, Jane Evrard, wife of the well-known conductor Gaston

Poulet, directed 'the fairies' orchestra' in the 1930s, recording music written for her ladies by Roussel, Schmitt and Rivier. Evrard felt a woman was innately inhibited from conducting an orchestra of men, 'which often lacks discipline and resents receiving orders from anyone not of its own kind'. Around the same time, Kathleen Riddick formed a London Women's String Orchestra and kept it afloat with money chipped in by her players. It was a sound investment so long as the war lasted and the ensemble was often heard over the BBC. Once the men came home, normal service was restored and the group lost all its work, leaving Riddick to eke out her career with the employees' orchestra of the Midland Bank. The surviving women's orchestras nowadays are mostly hardline US feminist groups, such as the Bay Area Women's Orchestra of San Francisco which plays music exclusively by female composers.

An unsatisfactory alternative for a woman conductor was to lead a choir. Margaret Hillis was pushed into starting the Chicago Symphony Chorus for Fritz Reiner after finding all orchestral avenues tightly closed. She has directed the chorus in hundreds of concerts and award-winning recordings in Chicago, without ever being given the chance to make a symphonic record of her own – despite deputizing successfully at several Solti concerts. Hillis has been confined to conducting the Chicago Civic Orchestra, a training group for the main band.

The pioneer women who led the first assaults on the podium tended to be more masculine than the men. Ethel Leginska, a concert pianist 'of considerable power', wore men's suits and would be mistaken for Paderewski in the half-light of a concert hall. Having run away at fourteen from Hull (where she was born plain Ethel Liggins) to Vienna, she married an American composer, Roy Emerson Whithorne, and fought him unavailingly for the custody of their infant son. Dusting herself off after the divorce, she formed a 100-man Boston Philharmonic Orchestra and a separate Women's Symphony Orchestra of Boston, wrote an opera, *The Rose and the Ring*, and directed performances of *Carmen*, before retiring to the West Coast in despair. Her activities overlapped those of Antonia Brico, a Dutch-born Californian who in the early 1930s was the first woman to conduct the Berlin Philharmonic and the Metropolitan Opera – where she was dismissed after two performances when a baritone, John Charles Thomas, refused to sing under a woman.

More resilient was the bombastic British composer Dame Ethel Smyth, of whom London musicians surmised that 'had she not been a woman, recognition would have come to her earlier, and possibly more easily, *as a conductor*'. Dame Ethel in full cry was a Boadicean figure of formidable proportions. Her most famous concert was conducted not with the baton but a toothbrush – leading fellow-inmates in a suffragette hymn at Holloway jail, where she was serving a two-month sentence in 1912 for heaving a brick through the Home Secretary's window. Anyone who could cow Virginia Woolf into submission would have no difficulty dealing with an orchestra, and Dame Ethel was much respected by her men. Her shortcomings as a conductor were technical rather than disciplinary for, while her beat was precise, it lacked the flowing grace essential to coherent music-making. She was anyway too occupied in creative social and sexual conquests to pursue a conducting career in any earnest.

The female conductor who achieved the greatest extent of male approval was the maidenly Frenchwoman, Nadia Boulanger, who enjoyed the confidence of Fauré and Stravinsky and gave private lessons to three generations of composers, mostly American. Shadowed by the memory of a short-lived sister of superior gifts, the long-lamented Lilli, Boulanger dedicated herself sternly to the unbending rigours of Roman Catholicism and neo-classicism, and the pounding rhythms of her Russian ancestors. She never gave herself to a man, abominated modernism and expelled any pupil she discovered was divorced.

Boulanger was steeped in the music of her church and played a vital role in the revival of Monteverdi, making a revelatory set of première recordings. She became the first woman to conduct the Boston Symphony, Philadelphia Orchestra and New York Philharmonic and, in Washington, DC, on 8 May 1938, gave the world première of Stravinsky's *Dumbarton Oaks*. As both teacher and conductor she made huge inroads into masculine domains but seemed unwilling to consolidate the gains for others of her sex, and habitually deferred to male authority. After Boulanger, there was no deluge and women waited for several decades before the liberationist movement shook the barriers and two female conductors commanded the attention of American opera-goers. When Sarah Caldwell conducted *La Traviata* at the Metropolitan Opera in January 1976 it was hailed as a social milestone, though Brico had been there long before and Caldwell had been labouring fruitfully for some years in Boston, where she had given a variety of important US premières, including Berlioz's *Les Troyens* and Schoenberg's *Moses und Aron* – all in her own productions.

The lightness of her musical touch belied a 300-pound girth that forced Caldwell to conduct sitting in an armchair. The critic Andrew Porter considered her 'the single Best Thing in American opera' and wrote that 'in a well-ordered world, Miss Caldwell would be treated as a national treasure, freed from financial and administrative cares, and enabled to concentrate all her spiritual, dramatic and musical fire on the performance of operas'. Unhappily, cash crises forced her into dubious decisions. After signing a 1982 agreement with the avaricious Marcos regime to provide opera in the Philippines, she was picketed by human rights campaigners in Boston. Soon afterwards she arranged to revive opera in Israel – in the midst of a Palestinian uprising. Caldwell has been neither wise nor lucky.

Eve Queler meanwhile was introducing New York audiences to early operas by Strauss and Puccini and making a fine recording of *Guntram* in Budapest. Judith Somogi had perceptively noted that a woman would stand a better chance conducting opera than concerts because in the pit she was less visible, and offensive, to conservative audiences. In 1990, the American Symphony Orchestra that Stokowski had created announced that a woman, Catherine Comet, was to be its principal conductor. But the ASO was no longer much of a pace-maker, having reduced its activities to six concerts a year. At the time of writing, no leading orchestra in any country has installed a woman as chief conductor, despite a rising tide of promising girl graduates from conducting courses at the conservatories.

The nearest that music has come to changing its ways is in London, where the violinist Iona Brown was chosen to direct the Academy of St Martin-in-the-Fields, the scholarly Jane Glover inherited the London Mozart Players and an effervescent Cuban-American, Odaline de la Martinez, formed a modernist ensemble of her own. Glover in particular made headlines by conducting opera at Glyndebourne, commentating in concert intervals on television and sacking two-thirds of her players in a sweeping reconstruction. Neither she nor the others, though, have yet gained a position with London's international orchestras.

The promising exception is a bespectacled young redhead called Sian Edwards, who in 1988, aged 28, became the first woman to conduct at Covent Garden and over the next three years joined the staff and rescued troubled productions. Thrust in to conduct *Il Trovatore* without rehearsal, she impressed senior members of the orchestra with her unflappability. 'It was very nice,' she laughed later. 'This way you don't tangle with anyone – you just come in and act like the icing on the cake.' She gave the world première of a British opera at the Munich Biennale and made a wider impact on the Orchestre de Paris and the Los Angeles Philharmonic.

London's orchestral community quickly cottoned on to her capabilities and engaged her for several concerts. 'She made a terrific impact in Mozart symphonies – full of confidence and authority,' said one of the players, 'but she came unstuck in a *Symphonie Fantastique* and our players are very unforgiving.' She was asked back for further concerts but there was no inkling of a position with any British orchestra. Although the Hallé, the Scottish and the BBC regional ensembles were desperately seeking a conductor who could raise them out of mediocrity, the vacancies were, in effect, closed to females.

A tree-climbing tomboy of Welsh ancestry, Edwards rebelled against

settled British ways and undertook a rigorous training at the Leningrad
conservatory after meeting the Estonian conductor Neeme Järvi. 'The
way he conducted was so exciting and magnetic that I asked him, how
do you do it? He said, I practise five hours a day, with an orchestra or
in front of a mirror. This was news to me. I had the British idea that
conductors were born, not made. In the Soviet Union I discovered that
they teach conducting just as they teach the violin or piano.'

The emotional depth-charges that Russians plant in music transformed
her perspectives and, on her return, a college performance of Tippett's
fourth symphony prompted the octogenarian composer to recommend
her to the Royal Opera House for a revival of *The Knot Garden*. Her
ascent until the age of thirty was eased by the approval of important
men. Simon Rattle sent her to Scottish Opera to cover his cancellation
and Bernard Haitink took her under his wing at Glyndebourne. Rattle
also urged British orchestras to recognize her potential as a likely leader
of the next generation. 'There are never enough good conductors to go
round,' he said. 'It's a matter of conductors growing with an orchestra,
having an opportunity to grow.' His appeal fell on deaf ears and early
in 1991 Edwards left Covent Garden to strike out independently in a
determined worldwide quest to capture a professional orchestra. The
sight of a woman conducting opera was now commonplace and welcome
in London, New York and other enlightened societies. But the real
barrier to female progress stood as firm as ever, and the prospect of a
woman standing tall in front of a major orchestra to conduct a symphony
still shimmers as a distant mirage.

*   *   *

The story of black conductors is brief and bitter, an account of pervasive
discrimination. After quarter of a century of equal rights, fewer than one
musician in a hundred in American orchestras is black. In Detroit, which
has a black majority population, the state legislature has threatened to
slash subsidies unless more than one black is brought into the symphony
orchestra.

Black musicians in America have long campaigned to be allowed to
audition behind a screen, asking to be judged only by the sound they
make rather than by their looks. In 1969 two black string players sued
Leonard Bernstein and the New York Philharmonic before the New York
State Commission on Human Rights for refusing to allow them to audition
unseen. Bernstein argued that he had to see how a man played before
hiring him, and won the case.

Unable to get into orchestras, blacks had no chance whatever of conducting them. In the 1920s a young British Guianan, Rudolph Dunbar,
came to study at the Juilliard School, paying his fees by playing the

clarinet in Harlem jazz bands. Unable to make headway in the concert hall, he came to Europe where he was fêted by Debussy's widow and gave a celebrated recital at the Salle Pleyel. Crossing the Channel he led an all-black dance band in fashionable London restaurants until, three years into the War, he attained his ambition and conducted the London Philharmonic at the Royal Albert Hall. After the defeat of Nazism, he also got to conduct the Berlin Philharmonic. Neither engagement led to anything more and Dunbar wandered off into introspective isolation, devoting 'much of his time and energies to waging war on the racism which thwarted his progress'.

The first black to become a music director was Henry Lewis, who in 1968 took charge of the New Jersey Symphony Orchestra. Lewis began playing the double-bass in the Los Angeles Philharmonic when he was 16 and, on military service, managed to conduct the Seventh Army Symphony Orchestra. In 1960 he married the soprano Marilyn Horne and made a name for himself as her husband, attracting most attention when he conducted her performances at the Met. He continued to work there long after their divorce but the stigma attached to a diva's husband never really faded. Andrew Porter in the *New Yorker* called him 'a conductor of no particular merits other than simple vitality' and on another occasion attacked 'the styleless, erratic conducting of Henry Lewis, on which the show foundered'. Lewis, for his part, has remained optimistic about the future for black conductors.

Little has happened to justify his hopes. A couple of blacks have conducting jobs in the American backwoods and a handful of youngsters have won apprenticeships with metropolitan orchestras but the general situation is, if anything, bleaker than it was in 1945. In Europe, Isaiah Jackson of Virginia has the inauspicious position of music director with the Royal Ballet in London, while James DePriest, a nephew of the contralto Marian Anderson, has concert engagements in Scandinavia. In an increasingly multi-racial continent, the podium is out of bounds to minorities.

The black conductor who came closest to piercing this wall of prejudice was a New Yorker called Dean Dixon, whose parents took him to Carnegie Hall as a kid and switched off the radio when pop songs were playing, to protect his precious ears. At 17 he formed the Dean Dixon Symphony Society and aroused enough interest for Eleanor Roosevelt, the First Lady, to get him a date with the New York Philharmonic in August 1941, after he had completed his doctorate in music at 26 years old. Unable to impose himself on a group of hostile white men, he assumed a remote and lofty attitude that won him their respect but no appreciable affection. 'He literally never raises his voice,' noted a *New York Times* reporter. 'His authority stems not from a sense of personal power but from his knowledge of the music. Dixon can play, and is familiar with the difficulties and limitations of every instrument in his orchestra.'

He received follow-up invitations from Toscanini's NBC Symphony Orchestra, Boston and Philadelphia but was unable to land a job and finally formed his own American Youth Orchestra. In 1948 he received a major award for outstanding contributions to American music and later that year left the United States for good. 'I kicked myself out of America,' he explained indistinctly, 'because helping a Negro in *my field*, a field which requires a certain intellectual background, which requires a *leadership* ability, goes against what America says we Negroes don't possess.'

After a stint with the Israel Philharmonic, he settled in Sweden with the Gothenburg Symphony Orchestra and guest conducted across Europe. He was popular in Paris, where in 1960 he gave the French première of Mahler's ninth symphony, and divided the latter part of his career between Frankfurt, where he led the radio ensemble, and Sydney where he worked with the symphony orchestra and helped inaugurate the new opera house. His recordings include interesting and arcane repertoire and his conducting courses at Salzburg were well-attended. Dixon's experiences had given him insights into human nature that he was keen to pass on. 'Dean Dixon took conducting very much from the psychological point of view,' recalled one student, Edo de Waart. 'He was always talking about the psychological side of it and how the conductor himself should not be excited but should get his players excited.'

Dixon finally returned to New York for an acclaimed series of summer concerts in 1970 and died five years later in Switzerland aged 61, a prophet without honour in his own country. His drive and determination, not to mention his very considerable natural gifts, would have won him leadership in any walk of life where opportunities were approximately equal. Had he taken a different course, he could have become a US senator, supreme court judge or captain of industry. In conducting, he was shoved to the sidelines: voluntarily exiled from his homeland, he was treated as an exotic curiosity wherever he went. He was alone of his kind, received with respect and kindness in humane societies which, however, did not wish to produce others like him. The black conductor was a musical anomaly that was not to be further encouraged.

Such tacit resistance to conductors of the wrong colour, sex and sexual orientation was not founded on racist or reactionary creeds, nor even on the personal tastes of powerful managers. There was never any question as to the cultural and emotional suitability of Dixon and Leginska to perform symphonic music, far less of their proven musical capabilities. This was simply a matter of business. Given the prejudices of record companies and the predominance of middle-class values in concert life, blacks, women and known homosexuals have been effectively shut out of the podium. A thaw of sorts is becoming discernible, and the chances of 'outsiders' are marginally better than they were a generation ago. But the art and its consumers are imprisoned by tradition and it will take a talent of immense proportions to break the barriers once and for all – a female Furtwängler, a gay Toscanini or a black Nikisch.

Formidable Ethel Leginska

CHAPTER 14

The Search for a Semi-Conductor

TYRANNY IS A habit, warned Dostoevsky in *The House of the Dead*: it may develop into a disease. As conducting reached the summit of its attainments, despotism became so addictive that it was accepted as a natural condition. To combat it might kill the patient, and isolated players were not prepared to risk their jobs in the attempt. When power was seized in Russia in the name of the downtrodden proletariat, orchestral musicians were infected by the revolutionary spirit and banded together to cast off the yoke of conductors. In 1922, Muscovite players gathered around Koussevitsky's former concertmaster, Lev Zeitlin, to form a conductorless orchestra. They called it Persimfans, an abbreviation of PERvyi SIMfonicheskii ANSambl, meaning First Symphonic Ensemble and suggesting itself as the model of future concert organization in the USSR. The players sat facing one another in a semi-circle, their backs to the audience. At rehearsal, 'there was a workshop atmosphere generated by proud artisans bound together in the common task of making good music', reported a visiting soloist, Joseph Szigeti. 'Each man had the right to have his little say on occasion . . . bickerings, backbiting, sycophancy had no place in their setup.'

Prokofiev was surprised to find they could cope undirected with his fidgety rhythms; 'the only difficulty lay in changing tempo, for here the whole ensemble had to feel the music in exactly the same way'. Darius Milhaud, another composer whose work they premièred, remarked tartly that 'a conductor would have obtained the same results, no doubt a little faster'. Zeitlin took the criticisms to heart, saying 'we are not opposed to conductors, only to *bad* conductors'. Otto Klemperer was invited to give a concert, in the middle of which he was sent to sit among the audience while the Persimfans played on their own. In a farewell speech, he asked rhetorically, 'Is a conductor really necessary?'

> In the last analysis I remain of the opinion that [he is]. First, there are new works of such complexity that an assured performance without a

conductor is scarcely possible. Secondly, however precisely detail is prepared in rehearsal, at the actual concert there is always an improvised 'something' . . . otherwise a performance is machine-like.

Persimfans flourished for a decade and spawned some imitators until Stalin's hand descended to disperse its individualists among state institutions or labour camps. Real democracy was inimical to people's democracy and the Persimfans experiment was never revived in the workers' paradise. Its next appearance was half a century later in the capital of capitalism, where a collective of 26 New Yorkers formed the Orpheus Chamber Orchestra, whose sparky concerts got them on to the grand maestros' label, Deutsche Grammophon.

The originator of Orpheus, Julius Fifer, developed such an allergy to conductors while playing cello in the opera pit that each night he would 'have to go home and play scales to cleanse my ears of the experience'. Orpheus needed twice to four times as much rehearsal as conducted ensembles, but what it spent on extra sessions was saved in star salaries. Interpretations were worked out by principal players elected by their sections, but every member had the right to voice an opinion during rehearsal. To avoid the blandness and monotony that Klemperer warned against, the players encouraged one another to take risks and indulge in large gestures. Orpheus, said Fifer categorically, 'does not get conducted. We don't need someone to wave their arms for us to understand a phrase.'

Orpheus has preserved its liberty for almost twenty years, a feat unique among enterprises of its kind. While it is common enough for fed-up instrumentalists to declare independence from large orchestras and form their own chamber groups, it is almost axiomatic that sooner or later a *primus inter pares* arises to dominate the ensemble and eventually conduct it. Player republics were neither motivated nor structured to resist the surge of a determined power-seeker. No vacuum is more abhorrent to nature than a power vacuum, and someone was always waiting to 'save' the venture from impending anarchy. Thus, the idealism that inspired such co-operatives became harnessed to the ambitions of an individual – never more so than by the future Robespierres of a freedom movement that called itself the Early Music Revolution.

London was a fertile hatching ground for small ensembles, drawn particularly from the ever-rumbustious London Symphony Orchestra – itself the product of a 1904 rebellion against Henry Wood. The most prolific of its offshoots branched out in 1959, when the leader of the LSO's second violins persuaded disaffected colleagues to join him for baroque concerts after evensong in a famous 18th-century church in

Trafalgar Square. 'At the outset,' said Neville Marriner, 'it was immensely democratic. Everyone talked at the same time during rehearsals, everyone threw in their bits. Now, of course, because of the success of the Academy, we have too many deadlines to meet and so it is a much more authoritarian affair.' The Academy of St-Martin-in-the-Fields developed into the world's most recorded orchestra. Its founder, a noted tormentor of music directors, has now conducted more discs than any maestro apart from Herbert von Karajan. Marriner's rise from radical to ruler was non-violent and unopposed, yet in many respects exemplified the trend by which egalitarianism gave way to managerial discipline.

The Academy's early efforts were inauspicious and it took ten years before Marriner had enough confidence to leave the LSO. Their concerts were poorly attended and thinly reviewed, though among the tarrying worshippers was an Australian heiress, Louise Dyer, who mothered the ensemble on her songbird label, L'Oiseau Lyre. Further recordings were made for Decca before the breakthrough came in 1970 with Vivaldi's *Four Seasons*, 'which did all the things that record companies dream of, like getting two golden discs and paying for all the unsuccessful recordings they had made that year'. The sessions were nightmarish. All morning in a Westminster church, the band was bedevilled by outside noise and internal inhibitions; their flamboyant New Zealander soloist, Alan Loveday, was unnaturally subdued. At lunchtime, having failed to record a single publishable bar, they slunk off to a bar of another kind, where the hospitality was so liberating that the *Seasons* spun round in the afternoon on a cloud of high spirits and shot straight into the best-selling charts. The record served as a calling-card and the Academy travelled behind it all over the world.

Marriner expanded the playing strength to more than seventy, taking on Sibelius suites and hiving off an Academy Chamber Ensemble to cover the smaller stuff. He clapped eyes on a disused pumping station in east London and re-envisaged it as a record and rehearsal studio, while building up a regular following as resident orchestra in the second South Bank hall. As conductor and owner, Marriner governed by the consent of colleagues who admired his acumen and lack of pretension. Stick in hand, he was still the same 'Nev', unexalted by wealth and sensitive to the feelings of fellow-musicians. When a refugee violinist was hauled off the train for questioning by Austrian border police, Marriner rode on to Vienna and announced quietly on arrival that his sold-out concert would not commence until the detained man was safely in his seat. He was too much a musician to stand apart from his players; he shared their robust humour and was colloquially plain-spoken – 'one of the lads'. His son, Andrew, followed his footsteps into the LSO.

The Vivaldi hit established the *Four Seasons* as aural wallpaper and, perversely, detached Marriner from his creation. 'Wherever we went, we were asked for the *Seasons*. I got very tired of jumping through the same hoop over and over again, and I could see the same thing happening with the Brandenburg concertos and some Haydn symphonies. So I decided to go back into symphonic repertoire, with a baton in my hand, and conduct symphony orchestras.'

Unable to convince London orchestras to take him seriously, he enlisted a high-powered American agent, Ronald Wilford, to land him full-strength ensembles in Minnesota and Stuttgart. Neither promoted him to the major league of symphonic maestros and he sensibly reverted to base and what he knew best. His fate was typical of chamber orchestra directors who, no matter how dominant in their field, seemed generically unsuited to the big time. Parallel ascents by the Londoner Boyd Neel, Karl Münchinger of Stuttgart and Rudolf Barshai of the Moscow Chamber Orchestra were to end in failure. They were regarded as semi-conductors, rather than full-blown maestros, and were never accorded star treatment by the record companies.

While concentrating on his own career, Marriner left the Academy's musical leadership to its first violinist, Iona Brown, and gave the players a share in running the company – only to have them overturn his expansion plans and abandon the pumping-station project. He took the setback quietly and returned to carry on business as usual. Reliability was the hallmark of his recordings and the secret of their consistent sales. People who bought a Marriner product knew they were getting value for money, honestly played music with no frills or missing notes. He had studiously assimilated the requirements of recording by watching masters at work. As a young violinist he had played throughout a hot August, three sessions a day, seven days a week, for Pierre Monteux and Antal Dorati who were working their way through the symphonic repertoire for US labels that refused to pay the prohibitive union rates of American orchestras. He acquired technical expertise from Dorati, who was brilliant at patching up a spotty performance with short retakes and bits of tape, and musical freedom and fantasy from Monteux, with whom he took private lessons. He rounded off his education by playing in the Philharmonia under Karajan, who produced 'astonishing orchestral playing, probably the best England ever had', but whom he found interpretatively unsatisfying. Karajan, he said, was 'meticulous in a way that sometimes can work to the music's disadvantage – though you will rarely find any flaws'.

Marriner aimed to achieve perfection within a free-flowing performance. He would record entire movements at a time, cleaning up any lapses at the end of a session. His musicianship appealed to some of the most discriminating soloists, among them the cerebral pianist Alfred

Brendel and the incorrigible violinist Henryk Szeryng, who enjoyed shaking less secure directors from their pedestal. A conscientious craftsman, Marriner would bring his craft home on time, and within budget. 'He taught me how to discipline his time so as to get the most out of his players . . . how to finish a rehearsal on the dot,' said the Academy's harpsichordist, who watched him intently, as Marriner had once watched Dorati and Monteux.

His matter-of-factness about the process of making music was much appreciated by cost-conscious producers, less so by some concert critics who complained that Marriner was efficient to the point of tedium, 'conducting like a machine for the performance of recorded music'. He confounded sceptics with elevating recordings of romantic works where one least expected him to excel – Beethoven's *Eroica*, for instance, and Samuel Barber's Adagio for Strings.

'We very deliberately moved away from the baroque period,' he remarked, 'because we could see there was a revolution coming in performing conventions.' The Academy had helped foster these changes. Marriner took guidance in performing style from a Cambridge harpsichordist, Thurston Dart, whom he once partnered in a recital duo. Dart, a professorial evangelist, believed in playing Bach and Handel at the dancing speeds of their epoch, rather than with the portentous respect that had encrusted their music. The Academy rolled off the weight of posterity and charmed its listeners with light and sprightly rhythms. 'We tried to observe historical accuracy,' said the conductor, although he used modern instruments and intonation.

Various of his players went one step further and experimented privately with period instruments. His harpsichordist, a Cambridge antiquarian of fundamentalist inclinations, seethed with unconcealed discontent at the middle road he was obliged to follow. 'Chris Hogwood and I don't agree very much about style,' Marriner would acknowledge. 'I know he suffered a great deal when he worked with us.'

While toiling in the service of St Martin, Hogwood recruited some of Marriner's players into his own ensemble, the Academy of Ancient Music. He also borrowed the Academy's premier record producer and made his first recordings for L'Oiseau Lyre and Decca in St John's, Smith Square, the Westminster church that Marriner favoured. While editing a *Messiah* for the Academy of St Martin to record, he was studiously planning his own version, on a scale that Handel might have recognized. Hogwood had seen a future in reinventing the past, and proposed to exploit it imperially.

The early music bandwaggon began to roll in post-industrial societies that were discovering real ale, wholewheat bread, carbonated spring water and open-toed sandals. Its basis was academic and its premise unarguable: to perform exactly what the composer wrote, in the way he wanted to hear it, on the instruments and in the style of his time. The effect was quicker, leaner, and lower pitched than modern audiences were accustomed to hear. It was also distinctly painful to sensitive ears. When museum instruments, or their replicas, were played by any but the most practised exponents, the sound could be as scraggy as a school band. True believers enjoyed seeing their neighbours wince. This was, in all but name, a campaign for real music, aimed at altering sonic perspectives and taking classical music out of massed philharmonic production.

In authentic instrument ensembles, all players were equally respected for a studious and sometimes seminal expertise, both technical and theoretical, at their particular instrument. The director was a colleague who led performances from either the keyboard or first fiddle. 'I'm for democracy to the point of anarchy,' declared Christopher Hogwood. 'Your oboe d'amore player is fully aware of the state of the art regarding his instrument, its technology and history. [As director], you accept what he feels best in the circumstances. You are the umpire between the players. No-one wants to get back to the maestro situation of a bunch of mice playing baroque instruments and a great conductor telling them to do it his way. Because that is the point where you lose touch with individual research.'

Such sentiments resounded pleasantly around the Cambridge halls where the movement gained a cultish following. Comradely feelings persisted, as with the Bolsheviks, until power came within grasp and dictators took control. The Finland Station of the early music revolution was situated somewhere in London or Hamburg, behind the higher windows of a crisis-ridden record industry.

Record barons had been caught flat-footed by the 1970s oil recession. Raw materials rose steeply and sales plummeted in economies hit by sweeping unemployment and double-figure inflation. The cost of recording a solo recital in New York soared to $6,000, an orchestral disc to $50,000 and an opera to $100,000 – prices that doubled again by the end of the decade. Neither pop nor classical sectors could find new stars or sounds and the release sheets looked stale and predictable. A misguided bid to replace stereo with quadrophonic sound, forcing hi-fi buffs to replace their amplifier and buy two extra speakers, was launched haplessly in mutually incompatible formats at the lowest ebb of customer confidence. The industry desperately needed a different type of sound, allied to a technological miracle.

Both could be glimpsed through the gloom. Decca and Philips were developing digital recording systems that captured sound clean of hiss or crackle and enabled the tiniest voice and instrument to project on record. Deutsche Grammophon, their PolyGram group partner, entrusted its musty Archiv label to Andreas Holschneider, a Hamburg University musicologist whose researches centred on performance practice in previous times. Holschneider made his own edition of Mozart's version of *Messiah* for Charles Mackerras to conduct in Vienna, but soon forsook modern orchestras for original instruments. His polished practitioners refurbished the sound of familiar classics by playing them half a tone lower down the diatonic scale on instruments of a distinctly different timbre. Digitally recorded, they achieved spectacular sales on ultra-clear compact disc. Success catapulted Holschneider to the presidency of DG and the esoteric area of period performance to best-seller status. Hogwood was christened 'the Karajan of early music' on coming third in the 1983 annual Billboard chart, behind Placido Domingo and Kiri Te Kanawa but ahead of any symphonic conductor. In the last classical Top Ten of 1989, his compatriot Roger Norrington had no fewer than three hits.

It does not take an accountant to appreciate why early music was so attractive to record companies. A *Messiah* conducted by Georg Solti in Chicago called for two hundred participants and four highly paid operatic stars. Hogwood, who wrote a Handel biography, used the composer's complement of 35 musicians, forty choristers and light-voiced soloists, substituting 'authentic' parsimony for audacious pomp. *Messiah* continued to shrink with each passing year until Harry Christophers and his choir, The Sixteen, whittled the oratorio down to living-room size with 18 players and 21 singers. On compact disc, Christophers' matchbox version cold be turned up to outblast the most leviathan assemblage.

The revolution stretched far beyond Baroque repertoire. By 1990, three early music ensembles had completed the Beethoven symphonies and concertos, a recording summit for which eminent symphonic conductors waited unavailingly all their lives. In concerto, the primitive fortepiano, which could never make itself heard above a full-sized orchestra, was restored intriguingly to circulation.

The early music revolution triumphed by means of a pact between fringe fanatics and leading industrialists. Once secure, it outlawed the kind of music-making people used to enjoy. Conductors no longer dared perform Bach with a modern orchestra, and almost all pianists removed the Goldberg Variations from their concert grand; virginals and harpsichords became compulsory for pre–1750 sonatas. Hogwood had Mozart's Requiem stripped down to the composer's last deathbed notes, erasing his pupil Süssmayr's completions. A massive *Messiah* was permissible only if it purported to re-create a historical event, such as Westminster Abbey's grandiose Handel commemorations of 1784 and after.

Proponents of catgut and raw reeds conquered one bastion after another. Hogwood conducted the Chicago Symphony, Trevor Pinnock took the pit at Salzburg and the Met. Glyndebourne, the summer picnic-ground of corporate society, consigned its Mozart triptych to a band that called itself, without a note of self-mockery, the Orchestra of the Age of Enlightenment. In these enlightened times, objections were inadmissible. Mackerras, who introduced period style to the Hamburg State Opera, parted company with Archiv after complaining that its antiquated instruments were being played neither pleasantly nor correctly. 'I was perhaps too ready to adopt practices which certainly were used by certain performers in Mozart's time or shortly after, but which perhaps Mozart himself might not have wanted,' he confessed. Despite his Hamburg breakthrough and illuminating Handel productions at the English National Opera, Mackerras was marginalized by the moguls of early music and their industry allies. Other old-style baroque stars – Münchinger, Karl Richter, Raymond Leppard – were driven off the turntable.

Marriner, who survived by sheer professionalism, despised the noises his former colleagues made. 'I cannot accept imperfections of intonation and articulation,' he said. 'I like the way [Hogwood] does *Messiah*, whereas I think his Mozart symphonies are pretty unacceptable. I cannot believe Mozart did not prefer to have his works performed by good players – and good players would always have made as many corrections to their intonation and ensemble as possible.' His strictures were echoed by modern instrumentalists who viewed old-instrument practitioners as dropouts from the exacting standards of their guild. Opera stars, too, were dismissive of the miniature voices that were invading the market in Mozart and Haydn.

Their queen, Emma Kirkby, an Oxford classics scholar, countered that the new order brought greater democracy and full employment. 'One of the great achievements of the early music revival,' she said, 'is that it has given the average-voiced singer an opportunity to perform. Apart from the one in a thousand who has a really unusual voice, most singers have to force the big sounds or develop an artificial amplifying technique. I find that reduces their individuality. Many older people have said to me, "You're so lucky: I had a voice like yours and was told there was no chance of a career." '

Much the same applied to early music conductors, who could not have imposed themselves on a large orchestra and shared a sense of parity and purpose with their players and followers. Modesty went out of the window the moment it conflicted with a record industry demand for stars who could personalize the products. Bespectacled, pallid figures were plucked from the college library or organ loft, photographed in a fashionable studio and plastered on to the cover of *Gramophone* magazine. A gulf opened between director and players and solidarity within the movement was shattered by promotions whose purpose was to help customers distinguish between Pinnock and Parrott, Koopman and Kuijken.

In marketing terms, this need was urgent since the bands had similar names and shared the same players. There were never enough period experts to go around and practitioners flitted nightly from one group to its rival. The Academy of Ancient Music that recorded Mozart symphonies with Hogwood had a front desk of Simon Standage, who was Pinnock's first violin in the English Concert, Monica Huggett, who occupied pole position in the Hanover Band and Amsterdam Baroque Orchestra, and Roy Goodman, leader of the Parley of Instruments and the Orchestra of the Age of Enlightenment. Playing flute and keyboard was Nicholas McGegan, who ran his own groups in Hungary and the United States. When Glyndebourne booked the OAE for the summer of 1989, there was strife while players were siphoned off by Norrington for a US tour and by Hogwood for a series of recordings.

All that separated one group from another was an arcane ethos stemming from the personal preferences of its conductor, whose function was rather like the manager of the national football squad – picking the best team for the engagement from whoever was available and uninjured around the country. It was also a proprietorial role, insofar as the Director – as most liked to be called – generally owned the company, or had a financial interest in it. Hogwood plunged much of his own money into the Academy before it paid him back. Ton Koopman played solo recitals between concerts to pay off his Amsterdam players.

The emergent personalities were predominantly British and, to a lesser extent, Dutch, since German scholarship took decades to recover from the Hitlerite doldrums. Britain possessed a solid musicological tradition, fortified by eminent refugees from Europe and enlivened by a gamut of periodicals. Its discoveries were transmissible in a common language to America. London was an important broadcasting and recording centre, where strong minds could make themselves heard. The local scene was ripe for change after dominance by the capricious Beecham and his bungling Sargent, men who did everything lavishly, regardless of historical validity. Into the musical bloodstream filtered iconoclasts like Thurston Dart whose tutelage, which so inspired Neville Marriner, kindled a firebrand in David Munrow, a Cambridge research student who played bassoon at the Shakespeare theatre in Stratford while delving deeper and deeper into the musical past. One night he walked into the pit with ten Elizabethan instruments of varying complexity and antiquity and played them all brilliantly in *The Taming of the Shrew*.

Munrow, said one of his tutors, 'did not just emerge into the field of medieval and renaissance music – he exploded into it'. Plucking crumhorns and sackbuts from the college vaults, he brought defunct cultures vibrantly to life in riveting lecture-recitals. The Early Music Consort that he formed with Hogwood and assorted friends in 1967 made records for

EMI, Decca and DG Archiv. His BBC series, called 'Pied Piper', drew a swelling column of innocent followers to its five-year trail of 655 programmes. His suicide at the age of 33 was blamed on overwork and the strain of worldwide tours, the price of success achieved too fast. Munrow brought period performance out of the university cloisters into the public domain. He was mourned, both as a glowing personality, and for what he might have yet achieved. 'I was absolutely convinced,' eulogized his concert agent, Jasper Parrott, 'that he would have made a very great career, initially as a choral conductor, but with chamber orchestra – putting together projects involving highly disciplined and musically developed groups of performers of . . . early music, or baroque music, but later of other types of music which had some thematic content.'

Parrott, a diplomat's son who had drifted into musical company at Cambridge, groomed Munrow's harpsichordist to fill his shoes. Christopher Hogwood lacked the Pied Piper's messianic fervour and rejected his 'inspired guesswork' approach, breaking away to form his more scholarly Academy three years before the tragedy. Where Munrow had made early music exciting, Hogwood proposed to make it universally acceptable by improving its intellectual and technical consistency and eradicating what he perceived as its 'wholefood image'. A bachelor collector of antique keyboards, his professional nickname, 'Hogweed', was reminiscent of the vegetarian faddists he meant to leave behind. Unable to find enough players at home to suit his style, he fought the Musicians Union for permission to recruit Dutchmen (Tom Koopman was simultaneously searching Britain for players to fill his Amsterdam Baroque Orchestra).

Hogwood's first leap was from Munrow's medievalism into Marriner's baroque and classical territory, which he roved initially with intentional roughness before settling for a cleaner sound that conformed to period practice but would not scare suburbanites. His approach was middle-of-the-road, erring on the side of blandness. Raw passion and playing gave way to respectability. 'Perhaps we went too far the other way in making it sleek and smooth, always dressing in white tie and tails, always playing in tune,' he conceded when rigorists in the movement accused him of selling out. Fringe culture was mortally offended when he accepted commercial sponsorship, notably from Suchard, a Swiss manufacturer of sugary, processed snack foods.

Questions were also raised about his historical assumptions when, in the later Beethoven symphonies, he doubled up the woodwind and brass – an excess for which Karajan had been castigated but which Hogwood justified as 'the kind of orchestra they used on the bigger occasions in Vienna'. This was symptomatic of the liberties that Hogwood and fellow-literalists felt able to take on the strength of their fundamentalist

credentials. 'I've tried to make this *Messiah* a *very personal statement* –
a statement of belief that goes beyond purely musical considerations,'
said the former Canterbury Cathedral chorister Trevor Pinnock, on
recording a larger-than-original oratorio. It could be said that Cecil B.
De Mille made a *personal statement* about the Bible in his epic interpretation of the Ten Commandments.

Hogwood went the whole hog in the Hollywood Bowl with a 400-
strong *Messiah* during the Los Angeles Olympics, and gave a semi-
staged performance of the oratorio in the Deutsche Oper for Handel's
tercentenary – 'a perfectly valid way of treating this work for a twentieth-
century Berlin audience', he insisted. 'I don't like to be doctrinaire.' The
true faithful spluttered at such liberties and accused the stars of apostasy.
Cologne's Reinhard Goebel, known as 'the Ayatollah of Baroque' and
leader of a back-to-Bach campaign, claimed that predatory foreign schol-
ars had not done their homework 'I was talking to Trevor [Pinnock] and
I asked him how was his German,' he told a journalist. 'He said he didn't
speak it at all. I said, "so how do you read the Bach documents? There
are volumes of vital information which only exist in German, and Baroque
German at that!" '

Purism, however, never made anyone's fortune, and it was the accommodating Brits who conquered America, overwhelming the native auth-
enticists, Joshua Rifkin and Noah Greenberg. Hogwood took over the
venerable Handel and Haydn Society in Boston, his flautist Nicholas
McGegan formed an orchestra on the West Coast, while Pinnock, with
DG backing, founded the Classical Band in the heart of New York. In
the old world, *Le Monde* noted that London was now '*sans doute la
capitale européenne où la musique – en particulier la musique ancienne –
est mieux servie*'.* It had become part of the established music scene,
sharing its gloss, its hype and its infatuation with power.

If Hogwood, as empire builder and super-smoother, has earned his tag
as the Karajan of early music, then Roger Norrington was its Bernstein
and John Eliot Gardiner its would-be Toscanini. Both were proper conductors who acquired their skill with modern orchestras and were accustomed to being obeyed.

Norrington had been through a chequered career before taking to the
podium. The son of an Oxford college administrator, he started out as a
tenor and formed a Schütz Choir before heading off to work in East
Africa for the Oxford University Press. With plenty of leisure to repent
his misrouting, he reverted to music, studied unrewardingly with Boult
and was fortunate to be named music director of Kent Opera, a new

---

*'without doubt, the European capital where music, particularly ancient music, is best served'.

company surviving on a shoestring in the London dormitory belt. Over the next 15 years he gained ever-widening attention with such coups as the revival of Monteverdi's *Coronation of Poppea*, one of the earliest extant operas. 'We didn't know what it would sound like,' he admitted, 'but when we discovered, it was wonderful.' Setting off at the age of fifty to make his way as a freelance, he devised a public form of musical exploration to which he gave the modish title of 'The Experience'. It involved booking a South Bank hall for the weekend and staging a programme that intermingled discussion, rehearsal, performance and audience participation. 'The concept is that you live with a piece and with its surroundings: the audience shares with me the sort of research I do,' he explained. 'You have to buy a ticket for the whole weekend. You really are expected to get into it like an EST weekend, and come out feeling differently about the composer and the piece.' As an ear-opening exercise, it recalled Bernstein's fiery perorations at Carnegie Hall.

Starting with Haydn he moved on to Beethoven and Berlioz, demonstrating how fresh the music could be made to sound when performed as the composer intended, on the orchestra of his time. 'What are modern instruments?' he challenged. 'The instruments we call modern often haven't changed in essence for as much as a century. We've got this strange museum culture – and it's up to us to change it. We're the revolutionaries, the iconoclasts. We're the ones who are making things new.'

In Beethoven, he rigidly followed the composer's metronome markings, something Toscanini purported to do but which Norrington demonstrated made sense only on an orchestra of authentic dimensions. His performances tended to be light, quick and lilting, a world away from the Italian's volcanic eruptions. Hogwood publicly rejected the metronome as a prime arbiter of interpretation. 'It has become the kiwi fruit of modern musicology,' he charged. 'And when you check the metronome enthusiast's recordings against the markings you find they are often out by a fair margin.'

For Berlioz, Norrington borrowed original brass bugles and arrayed his players in the Parisian seating plan, critically altering the sonority. This carried period reconstruction into a new sphere and far into the nineteenth century, earning the unprepossessing provincialist a full-page of coverage in *Time* magazine. He moved on to Schubert, Schumann and beyond, reaching the end of the line with Mahler's Fifth Symphony, where precise timing mattered less than spontaneous feeling. His conducting had a dramatic edge carried over from the opera pit and his boundless enthusiasm was infectious to musicians, critics and audience alike. He kept in touch with opera, conducted Britten at Covent Garden and contemplated staging seventeenth-century works, with Baroque gestures

and dance episodes choreographed by his second wife, Kay Lawrence –
'the missing link in the authenticity chain', he called it. EMI, which
had initially missed the early music boat, caught up with Norrington's
Beethoven cycle and set the pace with his 'authentic' Wagner overtures.

He would yield to members of his London Classical Players – many of
whom doubled as Hogwood's Academicians – on matters of technique
and liberally consulted them in rehearsals. He conducted with a baton –
a flagrant anachronism in much of what he performed – but envisaged
himself as being part of the musical process, rather than its external
dictator.

John Eliot Gardiner, on the other hand, was a conductor of an altogether more familiar type: autocratic, unyielding, choleric. Tales of his
temper littered the early music landscape. He changed staff with alarming
rapidity and ruled his ensembles severely. Musicians called him 'Jeggy',
though not to his face. He was at his best in a tight corner, when time
was running out in a film session or a singer was losing her voice: here
he could show qualities of leadership reminiscent of a bygone imperial
age. He was the great-nephew of a pro-consul of British music, the
composer Balfour Gardiner, who financed the première of Holst's *Planets*
and much else besides. Raised among the landed gentry, Gardiner continued to run his family's organic farm in Dorset, using neither pesticides
nor hormones – perhaps his only gesture towards open-toed idealists of
early music. 'This place is my bolt-hole,' he told a lady journalist, 'a place
to get shit on my boots.'

Egged on by record companies, each director promoted his personal
preferences as the last word in historical truth. 'If you say you're doing
something authentic,' warned an American scholar, 'what are the implications for what everyone else is doing?' If Hogwood's Mozart was accurate, then Gardiner's was presumably out of tune and Norrington apparently beat the wrong time. Goebel implied that all the rest were charlatans
and Harnoncourt went his own way, refusing to hear a word of criticism
when he introduced post-baroque instruments to his Monteverdi edition.
In terms of internal rhetoric, early music was the liveliest of arts as
directors recriminated with one another and fought for power as avidly
as philharmonic potentates.

The lessons of their success were not lost on symphonic conductors.
Riccardo Muti made a fetish of checking composer's manuscripts when
restaging *bel canto* works at La Scala. Claudio Abbado, recording a
Schubert cycle in 1986, had one of his players go through the autograph
scores removing alterations by previous editors, notably Brahms, to produce a pure text. 'A few minutes in the Gesellschaft der Musikfreunde
archives, where the world's largest collection of Schubert manuscripts are
kept, were enough to convince me that I could not record the symphonies ·

without investigating the differences between the manuscripts and printed scores,' wrote Abbado. No member of his profession had been troubled by such niceties before.

Bernard Haitink brought Nikolaus Harnoncourt to conduct the Concertgebouw and gave his records to Simon Rattle to admire. Rattle urged his Birmingham players to study earlier techniques and introduced period performance to Glyndebourne. As modern conductors assimilated the more sensible of their rules, the ground was cut from beneath the early music moguls. Their territory was finite, coming to a dead end with the early romantics – no matter how far Norrington might push, or Hogwood might talk of extending historical principles to Stravinsky and Shostakovich. With nowhere to expand within their field, many tried their hand with symphony orchestras, and most came unstuck. Hogwood, whose agent looked after Previn and Ashkenazy, found it easy to get into American podia, less easy to get asked back. He finally took on a chamber orchestra in St Paul's, working with the size of modern-instrument ensemble that was most responsive to his modest brand of leadership.

Harnoncourt guested around Europe and gained clout at Salzburg once Karajan was dead, but did not assume responsibility for a major institution. Gardiner is returning to modern orchestras after initial failures. Norrington claimed tremendous success with the Boston Symphony, but bombed at Cleveland's summer festival. The easy-going ways of early music proved his undoing when he entered a rehearsal with George Szell's old regiment dressed in T-shirt and shorts. At the next session, the orchestra turned out in three-piece suits and drowned his historical dialectics in derisive cat-calls. 'The latest research has proved,' mocked one violinist, 'that this guy is a complete jackass.'

He came close to winning a position with the Philharmonia, only to be undermined by EMI's reported unwillingness to record him with a large orchestra. At the bottom line, record companies wanted early music directors to give a different flavour to familiar music, cheaply and efficiently – not to encroach on well-defined maestro territory. Despite their commercial success, the feeling lingered that early music specialists were, at best, semi-conductors who excelled in their own small speciality but were no substitute for the genuine article. Every classical label was on red alert to sign up promising new conductors, yet none was prepared to gratify the romantic ambitions of its former revolutionaries. Podium talent was in critical short supply. But if a new breed of conductors was ever to emerge, it would have to come up by the traditional route.

CHAPTER 15

Where Have All the Conductors Gone?

WORD OF MOUTH can make or break a new conductor. Amateurs can tell by ear whether an unknown pianist is prodigious or merely proficient, but the particular skill of a conductor is so nebulous that a newcomer is judged by instinct. The players get a tingle in their fingers, the orchestral manager calls a friend or two and an enterprising agent starts hitting the phone and lunching in earnest. Once word gets about that a talent has been spotted, things can move frighteningly fast.

Scattered around the Royal Festival Hall one concert night in October 1983 were some of the world's leading managers and record producers, several of whom had crossed the Atlantic specifically for the purpose. Michael Tilson Thomas had pulled out of a Philharmonia performance of Mahler's Third Symphony at five days' notice, and the work was being entrusted to a 25-year-old Finn who had not studied it before the previous week, let alone performed it.

The orchestra was taking a serious risk, of a kind that had all but vanished from the music business. The vacancy that gave Leonard Bernstein his break when Bruno Walter caught flu was now more likely to be filled by a jet-propelled senior figure happy to pocket an extra twenty or thirty thousand dollars, the goodwill of a leading orchestra and sympathetic reviews. Agents, alerted to an emergency, would offer the slot to their top-earners, while orchestras looked for a familiar name who would not leave their audience feeling short-changed. Novices need not apply. In the course of Klaus Tennstedt's long chronicle of disasters, the London Philharmonic never once replaced the chronically sick music director with an untested youngster – even though its players were being numbed to death at times by middle-ranked, middle-aged substitutes of moderate repute. Safety first was the slogan.

In this instance, the Philharmonia passed up a number of recognizable names and went for a baby-faced Scandinavian with a blank career sheet. Esa-Pekka Salonen had caught the eye of a London agent, Joeske Van Walsum, by stepping in at a Gothenburg concert when news reached

Luciano Berio that his first wife had died. If Salonen could sightread Berio at rehearsal and conduct his music the following night, Van Walsum reckoned, he would sail through Mahler. If he bombed, on the other hand, the agent stood to lose light years of credibility. Frustrated rivals converged on the hall to witness the rarity of risk. 'They came flying round like vultures,' said Van Walsum. 'I was shit-scared. I would never have wanted to create that kind of buzz before a concert – it could all have gone so terribly wrong.'

To his immense relief, and the grudged applause of his competitors, Salonen directed the six-movement, ninety-minute symphony without turning a hair or missing a tempo change. He was appointed principal guest conductor of the Philharmonia and won a record contract with CBS. Six years later, aged 31, he was named music director in Los Angeles by another member of his first metropolitan audience. 'I was fortunate to be present at Esa-Pekka Salonen's London debut,' said Ernest Fleischmann, executive director of the LAPO, 'and knew immediately that this was an extraordinary talent.' His shimmering, youthful appeal would win the Los Angeles Philharmonic the first foreign orchestral residency at the Salzburg Festival in 1992.

Salonen seemed refreshingly different. Neither a go-getter nor money-grabber, he was more interested in composing ethereal pieces for fringe concerts than in conducting at Carnegie Hall. 'I see my role as a potential provocateur, rather than as a wunderkind conductor,' he said. In Finland he led a revolt against the polite music of state-subsidized composers typified by his near-namesake Aulis Sallinen, forming a radical 'Open Ears' society to project nastier noises.

In Sweden, where he conducted the radio orchestra, he drew a full house of under-twenties to a programme of Berio and Magnus Lindberg by telling readers of a pop publication that his next concert would be more interesting than Michael Jackson's. 'Contemporary music is the normal, right sort of communication for young people,' he felt – although some of them angrily defaced his placards.

His debut recording for CBS was a world première of esoteric music, Witold Lutosławski's Third Symphony, coupled with Olivier Messiaen's mammoth *Turangalîla*, a polytonal feast of love, divinity and exotic instruments. It sold in handfuls but won him prestigious prizes and an approach from the rock star Sting, gently declined, to make a joint record. 'Everyone keeps telling me that I programme such adventurous repertoire,' said Salonen. 'Yet my relation timewise to Messiaen and Lutosławski is almost exactly as Karajan's was to Richard Strauss – and I don't think that anyone thought Karajan was an outrageous avant-gardist.'

He awoke to music at the age of eight on hearing a Finnish rock singer called Kirka deliver a syncopated version of the finale of Beethoven's Ninth; his interest was reinforced by a Helsinki performance of *Turangalîla*. 'I have the worst possible background for an artist – urban middle-class,' he confessed. 'I can't even claim to have listened to the whispering of the trees as a child and received inspiration from nature.' He took up the horn, played in orchestras, wrote music criticism and composed. Any Nordic aridity in his makeup was dispelled in Mediterranean studies with the Italian modernist Francesco Donatoni. Contact with the French Messiaenists joined him to the mainstream of borderless Euromusic.

'I want to be a nurse for talented composers,' he said. 'To help them, give advice. To do something I believe in.' His involvement in new music was a tonic for jaded players and a nightmare for money-conscious managers. In London, *Turangalîla* played to a hall more than half empty. When he tackled Beethoven, it was with an irreverent shifting of emphases, presenting the symphonies slightly askew, with illuminating sidelights. As an interpreter, he matured appreciably with a Florence production of Debussy's *Pelléas et Mélisande* in 1989, in which 'the outlines emerged clear and distinct, the high points were perfectly graded and each musical reminiscence, however distant, struck home'.

'What interests me as a counterbalance to emotional artistry,' he once reflected, 'is a certain sullenness and dry matter-of-factness. I am not interested in exhibitionism.' This low-key, greyish perspective carried over into his public image. He was untouched by the efforts of journalists to make him sound interesting – in much the same way as Stefan Edberg, the Swedish tennis champion, would present a dull façade and reserve his explosiveness for the Wimbledon court. Salonen humbly acknowledged what the music business refused to accept: that most good conductors are interesting only when they conduct.

No-one can predict how far he will go, although his diary is full for years to come and his record company blazes with hype and confidence. The sum of his achievements so far is insubstantial, and to some extent disputable. Salonen, in his early thirties, is standing at the foothills of a conducting career. What makes him remarkable is that he stands there almost alone, the sole sprout in a wilderness, symbol of a profession in terminal decline. Where have all the conductors gone? demand musicians, managers and newspaper headlines. Where, indeed.

The crisis has finally come to roost. In the early 1990s, for the first time in more than a hundred years, the well of conductors has run dry. Karajan and Bernstein, the last of the potentates, are dead, Solti is nearing the end of the road and, while they are followed by a line-up of Abbados, Haitinks and Levines, the next age-group has failed to materialize. A decade ago, critics could write optimistically about 'a new generation' of conductors taking over major institutions. Today, top orchestras are unable to replace their music directors. It took the New York Philharmonic 18 months and the London Philharmonic more than two years to make an appointment. The next round of jobs will be almost impossible to fill.

Only four conductors born after 1950 have come into contention for front-rank positions. Judgement must be reserved on Salonen, who has yet to be tested in Los Angeles, and on Myung Wha Chung, who won the Bastille Opera by default when no-one else would touch it after Barenboim's dismissal. The sole achievers so far are Riccardo Chailly at Amsterdam's Concertgebouw and Simon Rattle in Birmingham. Together, they constitute the future of conducting. Behind them hover a tiny clutch of hopefuls consisting of Jukka-Pekka Saraste of Finnish Radio; a quiet Austrian, Franz Welser-Möst; the East German, Claus Peter Flor; an American at the Bournemouth Symphony, Andrew Litton; and the British woman Sian Edwards. None had given conclusive proof of outstanding ability by their early thirties – by which time Toscanini was revolutionizing La Scala and Mahler was running his second opera house. Even the wayward Furtwängler was chief conductor in Mannheim at 29 and in Berlin by the age of 35. Karajan was 27 when he took command at Aachen, Mehta 26 when he moved to Los Angeles. If a conductor possessed the spark of genius, he made it glow before his thirtieth birthday and was riding high at forty. There were no consolation prizes for late developers.

Gasps of incredulity were heard at the press conference where Riccardo Chailly, aged 32, was named music director of the Concertgebouw. His youth caused no consternation; Amsterdam liked them young. Willem Mengelberg was 24 and Bernard Haitink 32 when they took the helm. What mattered was that Chailly was being appointed on the strength of a single concert. All that was known of him was that he was biased towards opera, devoted to modern music and not in the slightest bit Dutch – qualities that contradicted every Concertgebouw convention. His four predecessors talked to the orchestra in its own heavy tongue and stood out rigorously against the frivolities of musical drama and any kind of experimentalism. Chailly simply walked into the venerable concert hall for an Italian concert of Berio, Bussotti and Petrassi and walked out as the new chief. 'I didn't even know the Concertgebouw were looking for a new conductor,' he said. His 1985 debut coincided with acrid exchanges between the podium and a progressive management in a dispute that severed Bernard Haitink's half-century connection with the house where he grew up.

'I was sorry to hear about his tension with the orchestra,' said Chailly. 'The exact opposite happened when I was there: the atmosphere was idyllic, an unexpected happy, happy meeting. There was an intensity of involvement in rehearsals, complete silence when I explained things to them, fantastic to see.' Unhappy at finding the hall barely one-tenth full, he accused the Dutch of being musically lazy and inaugurated a 'C' series of modern music at which he explained each piece verbally before conducting it. 'Avant-garde music is important for everybody,' he announced. 'It makes a great orchestra an even greater orchestra if it practises avant-garde music regularly, because it is extremely difficult and always presents a challenge. Furthermore, it is the duty of an orchestra and its conductor to keep the audience informed.'

These strictures went down well in principle with the serious-minded Dutch, though attendances remained small. Chailly sweetened the modernist medicine with a large dose of Mahler, whom Amsterdam adored, and a fancy for the symphonic music of his acolyte Alexander Zemlinsky, whom Chailly proclaimed 'the Mahler of the 1990s'. He possessed a stylish personality, was fluent in German and English and conversant with many aspects of continental culture and cuisine – the kind of cosmopolitan near-intellectual that educated Hollanders aspire to become. He wore kaleidoscopic sweaters of Italian design over a maturing embonpoint, sporting a well-tended brown beard and the public expression of a man well pleased with life's bounty. He was twice married and self-managed. Behind closed doors, he fought ferociously for his rights and rewards.

Chailly's background was operatic, with orchestral interludes. The son of a composer and sometime director of La Scala, he attached himself as a youth to the Abbado regime and learned the politics of Italian opera from the inside. Among his privileges was free entry to all concert rehearsals, where he was entranced by the Mahlerian magic of John Barbirolli. Leaving Milan with Abbado, he conducted opera at the Met, Vienna and Covent Garden before settling at the Teatro Communale in Bologna, where he aimed to outshine the tribal enemy, Riccardo Muti, and snatched a share of attention with a filmed *Macbeth* and an Italian *Ring*. Orchestrally, he came to the fore as conductor of West Berlin's radio symphony orchestra, blooming in the shade of Karajan's Philharmonic. The old conductor kept tabs on his activities and questioned him closely about each innovation, such as his espousal of Deryck Cooke's completion of Mahler's Tenth Symphony. Chailly urged the veteran to conduct it himself, but warned that its scherzo was tougher than the *Rite of Spring*. In that case, said Karajan, 'it's too late. *Sacre* for a conductor is something to be done at a certain time of your life, then you need the courage to leave it forever.'

He became fond enough of the breezy youngster to let him open the Salzburg festival in 1984, the first Italian to do so since Toscanini, but

Chailly's tenure was short-lasting. As Karajan's control waned, his nominees fell prey to long-repressed resentments. Unguarded remarks by Chailly about the working practices of the Vienna Philharmonic provoked an orchestral boycott that drove him from the festival in 1988. He retaliated by turning up in Vienna to conduct the rival Symphoniker. This was something of a sideshow in an occupation now firmly grounded at Amsterdam and Bologna and supported by the Decca record company. Chailly gave up guest conducting and was not seen in America or Britain for three years at a stretch. 'It was always my dream to have an old-fashioned career,' he said happily and, like Salonen and Simon Rattle, he avoided all but the most compelling extra-mural opportunities. He was friendly with Rattle, would exchange notes with him on new music and try to avoid clashes of repertoire.

Rattle also kept closely in touch with Salonen, with whom he shared orchestras in Los Angeles and London, a liking for the same sort of sounds and an outspoken derision for the business side of music. It was common knowledge that these three contemporaries would lead music into the 21st century, although which of them would cast the longest shadow was still unforseeable.

Simon Rattle can, in the eyes of his musical countrymen, do no wrong. Everything he touches strikes critical gold, every move he makes seems innately right. He has shunned the jet-shuttle, snubbed philharmonic overtures, struck out at commercialism and sustained a secure domesticity with the American soprano Elise Ross and their two small sons. When a Viennese emissary sidled up to him with an offer few maestros could refuse, he snarled: 'I don't do guest conducting.' His career has been 'old-fashioned' in the finest sense, spending his prentice years in a provincial city and raising its orchestra to international standard. Extending his contract into its second decade, he witheringly discouraged suggestions of upward mobility. 'It reflects the arrogance of other orchestras in other cities to suppose that I would want to leave a situation where the benefits are so magnificent and so obvious,' he said.

Rattle was 25 and footloose when the City of Birmingham Symphony Orchestra, bereft of both its conductor and manager after a players' rebellion, offered him its podium. Rattle, tousle-headed and untamed, said: 'Don't expect me to perform Beethoven.' Ten years later, the orchestra was world famous and Birmingham was building him the concert hall it had promised seventy years before to Adrian Boult. Rattle had charmed a million pounds a year out of the town hall and as much again in state funds from the Arts Council. The merest hint of his displeasure broke open the public purse, no matter which political party held the strings. In Birmingham, he became the figurehead of a post-industrial metropolis intent on softening its image – performing much the same role that Nikisch played in Wilhelminian Berlin and Stokowski in Philadelphia. Underlining his commitment, Rattle gave up commuting from London and moved his family from their terraced Georgian house in inner-city Islington to a modern Midlands domicile, with the benefits of surrounding countryside and better neighbourhood schools.

His conducting salary was reputedly the highest in the land, but he had turned down much fatter propositions from America and Europe. 'I'm basically monogamous,' he liked to say. The Birmingham orchestra, drooping when he took over, was rapidly rejuvenated, with remarkably little rancour, until its average age dropped below that of its young conductor. Rattle pulled in key players from London and plucked fresh talent, mostly girls, straight out of college. His empathy with the orchestra became almost wordless. 'They play like that only for Simon,' complained a visiting maestro. 'He has developed a shorthand language with that orchestra that no other musician can emulate.'

'I'm sure that's true,' agreed Rattle. 'We have built up a very strong mutual identification, tightly, closely together. It makes for enormous ease of working. So much of the ground level is unsaid.' He urged players to join a Contemporary Music Group and tinker with different techniques and tones, broadening their horizons alongside his own. 'I always tried to work on pieces that they didn't know,' he revealed. 'It meant that I could teach them the notes. The art of being a good conductor is that you should know everything better than the orchestra.' They were also encouraged to share his social concerns, going out into the community and bringing back underprivileged and disabled kids to their rehearsals. Rattle was profoundly moved to see deaf children beam as they touched the vibrating instruments in the ninth symphony that Beethoven, its stricken composer, was unable to hear.

The audience he built in Birmingham was young and open-minded, 'not only loyal, but willing to explore', he felt. Attendances rose by one-third to a phenomenal 98 per cent for some series, leaving Rattle free to perform more or less what he pleased. His tastes were eclectic and unconfined. The music he *adored* – a favourite verb – extended from Pierre Boulez, whose ascetic work he placed at the centre of a French season, to the finger-snapping *West Side Story* of his antipode Leonard Bernstein. Rattle made his own rules. He propagated the pointillism of Webern with appropriate conviction, yet reserved his most impassioned performances for symphonies by Rachmaninov and the big tune in Sibelius's fifth. 'I just play music that I like,' he said. 'I see pieces, I fall for them and I want to do them. The sadness is, there are so many pieces I desperately want to do and can't find space for on the programme.' He programmed Henze and Holliger, Gorecki and Goehr, living composers that London dared not inflict on its fickle public. Birmingham bristled with bold and colourful sonorities that left the nation's capital sounding stale.

Repeated bids to bring him to London as music director on the South Bank complex foundered on the rocks of his fidelity and commonsense. Two London orchestras fought a bruising battle for his hand, ignoring Rattle's protestations that he was simply not interested. He fell out with the Philharmonia and switched his seasonal appearances to the London Philharmonic, whose manager, John Willan, was formerly his record producer. By making his stronghold outside the cosmopolitan fray, he could afford to pick and choose from London's favours and be assured of a welcome whenever he accepted one.

Away from Birmingham, his only formal connection was with the Los Angeles Philharmonic, which he directed for a couple of weeks each winter as principal guest conductor. Angelenes had taken him into their homes when he came as a schoolboy player in a youth orchestra and Rattle responded with enduring warmth. He particularly liked playing for the Sunday afternoon audience, 'which seems to be all doctors and lawyers, people who have worked very hard during the week and are willing to put aside their Sunday for this'. Ernest Fleischmann twice offered him the top job but settled for much less. 'Morale goes up by leaps and bounds when he's around,' said Fleischmann. 'We'll do anything to make him happy.' In a seller's market, Rattle quickly became accustomed to getting his own way. When the dress rehearsal of his Los Angeles *Wozzeck* proved unsatisfactory, one sharp word from him behind closed doors yielded the extra $20,000 for another run-through. Finding that Mozart felt right to him only on early instruments, he obliged Glyndebourne (another company whose music directorship he declined) to replace the resident London Philharmonic Orchestra with a period ensemble. Such was Rattle's sway that the change was effected without friction.

At his Covent Garden debut in June 1990, he conducted Janáček's *Cunning Little Vixen* in a production sung in English – ignoring the house policy of original languages, the availability of surtitles and the inextricability of Janáček's sonorities from everyday Czech speech. An English-sung *Vixen* had been seen months before at the nearby Coliseum and it would have been a more effective use of public and private money to recreate the rural fable in the full vigour of its vernacular. However, neither Rattle nor his chosen cast were, apparently, willing to delve into authentic Janáček and, more remarkably, none of the critics took them to task for the missed opportunity. Rattle, it was tacitly agreed, could do no wrong.

The following month, he opened a Promenade concert with Brahms' climactic fourth symphony and followed it with John Adams' *Har-*

monium, a post-minimalist piece that meandered mildly across a vast orchestral parabola. If ever a concert descended from the sublime to the slightly ridiculous this was it, yet Rattle was applauded for his iconoclasm and one headline proclaimed his feat to have been 'legendary'. He was shortlisted annually for record awards and named a Commander of the British Empire by Margaret Thatcher's government as a symbol of national revival, though he made no secret of his loathing for Thatcherite inegalities. He remained a cheerful mop-top, cocking a snook at establishments of all kinds.

Music critics tumbled over one another's perfumed phrases in their effulgences of praise and normally sober judges issued startling verdicts. 'Simon Rattle is the most stunningly gifted young conductor I know,' said the severe pianist Alfred Brendel, while an octogenarian composer, Berthold Goldschmidt, described him as 'just possibly the greatest all-round conductor I have ever seen'. Given that Goldschmidt had worked with Klemperer, Furtwängler and Szell, and assisted Erich Kleiber in preparing the first performance of *Wozzeck*, his view warranted serious consideration. Rattle was not a better Bergian than Kleiber or profounder in Brahms than Klemperer, but he was already a more versatile musician than either would ever become, spanning Monteverdi to Messiaen and beyond within his sphere of command.

In terms of concrete accomplishments, he had notched up by the age of 35 the first performance of several enduring pieces, among them Nali Gruber's anarchic *Frankenstein!!*, the long-delayed first symphony by Peter Maxwell Davies and various Britten legacies from the Aldeburgh archives. More impressive still was his knack for liberating masterpieces from a cloud of half-baked prejudice. 'For me, Simon has put Mahler Ten on the map; he has proved once and for all that this is a very remarkable score,' said Brendel, of his youthful recording of the Deryck Cooke completion. Leonora Gershwin, the composer's testator, credited Rattle with 'the first successful *Porgy*' on witnessing a Glyndebourne triumph that had wealthy punters weeping openly at the love-tragedy of Catfish Row. 'Few Americans have realized it as yet,' wrote one of the singers, 'but at Glyndebourne that summer [of 1986] *Porgy and Bess* finally came of age.' 'People stopped saying it's not a real opera,' confirmed Willard White, who sang the title role. Orchestrally speaking, said Rattle, '*Porgy* is harder than *Wozzeck*; emotionally, it packs a punch equalled by very few works of art.'

It is this combination of commitment and self-confidence that has made Rattle such an exciting conductor. His wide-eyed innocence was unsullied by agents and managers, from whom he preserved a fiery independence. He would not listen to accepted opinion until he had formed his own and took counsel from a tiny circle of intimates who included his wife, the composer Oliver Knussen, Brendel, Fleischmann and his Birmingham partner Ed Smith, who was widely admired for his skill in keeping the orchestra and its conductor in top gear.

Rattle acknowledged two formative influences within the podium – 'my two old men', he called them fondly – each pulling in an opposite direction. Berthold Goldschmidt was a questing composer who used tone clusters in his piano sonata before Bartók discovered them and immersed his young friend in a Mahlerian mission of delving into the future. Rudolf Schwarz, a former deputy viola player in the Vienna Philharmonic and a survivor of the Belsen concentration camp, was rooted in a more conservative tradition; he taught Rattle the paramount importance of imposing his pulse on the music he played (by coincidence, Schwarz started his British career at Bournemouth and Birmingham, presaging his protégé's route). Rattle called regularly on both sages, remembered their birthdays with a telephone call from wherever he might be and brought Goldschmidt back in triumph to Berlin with a performance of his *Ciaconna Sinfonica*. He has also remained friendly with John Carewe, a conductor whose advice he sought in his late teens and continues to respect. 'A number of people claim to have set Simon on the road,' said Carewe, 'but he would always have got there himself. He is a phenomenon, just a simple Liverpool boy brought up the right way with all the right genes in place.'

As a child, while his father was away on long business trips in the Far East, young Simon was raised by his mother and by a sister, Susan, who was nine years his senior and handicapped by a slight muscular disability. She qualified as a librarian and would bring home records and scores. 'She had an extraordinary catholic taste,' said her brother, 'and stuffed Schoenberg and Bartók and Hindemith and whatever, that just came home and I just listened to it.'

'He would sit up in bed with these enormous orchestral scores in front of him, turning over reading . . . like other kids read a comic,' recalled his father, Denis. 'And he would call me or his mother or his sister and say, "look, look what they are doing with the flute, hahaha, isn't that funny?" ' He carefully copied out the percussion parts and on Sundays played them in a living-room concert to the accompaniment of a symphonic record on the gramophone. He played timpani in the Merseyside youth orchestra and became adept enough at the piano to perform a Mozart concerto.

Hearing a concert of Mahler's Second Symphony made him want to be a conductor. At fifteen he made national headlines by drumming up his own seventy-man orchestra for a charity event on behalf of Liverpool Spastic Fellowship. 'We thought he had a small concert in mind,' said a dumbstruck official. He got through Schubert's Unfinished Symphony,

Vaughan Williams' *Tallis Fantasia*, the Mozart clarinet concerto and Malcolm Arnold's *English Dances*. In the audience was Charles Groves, principal conductor of the Royal Liverpool Philharmonic, who involved him with the orchestra. After winning a national conducting competition and raising the youngest-ever baton at the Proms, he became Liverpool's associate conductor at the age of 22 and would have inherited the podium two years later but for the reservations of players who had known him in short pants – and his own decision to move away from the city where an excess of familiarity was breeding inevitable sentiments. A contemporary on the orchestra's staff, Ed Smith, had gone to Birmingham as manager and pressed his board to appoint Rattle as principal conductor.

His first act on taking the job was to get married; his second was to take a year off to read literature at Oxford, conducting only during college vacations. He was aware, unlike many maestros, of the rich and painful life that lay beyond music and manifested his social conscience in charity concerts and appeals for worthy causes that ranged from African drought to AIDS research. He was among the leaders of an artists' campaign protesting against Thatcherite erosions of civil liberties and homosexual rights. He did not inhabit an ivory tower.

After seven years in Birmingham Rattle took a second sabbatical, this time to Bali, where he sat at the feet of a gamelan teacher and played, together with his wife and son, in a village orchestra. 'They have no concept of a professional musician,' he found to his delight. 'The arts are so much part of people that there's no word for "art" or "culture" – it's taken for granted: everybody does it.' Determined not to be an absent father, he was forever nipping away from rehearsal to spend time with Sacha who, at seven years old, made a stage appearance in his Covent Garden *Vixen*. When James Levine asked him to conduct another Janáček opera at the Met, Rattle declined saying, 'I don't want to be away long from England when I have a young family and young orchestra to take care of.'

'What's the point of earning more in London,' he lectured musicians, 'if you never see the family you're supposed to be earning it for? Life can't be just playing music, morning, noon and night.' The strength to say No and the self-confidence not to regret it stemmed from a sense of priorities inculcated in early boyhood. 'His parents and sister are at the very root of his sanity,' confirmed Carewe. 'They are a powerful continuing influence on his life.'

Where that life might lead was indicated by a burgeoning relationship with the Berlin Philharmonic. Having rebuffed them for years with a demand to perform Mahler's Tenth on four rehearsals – only Karajan ever got those conditions – he undertook a three-rehearsal Mahler Sixth in November 1987 that blew away the artifice of Karajan's conceptualization. The ovation lasted long after the orchestra had left the stage, leaving Rattle to take his bows alone. Returning two years later for a Bartók concert, he called off a linked recording on finding that players were being hived off to a concurrent session with Barenboim. 'There is nothing extraordinary about wanting to record with the same players as you rehearse with,' he fumed. Although business managers were incensed, younger musicians liked his style and he was given an annual slot of six concerts in the Philharmonic schedules. It placed him in the exclusive company of Haitink, Levine, Ozawa, Kleiber, Mehta and Barenboim, the first of his generation to join the élite. One German magazine duly dubbed him 'the Karajan of the year 2000'. It was beginning to seem as if Rattle was truly infallible. And on the rare occasions that he failed with an orchestra, as he did with the Concertgebouw and Cleveland, it was put down as the musicians' fault. If an oddly paired programme left empty seats in the hall, the marketing department was blamed. Could Rattle really be that good?

The few chinks discernible in his shining armour were either tendentious, or lodged so deep within his character that they were mistaken for virtues. Some players, particularly in Berlin, complained that he never fixed them with his eye, never communicated the way a conductor should; on television, too, he avoided looking into the camera. Friends said he was inherently shy, protecting that part within himself that no-one was allowed to touch. Inviolability, though, was no fault in a conductor, who needed an inner retreat from which to draw the conviction to impose his outlook. Although widely read and ever curious, Rattle was uncomfortable in the company of intellectual heavy-weights, was bowled over by the mind of Boulez and irked by his own incapacity to master huge ideas and foreign languages. He made a virtue of these inadequacies, happily admitting that he was attracted to conducting 'by the thought of spending my life exploring a greater brain than mine'.

It was his encounters with the giants of music that provoked the sharpest doubts, particularly in America, where the hallelujahs of British critics raised musical hackles. His recording of Mahler's *Resurrection* Symphony, which won the 1988 *Gramophone* award for being 'in a spiritual class of its own', was taken to task in minute detail by the president of the US Mahler Society, who found that Rattle 'ignores many of Mahler's details and instructions and misinterprets others, especially in the first movement', throwing the symphony off balance from the fourth bar onwards. Another critic, in *High Fidelity*, slammed the performance as 'so bad, it's practically a joke' and the Birmingham players as 'a cautious, provincial group'.

Since this was the work that first inspired Rattle to become a conductor, his account of it was noteworthy as a measure of his mature ability. To the present writer, his interpretation sounded unidiomatic and stiff in the first two movements (though no stiffer than, say, Ozawa or Janssons), lacking the structural certainty that renders the redemptive finale inevitable, rather than merely impressive. 'It's a fine performance but it's not yet fully formed,' argued John Carewe, whose comment could have been applied to Rattle's general progress. Dazzling though he can be in contemporary and offbeat repertoire, he sometimes lacks the last degree of flexibility and penetration in the romantic mainstream, where he has to contend with a century of seasoned interpretation. Sensibly, he has refrained from recording other masterpieces until he has worked them to a higher pitch in the relative seclusion of his Birmingham laboratory. He took a six-week break to study Mahler's Ninth before taking it to the orchestra.

In a certain sense, he has become the prisoner of too many enthusiasms, lavishing – as Brendel has publicly warned – undue attention on ephemeral novelties at the expense of eternal creations. There are fears that Rattle spreads himself too thin across half a millennium of music, but he may need variety rather than discovery born of repetition to keep his enthusiasm bubbling over. Another arguable deficiency is an overdeveloped sense of loyalty, reflected in a hint of cronyism in the soloists he picks and in his unflagging sense of duty to old friends and playmates. Despite his professed reluctance to guest conduct, Rattle now splits himself seasonally between Birmingham, Los Angeles and Berlin; the London Philharmonic and London Sinfonietta; Glyndebourne and one or other of the London opera houses. He is diffusing precious energy and concentration among several institutions simply because each of them harbours people he loves – and loves working with. He may find it easy to say no to foreigners and bearers of gifts; to friends in need, he is a pushover. The streak of ruthlessness that distinguishes leaders in every walk of life runs thin in Rattle. He claims to do everything out of self-interest but the instances of generosity are too numerous, and creditable, to be denied.

He has backed several conductors younger than himself and urged orchestras to follow Birmingham's lead and take a chance with raw talent. 'There are never enough good conductors to go round,' he said. 'It's a matter of conductors growing with an orchestra, having an opportunity to grow. And I have been damned lucky. I know that. Most of what I have learned has been the result of the Birmingham experience.' Whether for want of courage or conviction, orchestras have not heeded his advice, beyond giving guest nights to his principal protégés, Paul Daniel and Sian Edwards. Behind them stretches a landscape bare of recognized conductors and the crisis deepens annually as senior figures retire and cannot be replaced.

*   *   *

Only Franz Welser-Möst, of the sparse next crop, seems to be cut out for something out of the ordinary. His name, to begin with, is counterfeit. So is his advertised Austrian patrimony and the serenity that led critics to liken him to Karl Böhm and credit him with a natural authority in Mozart and Bruckner. Welser-Möst loathed Böhm and all he represented, revoked his Austrian citizenship and spent his time with quirky composers like Gruber and Schwertsik of the Third Vienna School, who write dissident music to rude verses. 'Many people say it's primitive music. It's not,' he insisted. 'They have something that many of today's composers have lost, the connection to their roots. And they are not liked at all in Vienna.'

Nor is Welser-Möst. He had the unforgivable effrontery to walk out on the Vienna Symphony Orchestra simply because one of its players said, 'do we really have to play this shit?' on seeing Beethoven's first *Leonore* overture. Afterwards, said the young conductor, 'they came and argued that I shouldn't be such an idealist to expect that I can make music with everyone in the orchestra. I said, "I'll give you two tickets to my next concert with the London Philharmonic and you'll see it's possible." ' When, after rescuing a Rossini opera at the last moment, Vienna offered to reward him with an unrehearsed *Zauberflöte*, he bluntly refused, fed up with its condescension. 'I'm young and Austrian and successful abroad and that was enough for some people to give me trouble,' he complained.

In 1986 he returned his passport and left the country. His career break came in April of that year when the Spanish conductor Jesus Lopez-Cobos pulled out of a Mozart Requiem in London at two days' notice because his wife was dying. The London Philharmonic, in dire straits, gambled on a lad of 25 whom the agent Martin Campbell-White had never heard, but had heard good things about. Welser-Möst, it transpired, knew the Requiem from having sung in it as a boy. As he walked into the hall, straight off the plane, orchestral pranksters decided to test his mettle. Halfway into the session, a wind player raised his arm. 'Yes?' said Welser-Möst. The musician mouthed something soundlessly. The conductor called for quiet and asked him to repeat the comment. Once again, the player moved his lips, a hoary old trick designed to fluster a novice. Welser-Möst gazed back and said: 'You mean I don't speak loud enough? The reason I speak softly is so that you will listen.' The ensuing laughter was respectful, and players were soon talking of him as one to watch. 'He's a very level-headed chap who seems to know exactly where he is going – supremely self-confident, but in an almost naïve way,' said David Nolan, the orchestra's leader.

By the age of thirty, Welser-Möst had regular work in London and with the Deutsche Oper in Berlin, while learning his craft with a remote

Swedish orchestra at Norrkoeping. He shielded his obvious abilities behind a fatalistic lack of ambition. 'My philosophy in music-making is that I do as little as possible,' he said quietly. 'In music as in life, my main concern is to put my ego aside and let things happen.' Given the dearth of current talent, they were bound to happen for him rapidly.

The son of an overworked pulmonary specialist in Linz and his wife, a political activist, he had grown up, like Herbert von Karajan, in a middle-class, maternally dominated professional home. The lung-surgeon 'was always at the hospital, far away, working like hell; I hardly ever saw him'. When he was 12, his mother was elected to parliament for the right-wing People's Party and was away in Vienna for most of his adolescence. At 14 he was sent to music school for want of any compelling alternative, 'and suddenly discovered that this could be my life'. He began directing Bruckner masses at St Florian cathedral but dropped out of a conducting course at the Munich conservatory and seemed set to join the rank and file of orchestral violinists until, as he put it, 'the decision to be a conductor was made for me'.

On 19 November 1978, 150 years to the day after Franz Schubert's death, he was driving with friends to play the Trout Quintet in Steyr, where it was composed, when their car was involved in a motorway smash-up. The 18-year-old Franz broke three vertebrae and was unable to hold a violin again. He could still conduct, though. 'When I have a long opera like *Tristan*, or have to fight with an orchestra for a good result, it can give me pain,' he admitted. 'That maybe explains my way of working, letting the musicians do the work.'

While training the Austrian Youth Orchestra, his name was mentioned to a visiting dilettante – and his life changed overnight. Baron Andreas von Bennigsen was a scion of Hanover's oldest family, a distant relative of the Queen of England. As a child, he sat on the lap of Wilhelm Furtwängler, who had taken refuge from the Nazis with his maternal grandfather, the Swiss writer John Knittel. The two families were close enough for Bennigsen to receive the same baptismal name as Furtwängler's son. He founded a musical agency and formed a chamber orchestra in Austria in which he played violin. On hearing talk of a local conductor, he invited him over for a chat. 'He came by train to our Swiss home, very quiet, very humble, but I felt something in this boy. We had a three-hour conversation and I told him, "you must get all of Wilhelm Furtwängler's records, because my dream is to find his successor".' After hearing him perform Bruckner's fifth symphony, the baron formally proposed to become his agent, and was solemnly accepted.

He immediately changed the boy's surname from the unassuming Möst to the double-barrelled Welser-Möst. 'His family had connections in the town of Wels from the sixteenth century,' noted the baron. Months later, he changed his name again to von Bennigsen, adopting Franz as his son and heir. It was too late to change the name on his first recordings. 'I was too lazy to produce children,' laughed the baron, 'and I always wanted to have a gifted son, a prince. When I met Franzi . . . it was so natural. For my wife, too.' The conductor moved in with the Bennigsens and followed them to Switzerland and Liechtenstein, where he took citizenship in the ultimate tax haven. The baron kitted him out in new clothes and spectacles to make him look like a successful conductor. 'Nothing resembles Furtwängler, that's the strange thing,' he finally conceded. 'The only thing they have in common is that they bring music to people, *who don't know why they are taken by it*. Franzi, when he conducts, becomes like glass. The music goes through his body into the world – yet he makes it sound new.'

Welser-Möst continued to maintain his line of least resistance. 'I never really go for anything,' he insisted. 'My only aim is to make music, or rather to let music happen in the best possible way.' His leap into the major league came in September 1990 when the London Philharmonic picked him – ahead of Mehta and other fancied candidates – to be its resident music director at the South Bank Centre. He was given unprecedented authority over programme planning and the uncontested right to hire and fire players. 'We have found a huge talent, with both musical and political skills,' said the orchestra's manager, John Willan, 'and we mean to let him get on with it. Once he starts realizing what he can do, he'll be tremendous.'

Welser-Möst himself was more circumspect. He planned to retain a provincial position in Germany where he could perfect his repertoire in relative privacy. 'It will give me a possibility to work on myself in not too strong a spotlight – and that is still very necessary,' he conceded. 'My main purpose is to serve music by studying it properly. When it comes to performance, I try to put my ego aside and just let it happen.'

Among his few emergent contemporaries, Litton was still on a learning curve at an English seaside resort; Flor gained a slim foothold with a London orchestra; Edwards was hampered by her sex; and the Sibelius cycle that should have made the name of Jukka-Pekka Saraste sounded anaemic in comparison with Simon Rattle's blazing Birmingham recordings. One or two putative prospects glimmered in the liberated lands of eastern Europe, but overall the conductors' cupboard was barer than ever before. As he meandered on to the concert platform with a mild smile on his unassuming features, Franz Welser-Möst looked a little like a tabby-cat trapped in the creamery, with the open churns at his sole disposal.

* * *

Where had it all gone wrong? Never had there been so many courses for student conductors or televised competitions and masterclasses at which they could excel. American orchestras instituted a young conductors program, attaching assistants to the tails of their egregious maestros in the hope of training a successor. The summer schemes at Tanglewood and Sapporo were bursting with young hopefuls and Leonard Bernstein scoured the globe for wonderkids to whom he could act as a latter-day Koussevitsky, but the talent stubbornly refused to materialize. Pianists abounded in their youthful brilliance and each year Juillard turned out a fiddler who could play the Paganini caprices faster than Heifetz on skates. There were far too many star cellists for the limited number of concertos written for their instrument and the quality of wind playing rose in leaps and whoops. Yet conductors were nowhere to be found.

There was no single or obvious reason for the sudden shortage, rather a confluence of social and artistic factors. All the great conductors, without exception, came up through the opera system, rehearsing singers and chorus, learning to sustain a musical line and steadily gaining repertoire until the night their big chance came. Opera is the most hazardous form of music-making. Anything can go wrong, and usually does, if not with soloists, then with the chorus and orchestra, with falling props and rowdy audiences. By confronting such crises nightly at a tender age, the rising conductor tackled the unforeseen almost by instinct and was able to focus the brunt of his attention on developing a musical interpretation. Nowadays, tertiary education is required to enter such stately institutions and a repetiteur may not get to start before his mid-twenties. By the time he reaches the podium, if ever he does, his reflexes will have been slowed by age and his memory dulled. All his concentration will be directed at getting through the opera rather than stamping his mark on it.

When Nikisch, Mahler and Toscanini were making their way in the world, every market town had a theatre and every summer spa an operatic festival. Opportunities were legion for a would-be conductor and the scrappier the ensemble he found, the more he learned from improving it. He made his mistakes away from metropolitan eyes before a vacationing impresario put him on the first rung of the ladder. Summer opera was a popular entertainment and the conductor's task was to serve the leisured classes; Mahler's duties at his first summer job included walking the manager's baby around the municipal park. Learning to conduct was not a rewarding process.

The operatic grid that stretched across every wayside town was shattered in the First World War and devastated beyond repair by ensuing inflation and totalitarianism. A plethora of private companies was supplanted by government-supported institutions in state capitals in which employment was unionized and carried a safe pension. Opera was no longer a natural training ground for adolescents; and the status of conductor was frequently subordinated to non-musicians, as stage directors, state bureaucrats and singers asserted their rights.

As opera ceased to be a conducting school, symphony orchestras increased in number, and increasingly wondered why they could not find conductors. No alternative method of training conductors was devised to take the place of their natural greenhouse, the small-town stage. Tuition at the conservatories fell into the hands of failed conductors, few of whom had the patience and application of Hans Swarowsky in Vienna and Leningrad's Ilya Musin. To make matters worse, when talent was recognized but did not conform to a dogmatic regime, it was deliberately stunted. Libor Pešek made little headway in Communist Czechoslovakia, then blossomed late in Liverpool; Klaus Tennstedt withered in the provinces of East Germany; in the West, the Karajan hegemony blocked the way of conductors who refused to play by his rules.

In market economies, scarcity pushes up prices and heats up demand. The fewer conductors of proven ability, the more the lucky few can earn. A clique of successful conductors have become, for the first time in the history of their profession, seriously rich – just how seriously will be demonstrated shortly. Since wealth creates its own pressures – for no-one who has made a fortune ever wants to be poor again – the nouveau riche protect their prosperity by grabbing three music directorships when one would suffice and cornering every available window of media exposure. This makes it all the more difficult for newcomers to break through.

Today no more than a dozen conductors control all the world's top jobs. They might fight one another but always unite when faced by a threat to their common interest, as they did in the battle of the Bastille. It is obviously against their interest to share power too widely. Each conductor might have a protégé or two, but none will do much to remedy the alarming worldwide scarcity. Their concern is to manage known resources, not to increase them.

Behind the cartel of conductors stands a shadowy manipulator whose name is unknown outside the corridors of musical power and whose face is often unrecognized even within them. His strategy has helped concentrate power in the hands of the few and earn them rewards beyond the dreams of avarice. His aim has been to extend and perpetuate that power within an empire of his own making. A maestro might be master on his own podium, but this maestro-maker wanted to be master of them all.

CHAPTER 16

The Master of Them All?

HE SITS IN a darkened room across 57th Street from Carnegie Hall plotting the future course of conducting. His walls are bare of portraits, his desk free of paper. It could be the consulting room of a high-society psychoanalyst or plastic surgeon. The instruments of his practice – telex, fax machine and currency converter – are nowhere to be seen. The man himself is dressed anonymously in a dark-blue suit and quiet silk tie, able to blend into any background. He is sixtyish, tanned, trim and obviously fit. His only affiliation listed in *Who's Who in America* is to the New York Athletic Club. He has an almost pathological fear of publicity, jerks his head away when a flashbulb pops and avoids the press like a pestilence; his interview with the present author was, he claimed, his first in twenty years. He twice tried to cancel the appointment and subsequently denied the substance of our fifty-minute conversation (which, thankfully, is preserved on tape). He agreed to a photo session, then ducked out; he does not want anyone to recognize his face.

Ronald Wilford moves mysteriously through the music world, materializing unannounced in Berlin, Tokyo or London and vanishing before the purpose of his visit is apparent. The surprises he leaves behind are primed to go off weeks or months later. He operates with the stealth of a guerrilla fighter or secret agent. He is, in fact, an artists' agent. Wilford is president and principal shareholder of the 'largest classical music management firm in the world'.

Columbia Artists Management Inc. – CAMI for short – handles the careers of some eight hundred musicians, of whom the majority are singers, headed by Kathleen Battle and José Carreras. Instrumentalists on its books include Mstislav Rostropovich, Maurizio Pollini and Arturo Benedetti Michelangeli. Most of the names, though, are less familiar. CAMI is a vast warehouse of talent with a dozen separate divisions, and offices in New York, Los Angeles, Ottawa and Zurich. It supplies stars to the international opera stage and has-beens to the country circuit. CAMI caters to all tastes; no gig is too small or big for its fixers. 'Neither radio nor TV nor VCR technology can replace the companionship, accompaniment and sheer joy of hearing a fine musician perform on your stage, in your town, because you and your friends wanted it to happen,' wheedles its sales-blurb in *Musical America*, beside a directory of artists great, once-great or simply grateful to appear in the company of greatness.

CAMI's greatest asset is, however, never advertised. Its list of conductors is confidential, distributed only on request to bona fide orchestras. CAMI looks after more than one hundred active maestros, all of whom share the same manager. Ronald Wilford conducts the conductors. He is their king-maker and fortune-maker, guardian of their most intimate secrets and sins. He hoards conductors as others collect old masters, cornering the market in top talent. It is easier to count off, on the fingers of both hands, the few major figures he has *not* snared. He does not represent the self-managed Maazel and Mehta. Nor, for partisan reasons that will become apparent, did he sign up Solti, Barenboim and Boulez. He has also missed out – so far – on the generation of Rattle, Chailly and Salonen.

These exceptions apart, he manages the entire spectrum of conducting from the flashy Semyon Bychkov in Paris to sedate Herbert Blomstedt at San Francisco, from the ever-reliable Bernard Haitink to the mercurial Klaus Tennstedt and Carlos Kleiber, a catalogue that runs alphabetically from Claudio Abbado to the obscure Belgian, Ronald Zollman. Wilford's batons are planted strategically at the musical power points. His men direct the New York Philharmonic and Metropolitan Opera; three of the four London orchestras and the Royal Opera House; the Berlin Philharmonic and Deutsche Oper; the Vienna State Opera and three-quarters of the Vienna Philharmonic concerts; La Scala, Milan, and Houston Grand Opera; the Bavarian State Opera and Dresden Staatskapelle. In return for his discreet services, Wilford takes a twenty per cent cut of every conducting fee and contract – twice as much as most European agents. His clients feel he is worth every cent. Many have been with him all their working lives.

Political and emotional ruptures present no obstacle to his progress. He enjoyed the confidence of the Italian rivals, Muti and Abbado, *and* of their common adversary Sinopoli. He looks after the ultra-modernist German, Michael Gielen, and the arch-conservative Wolfgang Sawallisch. At the iciest Cold War temperatures, he attended to the Communist exiles Kubelik and Rostropovich and the Communist flag-wavers Kurt Masur and Vaclav Neumann with impartial fidelity and fairness. 'I learned a long time ago what one's fiduciary responsibility is,' he explained. 'When you are married, you don't necessarily have to do everything for the benefit of your wife. But when you have a fiduciary agency responsibility, which is what I have with these musicians, I must do only that which is in their favour. I have no problem separating. There are always jealousies. There will always be mistrust. I am sure that many of the people who do trust me don't trust me all the time. They have these thoughts – will I like this one more than the other? The answer is I don't, I don't play those games.'

The games he does play have changed the ground rules of conducting and forced neutrals to stay onside. Bernstein, who set up his own corporation and paid percentages to no-one, placed his protégés Michael Tilson Thomas and John Mauceri in Wilford's care. Maazel, no respecter of agents, was won over when Wilford, deploring the manner of his dismissal from Vienna, volunteered his candidacy as music director to prominent orchestras. Had his ploy succeeded, Wilford would have gained another satellite; either way, he made sure of future co-operation with an independent power-player. Mehta, who has not forgiven Wilford for snubbing him as a young man, was dismayed when the New York Philharmonic, on receiving his resignation, walked straight across the road to lunch with Wilford. 'Who do you think we should be interested in?' asked the Philharmonic board. Wilford suggested Colin Davis, Abbado and Haitink; when they backed out, he inserted Kurt Masur. The final choice, he would say, 'is up to the orchestra: I don't play God'.

He angrily denied allegations of pressure-selling by, for example, threatening to withhold guest stars unless an orchestra made his man music director. *Time* magazine, he said, went to every manager in America to ask if Wilford twisted their arms and came away with no story. In Chicago, the symphony manager said: 'The one time Ron Wilford told me to take somebody was Jim Levine and I didn't do it. I've been kicking myself ever since.' No-one criticizes him openly; even confidential comments are cautiously worded. Ronald Wilford is feared by managers, competitors and, apparently, by some of his own conductors. 'You can lose your music director if Wilford whispers in his ear that it is time to move on,' said an American orchestral chairman. 'If you got on the wrong side of him it could be very nasty,' warned a London concert organizer. No conductor has walked away from Wilford and prospered.

He has been called 'the most powerful man in music in America', but this does not begin to reflect the extent of his dominance. His tentacles stretch far beyond music into unrelated sectors, and beyond America to control musical supply in parts of Europe and Japan. The roll of companies registered at his address reveals that he is involved in the travel business, in television, theatre, real estate, festival management and much else. CAMI, under Wilford, is a mighty conglomerate – how mighty one cannot tell since, as a private company, its results are not published and its president refuses to reveal turnover. Wilford becomes visibly agitated when he is charged with being too powerful. 'There is no power,' he objects. 'Power does corrupt and I don't consider I am corrupt. A lot of the things I am accused of doing, I don't do. I have never told anybody who to engage. There is no power to exert in this business.'

That depends, of course, on one's perception of power. In Wilford's terms, he considers himself powerless because wilful conductors will not always obey him. 'I do wish I had the power they think I have. I do wish I could go to Kleiber and say, do this and this, and he would nod like a little puppy dog,' he mused. 'It would save me so much time.'

The only power he acknowledged was in growing the best grapevine. 'I know what is going on all over the world because of who I represent,' he gloated. 'This does cause certain people to have a problem. Sometimes they are not honest, but they have figured that if they deal with me I will eventually find out about it. If they are dealing with two or three conductors over the same job, my office will find out. So they have to play it a little – cool. That's the only time my position helps. If I'm good at what I do, does that mean I have power?' In an international business where minutes can make a difference between gaining or missing a vacant slot, it does. The man who gets first word of developments and has the resources to respond is the constant winner. Whatever his protestations to the contrary, Wilford's network of well-placed informants gives him an unbeatable advantage over competitors and isolated institutions. 'If only I had Mr Wilford's power . . .' lament European agents.

His power is rooted in a total dominance of CAMI – where, despite a pretence at partnership, he had absolute authority to hire and fire – and in the special status of his informants. By holding the cards of a hundred conductors, he has an earpiece and influence in every important musical boardroom and, when necessary, in the offices of ministers and presidents. 'I just sit here all day feeling nervous,' said Wilford recently. He has never betrayed a trace of anxiety. The day Ronald Wilford is seen looking worried, the rest of the music business will suffer heart failure.

Wilford is not an original thinker but an adapter of ideas, not a founder of empires but an expander of boundaries. The CAMI that he commands has existed since 1930, when Arthur Judson welded together seven competing agencies to exert an unbreakable arm-lock on musical America. 'The time has come,' declared CAMI's progenitor, 'to streamline the advancement of artists' careers by such corporation methods as have long been used in the distribution of refrigerators.'

For quarter of a century, until Congress challenged his monopoly, Judson applied industrial techniques to the marketing of music. Mass tastes were identified and sated, mass brands were invented and popularized. Music and artists were mass-produced with a minimum of risk and error. Judson, although privately sympathetic to new music, eliminated it from his menus unless a conductor was prepared to risk his own neck on it, as Stokowski and Mitropoulos were. He gave America the music that made him most profit, catering to every scale of performance from grand opera to school concerts, while running two of the Big Five orchestras on his own account. He blacklisted artists who offended him and threatened to withhold advertising from the *Herald Tribune* unless it sacked Virgil Thomson as music critic. His fortune was sunk into buying office blocks around 57th Street and, though rattled by the federal trust-busters and forced to resign his chairmanship in 1948, he clung on to America's biggest concert agency until he was 82.

Wilford came up on his blind side as a poacher, a fresh kid out of nowhere who approached a struggling orchestra in Portland, Oregon, offering to spice up its season with the stateless, penniless Klemperer and two underused Columbia artists, Mitropoulos and William Steinberg. 'It was the best conductors' list they ever had,' he recalled, and Judson 'didn't like me for that'. But the aging buccaneer recognized a kindred spirit and brought Wilford on board in 1958. Five years later Judson was voted out; formed a rival agency and lived to be 93. It took Wilford less than a decade after his departure to capture total control of CAMI in 1972. He was 44 years old, 'lean, mean and handsome', and about to marry Sara Delano Roosevelt Whitney, his third wife. The CAMI presidency gave him paramountcy in American music; the marriage gained him admission to America's upper crust.

His humble antecedents had been left far behind. Ronald Andrew Wilford was the second of seven children of a Greek janitor, born in the Mormon capital of Salt Lake City on 4 November 1927. His father looked after the maintenance and garbage of a city block and adhered to the Greek Orthodox faith; his mother was a devout Mormon, a religion that places heavy emphasis on family unity. 'I had a hard time knowing who I was,' confessed their second son, who grew up with a sense of being a permanent outsider. He failed to graduate from two universities, Utah and Stanford, married a childhood sweetheart, had a child and got divorced. He set up a theatrical agency and moved to New York, touring the Dublin Players and the French mime Marcel Marceau around middle America. According to one acquaintance, he speculated successfully, perhaps brilliantly, on Wall Street.

Unlike Judson, who started life as a violinist and claimed (unprovenly) to have played the American première of Richard Strauss's sonata, Wilford never studied music and could, by some accounts, not read a simple piano score. He enjoyed music and would weep at Puccini operas, but had no sense of its practical disciplines and artistic integrity. 'He is the only man to approach music purely as a business proposition,' said a financier who sat with him on several boards. Hired by CAMI to run its faltering theatrical side, he soon took over Judson's conductors division. The agency was at a turning point. It could not grow any larger in America without risking congressional interference. To avoid stagnation and decline, it needed to expand surreptitiously at home while cracking open sophisticated overseas markets where American agents, with their monoglot constraints and brash salesmanship, had never penetrated.

The key to both strategies was, Wilford realized, the podium. By managing the music directors, he could harness their orchestras to CAMI schemes. Nothing impeachable in that. And since many of the conductors he installed in America were imported from Europe, they could repay him with introductions to places of overseas influence. Judson was not particularly interested in what his conductors did outside the United States. Wilford was, passionately, and went all out to secure rights for worldwide management. Within four years, he had increased CAMI's list by a third to 73 conductors, and was heading for a target of between 90 and 110. Agents, whether musical, literary, insurance or secret, have two ways of getting clients: either they footslog around until they spot talent, or they lure it away from a competitor with golden promises. Everyone condemns the latter course as unethical, and everyone seizes it when the opportunity arises.

Wilford was not averse to a little fishing. He pulled a fast one on Klaus Tennstedt's German manager by persuading him to give up British rights in the conductor hours before the London Philharmonic, primed by CAMI, asked Tennstedt to be its chief. Several artists were introduced to him by European managers who entrusted their American engagements to Wilford, only to see their client swallowed up globally in CAMI's embrace. 'Wilford is not a man you can work *with*,' said an embittered British agent. 'You either work *for* him, or you're against him.' In fairness, he usually preferred developing fresh talent to trawling the slightly used, and had a network of informants who tipped him off about young men worth watching. André Previn was spotted by Schuyler Chapin, an executive at CBS, where the movie composer had recorded his Oscar-winners. Wilford, after touring Previn for a year with low-grade orchestras, agreed to manage him on condition that the conductor took his advice and put Hollywood behind him. 'Many people find Ron difficult, even abrasive – at least when it comes to business matters,' said Previn. 'He's always been wonderful to me – truly concerned, caring. And he's an absolute wizard in the business.'

Seiji Ozawa was introduced by Bernstein and Karajan. He happened to be sitting in the CAMI office when a call came through from San Francisco begging for someone to replace Dmitri Shostakovich, who had been pulled out by the Soviets. 'What about this guy?' said Wilford, pointing to the shy young Japanese. Riccardo Muti was recommended by Eugene Ormandy, a Judson veteran. James Levine was picked up by Wilford in his early twenties and nurtured until he was ripe for the Met, where Rafael Kubelik was about to pull out – on Wilford's advice. 'The people that are really very close to him,' said Previn, 'such as myself, Seiji Ozawa, Jimmy Levine and a few other people – we don't make a move without asking him. And that's curiously not because he's the great manipulator but because we absolutely trust him in his judgement.' By the time he became president of CAMI, Wilford had hand-reared a new generation of conductors.

'I have a fantasy, a fantasy,' he said, describing how he picked a potential maestro. 'It is dangerous because you can have an artist with a great deal of talent, but how do you know if he will have the discipline, or the character, or the insight? How do you know if he'll develop? I have believed in a lot of people who didn't make it – and it wasn't because they didn't have talent. Very few have one hundred per cent in all departments.' Those who did not live up to his expectations were smartly dropped and rarely heard of again. He ruthlessly pruned his list, shedding up to one-fifth of his conductors each year. 'It's the ones whose career we have been active with for years and years. Those are the ones we care about.'

Andrew Davis and Edo de Waart are the only recent conductors to have survived the Wilford chop with their careers intact. 'He indicated he could do certain things to help me that subsequently didn't transpire,' said Davis, who went back to his British agent and posts with the BBC and Glyndebourne. De Waart, a promising Dutchman who got bogged down in San Francisco, is recovering his morale with another British agent and the Minnesota orchestra. American managements were either too tiny or too timid to pick up Wilford's rejects.

His unseen hand gripped music in America more tightly than Judson's ever had. San Francisco, for example, took its music directors exclusively from CAMI: first Josef Krips, then Ozawa, de Waart and Blomstedt. When a CAMI conductor, the East German Gunther Herbig, fizzled out in Detroit, Wilford sent in the energetic Neeme Järvi to regalvanize the orchestra, while moving Herbig on to Toronto. No other agent could have responded so sleekly, to the satisfaction of all involved. Of the Big Five orchestras, he had music directors in three and associate conductors at the others. Every musical institution of any significance was infiltrated by a Wilford stooge.

When Rudolf Bing was retired from running the Met, he was promptly hired by Wilford to ease CAMI's dealings with his former staff. 'I think the role of manager found its high point in Ronald Wilford,' gushed Bing. 'He is one of those rare men in music who does not want fame. On the contrary he avoids it. Yet he dominates the field not only in his capacity as president of Columbia Artists Management but also in his most cunning ability to sniff out talent. Yet he need not search. They flock to him.'

As far as singers were concerned, his attractions became well-nigh irresistible when, with Bing at his beck and call and Levine as music director, Wilford had the run of the Metropolitan Opera. He organized its record contract with Deutsche Grammophon and installed one of his own deputies, Peter Gelb, to head the Met's media department. A subliminal message went out to the effect that if singers wanted to appear on records or videos from the Met, they would be well advised to enlist with CAMI. Jessye Norman led the rush in the late 1980s, shedding her long-suffering London agent. Inside the Met, Wilford was known as 'God'.

Gelb, who joined him from Ozawa's Boston Symphony, came up with the novel idea that CAMI should make promotional videos about its stars and sell them to television as 'intimate film portraits'. Credulous channels all over the world, including the BBC, France's Antenne Deux and America's Public Broadcasting System, swallowed the line and screened adulatory CAMI glossies without a murmur of editorial reservation. The programmes amounted to more than an hour's free advertising for Herbert von Karajan on his eightieth birthday and for Jessye Norman as a massively miscast Carmen. At the Met, meanwhile, Gelb heavily undercut Bayreuth in seeking to sell Levine's *Ring* to television with a CAMI-strong cast.

Gelb had other useful connections. His father, Arthur Gelb, was managing editor of the *New York Times* – 'an aggressive, often impetuous editor who involved himself in every aspect of cultural coverage', according to the media bible, *Variety*. Journalists complained of the 'ridiculous overcoverage' they were required to give to his son's CAMI clients. One stormy night in 1978, *Times* critics resigned en bloc in protest at Arthur Gelb's editorial interference in cultural affairs. When a scandal broke in Germany over a financial deal involving CAMI's senior conductor and the managing editor's son, the *New York Times* blacked out coverage, although its competitor *Newsday* carried full details. Arthur Gelb took early retirement in 1990 amid a huge shakeup of leisure coverage. Since the *New York Times* was the only American paper whose arts coverage carried nationwide clout, its sympathy for CAMI artists filtered back into the musical bloodstream to reinforce the agency's position. As for Wilford, he got the press he preferred in America, which was no press at all.

He was not infallible, but his faults were somehow ascribed to others while Wilford kept in the shadows. Levine was attacked for the inferior quality of his Met conductors, while Wilford cheerfully admitted to withholding his best batons from the company. 'Just because I manage you,' he told Levine, 'doesn't mean I have to help you for your opera house. When you ask for someone, my fiduciary responsibility shifts to him. It is not to the advantage of other conductors to go to the Met.' As pressure mounted on Levine, Wilford pulled Carlos Kleiber from his capacious hat to make a belated and sensational Met debut. Previn was not so lucky in Los Angeles. His tussle with Ernest Fleischmann (see Chapter 6) had been simmering noisily for a year and was known wherever musicians gossiped. An alert agent would have stepped in to defuse it long before the final explosion. But by the time Wilford got involved all he could do was threaten Fleischmann with a breach of contract suit that both of them knew would never stick. Previn was left naked in Hollywood, issuing rash statements that a caring manager would have suppressed in his best interest.

Wilford had too many conductors to treat them all like the only sons they longed to be. 'The vast majority of artists,' said a British agent, 'want a more personal relationship.' In going for all-out growth, Wilford had covered all the institutions but left individuals exposed. By moving out of America into a worldwide operation, he spread himself more thinly still.

The department that Wilford inherited from Judson contained a number of Europeans who were not receiving the attention they deserved. Otto Klemperer would be everlastingly grateful to Wilford for getting him work in America. Dmitri Mitropoulos, sacked by the New York Philharmonic, was consoled with other dates by his go-ahead agent, who played heavily on their common Greek ancestry and was distraught at his early death.

The same Hellenic connection brought him close to another unhappy conductor from the old world. Herbert von Karajan had been on Judson's books since 1938, and precious little good had come of it. His 1955 debut tour with the Berlin Philharmonic was disrupted by anti-Nazi demonstrators and he left America, he told a lover, on the brink of a nervous breakdown. His prospects there were nil and his efforts in Europe were dissipated – until Wilford came into the picture. The precise nature of their relationship is unfathomable, since neither shared its secrets with anyone else. For more than thirty years they were exceptionally close. 'I liked him very much,' said Wilford tersely. 'More than liked him. Adored him.' He saw Karajan as a musical idealist who sought power only as a means to achieve tonal perfection. Karajan presumably viewed Wilford as a pragmatist who pursued the last ounce of material benefit to be gained from music. Each identified in the other something of himself. It was a partnership so symbiotic that it was sometimes impossible to tell its partners apart.

'He is unique in the entire world of music,' said Wilford of Karajan. 'He overcame his provincial beginnings, learned languages, became an international figure . . .' The basic facts of their lives were remarkably similar. 'Do not ignore the bond of Greek blood,' said a record executive who watched them at close hand. Each stood like Onassis, the colossus of his trade.

'On the podium, others conduct, Karajan is being an artist,' said Wilford admiringly. 'Karajan, too, brings total attention to the smallest detail. He is a performer who brings the orchestra and the audience with him. He is the only one I know who can do it; and he didn't have it until he was fifty.' Karajan turned fifty in 1958, the year Wilford began directing his affairs.

Wilford's immediate benefit to Karajan was the ending of his American boycott and his admission to the land of plenty. CAMI brought him over that same year to conduct the New York Philharmonic, introduced him to the Met and arranged whatever tours and guest engagements he wanted. Artists who had led the campaign against him – mostly Jewish musicians and their friends – as well as conductors who had offended Karajan in some way, such as Solti, were placed outside the CAMI pale. Instead, Karajan supplied a roster of his latest favourites. These included the winners of his conducting competition, none of whom Wilford managed to make into stars, and singers of the stellar quality of Agnes Baltsa and Anna Tomowa-Sintow. His Salzburg stage director, Jean Pierre Ponnelle, joined CAMI, as did the pianists Christoph Eschenbach and Alexis Weissenberg.

The evolution of Anne-Sophie Mutter illustrates the tight-knit framework of the Karajan-Wilford clan. After her Berlin Philharmonic debut at 14, the dazzling violinist was consigned by Karajan to the trusty Michel Glotz for French representation and to Wilford for America, with an exclusive recording contract at Deutsche Grammophon. Her father, a newspaper publisher, kept tabs on her development but lost control when she hit America in a blaze of bare-shouldered CAMI publicity. Karajan sent her for tax advice in Monte Carlo to a middle-aged German lawyer, Detlef Wunderlich, who had successfully defended the industrial conglomerate Flick in heavy litigation. Wunderlich was also president of Karajan's film company, Telemondial, and became Mutter's husband. . . .

Wilford was given access to Karajan's citadels, swamping Salzburg and Berlin with CAMI artists. At a time when good singers were becoming scarce, he brought forth a crowd of Americans to shine in central roles, many of them bearing Karajan's personal seal of approval. Wilford went from strength to strength in Europe, to the alarm of native agents. He learned the ropes fast, and enough German to deal with Berlin senators in an attempt to sew up the Karajan succession. But his scheme came unstuck when an anti-Karajan faction in the Philharmonic learned that a visit they planned to Taiwan had been called off and replaced with a CAMI trip to Japan, because of exorbitant demands made on Karajan's behalf. A secret telex from Peter Gelb, leaked by the players to *Der Spiegel*, revealed Karajan's terms. He wanted 600,000 Deutschmarks (£200,000) to conduct two concerts and for ten of his films to be screened on Taiwan television at an additional cost of £200,000 – plus first-class air fares for an entourage of six. Since the Berlin Philharmonic chartered its own flight, the tickets would have gone into the conductor's bottomless pocket. A political squall blew up at the way the orchestra, which cost the city's taxpayers 19 million marks (£6.2 million) a year, was being run for private profit by an egomaniacal conductor and his American agents.

It was a set-up, said Gelb. He should have sensed the latent hostility and 'protected Karajan from himself'. The scandal, followed by a Social-ist-Green election victory, put CAMI on the rocks in Berlin and wrecked Wilford's hopes of crowning Levine as Karajan's heir. The success of Abbado was small consolation. Abbado belonged to Wilford in America only, not worldwide. Gelb, nevertheless, was soon back in Berlin, filming Abbado's 'first hundred days'.

When the wall opened between the two Germanies, Wilford, anticipa-ting reunification ahead of the politicians, made a raid on Dresden to instal Sinopoli as Staatskapelle conductor, with Levine close behind. The Silver Fox, as some called him, demonstrated that he had lost none of his sharpness with Karajan's demise.

The Taiwan tempest let a glimmer of light into the most lucrative aspect, dollar for dollar, of Wilford's operation. Whenever CAMI placed a music director, it would insist on exclusive touring rights. Anywhere the orchestra wanted to go, it flew CAMI. 'If I want to tour an orchestra with a conductor because I want to build him, then I want to do it in the US, Canada, South America, Europe and Japan, I have the facility to do that. I have found a way to do that. I want to be able to tour without another manager telling me, "No",' said Wilford with considerable vehemence.

On these tours, in addition to its share of the performing fees, CAMI took a commission on every airline ticket, hotel bed and meal supplied to the travelling orchestra. Some tours were fixed through CAMI Travel, giving the parent company an extra brokerage fee, others went through a mysterious CAMI middle man in Buenos Aires who struck cheapskate deals. The Berlin Philharmonic, aristocrats of the orchestral community, wound up in Midwestern fleapits blaming their conductor and his cohort for their unaccustomed discomfort. The New York hotel at which CAMI lodged one London orchestra had radiators that roared all night and a lobby like Heathrow airport on August bank holiday. Someone, muttered players, must be making a killing on this.

Wilford set great store by his tours. He bullied weaker music directors to do more than they instinctively wanted and, when the London Philharmonic balked at a fifteen-stop US whirligig, fearing for Klaus Tennstedt's health, he flew over in person to underwrite any possible losses. It was a tenet of his faith that conductors had to be kept moving, continuously exposed to potential new fans and record buyers. He was among the first to react to the growth of jet travel, pioneering the concept by which conductors could run three institutions at once and earn the cream of their income from guest appearances. 'Times have changed because of jets and the audience needs more variety on stage,' explained Seiji Ozawa, evidently echoing his master.

In his counsel to Karajan, though, Wilford pointed the other way. Karajan, at the time they got to know each other, was trying to be *Generalmusikdirector* of Europe, with positions in Berlin, Vienna, Salzburg, Milan, London and Paris. Over the next six years he dropped the peripherals one by one to focus solely on the Berlin Philharmonic and Salzburg Festival, extending his power by less obvious means. The parallel with Wilford is inescapable. Just as Wilford shed Judson's upfront management of orchestras to pull strings at a distance, so Karajan now removed himself from running institutions and aimed to dominate by proxy. Together, they conquered new markets, particularly Japan, exerting their influence with minimum visibility. Wilford even allowed local agencies to care for some of his conductors abroad, placing Previn with Jasper Parrott in London and Levine with the Munich firm of Karen Wylach, retaining an overview of their activities without being bothered with petty detail. He did not intend 'to conquer Europe or become multinational. . . . those are terms you can use with commodities but not with our field of endeavour', he said.

By putting his ear to Wilford's grapevine, Karajan could tap into any musical organization and colour its decisions. Whether he actually owned part of the agency cannot be verified unless CAMI opens its books. One insider speculates that it would have been typical of Karajan to demand payment in CAMI shares, increasing his corporate holdings rather than his already considerable financial worth. Whatever the case, and contrary to other long-standing connections, Karajan's links with Wilford grew ever closer and more involved right up to the day of his death. 'Their relationship was, to say the least, peculiar,' said an industry veteran. 'Karajan used Wilford to translate his ideas into hard cash. Wilford, when he smelled anything going, would go with it.'

Competitors were divided between those who feared Wilford as a machiavellian expansionist and others who perceived him as a lucky opportunist who had cottoned on to Karajan's commercial genius. The latter interpretation contained more sour grapes than credibility. It ignored Karajan's acute sensitivity to parasites and Wilford's advisory role in his transformation from mere conductor to plutocrat.

Wilford did not pretend to be a long-term planner. His knack was to take an existing concept, like CAMI, and mould it to his own specifications and the fluctuations in public taste. Some saw him as a small-scale Mark McCormack, the operator who signed up all the leading tennis players, followed by the ball-by-ball commentators, until he was able to run tournaments and make television 'documentaries' about his stars. McCormack's International Management Group, though, had to cover against a possible decline in tennis interest by branching into other sports and leisure sectors. These included music, where IMG signed up the top-earning Itzhak Perlman, and toured an open-space *Carmen* from London to Tokyo and Sydney. There were initially signs that McCormack planned to challenge CAMI's pre-eminence in the high-prestige concert hall but his gauntlet caused few tremors on 57th Street and not one maestro of substance was weaned away from Wilford. IMG may be the big racket at Wimbledon; in Salzburg it cannot get a game.

Wilford never had to move beyond his core speciality. If the market collapsed in conductors, the whole classical music industry would be ruined. His position was unassailable so long as he held on to his hundred-odd conductors. This he did by rotating talent and continuously searching for slack potential in his clients. 'There is always growth,' he believed. 'It's an evolution with all of them. They will all become better. There is always repertoire that they can do now or ten years from now.' If Ozawa took up Mahler, it was with Wilford's approval. If Previn returned to the piano, the move had been discussed with his mentor. No aspect of their development was left to chance.

'We advise on everything. The whole management of an artist is evolutionary, but without a plan. There is no formula. You can't say, be this way or that way, just be yourself. Be comfortable with who you are, don't be in stress, relax.' He read popular psychology, described himself as 'the doctor in the background', and prescribed every kind of intimate remedy, from tax shelters to posture lessons. 'You see mistakes that are made. Then you figure out why does somebody short with a particular body type approach the podium this way, in an unrelaxed way? You have to find out how each of these individuals functions best without any relation to anyone else. So I have to have the kind of mind that free-associates and identifies totally with them. I'm on their side in finding out what it is that makes them function best. That's my job.'

The mark of his attention could not be discerned on a maverick like Tennstedt, on the self-assured Marriner or the wavery Colin Davis; but on 'the people that are really very close to him' (in Previn's phrase), it was all too apparent. Conductors that Wilford raised from scratch assumed certain of his personality traits, as if by osmosis. They were secretive, acquisitive and conservative. Commercial and careerist priorities took precedence over concern for the good of the art. Faced with tough decisions of the kind that every music director has to make, they prevaricated until Wilford could be consulted, weakening their authority in the eyes of musicians and administrators. 'My artists don't think I am a son of a bitch, and I don't care what anyone else thinks,' he once said. 'My client is the artist – not the Philharmonic, not the Metropolitan Opera, not anyone else . . . And I *am* absolutely ruthless if it comes to telling an orchestra to go to hell if I feel something is unfair to an artist of mine. I really don't care because if I have an artist they want, they will have to book him.'

Interpretatively, the performance of his chosen few failed to deepen with maturity. On the contrary, it progressively lost the cutting edge of individuality that made Previn, Ozawa and Levine so compelling as young conductors. The music they now produced was safe and sometimes slack, product of a mid-life performing crisis. By refining a career to maximum efficiency, Wilford may have whittled away the conductor's special qualities and left him bare of personal reserves. Wilford denied the charge, of course, as indeed he denied having any perceptible influence on the state of music today. All that, he said, was a matter for the musicians. He merely advised, they decided.

Wilford's total involvement in a musician's life, together with his monolithic power, has positively repelled conductors of the younger generation. Rattle took a principal agent in London, Martin Campbell-White, and when in America used the tiny firm of Frank Salomon Associates, with fewer than a dozen artists on its books. Chailly looked after himself, Welser-Möst had his benevolent baron and Salonen placed his affairs worldwide in the hands of Joeske Van Walsum. Wilford's hopes for the future were pinned on Andrew Litton, whom Mstistlav Rostropovich discovered in Washington, and on the older and quieter American Kent Nagano, who made his name in France as a Messiaen interpreter. The thrust of Wilford's efforts in recent seasons has been aimed at establishing high profiles for the Russian, Semyon Bychkov, whom Karajan mischievously tipped as his successor, the Bulgarian Emil Tchakarov, another Karajan favourite, and the widely disputed gifts of Giuseppe Sinopoli. The Svengali of 57th Street staked a sizeable chunk of his reputation on their unproven promise and by 1990 many around the musical world felt he was starting to lose his touch. Should his current models fail to live up to over-hyped expectations, and if he cannot quickly raise another crop of youngsters, Wilford's aura will be fatally dented and he will end up following Judson into luxurious obscurity.

He will not succeed altogether in preserving anonymity, for the changes he has made to musical life are too lasting and far-reaching. Wilford was responsible for inventing the part-time music director. He turned orchestras into flying circuses and cloned a pack of conductors in his own image. With his alter ego Karajan, he raised the social status of the maestro and altered the economic structure of the entire musical world.

We are about to trespass on strictly private territory. Money is music's last taboo. The *New Grove Dictionary of Music and Musicians*, which has entries for conductors great and small, fastidiously overlooks Ronald Wilford. Joan Peyser's prurient biographies of Boulez and Bernstein, revealing everything she could discover of their sexual proclivities and, in Bernstein's case, activities, did not discuss what they earned and what they owned, how they came by it and with whose assistance. Karajan's investigators never examined his finances. Conservatories teach every aspect of musical practice and theory, but none has a course in the economic history and organization of music. These are deemed to be unseemly topics, offensive and unrelated to so refined and ethereal an art. The maestro's task is to commune with superior levels of spirituality, to shed light on cosmic mysteries. If he was seen to be pursuing material wealth as greedily as the stockbroker in row 16, his priestly myth would be dispelled. Jeffrey Archer and his publisher might brag in press releases of the 11 million dollars one has given and the other received for a sequence of novels. The six or seven figures paid for a David Hockney painting or a Schnabel are publicized as a mark of the artist's current standing and the investor's acumen. But the remuneration of musicians remains a well-kept secret, known only to two or three people in any organization. The player-chairman of the Berlin Philharmonic admitted recently that he had no idea how much his conductors were paid and no easy way of finding out.

When a German manager, Hans-Dieter Göhre, published the 1989 list of his artists in three specified price brackets, there was an outburst of consternation. 'It puts artists in the category of commodities,' complained David Sigall, chairman of the British Association of Concert Agents. 'It also creates values in people's minds that will colour their artistic judgement. Psychologically, it's bad for artists and bad for audiences.' Göhre was threatened with suspension from the European Association of Concert Agents. 'The prime thing about artists is their artistry, not their bloody money – I have never known an engagement to be turned down because of money,' said Joeske Van Walsum. It was not as if musicians' earnings in general were of an order to excite amazement among shipowners and agitation at the Inland Revenue. With the exception of the odd Patti and Caruso, no concert artist ever earned anything on the scale of Frank Sinatra or the Beatles. The secrecy that shrouded their fees was purely a matter of myth protection. Agents did not want to reveal the value of their products and performers did not want their audiences to calculate how much each movement was worth.

Göhre's list demonstrated that beginners and also-rans drew concert fees of between DM 2,000 and DM 10,000 (£700-£3,250), middle-rankers fetched up to DM 20,000 (£6,500) and stars, notably the violinists Itzhak Perlman and Pinchas Zukerman, opened negotiations at DM 20,000. German fees were roughly equivalent to UK payments, though well below the going rate in the United States, where Perlman was drawing $45,000 nightly. The publication was harmless enough, except that it underlined the economic unreality of a scale of payments which bore scant relevance to box office takings. Adding the cost of orchestra, conductor, hall and promotion, a top soloist would need to sell two thousand tickets at a hundred dollars each to justify his fee – an impossible proposition. A star was not paid more because he made a bigger profit for the promoter; on the contrary, he usually left a bigger loss, compensated partly by the lustre his presence added to the season as a whole.

There was one category, however, that even the glasnost-minded Göhre kept under wraps. 'Conductors,' said Göhre firmly, 'are different.' Their privacy could not be violated, their income was in a class of its own. A maestro might not receive as much for a night's work as Luciano Pavarotti's reputed $100,000 or score a freak hit like his 'Nessun dorma' but, in terms of total revenue, the top dozen music directors were making more out of music year by year than anyone else in the art. Adding up two full salaries in America and Europe, annual guest appearances at Salzburg, Lucerne and Tokyo, television fees and the rolling royalties from a hundred recordings or more, Muti or Previn, to name but two, would expect to make two million dollars in an average year.

The veil of secrecy surrounding their earnings can be pierced by a persistent researcher armed with the US Freedom of Information Act. American institutions are required by the IRS to enumerate their five highest paid beneficiaries. In 1990, the going rate for a music director at Big Five orchestras averaged out at $700,000 a year. Pittsburg was alleged to be paying Lorin Maazel close to one million, but accounts have not yet been filed. European wages are harder to crack but details leak out during disputes. Daniel Barenboim was to have been paid seven million francs (£1.2 million) for running the Bastille Opera in Paris; Wilford wanted seven hundred thousand Deutschmarks (£250,000) for Sinopoli to conduct two productions a year at the Deutsche Oper. Maazel made

$450,000 in Vienna in 1983. The conductorship of a German radio orchestra is worth around quarter of a million dollars for three months' work. Emoluments are closely guarded in secretive British society, but London orchestras would not pay much less than a German radio station.

Even an undemanding man like Abbado is an annual millionaire. He has reportedly taken just DM 140,000 (£48,000) in salary from the Berlin Philharmonic, plus DM 24,000 (£8,000) for a minimum of 24 concerts, a total of DM 332,000 (£110,000). Add to these a Vienna Opera salary not less than Maazel's, huge fees from Japanese tours and Salzburg appearances and the royalties from more than a hundred recordings in current circulation, and you have an income of at least seven figures in any currency you can name.

Traditionally, there have always been one or two maestros who demanded to be paid more than the rest. Toscanini, at his last London concert was paid five times more. Nikisch made the London Symphony Orchestra give him twice as much as Weingartner and six times more than British conductors (see Table 1). All that had changed now was that the wealth was far greater and being spread among a dozen conductors instead of just a couple – or so it seemed. However, with the help of various sources who were prepared to break silence over the precise earnings of conductors who are no longer alive, a more sweeping trend becomes apparent. In the past two decades, there has been hyper-inflation in conductors' fees, increases that are out of all proportion to general inflation and the economics of musical activity. The increase is notable in their salaries, but most strikingly in the fees that conductors command for guest performances. Any of the top dozen maestros can expect around twenty thousand dollars a night for appearing on a major American podium, slightly less in West European countries, and up to four times as much in Japan. Charles Dutoit is reported to receive 220 thousand francs (£22,500) for every concert with the Orchestre National de France; Lorin Maazel is allegedly paid $80,000 a night in Tokyo.

In 1910, the top fee in the United States was one hundred dollars, except for Mahler and Toscanini who got three hundred. By 1940 it had risen to five hundred dollars and by 1960 was creeping towards two thousand. This steady growth was roughly in line with US living standards. Between 1960 and 1990, the nightly fee for a top conductor increased twelvefold, while industrial earnings merely quadrupled. Put another way: in 1910, a top conductor earned ten times as much for a concert as a factory worker took home in a week. In 1990, he was paid fifty times as much.

Table 1 Sample of conductor's concert fees in London

1905	Felix Weingartner (LSO)	£52.10.0 (50 guineas)
	Frederic Cowen (LSO)	£15.15.0.
1912	Arthur Nikisch (Covent Garden)	£150
1913	Fritz Steinbach (LSO)	£87.3.0
	Arthur Nikisch (LSO)	£105
1921	Albert Coates (LSO)	£63
1950	Otto Klemperer (Philharmonia)	£110
1951	Thomas Beecham (Covent Garden)	£100–150
	Hans Knappertsbusch (Covent Garden)	£100–150
	Erich Kleiber (Covent Garden)	£200
1952	Malcolm Sargent (RPO)	£85
	Joseph Krips (LSO)	£100
1954	Joseph Krips (LSO)	£125
1958	Malcolm Sargent (RPO)	£115
1970	Otto Klemperer (Philharmonia)	£650
1972	Leopold Stokowski (LSO)	£500
	Jascha Horenstein (LSO)	£500
	Istvan Kertesz (LSO)	£500
1974	Eugen Jochum (LPO)	£275
	Adrian Boult (LPO)	£350
	John Pritchard (LPO)	£375
1975	John Pritchard (LPO)	£486
1977	John Pritchard (LPO	£575
1978	Eugen Jochum (LSO)	£1300
1979	John Pritchard (LPO)	£1000
1980	Karl Böhm (LSO)	£3000
1981	John Pritchard (LPO)	£2800

Table 2

	US industrial worker's average weekly wage	Conductor's average top US concert fee
1910	$9.74	$100
1930	$23.00	$300
1940	$28.07	$500
1960	$97.44	$1500
1970	$143.47	n/a
1980.	$267.96	$6–7000
1990	$400.33	$18–20,000

Otto Klemperer was paid $500 by the New York Philharmonic in 1936, and offered $1000 20 years later. Today, a run-of-the-mill conductor fetches $10,000 a night; a Barenboim or Giulini holds out for double that amount. It would take a car worker in their audience half a year to earn as much. On a global scale, the sums become literally fantastic. At the time of his death Leonard Bernstein's minimum fee was DM 40,000. In the post-Communist Prague spring of 1990, he was paid for a concert what a Czech schoolteacher would earn in 25 years.

Table 3 Sample of conductor salaries paid by US orchestras

		fee	number of concerts
New York Philharmonic			
1910	Gustav Mahler	$30,000	90–100
	('the highest ever paid to an orchestral leader')		
1924	Arturo Toscanini	$24,000*	15
1930	Arturo Toscanini	$110,000*	60
1936	John Barbirolli	$10,000	32
1986	Zubin Mehta	$638,830	32
1990	Kurt Masur	$700,000+	28–32
Boston Symphony			
1881	George Henschel	$10,000	
1910	Max Fielder	$18,000	
1940	Serge Koussevitsky	$75,000	75
1986	Seiji Ozawa	$381,000	
Chicago Symphony			
1910	Frederick Stock	$10,000	
1985	Georg Solti	$355,552	
1990	Daniel Barenboim	$710,000+	
Cincinnati Symphony			
1897	Theodore Thomas	$10,000	
1909	Leopold Stokowski	$4,000	
1911	Leopold Stokowski	$8,000	
1918	Eugène Ysaÿe	$25,000	
Philadelphia			
1912	Leopold Stokowski	$12,000	82
1938	Leopold Stokowski	$110,000	80+
1940	Eugene Ormandy	$50,000	100
1970	Eugene Ormandy	$100,000	
1990	Riccardo Muti	$400,000+	32

* the orchestra also paid Toscanini's taxes.
\+ reported approximation.

The figures for Britain (see Table 1) are somewhat sketchier because the orchestras have not kept comprehensive records, and a condition of our research was not to breach the confidence of living conductors. The ratios, though, are much the same as in America. Average manual earnings rose from £7.10s 5d in 1949 to £203.20 forty years later, a 27-fold increase. The average top conductor's fee, excluding Toscanini, Karajan and Bernstein, shot up from one hundred guineas to six thousand pounds, rising at exactly twice the rate of audience earnings.

Until the War, conducting fees in Britain were puny. A festival performance in Bradford paid £13, a Queen's Hall concert £20. Beecham often waived his fee to help out an orchestra. In 1951, the top London fee was Erich Kleiber's £200 to conduct *Wozzeck* at Covent Garden, more than twice what a local luminary like Malcolm Sargent could command. Two decades later the fees had not risen enormously. The excitements of Stokowski's Indian summer cost the London Symphony Orchestra £500 a night, the same as it paid Jascha Horenstein and the short-lived Istvan Kertesz. At the London Philharmonic, Adrian Boult was taking his last bows for £350. Otto Klemperer was satisfied in his last years with six or seven hundred pounds, rather less than some of his young soloists were demanding. Between 1950 and 1970 fees merely trebled. In the next twenty years, they increased tenfold. Eugen Jochum saw his London cheques quadruple in four years. John Pritchard went up from £375 in 1974 to £2,800 seven years later. The benefits trickled down to mediocre time-beaters, who received £150 per concert in 1970 and £1,500 twenty years later.

Whenever a concert is broadcast, the conductor gets an extra cheque of between one-third and three-quarters his original fee, a scale that varies from one European country to the next. Conductors in America, where live broadcasts died with Toscanini's memory lapse, can boost their income by linking concert rehearsals to record sessions. Conductors had suddenly struck gold dust. 'It's pure market forces,' said David Sigall. 'If people are prepared to pay huge amounts for certain conductors and singers, those individuals will earn astronomical fees.' The fact was, though, that the funny money was not confined to individuals but to an entire class of conductors, regardless of individual quality or, as racing tipsters would put it, current form.

What had conductors as a breed done to earn their fortune or, rather, what had been done for them? Two objective causes could be perceived. Television, with more channels to fill, broadcast a greater number of concerts, raising the public profile of conductors and hence their earnings potential. And, as senior statesmen retired or died, the alarming shortage of top-flight replacements created a rarity value that raised the price of the lucky stars and filtered down to the rest of the breed. These factors, however, were not sufficient to boost fees by several times the rate of inflation and turn maestros into annual millionaires. Conductors did not wear advertising on their sleeves like televised sportsmen – not yet, at any rate – nor was their scarcity as severe as the tenorial crisis, which left just three star singers in command of the *bel canto* roles and able to make or break an operatic season. There was nothing inherent in the instant fortune of conductors. It was artificially created.

Karajan showed them how to make money out of music, and Wilford in his shadow quietly sorted out the details. From the time he became president of CAMI, the price of conductors went soaring. The two facts are too closely linked to be coincidental or unintended. For every million dollars a conductor earned, CAMI became richer by $200,000. 'As one of the people who raised the ante, do not overlook Harry Kraut,' warned a veteran agent, pointing a finger at the shrewd director of Bernstein's Amberson Enterprises. Kraut, however, negotiated for one man. Wilford represented one hundred, and set the pay scale for the entire industry. He denied using his position to push up fees. 'I can try it, and I can be told, No. There's no answer to No,' he said. There was an answer, of course. He could withdraw his labour force, an implicit deterrent to any orchestra. He could (and did) simply fail to answer the telephone. 'If I have an artist they want, they will have to book him,' he said. Sooner or later everyone accepted Ronald Wilford's terms.

The wealthier maestros became, the further they drifted away from their musicians and orchestras. The prosperity of a music director counterpointed the penury of his ensemble. Until the Second World War, many symphony orchestras made a profit or broke even. Philadelphia used to distribute a dividend among its players at the end of a particularly healthy season. The LSO survived on its wits, the London Philharmonic on Beecham's. The Berlin Philharmonic was run as a commercial operation by the Wolff und Sachs agency.

Since 1945, despite an increase in audiences, orchestras have become reliant on state subsidy and corporate generosity. 'They play more often than ever before to full houses, all of them benefit from broadcasting, television, records and films – and all of them lose more and more money every year,' lamented a music publisher. The threat of closure hangs over all but the strongest. The Philharmonia narrowly avoided it twice. The BBC have disbanded three orchestras in the past decade. East Germany stands to lose at least half its 88 ensembles in the march of capitalism. In the wealthiest nation on earth, long-established civic orchestras teeter perpetually on the brink.

In 1986, the Oakland Symphony went into liquidation with debts of $965,000 after half a century of existence. Members of the New Orleans Symphony played for six weeks without pay to save their band. The 75-year-old San Diego Symphony, in booming computerland, cancelled the second half of its season with a deficit of $1.9 million, throwing its players out of work after they refused to take a wage cut. San Diego's British music director, David Atherton, drew a salary of $347,000 that year. The Detroit Symphony, after appointing a CAMI music director, tried to cut players' pay by 11 per cent because of a cash crisis. At Baltimore, while players went on strike over falling pay, David Zinman received $193,500 as music director. 'While conductors get excellent pay, orchestras are dying at the box-office and have troubles raising money,' said one observer.

Poor administration, limp publicity and boards of dilettantes were as much to blame for the crisis as priceless maestros, but the gulf between conductor and conducted was obviously greater than ever before. Rank-and-file players in London would work all hours of the day and night for £30,000 a year. Their music director made a million. Musicians at Welsh National Opera estimated that their standard of living had dropped from nine per cent above national average in 1975 to 16 per cent below it in 1990. Conductors in that period enjoyed an eightfold increase. The Oakland players, before they lost their jobs, made $13,000 for half a year's work; their conductors earned more than that in a night.

Nikisch and Strauss used to play cards with their men in rehearsal breaks. They belonged to the same class, shared the same interests. None of the legendary conductors became rich from his art. Mahler's estate (including the projected revenue from his symphonies) was valued for probate at 169,781 Austrian crowns, equivalent to £34,369, or less than £10,000. Toscanini never owned more than one house. Barbirolli shortened his life by working too much in his sixties to recover liquidity after losing his modest savings. He left a mere £36,307.

The post-Karajan conductor is made of more splendid stuff. He has two or three homes, drives a red Rolls-Royce or Lamborghini, collects Henry Moores and is clued in to every conceivable tax dodge. Leonard Bernstein once bought up twenty thousand head of cattle to cash in on a Reagan administration tax sweetener and was stuck with them when the price collapsed. Could anyone imagine Furtwängler or Klemperer becoming a cowboy in order to make money? One of Ronald Wilford's regular tasks was to remind Mstislav Rostropovich in Washington when he needed to nip over to Canada for the weekend to avoid US tax liability. Rostropovich was music director of the National Symphony Orchestra and a favourite at the Reagan White House. He earned $687,392 in 1986 and denied Uncle Sam a share of the loot; the orchestra, meanwhile, ran up a four million dollar deficit. 'Is he worth it?' demanded *The Washingtonian* magazine.

The company conductors kept has altered with their soaring status. Mahler's friends were artists and scientists. Toscanini's were mainly musicians, Furtwängler mixed with philosophers. A modern conductor cultivates the kind of people he meets at Davos and St Tropez. Earning as much as an IBM director, he has common interests with oilmen, stockbrokers and corporate lawyers. The circle of friends who turned out to celebrate Rostropovich's sixtieth birthday at the French ambassador's residence in Washington included the chairman of the World Bank, Robert McNamara, the business publisher Malcolm Forbes and the commodity trader Armand Hammer.

Some conductors consider social climbing to be part of their job. If a music director wants to stage an ambitious series, why sit through endless fund-raising meetings when he can call on a chum to finance the season with a single company cheque? Several 'commercial sponsorships' are conducted on a one-to-one basis between chairman and conductor. Abbado rallied Italian businessmen around the LSO; Mehta was magnificent at parting Wall Street from its wallet when the New York Philharmonic ran short of cash. The real expert at befriending the rich and mighty was, of course, Karajan, who drew first Siemens then Sony into his schemes by assiduously cultivating the company chairman. A conductor's connections became part of his attraction as much as, and sometimes more than, his musical abilities. One does not have to look far around the orchestral world to find a music director who was appointed for non-musical reasons.

Those are extreme cases, but every musician is affected by personal priorities in the music he makes. If a gifted artist like Abbado or Muti expends time and concentration on making money, whether for his orchestra or for himself, he will have that much less time and concentration to devote to music. Those who lament a lack of spirituality in modern performances need only ask what the conductors spend much of their time thinking about. Furtwängler could plumb the depths in Brahms because ideas and emotions were all that mattered to him; material possessions were of marginal consequence. Beecham added sparkle to whatever he touched, because he lived for the moment and could not be bothered with practicalities. He was not sure, he told an insolvency court, whether he owed a million pounds, or was owed a million. Toscanini never talked of money or banqueted with bankers. All were adept in the pursuit of power, but were uninterested in its potential for personal gain. The music they made was coloured by the values they held.

As we have seen, Karajan was the first conductor to build a corporate empire and shift the centre of gravity away from music itself. He could, said an associate, have been a great general, or industrialist; he just happened to be a conductor. Whether his influence was bountiful or baneful depends on one's point of view; but there is no doubt that he changed the way musical life is conducted and shifted the priorities of many in his profession. Alongside the post-Karajan conductor and his fingertip command of diverse tax and political structures, Nikisch looks like Neanderthal man, capable only of producing a musical performance.

The evolution of conductors as a mirror of society has yielded, in the avaricious end of millennium, a portrait of the maestro as corporate raider and media baron. The image is not true of all leading conductors, but of many. It will continue to change with the social climate and, perhaps, with the cleansing winds that Claudio Abbado has brought to Berlin. Ultimately, the conductor is the most flexible of musical creatures, adapting to whichever way the world turns, for better or worse. 'I don't see why people expect conductors to behave differently or better than the rest of the world,' said one pragmatic maestro.

In a matter of twelve decades, the conductor has risen from humble servant in a composer's court to be master of musical destiny. The composer, meanwhile, has become poor as a churchmouse and equally muted. Lutosławski, Ligeti and Birtwistle won their first freedom from financial worry in mid-life with the $150,000 Grawemeyer prize, an amount some maestros can make in a week. Conductors have come into a class of their own, a class that has diminished in numbers as its power has grown. Forty years ago, orchestras did not hesitate to drop an unsuitable music director, knowing that an equivalent was readily available. Nowadays, they cling to an unhappy relationship, fearing they might never find another. Conductors, in their pursuit of power, have won a position of temporary invincibility.

History, however, has plenty of warnings for tiny minorities who cling to power. Whatever their monetary prosperity, the future for conducting has never looked more bleak, with superficial interpretations in abundance and fresh blood in alarmingly short supply. If present trends persist, by the dawn of the next century there will be a dozen international orchestras with vacant podia. To survive as a living art, concert music will need to adapt quite rapidly, either by reverting to smaller works of music played by conductorless chamber orchestras, or by devolving most of the maestro's functions on to other functionaries. The first violinist, along with fellow section-leaders, may seize the interpretative prerogative from the podium – a possibility presaged in the early music movement – while the orchestral manager or executive director rules over programme-planning and personnel. This would reduce the role of the passing conductor to little more than that of a technician, waving his stick to obtain uniformity in those large-scale works where the players cannot hear and see one another.

Already, concertmasters in some European orchestras are flexing considerable artistic muscle and commanding high wages. Managers like Ernest Fleischmann in Los Angeles, John Willan at the London Philharmonic, the duopoly running the Vienna State Opera and the trinity in charge at Salzburg wield more artistic authority than ever a resident music director would have allowed. Taken several steps further, this will diminish the glamorous global conductor to the status of fairy atop a Christmas tree – decorative, but wholly detached from the real world, where real-life decisions are made. At the zenith of his visible power, the great conductor has paved the way to his own extinction.

APPENDIX

Conductors and their Careers

(all appointments are principal conductor, unless specified)

Claudio ABBADO
b Milan, 26.vi.1933; st.Vienna with Swarowsky; cond. La Scala orch. 1967–86; artistic director, La Scala 1972–86; music director, London Symphony Orchestra 1979–87; Vienna State Opera 1986–91; Berlin Philharmonic Orchestra 1989–; Salzburg Easter Festival 1994–. Premièred: Adagio fragment of Bruckner's 3rd symphony, reconstruction of Schubert's opera *Fierrabras*, works by Nono, Berio, Maderna.

Karel ANČERL
b Tučapy, Bohemia, 11.iv.1908; music director Prague Radio 1933–39; deported to Terezin and Auschwitz, where his wife and family were murdered; cond. National Theatre 1945–47, Prague Radio 1947–50; chief cond. Czech Philharmonic 1950–68; fled after Soviet invasion to Canada, principal cond. Toronto Symphony 1970–73; *d* Toronto 3.vii.1973.

Ernest ANSERMET
b Vevey, Switzerland, 11.xi.1883; founder-cond. Orchestre de la Suisse Romande 1918–67; *d* Geneva 20.ii.1969. Premièred: Stravinsky's *The Soldier's Tale, Pulcinella* and *Renard*.

Vladimir ASHKENAZY
b Gorky, USSR, 6.vii.1937; won Tchaikovsky Competition, Moscow, 1963, and emigrated in same year; guest cond. Philharmonia Orchestra, London 1981–85, Royal Philharmonic Orchestra 1986–, Radio Symphony Orchestra Berlin 1991–.

David ATHERTON
b Blackpool, NW England, 3.i.1944; founder-conductor London Sinfonietta 1968–73; Royal Liverpool Philharmonic 1980–83, San Diego SO 1981–86, Hong Kong Philharmonic 1989–, London Sinfonietta 1989–. Premièred: two significant operas, Henze's *We Come to the River* (Covent Garden) and Birtwistle's *Punch and Judy* (Aldeburgh), and many orchestral works with the Sinfonietta.

(Sir) John (Giovanni Battista) BARBIROLLI
b London, 2.xii.1899; cond. at Covent Garden 1929–33; New York Philharmonic 1936–42; Hallé Orchestra, Manchester 1943–70, Houston (Texas) SO 1961–67; married (1) Marjorie Parry (singer) (2) Evelyn Rothwell (oboist); *d* London 29.vii.1970. Premièred: Britten violin concerto and Sinfonia da Requiem, Vaughan Williams' 7th and 8th symphonies.

Daniel BARENBOIM
b Buenos Aires, 15.xi.1942, emigrated to Israel 1952, married (1) Jacqueline du Pré 15.vi.67
(2) Elena Bashkirova Kremer 1988; cond. English Chamber Orchestra from 1965, Orchestre
de Paris 1975–89, musical and artistic director Opéra Bastille 1987–89. Chicago Symphony
Orchestra 1991–; German State Opera, Berlin, 1992–. Premièred: Boulez's *Notations* (orch.
version).

(Sir) Thomas BEECHAM
b St Helens, Lancs, UK, 29.iv.1879; founded New Symphony Orch. 1908, Beecham
SO 1909–12, London Philarmonic 1932–39, Royal Philharmonic 1946; Beecham
Opera Company 1915–21; also conducted several seasons with Hallé Orchestra, LSO,
Royal Liverpool Phil and Seattle SO and staged numerous enterprises at Covent
Garden; married (1) Utica Welles 1903 (2) Betty Humby 1942 (3) Shirley Hudson
1959; *d* London 8.iii.1961. Premièred and edited works by Delius.

Franz BEIDLER
b 1872; married Isolde Wagner 20.xii.1900; assistant cond. at Bayreuth 1896–97 and
1901–2; cond. Moscow and St Petersburg 1902–5; cond. *Ring* at Bayreuth 1904,
Parsifal 1906; dismissed by Cosima 11.viii.1906 after quarrel with *Siegfried*; cond.
Hallé concert in Manchester 1908; thereafter made his living as businessman; *d*
Switzerland 1930.

Eduard van BEINUM
b Arnhem, Holland, 3.ix.1901; cond. Haarlem SO 1927–31; assistant cond. to Mengelberg with Concertgebouworkest 1931–45; chief cond. 1945–59; principal cond.
London Philharmonic 1948–49; *d* Amsterdam 13.iv.59.

Jiri BELOHLAVEK
b Prague, 24.ii.1946; chief cond. Brno State Philharmonic 1972–77, Prague Symphony
1977–89, Czech Philharmonic 1989–.

Leonard BERNSTEIN
b Lawrence, Massachusetts, 25.viii.1918; st. with Koussevitsky and Reiner; debut with NY
Philharmonic 14.xi.1943; NY City Center Orchestra 1945–48; music adviser Israel Philharmonic 1948–49; head of cond. dept. and orchestra at Berkshire Music Center 1951–55;
professor of music Brandeis University 1951–56; music director New York Philharmonic
1958–69; president LSO 1986–90; *d* New York 14.x.1990. Premièred: Messiaen's *Turangâlila*
symphony, much American music and all of his own.

Herbert BLOMSTEDT
b Springfield, Massachusetts, 11.vii.1927 but raised in Sweden; st with Igor Markev-
itch and Bernstein; Norrkoeping SO 1954–61, Oslo Philharmonic 1962–68, Danish
Radio 1967–77, Swedish Radio 1977–82, Dresden Staatskapelle 1975–89, San Francisco Symphony 1986–; Swedish citizen, lives in Switzerland.

Karl BÖHM
b Graz, Austria, 28.viii.1894; junior cond. Bavarian State Opera, Munich 1921–27;
Darmstadt 1927–31; Hamburg State Opera 1931–33; Dresden 1934–43; Vienna
1944–45; cond. opera in Buenos Aires 1950–54; Vienna State Opera 1954–55; thereafter regular guest cond. with Vienna and Berlin Philharmonics, NY Met. etc.;
president London Symphony Orchestra 1977–81; *d* Salzburg 14.viii.1981. Premièred:
Strauss's *Die schweigsame Frau, Daphne*.

Nadia BOULANGER
b Paris, 16.ix.1887; st. with Fauré, taught at Conservatoire and the American Conservatory at Fontainebleau, *d* Paris 22.x.1979. Premièred: Stravinsky's *Dumbarton
Oaks*.

Pierre BOULEZ
b Montbrison, France, 26.iii.1925; st. with Messiaen and René Leibowitz in Paris and Darmstadt; director of music for small Renaud Barrault theatre 1946–52; founded Domaine Musical seasons 1954–58; cond. Südwestfunk, Baden-Baden 1959–65; principal cond. BBC SO 1969–75, New York Philharmonic 1971–77; cond. centenary Bayreuth Ring 1976; founder-director Ensemble Intercontemporain 1975–, and Institut de recherche et de coordination acoustique musique (IRCAM) 1977–. Premièred: complete three-act *Lulu*, Stockhausen's *Gruppen*, own works and those of Xenakis, Berio, Birtwistle and others.

(Sir) Adrian (Cedric) BOULT
b Chester, UK, 8.iv.1889; st with Nikisch; City of Birmingham SO 1924–30, BBC SO 1931–50, London Philharmonic 1951–57; retired 1979; *d* London 22.ii.1983. Premièred: Vaughan Williams' 3rd, 4th and 6th symphonies, Holst's *Planets* and much other British music.

Hans (Guido) von BÜLOW
b Dresden, 8.i.1830; married (1) Cosima Liszt 18.viii.1857 (divorced 1870) (2) Marie Schanzer 29.vii.1882; cond. Munich court opera 1864–69, Meiningen court orchestra 1880–85, Hannover 1887, Hamburg opera 1887–88, Berlin Philharmonic Orch. 1887–92, Hamburg Philharmonic concerts 1888–93; *d* Cairo 12.ii.1894. Premièred: Wagner, *Die Meistersänger von Nürnberg, Tristan und Isolde*, Brahms' 4th symphony.

Semyon BYCHKOV
b Leningrad, 30.xi.1952; st with Ilya Musin; left USSR 1975; music director Grand Rapids SO 1980–85, Buffalo Philharmonic 1985–89, Orchestre de Paris 1988–; his second wife is the French pianist Marielle Labècque.

Sarah CALDWELL
b Maryville, Missouri, 6.iii.1924; formed Boston Opera Group 1957.

Riccardo CHAILLY
b Milan, 20.ii.1953; asst cond. La Scala 1972–74; founded Montepulciano festival 1976; West Berlin radio SO 1982–90; Teatro Communale di Bologna 1986-; Concertgebouworkest, Amsterdam 1988-. Premièred: Berio's *Formazioni*; Zemlinsky, *Die Seejungfrau*.

Myung-Whun CHUNG
b Seoul, South Korea, 22.i.1953; Saarlandischer Rundfunk 1984–90; Bastille Opera, Paris, 1989-.

Walter DAMROSCH
b Breslau, Germany, 30.i.1862; son of Leopold D who founded New York Symphony Society, which he cond. 1885–1927; formed Damrosch Opera Company 1894–99; cond. NY Philharmonic 1902–3; *d* New York 22.xii.1950.

Andrew DAVIS
b Ashridge, Herts, UK, 2.ii.1944; associate cond. Philharmonia 1973–75; Toronto SO 1975–88; BBC SO and Glyndebourne Festival 1989-.

(Sir) Colin DAVIS
b Weybridge, Surrey, UK, 29.ix.1927; assistant cond. BBC Scottish Orch. 1957–59; Sadler's Wells Opera 1961–65; BBC SO 1967–71; Royal Opera House Covent Garden 1971–86; Bavarian Radio SO 1987–91; principal guest Boston SO 1972–83; Premièred: symphonies and operas by Tippett.

Victor DE SABATA
b Trieste, 10.iv.1892; Monte Carlo Opera 1918–30; La Scala 1929–53; *d* Santa Margherita Ligure 11.xii.1967. Premièred: Ravel's *Les enfants et les sortilèges*. Composed: operas and orchestral works.

Dean DIXON
b New York, 10.i.1915; founded American Youth Orchestra 1944–49, cond. Israel Philharmonic 1950–51, Gothenburg SO 1953–60, Frankfurt Radio 1961–70, Sydney Symphony Orch. 1964–67; *d* Zug, near Zurich 3.xi.1976.

Christoph von DOHNÁNYI
b Berlin, 8.ix.29, grandson of composer Ernst (Ernö) von Dohnányi; opera cond. Frankfurt/M, Lübeck and Kassel 1952–66; music director Cologne Radio SO 1964–70, Hamburg State Opera 1977–84, Cleveland Orchestra 1984–; married to soprano Anja Silja.

Charles DUTOIT
b Lausanne, Switzerland, 7.x.1936; Berne SO 1963–67; Zurich Radio 1967–75; Gothenburg SO 1975–77, Montreal Symphony 1977–; Orchestre Nationale de France 1991– his second wife (of three) was the pianist Martha Argerich.

Sian EDWARDS
b West Sussex, UK, 1959; won Leeds conductors competition 1984; first woman to conduct at Covent Garden 29.iv.88. Premièred: Mark-Antony Turnage's *Greek*.

Claus Peter FLOR
b Leipzig, Germany, 1953; chief conductor Suhler Philharmonic 1980–83, Berlin Symphony Orchestra 1984–90.

Ferenc FRICSAY
b Budapest, 9.viii.1914; st with Bartók and Kodaly; cond. at Szeged 1934–44; music director city opera of Berlin 1948–52 and RIAS orchestra 1949–54; Houston SO 1954–55; Bavarian State Opera, Munich 1956–58; *d* Basel, Switzerland 20.ii.1963. Premièred: Von Einem's *Dantons Tod*.

Wilhelm FURTWÄNGLER
b Berlin, 25.i.1886; moved to Munich 1894; repetiteur Breslau 1905, Zurich 1906, Munich 1908; third cond. Strasbourg 1910; cond. Lübeck 1911–15; chief cond. Mannheim 1915–20; Berlin Philharmonic debut 14.xii.1917; Berlin Staatskapelle 1920–22; concert director Gesellschaft der Musikfreunde in Vienna 1921–54; chief conductor Leipzig Gewandhaus 1922–28, Berlin Philharmonic 1922–45, 1952–54; married (1) Zitla Lund 1923, separated 1931 (2) Elisabeth Ackermann 1943; one son; *d* Baden-Baden 30.xi.1954. Premièred: Schoenberg's Variations for orchestra op 31, Bartok's 1st piano concerto, Hindemith's Mathis suite, Strauss's Four Last Sings. Composed: 2 symphonies, piano concerto, Te Deum, etc.

John Eliot GARDINER
b Fontmell Magna, Dorset, UK, 20.iv.1943; founder-conductor Monteverdi Orchestra 1968–; music director Opéra de Lyons 1983–89; Norddeutsche Rundfunk 1984–90.

Carlo-Maria GIULINI
b Barletta, Italy, 9.v.1914; cond. RAI orchestra Rome 1946–50, Milan 1950–52; joined La Scala 1952–56; Vienna Symphony Orchestra 1973–78, Los Angeles Philharmonic 1978–84.

Jane GLOVER
b Helmsley, Yorks, UK, 13.v.1949; cond. Wexford Festival, Ireland 1975; music director Glyndebourne Touring Opera 1981–85; artistic director London Mozart Players 1984–90; Huddersfield Choral Society 1988–90.

(Sir) Reginald GOODALL
b Lincoln, England, 13.vii.1901, Covent Garden staff 1946–; *d* London 1990. Premièred: Britten's *Peter Grimes*.

Bernard HAITINK
b Amsterdam, 4.ii.1929; permanent cond. Netherlands Radio orchestra 1956–61; artistic director Concertgebouworkest 1961–86 (two seasons in tandem with Eugen Jochum); London Philharmonic 1967–78; opera debut at Glyndebourne 1972, music director there 1977–87, Royal Opera House Covent Garden 1987–;

Nikolaus HARNONCOURT
b Berlin, 6.xii.1929; cellist in Vienna Symphony Orchestra 1952–69; formed Concentus Musicus Wien 1957.

Günther HERBIG
b Usti-nad-Labem, Czechoslovakia; Weimar national theatre 1957–62, Potsdam theatre 1962–66, Berlin (East) Symphony Orchestra 1966–72 and 77–84, Dresden Philharmonic 1970–77, Detroit Symphony 1984–89, Toronto Symphony 1989–91.

Christopher HOGWOOD
b Nottingham, UK, 10.ix.1941; co-founder (with Munrow) Early Music Consort 1967; founded Academy of Ancient Music 1973.

Jascha HORENSTEIN
b Kiev, 6.v.1898; debut Vienna 1923; chief cond. Dusseldorf Opera 1926–33; *d* London 2.iv.1973. Premièred: Berg's *Lyric Suite*.

Eliahu INBAL
b Jerusalem, 16.ii.1936; chief cond. Frankfurt Radio SO 1974–.

Mariss JANSONS
b Riga, Latvia, 14.i.1943; st with his father Arvid Jansons (1914–84) adn Mravinsky; Oslo PO, 1979–.

Neeme JÄRVI
b Talinn, Estonia, 7.vi.1937; st with Mravinsky; Estonian Radio Orchestra and state opera 1963–80; Gothenburg Symphony Orch. 1981–85, Scottish National Orch. 1984–88; Detroit Symphony 1990-. Premièred: 3 symphonies by Arvo Pärt, several by Eduard Tubin.

Eugen JOCHUM
b Babenhausen, Bavaria, 1.xi.1902, cond. Munich, Kiel, Mannheim and Duisburg; Hamburg State Opera and Phil. Orch. 1934–49; Bavarian Radio Orch., Munich 1949–60; joint chief conductor at Concertgebouw 1961–3; Bamberg Symphony 1969–73; *d* Munich 26.iii.1987.

Herbert von KARAJAN
b Salzburg, Austria, 5.iv.1908; cond. Ulm 1928–33; Aachen 1934–38; Berlin State Opera and Staatskapelle 1938–42; Philharmonia 1947–55; Vienna SO 1951–55; music director Berlin Philharmonic Orchestra 5.iv.1955–24.iv.1989; director Vienna State Opera 1956–64, Salzburg Festival 1956–60, thereafter dominant board member; founded Easter and Whitsun festivals at Salzburg; *d* Anif nr Salzburg 16.vii.89. Premièred: peripheral works by Orff, von Einem, etc.

Herbert KEGEL
b Dresden, Germany, 29.vii.1920; cond. Leipzig radio choir 1953; chief cond. Leipzig radio orchestra 1960; chief cond. Dresden Philharmonic Orchestra 1977–.

Rudolf KEMPE
b nr Dresden, Germany 14.vi.1910; played oboe in Leipzig Gewandhaus Orch., cond. debut Leipzig Opera 1935; music director Chemnitz opera 1943–48, Weimar national theatre 1948–49, Dresden state opera 1949–52, Bavarian state opera, Munich 1952–54, chief conductor Royal Philharmonic Orchestra, London 1961–75; *d* Zurich 12.v.1976.

Istvan KERTESZ
b Budapest 28.viii.1929; cond. Györ 1953–55, Budapest Opera 1953–57, music director Augsburg, West Germany 1958–64; London Symphony Orchestra 1965–68; drowned in the Mediterranean off Israeli coast 16.iv.1973.

Carlos KLEIBER
b Berlin, 3.vii.1930, son of Erich Kleiber; junior cond. Duisburg and Düsseldorf 1956–64, Zürich 1964–66; cond. Württemburg State Opera, Stuttgart 1966–68.

Erich KLEIBER
b Vienna, 5.viii.1890; cond. Düsseldorf and Darmstadt; music director Berlin Staatsoper 1923–34; *d* Zurich 27.i.1956. Premièred: Berg's *Wozzeck*.

Otto KLEMPERER
b Breslau, Austro-Hungary, 14.v.1885; st. Berlin with Fried and Pfitzner; cond. German Theatre Prague 1908–10, Hamburg 1910–12, Strasbourg 1914–17, Cologne 1917–24, Wiesbaden 1924–27, Kroll Opera Berlin 1927–31; Los Angeles Philharmonic 1933–39, Budapest Opera 1947–50, Philharmonia Orchestra London 1951–72; *d* Zurich 6.vii.1973. Premièred: Schoenberg/Brahms piano quartet; Zemlinsky's *A Florentine Tragedy*. Composed: symphonies, 9 string quartets and an opera.

Hans KNAPPERTSBUSCH
b Elberfeld, Germany, 12.iii.1888; assistant to Richter and Siegfried Wagner at Bayreuth; opera cond. Elberfeld 1913–18, Leipzig 1918–19 and Dessau 1919–22; Bavarian State Opera 1922–36; thereafter regular cond. with Vienna State Opera, Vienna Philharmonic, Salzburg and Bayreuth festivals; *d* Munich 25.x.1965.

Kiril KONDRASHIN
b Moscow, 6.iii.1914; principal cond. Moscow Philharmonic 1960–75 when he defected in Holland and joined the Concertgebouw as associate conductor; *d* Amsterdam 7.ii.1981. Premièred: Shostakovich's *Babi Yar* symphony and 2nd violin concerto.

Serge KOUSSEVITSKY
b Vishy-Volochok, 26.vii.1874; double-bass player 1894–1905; own orchestra in Russia 1909–15; State Symphony orchestra, Petrograd 1917–20; Koussevitsky Concerts, Paris 1922–24; Boston SO 1924–49; *d* Boston 4.vi.1951. Premièred: Skryabin's *Prometheus*, Mussorgsky/Ravel, *Pictures at an Exhibition*, Stravinsky's *Symphony of Psalms*, Roussel's 3rd symphony, Prokofiev's 4th, Honegger's 1st, Copland's 3rd, Martinu's 1st and 3rd, Schoenberg's *Theme and Variations* op 43, etc. Composed: concerto for double-bass.

Clemens KRAUSS
b Vienna, 31.ii.1893; cond. Riga, Nuremberg, Stettin and Graz 1913–22; Vienna Tonkünstler concerts 1923–37; director of Frankfurt opera and Museum concerts 1924–29; director of Vienna State Opera 1929–34; chief conductor Vienna Philharmonic 1929–32; music director Bavarian State Opera in Munich 1937–44; married Strauss singer Viorica Ursuleac; *d* Mexico City 16.v.1954. Premièred: Strauss, *Arabella*, *Friedenstag* and *Die Liebe der Danae*.

Josef KRIPS
b Vienna, 8.iv.1902; cond. Volksoper (1921), Aussig and Dortmund; Karlsruhe 1926–33; staff cond. Vienna State Opera 1934–38 and 1945–47; Belgrade 1938–39; London SO 1950–54, Buffalo Phil. 1954–63; San Franscisco SO 1963–70; *d* Geneva 13.x.1974.

Rafael KUBELIK
b Býchory, Czechoslovakia, 29.vi.1914, son of Jan Kubelik (1880–1940); chief cond. Brno National Theatre 1939–41, Czech Philharmonic 1942–48, founded Prague Spring Festival 1946, exiled after Communist putsch in 1948, Chicago SO 1950–53, Covent Garden 1955–58, Bavarian Radio SO 1961–85, Metropolitan Opera NY 1973–74; married (1) Czech violinist Ludmilla Bertlová for whom he wrote a concerto and (2) Australian soprano Elsie Morison; returned to conduct Czech Philharmonic at Prague Spring 12.v.1990. Premièred: Schoenberg's *Jakobsleiter*. Composed: two operas, three symphonies, Czech Requiem (1968) and string quarterts.

Hermann LEVI
b Giessen, Germany, 7.xi.1839; dir. Munich court theatre 1872–96; *d* Munich 13.vi.1900. Premièred: Wagner's *Parsifal*.

James LEVINE
b Cincinnati, 23.vi.1943; assistant cond. at Cleveland 1964–70; music director, Metropolitan Opera, New York 1975–.

Andrew LITTON
b New York, 16.v.1959; Bournemouth Symphony Orchestra 1988–.

Lorin MAAZEL
b Neuilly, France, 6.iii.1930; conducted NBC orchestra at 11 years old and NY Philharmonic at 12; cond. Pittsburgh Symphony 1949–52; first American to conduct at Bayreuth 1960; music director West Berlin Duetsche Oper 1965–71 and radio symphony orchestra 1965–74, Cleveland Orchestra 1972–82, Vienna State Opera 1982–84, Pittsburgh Symphony 1988–; also closely associated with New Philharmonia (London), Orchestre Nationale de France and Berlin Philharmonic.

(Sir) Charles MACKERRAS
b Schenectady, NY, 17.xi.1925 and raised in Australia; st. with Talich in Prague 1947–48; principal cond. Sadlers Wells Opera (later English National Opera), London 1970–80; Sydney SO 1982–88; Welsh National Opera 1987–90.

Gustav MAHLER
b Kalischt, Austro-Hungary, 7.vii.1860; opera cond. Laibach 1881, Olmütz 1882, Kassel 1883–85; 2nd cond. Leipzig 1886–88; Royal Hungarian Opera, Budapest 1888–91; Hamburg City Opera 1891–97; director, Vienna Court Opera 1897–1907; Vienna Philharmonic Orchestra 1898–1901; cond. New York Metropolitan Opera 1908-9; New York Philharmonic Society 1909–11; married Alma-Maria Schindler 1901; *d* Vienna 18.v.1911. Premièred: 8 of his own symphonies, Busoni's *Berceuse élégiaque*, Zemlinsky and others. Composed: 9 complete symphonies, *Das Lied von der Erde* and many songs.

(Sir) Neville MARRINER
b Lincoln, UK, 15.iv.1924; founder-conductor Academy of St Martin-in-the-Fields 1958–; Minnesota Orch. 1979–86.

Kurt MASUR
b Brieg, German Silesia, 18.vii.1927; repetiteur Hallé 1948–51; cond. Erfurt 1951–53, Leipzig state opera 1953–55; Dresden Philharmonic 1955–58 and 1967–72; Schwerin state opera 1958–60; Komische Oper, Berlin 1960–64; Leipzig Gewandhaus 1970–; New York Philharmonic 1991–; Premièred: Frank Martin's *6 monologues from Jedermann*.

Zubin MEHTA
b Bombay, India, 29.iv.1936; music director Montreal Symphony Orchestra 1960–62, Los Angeles Philharmonic 1962–77, New York Philharmonic 1978–91, musical adviser

to Israel Philharmonic, 1962–77, thereafter conductor for life; married (1) Carmen Lasky (2) Nancy Kovack.

Willem MENGELBERG
b Utrecht, Netherlands, 28.iii.1871; music director in Lucerne 1891–95, Concertgebouworkest Amsterdam 1895–1945 (when banned for Nazi collaboration), Frankfurt Museum Concerts 1907–22, New York Philharmonic 1922–30; *d* in exile at Chur, Switzerland 21.iii.1951. Premièred: Bartok's 2nd violin concerto, and gave first integral cycle of Mahler symphonies (1920).

Dmitri MITROPOULOS (orig. Dmitropoulos)
b Athens, Greece, 1.iii.1896; asst. cond. Berlin State Opera 1921–24; cond. Athens Symphony Orchestra 1924–36, Orchestre Lamoureux, Paris 1932, US debut Boston 24.i.1937, Minneapolis Symphony 1937–49, New York Philharmonic 1949–58; Metropolitan Opera, NY 1958–59; US citizen 1946; *d* La Scala, Milan 2.xi.1960. Premièred: Samuel Barber's *Vanessa*.

Pierre MONTEUX
b Paris, 4.iv.1875; cond. Ballets Russes 1911–17; Boston SO 1919–24; assoc. cond. Concertgebouw 1924–34; cond. Orch. Symphonique de Paris 1929–38, San Francisco SO 1936–52; London SO 1961–64; *d* Hancock, Maine 1.vii.1964. Premièred: Stravinsky's *Petrouchka, Le Sacre du Printemps, Le Rossignol*, Debussy's *Jeux*, Ravel's *Daphnis et Chloé*.

Felix MOTTL
b nr Vienna, 24.vii.1856; assistant at Bayreuth 1876, cond. Munich Court Opera 1903–11; *d* Munich 2.vii.1911. Premièred: complete 5-act version of Berlioz's *Les Troyens*.

Yevgeny MRAVINSKY
b St Petersburg, 4.vi.1903; Kirov Ballet 1932–38; Leningrad Philharmonic 1938–88; *d* Leningrad 20.i.1988. Premièred: Shostakovich's symphonies 5, 6, 8, 9 and 10, and Prokofiev's 6th symphony.

Charles MÜNCH
b Strasbourg, Alsace-Lorraine, 26.ix.1891; concertmaster there 1919–26 and with Leipzig Gewandhaus 1926–32; cond. Orchestre de la Société Philharmonique de Paris 1935–38, Conservatoire Orch. 1938–46, Boston SO 1949–62; *d* Richmond, Virginia 6.xi.1968. Premièred: Martinu's 6th symphony, music by Honegger and Roussel.

Riccardo MUTI
b Naples, 27.vii.1941; Maggio Musicale, Florence 1969–80; Philharmonia Orch. London 1972–82; Philadelphia Orch. 1980–92; La Scala, Milan, 1986–.

Kent (George) NAGANO
b Moro Bay, California, 22.xi.1951; second conductor Opera Company of Boston 1977–79; music director Berkeley (Cal.) SO 1978; principal guest conductor of Boulez's Ensemble Intercontemporain 1985–; chief cond. Opéra de Lyon 1989–; music director Hallé Orchestra, 1991–. Premièred (with Ozawa): Messiaen *St. François d'Assise*.

Vaclav NEUMANN
b Prague, 29.ix.1920; violist in Czech Philharmonic, took up baton after Kubelik's departure in 1948 Communist putsch; chief cond. Prague Symphony Orchestra 1956–63, Prague Philharmonic 1963–64, Berlin Komische Oper 1957–60, Leipzig Opera (and Gewandhaus concerts) 1964–67, Württemburg state theatre, Stuttgart 1970–71, Czech Philharmonic Orchestra 1968–89.

Arthur NIKISCH
b Lébényi Szent-Miklos, Austro-Hungary, 12.x.1855; 2nd cond. Leipzig Opera 1878, 1st cond. 1882–89; Boston Symphony Orchestra 1889–93; Royal Hungarian Opera, Budapest 1893–95; Leipzig Gewandhaus concerts and Berlin Philharmonic Orchestra 1895–1922; Hamburg Philharmonic concerts 1897–1922; London Symphony Orchestra 1905–13; *d* Leipzig 23.i.1922. Premièred: Bruckner's 7th; Delius's *On hearing the first cuckoo in spring;* Reger's violin concerto.

Roger NORRINGTON
b Oxford, 16.iii.1934; founded Schütz Choir 1962; music director Kent Opera 1969–84; founded London Classical Players 1978.

Eugene ORMANDY
b Budapest, 18.xi.1899 as Eugen Blau, emigrated to US 1921 working as concertmaster in NY theatre orchestra; music director Minneapolis SO 1931–36, Philadelphia Orch. 1938–80; *d* Philadelphia 12.ii.1985. Premièred: Rachmaninov's Symphonic Dances and Bartok's 3rd piano concerto.

Seiji OZAWA
b Hoten, Manchuria, China (of Japanese parents), 1.ix.1935; music director Ravinia Festival (Chicago) 1964–68, Toronto Symphony 1965–69, San Francisco SO 1970–77, Boston SO and Berkshire Music Center, 1972–. Premièred: Messiaen's *St François d'Assise*, Panufnik's *Sinfonia Votiva*.

Libor PEŠEK
b Prague, 22.vi.1933; founder-cond. Prague Chamber Harmony 1959, Sebastian Orchestra 1965; music director State Chamber Orchestra, Czechoslovakia 1969–77, Frysk Orkest (Holland) 1969–75, Overijssels Orkest (Holland) 1975–79, Slovak Philharmonic, Bratislava 1981–82; Royal Liverpool Philharmonic 1987–.

Trevor PINNOCK
b Canterbury, Kent, England, 16.xii.1946; founder-director The English Concert 1972–.

Georges PRÊTRE
b Waziers, France, 14.viii.1929; music director Opéra Comique, Paris 1955–59, associate cond. of Royal Philharmonic Orchestra on Beecham's death 1962–64, Vienna Symphony Orchestra 1986–. Premièred: Poulenc's *La voix humaine*.

André PREVIN
b Berlin, 6.iv.1929 as Andreas Ludwig Priwin; St. Louis SO 1962–67; Houston SO 1967–69; London SO 1968–79; Royal Philharmonic Orch. 1985–91; Pittsburg SO 1976-86; Los Angeles Philharmonic 1986–90. Composed and premièred: concertos, music for Tom Stoppard play, *Every Good Boy Deserves Favour.*

(Sir) John PRITCHARD
b London, 5.ii.1921; Royal Liverpool Philharmonic 1957–63, London Philharmonic 1962–66, Glyndebourne 1967–77, Cologne Opera 1969–77, Belgian Opéra Nationale 1981–89, BBC Symphony Orchestra 1982–89, San Francisco Opera 1986–89; *d* San Francisco 5.xii.1989.

Eve QUELER
b New York, 1.i.1936 (as Eve Rabin); formed Opera Orchestra of New York 1971–;

Karl RANKL
b Gaaden, Austro-Hungary, 1.x.1898; st. with Schoenberg and Webern; cond. Reichenberg, Königsberg, Berlin State Opera and Wiesbaden 1925–33, leaving Germany on Hitler's ascent; then music director at Graz 1933–37 and the German Theatre in

Prague 1937–38; chief conductor at Covent Garden 1946–51; Scottish National Orchestra 1952–57, when he went to Australia to lead the Elizabethan Opera Company; d St Gilgen, Austria 6.ix.1968. Premièred: Krenek's *Karl V*. Composed: several operas.

Simon RATTLE
b Liverpool, UK, 19.i.1955; principal conductor City of Birmingham Symphony Orchestra 1980–; principal guest conductor Los Angeles Philharmonic 1983–; Premièred: H. K. Gruber's *Frankenstein!!!*, Maxwell Davies's 1st symphony and other British works.

Fritz REINER
b Budapest, 19.xii.1888; Budapest People's Opera 1911–14, Dresden Court (later State) Opera 1914–21, Cincinnati SO 1922–31, Pittsburg SO 1938–48, Chicago SO 1953–62; d New York 15.xi.1963. Premièred: Copland's clarinet concerto.

Hans RICHTER
b Györ, Austro-Hungary, 4.iv.1843; court cond. Munich 1868–70; Royal Hungarian Opera 1871–75; 2nd cond. Vienna Court Opera 1875, 1st cond. 1880–99; Vienna Philharmonic concerts 1877–98; cond. inaugural *Ring* cycle, Bayreuth, Aug. 1876; Richter Concerts, London 1878–99; dir. Birmingham Festival 1885–1909; Hallé Orchestra, Manchester 1899–1911; d Bayreuth 5.xii.1916. Premièred: Wagner's *Ring*, Brahms's 2nd and 3rd, Bruckner's 1st, 3rd, 4th and 8th symphonies, Elgar's *Enigma Variations* and 1st symphony.

Hans ROSBAUD
b Graz, Austria, 22.vii.1895; directed Mainz city orchestra and conservatory 1921–30, Frankfurt radio and museum concerts 1928–37; music director at Münster 1937–41 and at Strasbourg 1941–44; Munich Philharmonic 1945–48; Southwest German radio orchestra, Baden-Baden 1948–61; Zurich Opera 1950–58; also principal conductor at summer festivals of Donaueschingen and Aix-en-Provence; d Lugano, Switzerland 29.xii.1962. Premièred: Schoenberg's *Moses und Aron*, Boulez's *Le marteau sans maître*, *Bartok's 2nd piano concerto*.

Mstislav ROSTROPOVICH
b Baku, USSR, 27.iii.1927; conducting debut 1960; music director National Symphony Orchestra, Washington DC 1987–.

Gennady ROZHDESTVENSKY
b Moscow, 4.v.1931; cond. at Bolshoi 1951–70; BBC SO 1978–81; Vienna SO 1981–84; USSR Ministry of Culture Orch. 1984–; Stockholm Philharmonic 1989–. Premièred: Schnittke's 5 symphonies.

Vasily SAFONOV
b Itsiursk, Russia, 6.ii.1852; established popular concertsa in Moscow 1890–1905, cond. New Philharmonic 1904–6; d Kislovodsk 27.ii.1918.

Esa-Pekka SALONEN
b Helsinki, Finland, 30.vi.1958; principal cond. Swedish Radio SO 1985–; Los Angeles Philharmonic 1990–.

Kurt SANDERLING
b Arys, Germany, 9.ix.1912; cond. Moscow Radio 1937–41, Leningrad Philharmonic 1941–60; founder-conductor Berlin Symphony Orchestra 1964–77.

(Sir) Malcolm (Harold Watts) SARGENT
b Stamford, Lincs, UK, 29.iv.1895; chief cond. Royal Choral Society 1928–67; Courtauld-Sargent concerts 1929–40; Hallé orchestra 1939–42; Royal Liverpool Philhar-

monic 1942–48; BBC Symphony Orchestra 1950–57; *d* London 3.x.1967. Premièred: Walton's *Belshazzar's Feast* and *Troilus and Cressida*; Vaughan Williams's 9th symphony.

Wolfgang SAWALLISCH
b Munich, 26.viii.1923; opera cond. Wiesbaden 1957–59 and Cologne 1959–63; music director Bavarian State Opera 1971–92; Philadelphia Orchestra 1992–.

Franz SCHALK
b Vienna, 27.v.1863; st with Bruckner; cond. Graz 1889–95, Prague German Theatre 1895–98, NY Met 1898–99 (giving first uncut US *Ring*), Berlin Royal Opera 1900, Vienna *Gesellschaft der Musikfreunde* 1904–21; dir. Vienna State Opera 1919–29 (to 1924 jointly with Richard Strauss); *d* Edlach 2.ix.1931. Misedited Bruckner symphonies. Premièred: own revision of Bruckner's 5th, Strauss's *Die Frau Ohne Schatten*, 2 movements of Mahler's 10th symphony.

Hermann SCHERCHEN
b Berlin, 21.vi.1891; cond. Riga SO 1914–16; Königsberg Radio SO 1928–33 when he left Germany; Collegium Musicum Winterthur (Switzerland) 1922–47; US debut 1964; *d* Florence 12.vi.1966. Premièred: Dallapiccola's *Il prigionero*, Henze's *König Hirsch*.

Ernst von SCHUCH
b Graz, Austria, 23.xi.1846; cond. Dresden Court Opera 1873–1913; *d* Kötzschenbroda, Saxony 10.v.1914. Premièred: Strauss operas, *Feursnot, Elektra, Salome* and *Rosenkavlier*.

Tullio SERAFIN
b near Venice, 8.xii.1878; principal cond. at La Scala 1909–14, 1917–18; chief cond. Rome Opera 1934–43; also cond. at Met and Chicago; *d* Rome 2.ii.1968.

Giuseppe SINOPOLI
b Venice, 2.xi.1946; st Vienna with Swarowsky; founded Bruno Maderna ensemble 1975; Philharmonic Orchestra 1984–; Santa Cecilia Orch. Rome 1980s; Deutsche Oper, Berlin 1990; Dresden Staatskapelle 1992–. Premièred: modern Italian music. Composed: opera, *Lou Salomé*.

Leonard SLATKIN
b Los Angeles, 1.ix.1944; music director New Orleans Philharmonic 1977–79, St Louis SO 1979–.

(Sir) Georg SOLTI
b Budapest, 21.x.1912; repetiteur at Budapest Opera 1930–39 and Salzburg Festival 1937; opera cond. debut Budapest 11.iii.38; 1st prize Geneva int'l piano competition 1942; chief cond. Bavarian state opera 1946–52; music director Frankfurt Oper 1952–61; Covent Garden 1961–71; Chicago SO 1969–91; London Philharmonic 1979–83; UK citizen 1972; artistic director Salzburg Easter Festival 1991–93; conducted first recorded *Ring* cycle 1958–68. Premièred: Lutosławski's 3rd symphony, Tippett's 4th, Martinu's 1st violin concerto.

Judith SOMOGI
b NY, 13.v.1937; *Kapellmeisterin* Frankfurt Opera 1982–86; *d* 3.iv.86.

Leopold (Boleslawowicz Stanislaw Antoni) STOKOWSKI
b Marylebone, London, 18.iv.1882; Cincinnatti SO 1909–12, Philadelphia Orch. 1912–38, NBC SO (with Toscanini) 1942–44, Hollywood Bowl, Houston SO, founded American SO 1962; married (1) Olga Samaroff (2) Evangeline Johnson (3) Gloria Vanderbilt; *d* 13.ix.1977, Nether Wallop, Hampshire, UK, and buried in Marylebone

cemetery, East Finchley, London. Premièred: Ives' 4th symphony, Varèse's *Amériques*, Rachmaninov's 4th concerto, Paganini Rhapsody, 3rd symphony; Schoenberg's piano and violin concertos; Martinu's 4th piano concerto, Panufnik's *Universal Prayer*; Havergal Brian's 28th symphony, Bruch's 2-piano concerto, Copland's Dance Symphony, Cowell's 6th and 12th symphonies and music by many other composers from Amfiteatrov to Zemachson.

Fritz STEINBACH
b Grünsfeld, Germany, 17.vi.1855; succeeded Bülow at Meiningen 1886–1902; directed conservatory in Cologne 1902–1914; *d* Munich 13.viii.1918.

William (Hans Wilhelm) STEINBERG
b Cologne, 1.viii.1899; chief cond. Cologne Opera 1924–25, Prague German Theatre 1926–29, Frankfurt Opera 1929–33, when he left Germany; co-founded Palestine Symphony Orchestra (later Israel Philharmonic) 1936–38; music director Buffalo SO 1945–52, Pittsburgh SO 1952–76, Boston SO 1969–72; *d* New York 16.iii.1978. Premièred: Schoenberg's *Von Heute auf Morgen*.

Richard (Georg) STRAUSS
b Munich, 11.vi.1864; assistant to Bülow at Meiningen 1885, cond. Meiningen 1886, Munich Court Opera 1886–89, Weimar Court Opera 1889–94, Berlin Court Opera 1898–1918, co-director (with Franz Schalk) Vienna Court Opera 1919–24; married Pauline de Ahna 1894; *d* Garmisch-Parntekirchen 8.x.1949. Premièred: Humperdinck's *Hansel und Gretel*, and his own orchestral works. Composed: 15 operas, and many orchestral and chamber works.

Yevgeny SVETLANOV
b Moscow, 6.ix.1929; chief cond. Bolshoi Theatre 1962–64; music director USSR state symphony orchestra 1965–89. Composed: symphony and piano concerto.

Hans SWAROWSKY
b Budapest, 16.ix.1899; chief cond. Krakow Philharmonic 1944–45. Vienna Symphony Orchestra and Graz Opera 1947–50; thereafter indifferent guest conductor and influential teacher whose pupils included Abbado and Mehta; *d* Salzburg 10.ix.1975.

George SZELL
b Budapest, 7.vi.1897; cond. Berlin, Prague, Darmstadt, Düsseldorf 1917–24; Berlin State Opera 1924–30; chief cond. Prague German Theatre 1930–36; Scottish Orchestra 1937–39; conductor of Cleveland Orch. 1946–70; *d* Cleveland 30.vii.1970.

Vaclav TALICH
b Kromeriz, Bohemia, 28.v.1883; opera cond. Pilsen 1912–15; chief cond. Czech Philharmonic 1918–41; Stockholm Philharmonic 1931–33; National Opera, Prague 1935–44; founder-cond. Slovak Philharmonic, Bratislava 1949–52; *d* Beroun, Czechoslovakia 16.iii.1961. Premièred: Janáček's Sinfonietta and the major orchestral works of Suk and Novak.

Jeffrey TATE
b Salisbury, England 29.iv.1943; principal cond. Royal Opera House, Covent Garden 1986–, English Chamber Orchestra 1985, Rotterdam Philharmonic 1991–.

Yuri TEMIRKANOV
b Nalchik, USSR, 10.xii.1938; Leningrad SO 1968–76; Kirov Opera Leningrad 1976–89; Leningrad Philharmonic 1989–.

Klaus TENNSTEDT
b Merseburg, Germany, 6.vi.1926; concertmaster Hallé Opera 1945; deputy conductor Karl Marx-Stadt 1954–58; Dresden Landesoper 1958–60, Schwerin Staatsoper

1960–69; Kiel Opera 1975–75; North German Radio Symphony Orchestra, Hamburg 1979–82; Metropolitan Opera debut 14.xii.1983; London Philharmonic Orchestra 1983–87.

Michael TILSON THOMAS
b Hollywood, 21.xii.1944; music director Buffalo Philharmonic 1971–79; London Symphony Orchestra 1988–.

Heinz TIETJEN
b Tangier, 24.vi.1881; studied with Nikisch; cond. Trier 1902–21; intendant Breslau 1922–25 and Berlin Städtische Oper 1925–29 and 1948–54; general intendant of all Prussian state theatres 1930–35, artistic director (and cond.) Bayreuth festivals 1931–44; produced Wagner operas at Covent Garden 1950–51; intendant (and cond.) Hamburg State Opera 1954–59; d Baden-Baden 30.xi.1967.

Arturo TOSCANINI
b Parma, Italy, 25.iii.1867; debut aged 19 conducting Aïda in Rio; music director at La Scala 1898–1908; artistic director at NY Metropolitan Opera 1908–15, displacing Mahler; artistic director at La Scala 1921–29; conducted at Bayreuth and Salzburg until the Nazis took over; conducted New York Philharmonic and Symphony orchestras 1920–26, NBC Symphony Orch. 1937–54; d New York 16.i.1957, buried in Milan. Premièred: Puccini's Turandot, Barber's Adagio for strings.

Edo De WAART
b Amsterdam, 1.vi.1941; played oboe in Amsterdam Philharmonic and Concertgebouworkest; won Mitropoulos competition 1964; founded Netherlands Wind Ensemble 1966; chief cond. Rotterdam Philharmonoic 1973–79, San Francisco Symphony 1977–85, Minnesota Orchestra 1986–.

Bruno WALTER (Schlesinger)
b Berlin, 15.ix.1876; assistant at Cologne 1893, Hamburg 1894–96, 2nd cond. Breslau and cond. Pressurg 1897, Riga. 1898–1901, 2nd cond. Vienna 1901–11, Munich 1911–22, Bruno Walter Concerts in Berlin 1922–35, Charlottenburg Opera, Berlin, 1925–29, Leipzig Gewandhaus 1929–33, Vienna State Opera 1936–38, New York Philharmonic 1947–49; d Beverly Hills, California 17.ii.1962. Premièred: Mahler's Das Lied von der Erde and 9th symphony, Pfitzner's Palestrina, Weill's 2nd symphony.

(Paul) Felix von WEINGARTNER
b Zara, Austria, 3.vi.1863; cond. Königsberg 1884, Danzig 1885–87, Hamburg Opera 1887–89, Mannheim 1889–91, Berlin Royal Opera 1891–98 and Royal Orchestra 1891–1907, Kaim Concerts Munich 1898–1905, dir. Vienna Court Opera 1907–11, Hamburg Opera (again) 1912–14, Darmstadt 1914–18, mus. dir. Vienna Volksoper 1919–24, dir. Basel Conservatoire 1927, cond. Vienna State Opera 1934–38 (including 1935 season as mus. dir.); d Winthertur, Switzerland 7.v.1942. Composed: 7 operas, 7 symphonies.

Franz WELSER-MÖST
b Linz, Austria, 16.viii.1960; Norrkoeping SO 1985–; music director London Philharmonic 1990–.

(Sir) Henry (Joseph) WOOD
b London, 3.iii.1869; founder-cond. Promenade concerts 1895–1944; d Hitchin, Herts, UK 19.viii.1944. Premièred: Schoenberg's Five Orchestral Pieces and many works by British composers.

Alexander (von) ZEMLINSKY
b Vienna, 14.x.1871; cond. at Vienna Volksoper 1904–7 and at Court Opera 1908–11, music director New German Theatre in Prague 1912–26, senior conductor, Kroll

Oper Berlin 1927–32; emigrated to US 1939; *d* Larchmont, NY 15.iii.1942. Premièred: Schoenberg's *Erwartung*, Korngold's *Der Schneeman*. Composed: 7 operas, Lyric Symphony, string quartets, songs.

David (Joel) ZINMAN
b New York, 9.vii.1936; music director Netherlands Chamber Orchestra 1964–77, Rotterdam Philharmonic 1979–82, Rochester Philharmonic 1974–85, Baltimore Symphony Orch 1984–.

Notes

For the meaning of abbreviations, see Source List and Bibliography, p. 360. AI refers to author interviews.

Introduction
The Making of a Myth

p1, l27: Barenboim, sleeve note to DG 427 778–2
l29: FLE 271–2
p2, l7: KELLER 22
l13: Galway AI
l22: BUSCH 59
l28: BBC/GER/68
l32: EPST 65
l32: CANE 460
p3, l10: CANE 458
l16: OSBK 139
l21: André Malraux
l28: Hanno Rinke, 'The Boundless Vitality of Leonard Bernstein', DG press release, July 1990

p3, l35: Salzburg press conference, 29.vii.1989
p4, l42: *ST*, April 1990
p6, l35: GSAI
p7, l11: RFAI
l33: SRAI
l36: RMAI
p8, l2: Galway AI
l11: BBC/GER/6821
p9, l7: DORA 9–10
l20: Ladislav Sip AI
l26: CUM 232
p10, l34: *CM*, 12.v.90, p. 3.
l40: OCON
l43: HEINS 82
p11, l3: CULR
l34: *Leben des Galilei*, sc 13

Chapter 1
The Tears of a Clown

p12, l1: Benjamin Britten, *Music Survey*, Spring 1950, p. 247
p13, l31: LEBAN 77
p14, l25: *idem*, p. 187
p15, l16: *Le chef d'orchestre, théorie de son art*, Paris, 1855
l17: See GALK 553, fn 31
l34: 'Über das Dirigieren', in *Neue Zeitschrift für Musik*, issues of 26.xi.1869 to 21.i.1870.

p17, l7: BUL ix
l19: SCHN 165
l25: MANNH 3
l37: MANNH 5
p18, l1: Proceedings of the British Association for Advancement of Science conference, September 1988.
l31: BUL 46–52
l37: BUL 69
l42: BUL 169

p19, l2: BUL 171
l40: SKEW 17
p20, l19: ADA
l23: BULC 212
l27: WAGCD1, 19.iii.1869
l30: *idem*
l33: WAGML, p876
l42: WAGCD1, 8.i.1869
p21, l22: BARW 207
l28: SKEW 85
l41: BARW 214
p22, l2: STRR 128
l7: BULC 243
l13: BULC 95
l19: BULB 552
l34: WAGCD2, 975–6
l35: WAGCD2, 978
p23, l12: STRR 122
l20: TCHL 472
l27: LEBR 78

p23, l40: BULB 313
l42: SMY 279
p24, l10: STRR 121
l23: SPEY 180
l42: WEIC 217–8
p25, l4: PAN 70
l11: WEI 163
l26: STRR 121
l28: WOO 69
l32: STRR 50
l42: WALTV 39
p26, l9: DAM 81
l11: BULC 385
l36: STAN 142
l41: MAY 30
p27, l18: STAR 80
l24: SBER 46
l36: WEI 198
p28, l7: STRERE 54
l17: BULB 545–9
l40: BULC 408

Chapter 2
Honest Hans and the Magician

p30, l5: NIK 214
l16: NIK np
l22: DAM 338
l25: SCMMI 390 *idem*
p31, l6: see NIK 209–10
l10: NIK np
l16: HEYKC 115
l20: WOOD 211
l25: NIK 45
l26: BOUT 14
p32, l5: BOUC x
l10: BBC/GER/69
l20: NIK np
l24: FLE 149
l26: PEV
l34: STU 51
l41: PEART 31
p33, l2: ROG 74
l5: BUSCH 59
l16: BUSCH 60
l18: STU 51
l22: ROG 75
l28: MON-50
l30: WEI 58
l33: STU 52
l38: GERH
p34, l30: NEU 66–7
l36: WEINK 109
l39: STRR 144

p35, l20: MAHLET 109
LEBMR 40
l26: BLAUU 53
l31: See WEI 235
l37: GAI 138
p36, l32: LEBAN 172–3
l42: NET 224
p37, l13: SPEY 55–7
l18: WAGCD, 821
l20: SCHO 178
l33: KLMUM 169
l36: KENHA 129
l41: MOORELG 233
p38, l10: KLMUM op. cit.
l12: MOORELG
l15: op. cit.
l22: LEBAN 231
l28: CAMDEN 43
l32: review 30.iv. 1903
l43: See LEBMR 141
p39, l5: BAUE 92
l12: CARD 15
l18: BEECH 47–8
l20: CUM 232
l22: CARD 16
l24: CUM 230
l30: FUL 209–10
l36: GRAF 250
l39: STU 52

p40, l2: SCHOELET 45
  l3: BOUT 41
  l42: KUNA 27
p41, l4: *The Conductor Magazine*,
  September 1983, p.11
  l12: OSBK 51–2

Chapter 3
Masters of the House

p44, l1: LEBMR 7
  l18: MAHLET 25
  l21: LEBMR 82, 174
  l24: Prague lecture, 25.iii.1912;
  LEBMR 315
  l33: BLAUD 154–5
p45, l35: MAHLET 393
  l42: *News about Mahler
  research*, No 21, April
  1989, pp. 7–11
p46, l11: *GRAM* 185
  l13: LEBMR 59
  l19: MAHLET 117
  l26: *GRAM* 221
  l31: BAUE 28
  l36: LEBMR 60
  l41: *GRAM* 185
p47, l4: BLAUD 186
  l17: LEBMR 75
  l18: BAUE 51
  l22: BLAUU 123
  l24: WALTV 97
p48, l18: BAUE 51
  l35: *GRAM* 452
p49, l16: MAHALM 116
  l19: MAHALM 136
  l20: BAUE 104
  l29: BAUE 116
  l37: BLAUD 219–20
p50, l44: LEBMR 108
  l8: LEBMR 118
  l17: LEBMR 117
p51, l4: *idem*
  l5: STEF 46
  l35: *GRAM* 600
p52, l32: LEBMR 305
p53, l4: BLAUU 123
  l5: LEBMR 208
  l6: MAHALM 92
  l10: MAHALM 93
  l15: LEBMR 181
  l21: LEBMR 316
  l27: MAHLET 304

p41, l14: Hugo Cole, 'The Shy
  Conductor', Gdn, 3.vii.87,
  np
  l19: BBC/GER/69
  l38: last issued by DG in
  centenary BPO album

p53, l32: LEBMR 213–14
p54, l2: WEISS 99
  l5: WILH 129
  l10: BOUT 42
p55, l13: WEI 258
  l41: BHAI
p56, l10: see *GRAM*, xi/89, p.822
  l13: Philips 416 211–2 sleeve
  note
  l16: MAHALM 69
  l27: STRAVE 61
  l38: 50th birthday tribute (sic)
  in *Der Auftakt*, Prague,
  October 1921
  l41: WEBZEM, 38
p57, l2: HEYKI 249
  l25: HEYKC 69
  l28: *idem*
p58, l6: SCHOELET 192
p58, l15: Peter Horensteins, letter
  to NL
  l32: TILL 151
  l33: CARD 278
  l37: *GRAM* v/85, 1316
p59, l11: LEGGE 191
  l14: HOLMES
  l32: HEYKI 62
p60, l18: 'The Real Mahler'
  l33: BGAI
  l37: WALGM 4–5
  l40: Eleanor Rosé AI
p61, l4: MAHLET 189
  l10: WALTV 125
  l20: MAHLET 235
  l23: WALTV 135
  l30: WALTV 180
  l41: CARD 251
  l42: SCHO np
p62, l7: AMAI
  l17: Eleanor Rosé, AI
  l25: BERG 457
  l28: MENU 126
  l33: AMAI

p63, l2: WALTV 380
l18: LEBMR 46–7
l20: *idem*
l29: WILH 202
p64, l13: HEYKC 146–7

Chapter 4
Facing the Dictators

p66, l13: DAVEN 85
l19: PAD 137
l21: DORA 308
l22: SHO 161
l24: OCON 132
p67, l26: OCON 98–9
l27: HOLMES
l29: CHOTZ 34–35
p68, l4: DAVEN 395
l16: DAVEN 391
l24: SACCHI 179
l34: OCON 103
p69, l11: SACHTOS 22
l24: TAUB 46
l37: WALK 449
p70, l30: SACCHI 110
l35: SACHTOS 86
p71, l3: SACCHI 116
l11: *NYT*, 2.ii.08, p.8
l22: GATTI 159–62
l32: HORO 65
p72, l10: HEYKC 113
l11: OSBK 68
l24: FURT 45–6
p73, l15: FURT 17
l18: See HORO 313, 154
p74, l2: TAUB 107
l4: DAVEN 257
l24: TAUB 309
l26: SACHTOS 227
p75, l2: TOSN
l11: CHOTZ 120
l16: MFI
l18: CONA 292
l21: NICHRAV 48–9
l24: VOLKOV 17
l30: MFI
l33: SHO 168
l36: OCON 134
l40: HORO 368–9
p76, l3: *Time* 4.iv.35
l8: VINT 45
l12: PVT 206
l30: EWE 37

p64, l31: WALGM 60
l41: LEBMR 226
p65, l8: 'The Real Mahler'
l17: GATTI 148
l22: MAHLET 319

p76, l33: STEF 126, 14, 16
l36: HORO 167
p77, l4: See ANTEK 88–90
l11: DAVEN 166
l16: CHOTZ 33
l22: SACHTOS 139
l29: PRIM 94
l34: EWE 46
l35: CHOTZ 112
l37: DORA 310
p78, l6: ANTEK 88–90
l14: CHOTZ 117
l16: RUB2 505–6
l32: BULLOCK 376
l34: WAITE 11
p79, l5: SACHIT 208
l7: CHOTZ 90
l15: SACHIT 169
l17: LOCH 256
l41: SACHIT 209
p80, l23: CHAMB 110
p81, l11: SACHIT 229
l14: SACHIT 227
l25: JORD 175–84
l39: *Life*, 13.ix.1943, np
p82, l7: SACHTOS 290
l12: DAVEN 297
l15: SACHTOS 229
l30: WAGWIN 89
l32: SACCHI 168
p83, l5: OCON 95
l12: Freiburg in Breigau
(Friedrich Wagner'sche
Buchandlung) 1854
l16: HÖCKER 7
l29: FURT 118
l32: Luigi Bellingardi, sleeve
note to DG recording
427–783–2
l34: FURT 65
l36: FURT 82
l38: *idem*
p84, l1: BBC April 1947; see
interview FURTGB 38

p84, 14: *idem*
18: *idem*
111: GEI 16
114: FURTGB 39
118: Berthold Goldschmidt, 'The Conductor's Mirror', *TLS*, 28.vii.89, p. 826
129: WALTBR 149
134: FLE 272
p85, 15: WALTBR 189
17: RIESS 62
113: CAMDEN 117
119: Joachim Kaiser, sleeve note to DG recording 427–781–2
135: FURTGB 14–15
139: VAUK 144
142: HOTTER 237
p86, 17: PIAT 105
119: CLARE 153
120: RIESS 73
132: FURTUS 11
143: BGAI
p87, 12: SACHTOS 176
111: FURT 45–6
122: *Vossiche Zeitung*, 11.iv.1933; WULF 80–82
125: *idem*
127: *idem*
137: SCHN 110
p88, 17: RIESS 102
119: GEI 140
124: *Deutsche Allgemeine Zeitung* 25.ix.1934; HÖCKER 82–4
p89, 110: RIESS 68
124: GOEB 54
130: GOEB 90

p89, 136: FURTAB
p90, 114: FURTUS 54
119: LANG 30
121: RIESS 169
134: SCHOELET 238
136: RIESS 181
p91, 12: FURT 161
16: Elisabeth Furtwängler, sleeve note to DG recording 427–778–2
18: *idem*
117: HÖCKER 90
124: FURTUS 83
130: CLARE 86
142: CARD 247–8
p92, 113: JAHR 58
132: See, hilariously, Unger 229–30
p93, 110: Interview with John Holmes, ms *IND*, 26.i.88
112: Sian Edwards, *GRAM*, Mar 88, p. 1287
117: *CM*, 12.viii.89, pp.14–16.
133: NYT, 12.vi.88, np
p94, 140: Masur, *ST*, 18.ii.90, p. C7
p95, 114: TT, 3.ii.90, np
122: AI
134: VAUK 144
140: John Goldsmith of Unicorn Records, AI
p96, 14: NYT, 16.xii.67
112: See KLAW 73–87
122: OCON 138
138: Richard Taruskin
141: FISCH 147
p97, 11: BGAI
16: HOLMES

Chapter 5
The Karajan Case

p99, 132: VAUK 135
137: VAUK 134
p100, 15: LEGGE 222
111: LEGGE xi
122: *idem*
123: LEGGE 223
128: LEGGE 224–5
132: CLARE 201
p101, 16: KAR 70
19: AI
129: LEGGE 73

p102, 16: GOEB 271
129: PRIE 52
p103, 110: SPEE2 288–9
137: See BACK 381, PRIE 19
p104, 13: VAUK 108
129: NYO, 2.xii.67
p105, 138: GOEB 205
p106, 15: GOEB 161
16: See FURTUS 73–9
122: BACK 390–1
126: VAS 211

p107, l11: HAEU 80, VAUK 132
125: KAR 61
135: VAUK 140
p108, l6: Justice Dept source
129: BOEH 52–3 and PRIE 31
139: BGAI
141: BGAI
p109, l10: PRIE 30–32
114: PRIE 131
119: BOEH 141
125: BERK 304, 317
133: Interview in *Die Zeit*, Hamburg, 15.xii.78
p110, l4: *New York Post*, 24.ii.89
19: VAUK 222
113: BING 256
p111, l5: Elisabeth Schwarzkopf, AI
119: CULP 195
127: VAUK 152
142: CULP 201
p112, l2: AI
18: Peter Csobidi, *Karajan, oder die kontrollierte Ekstase*, Vienna (Neff Verlag), 1988
120: Peter Heyworth, 'Karajan: The English Connection', *Philharmonia Yearbook*, London, 1988, p. 37
137: 'Karajan in Salzburg' – CAMI productions, 1988
p113, l1: Sam H. Shirakawa, 'Birgit Nilsson: The Legend Speaks', *Opera Monthly*, June 1988, p.34
l78: *DG Karajan Magazine*, April 1988 (Domingo and Baltsa)
110: CM, 1.x.88, p. 33
112: VAUK 47
118: STRE 150
120: VAUK 143
121: AI
124: Edward Rothstein 'Twilight of the God', VF, December 1989, p. 117
118: Letters sold at Sotherby's London, 10 May 1990
p114, l7: Gdn 21.vii.89
132: BETHGE 194
139: See PEUK 67–81
142: 'Herbert von Karajan by

Michel Glotz' – *DG Salzburg Journal 1988*
p115, l1: Britannia Music advertisement, ST, 5.vi.88
l2: Richard Osborne 'The Consummate Professional' – *DG Salzburg Journal 1989*
l5: KARDG p. xi XI
l8: DG VHS (no) and BBC interview 3.iv.88 'Karajan at Eighty'
l17: Heyworth art. cit. 39
l20: Christopher Raeburn, AI
l24: Berlin Philharmonic players, AI
l40: Strehler to Gitta Sereny, AI
l43: LEGGE 224
p116, l13: BACK book-jacket and *Wochenpresse*, 21.vii.89
l19: KAR 88
l29: KAR 91
p117, l8: ZMI
l21: POR3, 338
l26: Fegus McWilliam, AI
l36: KARANEK 37
l40: STRE 136–8
p118, l2: *ST*, 30.i.83, p. 13
l9: Interview with *The Times*, 28.iii.1988. p.15
l44: *CM*, 20.viii.88, p. 5
p119, l33: 1989 figure – source: DG President Holschneider, AI
l43: *DTel*, 11.iv.88
p120, l1: BERGMAN 243
l7: Press conference at Anif, 29.vii.87
l22: STA, 2.viii.89, p.1
l41: KAR 71
p121, l35: Salzburg press conference, April 1981
l42: Anif press conference, 29.vii.1987
p122, l4: *idem*
l14: *idem*
l18: interview with *The Times*, 5.iv.88, np
l25: BERGMAN 243
l38: interview with Humphrey Burton, BBC-2, 3.iv.1988

p122, l43: OSBK 131
p123, l5: KAR 110
l5: *TT*, 5.iv.88, art. cit.
l28: Letter offer for sale at Southerby's New York December 1990.
p124, l27: *ST*, 30.i.83, art. cit.
p125, l12: AI, ST, 00.ii.89
l33: *VF*, art. cit.
l38: 'Karajan's Salzburg' video
p126, l2: *VF*, art. cit.
l80: sleeve note to EMI CMS 7 633 16 2
l12: KAR 127–45
l33: RCAI
l39: BBC interview, quoted in *STel*, 23.vii.89, np
l42: *GRAM*, Sep 89, p. 614
p127, l3: KAR 130
l11: Alan Blyth, *DTel*, 5.iv.88, p. 14

p127, l18: STRAVD 89
l28: KAR 129
l43: POR 3 339
p128, l2: VAUK 28
l8: *LRB*, 8.ii.90, p. 21
l20: *STel*. 23.vii.89
l27: *NR*, 7.xi.88, p. 30
l35: *ST*, 23.vii.89, p. C9
l39: CAIRNS 165–7
p129, l4: *GRAM*, ix.89, p. 408
l31: CDAI
l34: MATT 285
l36: MATT 391
p130, l7: OSBK 101
l23: RCAI
l35: Csobidi op. cit.
l37: OSBK 139
p131, l3: KAR
l7: HIBBERT 288
l15: CDAI

Chapter Six
'A Starving Population and an Absentee Aristocracy'

p132, title: Benjamini Disraeli to the House of Commons, 16.ii.1844: 'Thus you have a starving population, an absentee aristocracy and an alien Church, and in addition the weakest executive in the world. That is the Irish Question.'
p133, l6: *NYT*, 1.iii.88, p. C25
l18: *Chicago* magazine, October 1989, p. 139
l20: Ernest Fleischmann, 'The Orchestra is Dead: Long Live the Community of Musicians'; Cleveland address, 16.v.87
p134, l5: Carter AI
l8: MONT 115
l42: dedication in the score
p135, l2: SCHOELET 22
l9: STRAVLET 217
l19: SLONPP 76
p136, l12: DICK 46–8
l14: COH 214
l22: STRAVLET, 223
l22: *idem* 362
l25: *idem* 249

p136, l32: London press conference, 6.xii.89
p137, l40: Linda Corman, 'Confessions of a Conductor', *Boston* magazine, November 1986, pp. 188–255
l42: HART 185
p138, l5: *Fanfare* magazine, May-June 1986, np
l15: Corman, art. cit.
l19: Corman, art. cit.
l29: EPST 227–8
l31: Corman art. cit.
l39: Corman art. cit.
p139, l4: DG press release, vii.88
p140, l37: Corman art. cit.
l9: CHAS ix
l30: DANIEL 24
p141, l3: OCON 285
l16: See *MT*, August 1984, pp. 433–5
l19: issue of 4 March 1911, p. 6
l24: DANIEL 78
l38: CHAS 53–4
p142, l1: DANIEL 112

p142, l17:   related by Mischakoff to
             RFAI
p143, l11:   CHAS 88
       l31:   See Biographies p. 329 and
             DANIEL pp 1040–50
       l35:   STRAVLET 430–35
       l37:   Panufnik AI
p144, l4:   see GOULD pp. 00–00
       l9:   OCONN 284
       l13:   PIAT 183
p145, l8:   CHAS 174
       l11:   STRAVE 145–6
       l21:   DANIEL 357
       l33:   DANIEL 356–71
       l43:   *idem*
p147, l2:   Daniel AI
       l5:   DANIEL
       l8:   CHAS 159–60
       l9:   OCON 285
       l16:   Daniel AI
       l28:   OCON 301

p147, l41:   PVT 154–5
p148, l8:   REIS 63
       l38:   CM issue no. 1, ix.1976
       l40:   RUTT 60
p149, l22:   PEART 193
       l36:   ST, see MORT 183
       l42:   API
p150, l6:   EMI TC-SLS 5225 (1973)
       l10:   RUTT 25
p151, l2:   RUTT 210
       l15:   API
       l26:   Ernest Fleischmann, AI
       l30:   *TT*, 22.vi.90 p. 22
       l38:   *TT*, 19.vi.87, p. 20
p152, l7:   AI
       l20:   press statement 27.xi.86
       l25:   *LA Times* magazine,
             8.x.89, p. 18
       l29:   loc. cit. p. 10
       l33:   loc. cit.
       l39:   AI

Chapter 7
The Gremlin in the Garden

p154, l2:   MOORE 478
p155, l29:   SHO 35
       l35:   REID 17
p156, l12:   REID 30
       l21:   AI
       l31:   TOYE 227
       l39:   CHIS 45–8, 373
       l40:   CARDB 28
p157, l7:   OCON 77
       l10:   BEEP 168
       l15:   COAT 122
       l21:   SHO 41
       l27:   BBC recorded tribute,
             1979
       l32:   PRIM 90
p158, l10:   SHO 34
       l14:   SMYBEE np
       l18:   RONA 26
       l23:   BEEST 66
       l33:   *ST*, 9.x.32
p159, l3:   TOYE 227
       l9:   BEEP 66
       l14:   KENBA 189
       l29:   BEEP 100
       l31:   TAYL 166
       l32:   KENBA 188
p160, l13:   KENBA 117
       l25:   KENBA 169

p160, l37:   LEGGE 61
       l40:   TILL 34
p161, l2:   AI
       l23:   STRE 233–7
       l30:   RCAI
p162, l28:   REID 108
       l34:   GLOV227–8
p163, l15:   TOYE 90
       l24:   BEEST np
p164, l3:   BEEP 14
       l30:   LANGD 27–8
       l34:   HALT 119
p165, l8:   HALT 108
       l15:   HALT 106
       l17:   KENBR 65
       l25:   DROG 237
       l33:   HALT 107
       l36:   HALT 108
       l38:   REID 236
p166, l9:   RKI
       l20:   HARE 159
       l28:   SAVAGE 153
       l34:   DROG 244
p167, l43:   *TT*, 27.vi.56
       l5:   DROG 245
       l9:   RKI
       l18:   RKI
       l24:   HALT 251

p167, 126: Lady Beecham, AI
136: *Opera*, June 1990, vol 41/6, p. 644
p168, 114: GSAI
120: GSAI
134: DROG 251
135: GSAI
p169, 12: Salzburg press conference, August 1989
110: GSAI
116: GSAI
120: Perahia AI
126: *Time* magazine, 7.v.73
130: GSAI
138: CDAI
140: CULP 189
142: See LEBMR ix
p170, 110: GSAI
114: *TT*, 9.ix.88
123: GSAI
134: SAVAGE 169
143: LANGD 102
p171, 14: Nilsson, *Opera Monthly* interview

p171, 112: *Time*, loc. cit.
122: Rodney Friend, AI
134: *Ovation*, Nov 1987, p.13
135: *Time*, loc. cit.
137: *OBS*, 12.vi.88, p.14
p172, 19: *Time*, loc. cit.
124: DROG 325
135: Peter Heyworth, quoted in unsigned OBS profile by Gillian Widdicombe, nd
139: *OBS*, loc. cit.
p173, 118: DROG 336
125: 1982 press conference.
136: HOLMES, Davis entry
138: HOLMES, Loc cit.
141: Harold Rosenthal, articles in *Opera* and *CM*
p174, 110: BHAI
118: BHAI
120: Bill Webster AI
131: RFAI
140: RFAI
p175, 19: BHAI
112: *TT*, 31.i.90, p.13
p176, 12: GSAI

Chapter 8
Collapse of the Conducting Composer

p178, 120: RFAI
134: VIN 240
16: William Lincer, PEYBER 290
127: MTTI
133: GRAD 285
139: NYT, 15.xi.43
p180, 16: GRUEN 26–7
118: *NYT*, 19.v.69
129: GRUEN 273
140: PEYBER 292
p181, 18: GRAD 255
113: GRUEN 27–8
120: *STel*, 15.vii.90, Review I
123: EPST 65
128: RFAI
137: *NYT*, 19.v.69
p182, 12: *High Fidelity*, Sept 1967
13: DICK 100
16: *High Fidelity*, loc.
18: BERNH 316
114: witnessed by the author
117: BERNH 313
127: *ST*, ix.88

p183, 13: *NYT*, 15.i.70
114: *NYT*, 16.i.70
117: WOLFE 109
127: *NYT*, 22.x.80, see ROBBER 66
132: MTTI
141: GRUEN 28
p184, 138: AI
p185, 13: quoted PEYBOU 257
18: William Glock, AI
116: HEYKC 120
118: PEYBOU 256
132: 'Pierre de Resistance', interview: GDN, 13.i.89, p. 21
135–37: all quotes: PBAI
143: PEYBOU 182
p186, 19: PBAI
110: PEYBOU 168
115: published in *The Score*, May 1952; revised in BOULN 268–76
131: PBAI
138: PBAI

p186, 143: *e e cummings ist der dichter* (1970)
p187, 16: DUFF 179
17: BOULOR 443
110: STRAVEX
113: BOULOR 442
116: BOULOR 443
143: PBAI
p188, 14: DUFF 200–1
111: PBAI
121: PBAI
136: Joan Peyser
p189, 15: PBAI

p189, 16: Glock AI
18: HEYKC 123
141: *Gdn*, 13.i.89, loc. int.
p190, 14: *OBS*, 89, nd
113: introduction to LB Edition, DG 1990
124: loc. cit.
131: *TT*, 1.viii.89
p191, 16: MTTI
119: LEBAN 329
124: DG internal document, copy in author's possession

Chapter 9
Strange Tales from the Vienna Woods

p193, 126: GEI 302
p194, 11: DAM 353/LEBAN 186
113: JERGER 74
124: HEYKC 114
134: letter of 18.ii.1942, see STRR
p195, 111: CUL 190
118: Interview in *Bunte* magazine, May 1987
p196, 13: *TT*, 11.ix.87
116: ORF/IS/88
117: Werner Resel, *Jerusalem Post* interview, ix.88
p198, 115: *idem*
135: GRAD 52
138: GRAD 54
p199, 12: GRAD 57
118: PEYBER 370
130: MATT 19–20
134: quoted in sleeve notes for CBS 77416
p200, 19: statement in Vienna, 27.ix.88
114: GRAD 103
116: GRAD 106
124: *NYO*, 26.xi.79
143: ORF/IS/88
p201, 16: MATT 7
112: Leonard Bernstein, 'Mahler: his time has come', *High Fidelity* magazine, September 1967
119: PEYBER 435
131: GRAD 100
p202, 13: Resel, art. cit.

p202, 112: LMAI
121: LMAI
130: LMAI
138: Hubert Deutsch, AI
p203, 15: John Holmes, AI
122: Richard Bassett, 'The man who wanted to be Mr Vienna,' TT, 13.vii.84, p.19
143: AI
p204, 112: LMAI
120: LMAI
138: LMAI
143: Deutsch AI
p205, 119: Seefehlner AI
124: TT, loc. it.
127: CULP 192
132: *Gdn*. 18.ix.1987
p206, 126: LMAI
134: LMAI
p207, 11: *Gdn*, *idem*
12: *idem*
16: *CM* 21.ix.89, p.15
121: AI
125: press conference, 23.x.89
p208, 130: Holschneider AI
p209, 18: Ewing, AI
114: Will Crutchfield, 'James Levine, new era at the Met', cover story, *NYT* magazine, 22.ix.85, p.34
118: *idem* p 36
121: Peter G. Davis, 'Jimmy's Met', *New York* magazine, 20.iv.87; CM, 23.ix.89, pp.52–61

p209, l35: *NYT*, 11.xi.90, p.27
p210, l7: MAYER 341
l10: Crutchfield, p.23
l18: Donal Henahan 'Casting a critical eye at the Met's casting', NYT, 27.xi.88, p.H27
l23: Davis, loc. cit.
l38: Davis, loc. cit.
l39: Barry Millington, *OBS*, 7.v.89
l40: op.cit.
p211, l7: *CM*, 23.ix.89, p.5

p211, l20: Edward Greenfield, Gdn, 21.viii.87, p15
l27: loc. cit.
p212, l3: *GRAM*, Aug 87, p.269
l10: loc. cit.
l15: see, for example, H. Boese & A. F. Rottensteiner, *Botschafter der Musik: Die Wiener Philharmoniker*, Wien (Bundesverlag), 1967
l19: Resel, int. cit.

Chapter 10
Formula Uno

p214, l14: *taz*, 10.x.89, p.5
p215, l11: OSBK 71
l90: AI
p216, l3: BEAVAN 5
p218, l29: Anthony Camden, AI
p219, l21: all LSO players quotes, AI
p222, l30: RCAI
: all Muti quotes RMAI, and AI, unless specified
p223, l32: Peter Heyworth, OBS 18.xii.89, p.41
p218, l3: RCAT
p225, l25: PETTIT 177
p226, l40: Salzburg press conference, 29.vii.89
p227, l24: PBAI
l36: PHInq 30.iii.1990. p 1a
l36: RMAI

p228, l1: Edward Greenfield, Gdn, 25.iii.88, np
l7: Barry Millington, *TT*, 14.iii.90, np
l9: Hilary Finch, *TT*, 7.vii.88
l12: Paul Griffiths, *TT*, 22.ii.88
l21: CM, 26.xi.88, p. 15
l27: AI
l37: DG press information, 4/1989
p229, l16: Dino Villatico, sleeve-note to DG 415 984–2
l24: POR3, 340
l26: Richard Morrison, *TT*, 9.v.89
l39: LEBMR 125
l42: Villatico, loc. cit.
p230, l8: AI

Chapter 11
The Mavericks

p231, l20: Letter to the author
l27: Ernest Fleischmann, AI
p232, l6: John Goldsmith, AI
l10: *New Grove*, 'Horenstein'
l20: LANG 229
l31: *Aktuelt*, Copenhagen, May 1962
p233, l3: Günther Breest, AI, Dec 89
l37: BGAI
l41: HALT 175–7
l43: HARE 168
p234, l5: LANGDON 45
l10: BLAU 103

p234, l11: *idem*
l14: SAVAGE 128
l43: MATT
p235, l2: RCAI
l5: AI
l27: AI
l29: OSBKC 65
l31: VF Feb 88, p48
p236, l35: all players' quotes are AI
p237, l36: all Tennstedt quotes are KTAI
p238, l39: SRAI
p240, l35: *ST*, Magazine , June 85
p241, l20: the account of Tennstedt's

collapse is based on
conversations with those
present

p241, 120: Tim Page, *New York Newsday*, 21.i.1988

Chapter 12
Insider Dealing

p244, 120: VAUK 260
　　　　124: VAUK 69
　　　　130: See *CM*, 20.viii.88.
p245, 13: HARE, p. 279
p246, 118: HART 24
　　　　128: AI, May 1982
　　　　129: HART 85
　　　　132: HOLMES 40
p247, 119: BOO 216
　　　　123: HART 9
p248, 114: AI, CM, 22.i.83, p. 7
　　　　128: AI, *idem*
p249, 122: *TT*, 3.vi.89, p. 31
　　　　127: BOO 135
p250, 132: *R&R*, April 1978, p.20
p251, 116: *CM*, 17.ix.88, p.5

p252, 15: press conference, 16.i.89
　　　　123: *TT*, 3.vi.89, p.31
　　　　143: *Gdn*, 23.v.89. np
p253, 120: *CM*, 17.vi.89, p.5
　　　　143: BOO, 194
p254, 132: AI, 1989
　　　　　　AI, Rodney Friend, 1983
　　　　140: RFAI
p255, 14: *NR*, 13.vii.89, p.28
　　　　116: *CM*, 6.vi.87. p.9
　　　　126: RUB2, p.597
p256, 11: *WSJ*, 2.v.89, p.1
　　　　17: op. cit.
　　　　121: AI, ST, 21.xi.82. p.5
　　　　143: PAR 165
p257, 13: AI

Chapter 13
Left Outside

p259, 17: communicated to the
　　　　　　author by Eleanor Rosé
　　　　119: DICK 97
　　　　134: DG press information
　　　　140: SHERM 227
p260, 12: TOR 196
　　　　145: SHERM 228
　　　　19: SHERM 235
　　　　117: SHERM 246 (30.xi.1945)
　　　　129: SCHOELET 263
　　　　134: PVT 185
　　　　142: EWE 112
p261, 16: SMIT 237
　　　　113: SCHO 349
　　　　117: *NYT*, April 1956, nd
　　　　124: PEYBER 59
　　　　126: *ST* magazine, May 89. 'A
　　　　　　Life in the Day'
　　　　139: DICK 97
p263, 12: SEL 361–2
　　　　112: *Cultural Trends*, 1990:7,
　　　　　　p37

p263, 121: INTX, June 1989, p.35
p264, 12: *The Republic*, Book V
　　　　117: WOOD np
　　　　132: DANIEL 852
　　　　136: AMM 174
p265, 17: HOL 178
　　　　126: WOO 261
　　　　143: SHO 146
p266, 143: *NYO*, 23.v.83
　　　　198: *NYO*, 10.iii.73
p267, 132: SEAI
　　　　140: AI
p268, 110: SEAI
　　　　122: SRAI
　　　　135: See *CM*, 3.vi.89, p.5
p269, 113: *IND*, obituary, 5.vii.88
　　　　123: POR3 156
　　　　125: POR3 480
p270, 18: EWE 277
　　　　131: HART 199

Chapter 14
The Search for a Semi-Conductor

p272, 12: pt II, chapter 3
    118: SZIG 220
    121: SCUSSR 46–7
    124: *idem*
    125: *idem*
p273, 13: HEYKI 318
    112: Fifer, AI 1987
    123: AI
p274, 15: all Marriner quotes: NMAI
p276, 14: *Ovation*, Dec 1983, p.17
    110: Tom Sutcliffe, *Gdn*, 21.ii.88
p277, 121: CHAI
    132: EPST 200
p278, 118: Decca/London 414 396–2
    119: See HOGW
    120: L'Oiseau Lyre 411 858–2
    124: Hyperion CDA 66251/2
    125: Hogwood (Decca), Norrington (EMI) and Hanover Band (Nimbus)
    139: L'Oiseau Lyre 411 712–2
    141: See HOGW 232–51
p279, 19: interview with Arthur Jacobs for EMI, May 1989
    121: NMAI
    134: Kirkby AI
p280, 142: Sir Anthony Lewis, *Early Music*, July 1976, p.376
p281, 114: *The Listener*, 19.v.1977, p.659

p281, 118: *Ovation*, Dec 1983, p.17
    122: *GRAM* May 88, p.1573
    135: CHAI
    143: *GRAM*, February 1990, p.1437
p282, 14: *GRAM*, November 1988, p.734
    113: CHAI
    121: *Gdn*, 9.vi.89
    130: *Le Monde*, 29.iv.88
p283, 17: EMI press release, December 1986
    116: James Oestreich, 'Not what he seems – exploding the myths about Roger Norrington' – *Connoisseur*, January 1990. p.67
    125: *GRAM*, April 1989, p.1553
    134: *GRAM*, February 1990, p.1437
    141: 21.iii.88, p.42
p284, 14: *TT*, 28.iv.89, p.20
    128: Fiona Maddocks, IND, 13.xii.86
    130: South Bank brochure for 'Sounds in Time', 1990
p285, 14: sleeve note to DG 453 654–2
    131: Oestreich, loc. cit.

Chapter 15
Where Have All the Conductors Gone?

p287, 18: Van Walsum, AI
    117: CBS press release
    122: *Pulse* magazine, July 1988, p.41
    130: loc. cit.
    132: CBS M2K42271
    142: *Keynote*, March 1988, p.24
p288, 15: *Blue Wings* (Finnair in-flight magazine), December 1986
    111: *Pulse*, loc. cit.
    119: Review by Julian Budden, *IND*, 10.v.89, np

p288, 121: *Blue Wings*, loc. cit.
    143: see HART
p289, 135: *CM*, 6.viii.88, p.19
p290, 13: RCAI
    110: interview with Meeno Feenstra, Decca 1988
    115: RCAI
    141: RCAI
    110: RCAI
    126: SRAI
    131: *Birmingham Post*, nd
    135: KENRAT 104
p292, 19: *NYO*, 8.ii.88 np

p292, l16: AI
l19: SRAI
l24: CTV/RAT/88
l31: SRAI
l42: SRAI
p293, l21: SRAI
l24: Fleischmann AI
p294, l4: *Gdn*, 30.vii.90
l12: KENRAT 211
l15: Goldschmidt AI
l29: KENRAT 211
l34: Damon Evans, 1987 Glyndebourne programme book, p.147
l35: White AI
l37: SRAI
p295, l5: SRAI
l22: Carewe AI
l29: CTV/RAT/88
l34: CTV/RAT/88
l42: KENRAT 36
p296, l25: SRAI
l31: SRAI
l34: SRAI
l38: Carewe AI

p297, l6: reported to the author by players
l11: *Spie*
l30: CTV/RAT/88
l34: EMI EL 27 0598 3
l38: *GRAM*, Oct 1987 Gerald S. Fox, *American Record Guide*, Vol 51, No 6, November-December 1988, pp. 53–4
l41: David Hurwitz; July 1988 issue, pp. 63–4
p298, l6: Carewe AI
l16: KENRAT 212
l38: SRAI
p299, l11: WMAI
l19: WMAI
l23: WMAI
l41: David Nolan, AI
p300 : all quotes WMAI
l40: Andreas von Bennigsen, AI
p301, l16: Andreas von Bennigsen, AI
l19: WMAI
l26: John William, A1
l32: FWMAI

Chapter 16
The Master of Them All

p304, l8: 1987 edition, p.3491, col 2
l22: *Musical America*, 1987 edition, p.88
p305, l3: *idem*, p.97
l8: copy in author's possession
p306, l6: RWAI
l19: Andrew Decker, 'Classical String Puller', *Manhattan Inc.* magazine, September 1989, pp. 154–162
l21: RWAI
l28: RWAI
l32: AI
l33: AI
l35: *NYT*, quoted in RUTT 60
p307, l4: RWAI
l10: Decker, loc. cit.
l18: RWAI
l24: *CM*, 12.v.90, p.31
l30: Decker, loc. cit.
l39: HEINS 153
p308, l17: Decker, loc. cit.

p308, l31: Decker, loc. cit.
l38: Unrecorded in the Strauss *Werkverzeichnis*
l42: AI
p309, l38: RUTT 69
l43: HART 170
p310, l8: Decker, loc. cit.
l17: RWAI
l21: RWAI
l24: Davis AI
p311, l3: BING2, 185
l16: CAMI Video sales pitch, 1988
l27: *Variety*, 30.v.1990, pp. 1 and 45: 'Culture Shock at the New York Times'
l29: *Variety*, loc. cit.
p312, l4: RWAI
l18: David Sigall, AI
l24: Lotte Klemperer, AI
l33: letter to Mary Roblee, sold at Sotheby's, 17.v.90

p312, l39: Edward Rothstein, 'Twilight of the God', *VF*, February 1990, p.120

p313, l6: VAUK 181–2

l7: AI

l13: VAUK 23

p314, l8: *Spie*, 4.iv.88

l7: Decker, loc. cit.

l33: RWAI

l14: Paul Hume, 'Do Jet-set conductors lower quality?' WP, 30.iv.1972, np

p315, l31: RWAI

l43: AI

p316, l27: RWAI

l43: RWAI

p317, l11: 1971 interview quoted in Decker, loc. cit.

l16: RWAI

p318, l32: AI

l38: Sigall AI

l43: Van Walsum AI

p319, l23: Göhre AI

l33: I am indebted for recent figures to research by Scott Duncan published in the *Baltimore Evening Sun* on 13.iv 1988 and the OCSM Newsletter, January 1989, vol. 2.

Table 2: US Department of Commerce, *Historical Statistics of the United States, Colonial times to 1970*, part 1, pp. 169–70; and US Bureau of Labor Statistics monthly bulletin, March 1990

p321, l43: confirmed by Bernstein staff

p323   : figures from: REIDSAR 246–7

HALT 177

LSO archive

London Philharmonic archive

LSO archive

p323, l28: Sigall AI

p324, l9: AI

l15: RWAI

l18: Ronald Wilford, 1971 interview

l31: ROTH 116

l43: Duncan, art. cit.

p325, l14: *Gdn*, 9.viii.90, p.26

l16: *Musical America*, July 1987, p.30

l21: BLAUD.

l24: REIDBA 379

l36: Duncan, art. cit.

l38: *ST* magazine, 13.ix.1987, p.66

p326, l5: loc. cit.

Sources for tables 1 and 3:

Herbert Kupferberg, *Those Fabulous Philadelphians*, NY 1969

John H. Mueller, *The American SO*, Indiana UP, 1951

Lotte Klemperer

LSO Archive

LPO Archive

H. Foss and V. Goodwin, *London Symphony*, 1954

Acknowledgements

Many of the individuals and institutions listed below were exceptionally helpful in furthering my researches and deserve more than this formal expression of thanks. I am particularly grateful to the British Council and (post-Communist) Czechoslovak Ministry of Culture for facilitating a fact-finding visit; to the Austrian and Swiss national tourist offices; to the *Sunday Times* for sustaining some of my more esoteric preoccupations; and to a variety of confidential informants in the musical community who, for reasons that will be apparent by now, cannot be thanked by name. Apart from principal interviewees, who are acknowledged in the source list and chapter notes, other advice and assistance was received from:

UK: John Amis, Peter Andry, the late Herman Baron, Garrick Bond, John Dennison, Steve Boyd, Isabella De Sabata, Massimo Freccia; Clive and Penny Gillinson, Bruce Campbell, Jane Compton (LSO); Berthold Goldschmidt; Dr Jeffrey Graham (Dept of Health); Judy Grahame, Lucy Colyer (London Philharmonic); Peter Heyworth Graeme Kay, Jane Krivine, Aubrey Levey, Glynn Macdonald, James Mallinson, Graham Melville-Mason, Donald Mitchell, Andrzej and Camilla Panufnik, Dieter Pevsner, Christopher Raeburn, Tony Rennell, Eleanor Rosé, Naresh Samani, Gitta Sereny, Daniel Snowman, Joeske Van Walsum, Christel Wallbaum, Christine Walker, Dr Michael Weitzmann, Katherine Wilkinson (London). Andrew Burn, Brendan Carroll, Brian Pridgeon (Liverpool). Ed Smith (Birmingham).

US: Dr. Elliott Galkin (U. of Maryland, Baltimore); Gilbert E. Kaplan, Hermann Lowin, Gail Ross, Edward Rothstein, Frank Salomon, Patrick J. Smith, Mrs Dorli Soria (New York), Benjamin Zander (Boston), Ernst W. Korngold (Hollywood), Nicolas Slonimsky, Ernest Fleischmann, Peter Hemmings (Los Angeles).

Australia: John L. Holmes (Canberra), Michael Smith (Melbourne).

Austria: Dr Herta Blaukopf, Dr Wolfgang Herles, Prof. Hans Landesmann (Vienna).

Canada: Michael Crabb, Judith Melby (CBC Toronto), Walter Homburger (Toronto Symphony).

Czechoslovakia: Dr Jitka Slavikova (Prague), Dr V. Holecek (Czech Philharmonic), Professor and Mrs Jiri Rychetsky (Humpolec).

Denmark: Dr Knud Martner.

France: Baron Henri-Louis de La Grange, the late Maurice Fleuret, Astrid Schirmer.

Germany: Hellmut Stern, Fergus McWilliam, Helmut Rosenthal, Sylvia Hertel (Berlin), Klaus Schulz (Aachen), Peter Girth, Cees Mulderij, Dr Andreas

Holschneider, Dr Jochen Schürmann (Hamburg), Inge Tennstedt (Kiel), Peter Gürtler (Leipzig).

Israel: Advocates Moshe and Jonathan Kahn, Tatiana Hoffmannova.

Italy: the late Anna Mahler (Spoleto), Eugene Rizzo (Rome), Herbert Stuppner (Dobbiaco).

Netherlands: Mrs Desi Halban, Dr. H. J. Nieman; Sjoerd van den Berg (Concertgebouworkest).

Sweden: Ake Holmquist.

Switzerland: Franz Blum (Swiss national tourist office), Ulrich Meyer (Lucerne Festival), Lotte Klemperer.

Japan: Nobuko Albery, Tim Jackson.

Source List and Bibliography

Unpublished sources

i Author's taped interviews:

AMAI	Anna Mahler, Los Angeles and London, 1986–88
BGAI	Berthold Goldschmidt, London, 1987–90
BHAI	Bernard Haitink, Edinburgh and London, 1983–90
CDAI	Christoph von Dohnányi, London, April 1989
CHAI	Christopher Hogwood, London, April 1983
GSAI	Sir Georg Solti, Salzburg and London, 1989–90
KTAI	Klaus Tennstedt, London and Kiel, 1984–90
LMAI	Lorin Maazel, Vienna and London, 1984–5 and 1987
MRAI	Mstislav Rostropovich, London and Washington, 1986–7
NMAI	Neville Marriner, London, 1984 and 1989
PBAI	Pierre Boulez, Paris and London, 1985–6
RCAI	Riccardo Chailly, Salzburg, August 1988
RFAI	Rodney Friend, London, 1985–90
RMAI	Riccardo Muti, Ravenna, July 1986
RWAI	Ronald Wilford, New York, January 1988
SEAI	Sian Edwards, London, June 1990
SRAI	Simon Rattle, London, Birmingham and Los Angeles, 1987–90
WMAI	Franz Welser-Möst, London, April 1990

ii Author's transcribed interviews:

API	André Previn, London, November 1983
BGI	Berthold Goldschmidt, London, July 1989
DBI	Daniel Barenboim, Paris, November 1982
JDI	John Denison, London, December 1987
MFI	Massimo Freccia, London, April 1988
MTTI	Michael Tilson Thomas, London, June 1990
RKI	Rafael Kubelik, London, June 1983
ZMI	Zubin Mehta, Berlin, February 1989

Other interviewees are named individually in the footnotes.

iii Manuscript sources:

CZPHIL	Czech Philharmonic archive, Prague
MAHB	Bibliothèque Gustav Mahler, Paris
MAHJ	Gustav Mahler letters, National Library, Jerusalem
PEV	Pevsner family archives, London
TOSN	Toscanini collection, New York Public Library, New York
VPHIL	Vienna Philharmonic archive, Vienna

iv Broadcast sources:
BBC/GER/69   David Gerver, 'The conductor and the orchestra: the human relationship; prod. Daniel Snowman. BBC Third Programme, 28.iv.1969
BBC/MAH/88   Norman Lebrecht, 'The Real Mahler; prod. Daniel Snowman. BBC Radio 4, 25.xii.1988
CTV/RAT/88   Jim Berrow, 'Rattle on the Record', Central Independent Television documentary, screened 15.iv.1988
ORF/IS/88   Austrian television coverage of Vienna Philharmonic visit to Israel, transmitted 29–30.ix.1988

Published Sources

i Newspapers, magazines and periodicals

CM	*Classical Music*, London
DM	*Die Musik*, Berlin
Gdn	*The Guardian*, London
GRAM	*Gramophone* magazine, Harrow, UK
IND	*The Independent*, London
INTX	*Intersect*, Tokyo
LRB	*London Review of Books*
MT	*Musical Times*, London
NR	*New Republic*, New York
NYO	*The New Yorker*
NYT	*The New York Times*
OBS	*The Observer*, London
Opera	*Opera* magazine, London
PHInq	*Philadelphia Inquirer*
PRE	*Die Presse*, Vienna
R&R	*Records and Recording*, London
Spie	*Der Spiegel*, Berlin
ST	*The Sunday Times*, London
STA	*Der Standard*, Vienna
STel	*Sunday Telegraph*, London
Time	*Time* magazine
TT	*The Times*, London
VF	*Vanity Fair*, New York
WP	*Washington Post*
WSJ	*Wall Street Journal*, New York

ii Principal books consulted

AMM   Christine Ammer, *Unsung, a history of women in American music*, Westport, Conn. (Greenwood Press), 1980.
ANTEK   Samuel Antek and Robert Hupka, *This was Toscanini*, New York (Vanguard), 1963.
ATKBA   Harold Atkins and Peter Cotes, *The Barbirollis, a musical marriage*, London (Robson), 1983.

BACK   Robert C. Bachmann, *Karajan, Anmerkungen zu einer Karriere*, Düsseldorf (Econ Verlag), 1983.

BARW   Herbert Barth, Dietrich Mack, Egon Woss, *Wagner, a documentary study*, London (Thames & Hudson), 1985.

BAUE   Natalie Bauer-Lechner, *Recollections of Gustav Mahler*, transl. Dika Newlin, London (Faber Music), 1980.

BEAVAN   Peter Beavan, *Philharmonia Days*, London (Peter Beavan), 1976.

BEECH   Sir Thomas Beecham, *A Mingled Chime; leaves from an autobiography*, London (Hutchinson), 1944.

BEEP   H. C. Procter-Gregg (ed.), *Sir Thomas Beecham, conductor and impresario, as remembered by his friends and colleagues*, Kendal (privately printed), 1972.

BEEST   Harold Atkins and Archie Newman, *Beecham Stories*, London (Robson Books), 1978.

BERG   *The Berg-Schoenberg Correspondence*, ed. Juliane Brand, Christopher Hailey and Donald Harris, London (Macmillan), 1988.

BERGMAN   Ingmar Bergman, *Magic Lantern*, London (Hamish Hamilton), 1988.

BERK   George E. Berkeley, *Vienna and its Jews; the tragedy of success 1880–1980s*; Cambridge, Massachussetts (ABT Books), 1987.

BERNH   Leonard Bernstein, *The Unanswered Question: six talks at Harvard*, Cambridge (Harvard University Press), 1976.

BETHGE   Eberhard Bethge, *Dietrich Bonhoeffer*, London (Fount), 1977.

BILL   *Johannes Brahms und Theodor Billroth in Briefwechsel*, Vienna, 1935.

BING   Sir Rudolf Bing, *5,000 Nights at the Opera*, London (Hamish Hamilton), 1972.

BING2   Sir Rudolf Bing, *A Knight at the Opera*, New York (G Putnam's Sons), 1981.

BLAU   Kurt Blaukopf, *Grosse Dirigenten*, Teuffen (Verlag Arthur Niggli), 1957.

BLAUD   Kurt Blaukopf (ed.), *Mahler: A Documentary Study*, New York (Oxford University Press), 1976.

BLAUU   Herta Blaukopf (ed.), *Gustav Mahler: Unbekannte Briefe*, Vienna (Paul Zsolnay Verlag), 1983.

BOEH   Karl Böhm, *Ich erinnere mich ganz genau*, Vienna (Verlag Fritz Molden), 1974.

BOO   Martin Bookspan and Ross Yockey, *Zubin Mehta*, NY (Harper & Row), 1978.

BOUC   Adrian C. Boult, *Thoughts on Conducting*, London (Phoenix House), 1963.

BOUT   Adrian C. Boult, *My Own Trumpet*, London (Hamish Hamilton), 1973.

BOULN   Pierre Boulez, *Notes of an apprenticeship*, transl. Herbert Weinstock, New York (Alfred A. Knopf), 1968.

BOULOR   Pierre Boulez, *Orientations: collected writings*, transl. Martin Cooper, London (Faber and Faber), 1986.

BRO   Donald Brook *Conductors Gallery*, London (Rockliff), 1945.

BROI   Donald Brook, *'International Gallery of Conductors*, London (Rockliff), 1951.

BUL   Marie von Bülow (ed.), *The Early Correspondence of Hans von Bülow*, transl. Constance Bache: London (T. Fisher Unwin), 1896.

BULB   Marie von Bülow (ed.), *Hans von Bülow: Ausgewahllte Briefe* (Volksausgabe), Leipzig (Breitkopf & Härtel), 1919.

BULC   Richard Count du Moulin Eckart (ed.) *Letters of Hans von Bülow*, transl. Hannah Waller, New York (Alfred A. Knopf), 1931.

BULLOCK   Alan Bullock, *Hitler, a study in tyranny*, 2nd rev. edn, London (Penguin Books) ed. J. Burton, 1962.

BURSTO   K. V. Burian, *Stokowski*, Prague (Editio Supraphon), 1976.

BURW   ed. J. Burk, *Die Sammlung Burrell: Richard Wagner Briefe*, ed. Frankfurt, 1953.

BUSCH   Fritz Busch, *Pages from a Musician's Life*, London (J. M. Dent), 1953.

BUSL   Ferrucio Busoni, *Letters to his Wife*, London (Edward Arnold), 1938.

CAIRNS   David Cairns, *Responses*, London (Secker and Warburg), 1973.

CAMDEN   Archie Camden, *Blow by Blow*, London (Thames), 1982.

CANE   Elias Caretti, *Crowds and Power*, London (Penguin Books) 1973.

CARD   *Cardus on Music, a centenary collection*, ed. Donald Wright, London (Hamish Hamilton), 1988.

CARDB   Neville Cardus, *Sir Thomas Beecham*, London (Collins), 1961.

CHAMB   Anne Chambers, *La Sheridan: adorable diva – Margaret Burke Sheridan, Irish prima donna 1889–1958*, Dublin (Wolfhound Press), 1989.

CHAS   Abram Chasins, *Leopold Stokowski*, London (Robert Hale), 1981.

CHIS   Anne Chisholm, *Nancy Cunard*, London (Penguin), 1981.

CHOTZ   Samuel Chotzinoff, *Toscanini, an intimate portrait*, London (Hamish Hamilton), 1956.

CLARE   George Clare, *Berlin Days, 1946–1947*, London (Macmillan), 1989.

COAT   Eric Coates, *Suite in four movements*, London (Heinemann), 1953.

COH   Harriet Cohen, *A Bundle of Time*, London (Faber), 1969.

CONA   Marcello Conati, *Interviews and Encounters with Verdi*, transl. Richard Stokes, London (Gollancz), 1984.

CULP   John Culshaw, *Putting the Record Straight*, London (Secker and Warburg), 1982.

CULR   John Culshaw, *Ring Resounding*, London (Secker and Warburg), 1967.

CUM   Gerald Cumberland, *Set down in Malice*, London (Grant Richards Ltd), 1919.

DAM   Walter Damrosch, *My Musical Life*, New York (Scribner's), 1926.

DANIEL   Oliver Daniel, *Stokowski, a counterpoint of view*, New York (Dodd, Mead), 1982.

DAVEN   Marcia Davenport, *Too strong for Fantasy*, London (Collins), 1968.

DICK   Harry Ellis Dickson, *Gentlemen, more dolce please!*, 2nd edn, Boston (Beacon Press), 1974.

DORA   Antal Dorati, *Notes of Seven Decades*, London, (Hodder and Stoughton), 1979.

DRES   Dettmor Dressel, *Up and Down the Scale*, London (Selwyn Blount), 1937.

DROG   Lord Drogheda, *Double Harness*, London (Weidenfeld and Nicolson), 1978.

DUFF   Richard Dufallo, *Trackings: Composers speak with RD*, New York (Oxford University Press), 1989.

EPST   Helen Epstein, *Music talks: conversations with musicians*, New York (Penguin Books), 1987.

EWE   David Ewen, *Dictators of the Baton*, 2nd edn, Chicago (Ziff-Davis), 1948.

FISCH   Dietrich Fischer-Dieskau, *Echoes of a Lifetime*, London (Macmillan), 1989.

FLE   Carl Flesch, *The Memoirs of Carl Flesch*, transl. and ed. Hans Keller, New York (Macmillan), 1958.

FRANK   David Franklin, *Basso Cantante*, London (Duckworth), 1969.

FUL   J. A. Fuller Maitland, *A Doorkeeper of Music*, London (Edward Arnold), 1929.

FURT   Wilhelm Furtwängler, *Notebooks 1924–54*, transl. Shaun Whiteside, ed. Michael Tanner, London (Quartet Books), 1989.

FURTAB   Wilhelm Furtwängler/Walter Abendroth, *Gespräche über Musik*, Zürich (Atlantis Verlag), 1948.

FURTGB   John Squire and John Hunt, *Furtwängler and Great Britain*, UK (Wilhelm Furtwängler Society), 1985.

FURTL   A.-V. Listewnik und Hedwig Sander, *Wilhelm Furtwängler*, Leipzig (Edition Peters), 1986.

FURTUS   Daniel Gillis, *Furtwängler and America*, New York (Manyland Books Inc.), 1970.

GAI   Fred W. Gaisberg, *Music on Record*, London (Robert Hale), 1946.

GALK   Elliott W. Galkin, *A History of Orchestral Conducting in Theory and Practice*, New York (Pendragon Press), 1988.

GATTI   Giulio Gatti-Casazza, *Memories of the opera*, London (John Calder), 1977.

GEI   Bertha Geissmar, *The Baton and the Jackboot*, London (Hamish Hamilton), 1944.

GERH   Eleno Gerhardt, *Recital*, London (Methuen), 1937.

GLOV   J. M. Glover, *Jimmy Glover and his friends*, London (Chatto & Windus), 1913.

GOEB   *The Goebbels Diaries*, transl. and ed. Fred Taylor, London (Hamish Hamilton), 1982.

GOULD   ed. Tim Page, *The Gienn Gould Reader*, New York (knopf), 1984.

GRAD   Peter Gradenwitz, *Leonard Bernstein: the infinite variety of a musician*, Berg (Leamington Spa/New York), 1987.

GRAF   Max Graf, *Composer and Critic*, New York (Philosophical Library), 1945.

GRAI   Henry-Louis de La Grange, *Mahler*, vol. 1, London (Gollancz), 1973.

GRUEN   John Gruen, *The Private World of Leonard Bernstein*, New York (The Viking Press), 1968.

GRU   Richard Grunberger, *A Social History of the Third Reich*, London (Pelican Books), 1974.

HAEU   Ernst Haeusserman, *Herbert von Karajan*, Gütersloh (C Bertelsmann Verlag), 1968.

HAGG   B. H. Haggin, *The Toscanini Musicians Knew*, New York (Horizon Press), 1967.

HALT   Montague Haltrecht, *The Quiet Showman: Sir David Webster and the Royal Opera House*, London (Collins), 1975.

HAM   Die Hamburgische Staatsoper, 1678–1945, hrsg. Max W. Busch und Peter Dannenberg, Zürich (M & T Verlag), 1988.

HARE   George, Earl of Harewood, *The Tongs and the Bones*, London (Weidenfeld and Nicolson), 1978.

HART   Philip Hart, *Conductors, a new generation*, London (Robson Books), 1980.

HEINS   H. W. Heinsheimer, *Fanfare for 2 pigeons*, New York (Doubleday), 1949.

HERZF   Friedrich Herzfeld, *Wilhelm Furtwängler, Weg und Wesen*, Leipzig (Goldmann), 1941.

HERZK   Friedrich Herzfeld, *Herbert von Karajan*, Berlin (Rembrandt Verlag), 1962.

HERZM   Friedrich Herzfeld, *Magie des Taktstocks*, Berlin (Ullstein), 1953.
HEYKC   Peter Heyworth (ed.), *Conversations with Klemperer*, rev. 2nd edn, London (Faber and Faber), 1985.
HEYKI   Peter Heyworth, *Otto Klemperer*, vol. 1, Cambridge (Cambridge University Press), 1983.
HIBBERT   Christopher Hibbert, *Benito Mussolini*, London (Longmans Green), 1962.
HÖCKER   Karla Höcker, *Wilhelm Furtwängler: Dokumente – Berichte und Bilder – Aufzeichnungen*, Berlin (Rembrandt Verlag), 1968.
HOGW   Christopher Hogwood, *Handel*, London (Thames and Hudson), 1984.
HOLMES   John Holmes, Conductors on Record, London (Victor Gollancz), 1982.
HORO   Joseph Horowitz, *Understanding Toscanini*, New York (Knopf), 1987.
HOTTER   Penelope Turino, *Hans Hotter – Man and Artist*, London (John Calder) 1983.
HUNTKAR   John Hunt, *From Adam to Webern: the recordings of von Karajan*, London (self-published), 1987.
JAHR   *Jahrbuch der Deutschen Musik, 1943*, Leipzig/Berlin (Breitkopf und Härtel/Max Hesses Verlag), 1942.
JERGER   Wilhelm Jerger, *Die Wiener Philharmoniker*, Vienna (Wiener Verlagsgesellschaft), 1942.
JORD   Ruth Jordan, *Daughter of the Waves: Memories of growing up in pre-War Palestine*, New York (Taplinger), 1983.
KAR   Herbert von Karajan, *My Autobiography*, as told to Franz Endler, transl. Stewart Spencer, London (Sidgwick & Jackson), 1989.
KARANEC   *Anekdoten um Herbert von Karajan, gesammelt und erzählt von Christian Spiel*, Munich (Bechtle Verlag), 1968.
KARDG   *Herbert von Karajan: Der grosse Bildband*, Hamburg (Polydor), 1983.
KARPIC   *Herbert von Karajan: Der grosse Bildband*, Hanover (Polydor), 1983.
KELLER   Hans Keller, *Criticism*, London (Faber & Faber), 1987.
KENBA   Michael Kennedy, *Barbirolli*, London (Hamish Hamilton), 1971.
KENBO   Michael Kennedy, *Boult*, London (Hamish Hamilton), 1987.
KENBR   Michael Kennedy, *Britten*, London (Dent), 1981.
KENHA   Michael Kennedy, *The Halle Tradition, a century of music*, Manchester (Manchester University Press), 1960.
KENRAT   Nicholas Kenyon, *Simon Rattle; the making of a conductor*, London (Faber and Faber), 1987.
KLAW   Harold L. Klawans, *Toscanini's Fumble, and other tales of clinical neurology*, London (Bodley Head), 1988.
KLEIN   Herman Klein, *Thirty years of musical life in London*, New York, 1903.
KLEM   Martin Anderson ed., *Klemperer on Music: Shavings from a Musician's Workbench*, London (Toccata Press), 1986.
KLMUM   Herman Klein, *Musicians and Mummers*, London, 1925.
KUNA   Milan Kuna, *Václav Talich*, Prague (Panton), 1980.
LANG   Klaus Lang, *Lieber Herr Celibidache . . .* , Zurich (M&T), 1988.
LANGD   Michael Langdon (with Richard Ford), *Notes from a low singer*, London (Macrae), 1982.
LEBAN   Norman Lebrecht, *The Book of Musical Anecdotes*, London (André Deutsch), 1985.
LEBD   Norman Lebrecht, *Discord, conflict and the making of music*, London (André Deutsch), 1982.

LEBH   Norman Lebrecht, *Hush! Handel's in a Passion*, London (André Deutsch), 1985.

LEBMR   Norman Lebrecht, *Mahler Remembered*, London (Faber and Faber), 1987.

LEGGE   Elisabeth Schwarzkopf, *On and off the record, a memoir of Walter Legge*, London (Faber and Faber), 1982.

LEID   Frida Leider, *Playing my Part*, transl. Charles Osborne, London (Calder and Boyars), 1966.

LOCH   Louis P. Lochner, *Fritz Kreisler*, London (Rockliff), 1951.

MAHALM   Alma Mahler, *Gustav Mahler, Memories and Letters*, 2nd edn, transl. Basil Creighton, London (John Murray), 1968.

MAHLET   *Selected Letters of Gustav Mahler*, ed. Knud Martner, London (Faber and Faber), 1979.

MANND   Hermann Kester (ed.), *The Diaries of Thomas Mann*, transl. Richard and Clora Winston, London (André Deutsch), 1983.

MANNH   Heinsich Mann, *Man of Straw*, London (Penguin Books), 1986.

MATT   Helena Matheopoulos, *Maestro*, London (Hutchinson), 1982.

MAY   Florence May, *Life of Brahms*, London, 1905.

MAYER   Martin Mayer, *The Met: 100 years of grand opera*, New York (Thames and Hudson), 1983.

MENU   Yehudi Menuhin, *Unfinished Journey*, London (Macdonald & Jane's), 1976.

MONT   Doris Monteux, *It's all in the music; the life and works of Pierre Monteux*, London (William Kimber), 1965.

MOORE   Gerald Moore, *Am I too Loud?*, London (Hamish Hamilton), 1952.

MOORELG   Jerrold Northrop Moore, *Edward Elgar, a creative life*, Oxford (OUP), 1984.

MORT   John Mortimer, *Character Parts*, London (Penguin Books), 1987.

NAB   Nicolai Nabokov, *Bagazh*, New York (Atheneum), 1975.

NET   Reginald Nettel, *The Orchestra in England; a social history*, London (Jonathan Cape), 1948.

NEU   Angelo Neumann, *Personal Recollections of Wagner*, London (Constable), 1909.

NICHRAV   Roger Nichols, *Ravel Remembered*, London (Faber and Faber), 1987.

NIK   Heinrich Chevalley (hrsg.), *Arthur Nikisch, Leben und Wirken*, Berlin (Verlag Ed Bote & G. Bock), 1922.

NIKDET   Arthur Dette, *Nikisch*, Leipzig (Lothar Joachim), 1922.

OCON   Charles O'Connell, *The Other Side of the Record*, NY (Alfred A. Knopf), 1947.

OSBK   Richard Osborne, *Conversations with Karajan*, Oxford (OUP), 1989.

PAD   I. J. Paderewski and Mary Lawton, *The Paderewski Memoirs*, London (William Collins), 1939.

PANUF   Andrzei Paner frisk, *Composing myself*, London (Methuen), 1985.

PAR   Jasper Parrott, *Ashkenazy Beyond Frontiers*, London (Collins), 1984.

PEART   Maurice Pearton, *The LSO at 70*, London (Gollancz), 1974.

PETTIT   Stephen Pettit, *Philharmonia*, London (Robert Hale), 1986.

PEUK   Detlev J. K. Peukert, *Inside Nazi Germany; conformity, opposition and racism in everyday life*, transl. Richard Deveson, London (Penguin Books), 1989.

PEYBER   Joan Peyser, *Bernstein, a biography*, New York (Beech Tree Books), 1987.

PEYBOU   Joan Peyser, *Boulez: composer, conductor, enigma*, London (Cassell), 1976.

PIAT   Gregor Pintigorsky, *Cellist*, New York (Doubleday), 1965.
POR1   Andrew Porter, *A Musical Season*, London (Gollancz), 1974.
POR3   Andrew Porter, *Musical Events, a chronicle, 1980–1983*, London (Grafton), 1988.
PRIE   Fred K. Prieberg, *Musik im N.S.-Staat*, Frankfurt (Fischer Taschenbuch Verlag), 1982.
PRIM   William Primrose, *Walk on the North Side*, Provo, Urah (Brigham Young University Press), 1978.
PVT   Tim Page and Vanessa Weeks Page, *Selected letters of Virgil Thomson*, New York (Summit Books), 1988.
REID   Charles Reid, *Thomas Beecham, an independent biography*, London (Gollancz), 1962.
REIDBA   Charles Reid, *John Barbirolli*, London (Hamish Hamilton), 1971.
REIDSA   Charles Reid, *Malcolm Sargent*, London (Hamish Hamilton), 1968.
REIS   Claire R. Reis, *Composers, conductors and critics*, New York (Oxford University Press), 1955.
RIESS   Curt Riess, *Wilhelm Furtwängler, a biography*, transl. Margaret Goldsmith, London (Frederick Muller Ltd), 1955.
ROBBER   Paul Robinson, *The Art of the Conductor: Bernstein*, London (Macdonald), 1982.
ROBKAR   Paul Robinson, *The Art of the Conductor: Karajan*, London (Macdonald), 1975.
ROBSTO   Paul Robinson, *The Art of the Conductor: Stokowski*, London (Macdonald), 1977.
ROG   Clara Kathleen Rogers, *The story of two lives*, Boston (privately printed), 1932.
RONA   Sir Landon Ronald, *Myself and others*, London (Sampson Low, Marston & Co.), nd.
ROTH   Ernst Roth, *The Business of Music; reflections of a music publisher*, London (Cassell), 1969.
RUB1   Arthur Rubinstein, *My Young Years*, London (Jonathan Cape), 1973.
RUB2   Arthur Rubinstein, *My Many Years*, London (Jonathan Cape), 1982.
RUTT   Helen Ruttencutter, *Previn*, London (Michael Joseph), 1985.
SACCHI   Filippo Sacchi, *The Magic Baton*, London (Putnam), 1957.
SACHIT   Harvey Sachs, *Music in Fascist Italy*, London (Weidenfeld and Nicolson), 1988.
SACHTOS   Harvey Sachs, *Toscanini*, Philadelphia (J. B. Lippincott), 1978.
SAVAGE   Richard Temple Savage, *A Voice from the Pit: reminiscences of an orchestral musician*, Newton Abbott (David & Charles), 1988.
SAWYER   C. Sawyer-Lauçanno, *An invisible spectator; a biography of Paul Bowles*, London (Bloomsbury), 1989.
SCHN   Artur Schnabel, *My life and music*, London, 1961.
SCHO   Harold Schonberg, *The Greor Conductors*, New York (Simon & Schuster), 1968.
SCHOELET   Arnold Schoenberg, *Letters*, ed. Erwin Stein, transl. Eithne Wilkins and Ernst Kaiser, London (Faber and Faber), 1964.
SCHUS   Willi Schuh, *Richard Strauss: A chronicle of the early years, 1864–1898*, transl. Mary Whittall, Cambridge (CUP), 1982.
SCMM   Percy Scholes, *The Mirror of Music*, 2 vols, London, 1947.
SCUSSR   Boris Schwarz, *Music and Musical Life in the Soviet Union*, London (Barrie & Jenkins), 1972.
SEL   George Seltzer (ed.), *The professional symphony orchestra in the United States*, Metuchen, NJ (The Scarecrow Press, Inc.), 1975.

SHERM John K. Sherman, *Music and Maestros, The story of the Minneapolis Symphony Orchestra*, Minneapolis (University of Minnesota Press), 1952.

SHO Bernard Shore, *The Orchestra Speaks*, London (Longman, Green & Co.), 1938.

SKEW Geoffrey Skelton, *Richard and Cosima Wagner; Biography of a marriage*, Boston (Houghton Mifflin Co.), 1982.

SLONPP Nicolas Slonimsky, *Perfect Pitch, a life story*, New York (OUP), 1988.

SMY Ethel Smyth, *Impressions that remained; memoirs*, London (Longman, Green & Co.), 1919.

SMYBEE Ethel Smyth, *Beecham and Pharoah*, London, (Chapman & Hall), 1935.

SPEE1 Albert Speer, *Inside the Third Reich*, London, (Waterford and Nicholson).

SPEE2 Albert Speer, *Spandau, the secret diaries*, transl. Richard and Clara Winston, New York (Pocket Books), 1977.

SPEY Edward Speyer, *My life and friends*, London (Cobber-Sanderson), 1937.

STAN Charles Villiers Stanford, *Pages from an unwritten Diary*, London (Edward Arnold), 1914.

STAR Edith Stargardt-Wolff, *Wegbereiter grosser Musiker*, Berlin, 1954.

STEF Paul Stefan, *Arturo Tosconini*, trans. Eden and Cedar Paul, New York (Blue Ribbon Books), 1936.

STRAVD Igor Stravinsky and Robert Craft, *Dialogues*, London (Faber Music), 1982.

STRAVE Igor Stravinsky and Robert Craft, *Expositions and Developments*, London (Faber Music), 1981.

STRAVLET *Stravinsky, Selected correspondence*, vol. 1, edited and with commentaries by Robert Craft, London (Faber Music), 1982.

STRE Wolfgang Stresemann, *. . . und Abends in die Philharmonie; Errinerungen an große Dirigenten*, Munich (Kristall bei Langen Müller), 1981.

STREBE Wolfgang Stresemann, *The Berlin Philharmonic from Bülow to Karajan*, Berlin (Stapp Verlag), 1979.

STRR Richard Strauss, *Recollections and Reflections*, transl. L. J. Lawrence, London (Boosey & Hawkes), 1953.

STU Joachim Stutchewsky, *Hayyim lelo pesharot (A life without compromises)*, Tel Aviv (Sifriat Hapoalim), 1977.

SZIG Joseph Szigeti, *With Strings Attached*, London (Cassell), 1949.

TAUB Howard Taubman, *Toscanini*, London (Odhams), 1951.

TAYL A. J. P. Taylor, *A Personal History*, London (Coronet), 1984.

TCHI Modest Tchaikosky, *The life and letters of Peter Blyich Tchaikosky*, London (John Lane), 1905

THA Werner Thärichen, *Paukenschläge: Furtwängler oder Karajan?*, Zürich (M&T Verlag), 1988.

TILL Malcolm Tillis, *Chords and Discords: the life of an orchestral musician*, London (Phoenix House), 1960.

TOR Paul Tortelier in conversation with David Blum, *A Self-Portrait*, London (Heinemann), 1984.

TOYE Francis Toye, *For what we have received*, London (William Heinemann), 1950.

UNGER Heinz Unger, *Hammer, sickle and baton: the Soviet memoirs of a musician*, co-written with Naomi Walford, London (The Cresset Press), 1939.

VAS   Marie 'Missie' Vassiltchikov, *Berlin Diaries, 1940–45*, London (Chatto & Windus), 1985.

VAUK   Roger Vaughan, *Herbert von Karajan, a biographical portrait*, London (Weidenfeld and Nicolson), 1986.

VINT   John Vinton, *Essays after a dictionary*, Lewidburg (Bucknell University Press), 1977.

VOLKOV   Solomon Volkov, *Testimony: the memoirs of Shostakovich*, transl. Antonina W. Bouis, London (Hamish Hamilton), 1979.

WAGCD   Cosima Wagner's *Diaries*, ed. Martin Gregor-Dellin and Dietrich Mack, trans. Geoffrey Skelton, 2 vols, London (Collins), 1978–80.

WAGF   Friedelind Wagner and Page Cooper, *Heritage of Fire*, New York (Harper & Brothers), 1945.

WAGML   Richard Wagner, *Mein Leben*, Munich, 1911.

WAGWIN   Friedefind Wagner and Page Cooper, *Heritage of Fire*, New York (Harper & Bros.), 1945.

WAITE   Robert G. L. Waite, *The Psycopathic God: Adolf Hitler*, New York (Basic Books), 1977.

WALGM   Bruno Walter, *Gustav Mahler*, transl. James Galston, London (Kegan Paul, Trench, Trubner & Co.), 1937.

WALK   Frank Walker, *The Man Verdi*, London (J. M. Dent), 1962.

WALTBR   Lotte Walter Lindt (hrsq.), Bruno Walter Briefe, 1894–1962, Frankfurt (Fischer), 1963.

WALTV   Bruno Walter, *Theme and Variations; an autobiography*, transl. James A. Galston, New York (Alfred A. Knopf), 1946.

WEBZEM   Horst Weber, *Alexander Zemlinsky*, Vienna (Verlag Elisabeth Lafite), 1978.

WEI   Felix Weingastner, *Buffets and Rewards*, London, 1937.

WEIC   Felix Weingartner, *On Conducting*, London, 1901

WEINK   Bernd Weinkauf, *Briefe, das Gewandhaus zu Leipzig betreffend*, Leipzig (Mitteldeutscher Verlag), 1987.

WEISS   Adolf Weismann, *Der Dirigent im 20 Jahrhundert*, Berlin (Im Prophyläen Verlag), 1925.

WILH   Kurt Wilhelm, *Richard Strauss, an intimate portrait*, transl. Mary Whittall, London (Thames and Hudson), 1989.

WOLFE   Tom Wolfe, *Radical Chic and Mau-Mauing the Flak Catchers*, New York (Farrar, Straus), 1970.

WOO   David Woodridge, *Conductor's World*, London (Barrie & Rockliff), 1970.

WOOD   Henry J. Wood, *My life of music*, London (Victor Gollancz), 1938.

WEIC   Felix Weingartner, *On Conducting* London, 1901.

WULF   Joseph Wulf, *Musik im Dritten Reich: Eine Dokumentation*, Gütersloh (Sigbert Mohn Verlag), 1963.

Index